Writing:
A Workshop Approach

LaRene Despain
University of Hawaii at Manoa

Mayfield Publishing Company
Mountain View, California
London ■ Toronto

To: Bob Despain
Suzie Jacobs
Shirley Kahlert—
Who taught me how to teach writing

Library of Congress Cataloging-in-Publication Data

Despain, LaRene.
    Writing: a workshop approach / LaRene Despain
        p.   cm.
    Includes index.
    ISBN 0-87484-988-8 (paper)
    1. English language—Rhetoric   I. Title.
PE1408.D467   1991
808'.042—dc20   91-33509
                                         CIP

Manufactured in the United States of America

10 9 8 7 6 5 4 3 2 1

Mayfield Publishing Company
1240 Villa Street
Mountain View, California 94041

Sponsoring editor, Thomas V. Broadbent; managing editor, Linda Toy; production editor,
Carol Zafiropoulos; manuscript editor, Loralee Windsor; text and cover design, Lisa Mirski;
illustrator, Robin Mouat; cover illustration, Michele Collier. This text was set in 10½/13 Janson
by T:H Typecast, Inc. and printed on 50# Finch by Maple-Vail Book Manufacturing Group.

Acknowledgments and copyrights continue at the back of the book on page 365, which
constitutes an extension of the copyright page.

Preface

This textbook presents a workshop method of teaching based on the belief that because writing is a process which students must learn by practice, a writing class should itself be part of that process. Thus, students using this book are expected to spend much of their in-class time thinking about, planning, discussing, even writing their papers. In one sense, the students' writing is the real textbook for the course.

The book's eight sequenced assignments lead the student through two types of writing: experience based (Part One) and data based (Part Two). The assignments thus range along a continuum from narrative to expository, and the gap between the two types is bridged by illustrative writing which uses narrative material to support a thesis. Each assignment goes through a cycle with three main parts: *Getting Started*, *Writing a Draft*, and *Reworking the Draft*. Under these headings, students are guided through the process of thinking, planning, drafting, getting feedback from their fellow writers, redrafting, and final editing. In each section, Writing Activities help move the students ahead on their actual drafts.

Much of the current research on writing suggests that a process like the one described above is too tidy—that instead of moving through discrete stages, writing is actually a recursive process where thinking, drafting, and revising go on simultaneously. Although I recognize this both in my own writing and in that of my students, a textbook must handle one idea, one skill, at a time. Hence the divisions into what might be arbitrary stages. Moreover, my experience in teaching has shown that the concept of writing as a process with stages—the concept that one can try, then try again—is both a revelation and a salvation for students for whom writing is a daunting, seemingly impossible task.

All of the assignments and techniques suggested in the text have been used many times in writing classrooms in Hawaii, China, Massachusetts, and Utah. The sample student essays in the text are the result. The sample papers not only stimulate thinking but also give students a clear idea of what is expected in a given assignment. Written as they are by peers, they have two advantages: relatively simple structures and material familiar to students. When students are first trying their wings, sample essays that are complex and not closely related to the task at hand can inhibit rather than aid their efforts. In both language and structure, the samples reproduced in the text are simple but not simplistic: they will not patronize even your best students. The samples are sensitive and thoughtful, the language simple but efficient and occasionally even beautiful.

One of the most often-heard questions from students in a writing class is "What do you want?" The real answer to this question—a good piece of writing—is not specific enough. Yet answering in more detail might inhibit or confuse the student. A variety of sample papers can provide an objective answer to this question without boxing students into a particular form or structure.

One of the major ways in which a workshop writing class differs from a more traditional one is in its emphasis on *drafts*. In each chapter, some general principles are introduced, ranging from the use of sensory detail and dialogue in the first chapters to different ways of handling opposing arguments in the last one. At all times, however, the students' own ideas and writing are central. The emphasis on drafts makes the process of learning more manageable for the student. What is written in a draft is not engraved in stone and is easy to change. Thus the student is encouraged to try to write something—first maybe only jumbled ideas—then to try to make this something into a form capable of communicating meaning.

Each chapter has a section on revision that shows, mainly by presenting and analyzing student writing, how the paper assigned in the chapter can be made clearer, more exciting, more convincing. Undoubtedly, there is more material here than can be considered in detail in class. Each instructor can select whatever seems most useful to address the needs of a particular group. Obviously, using preselected revision samples and exercises can never take the place of the time-honored practice of reproducing pieces of writing produced in the class. But carefully prepared material for revision can focus attention on common problems.

This text places special emphasis on the sharing of drafts with other students in the class. The literature on peer response is large, and many instructors will already have techniques that work well for them. For each assignment the text gives suggested peer-response exercises. The type of response desired is not teacherly criticism of grammar, mechanics, and so on, but what might be called "reader-based" comments—that is, comments on content and structure: Is the paper interesting? Does it really contain experiences instead of generalizations? Are there places where the material is not interesting, needs more development, is hard to follow? Students are asked to point out successes as well as places which need improvement. The Instructor's Manual discusses ways of training students in peer-response techniques to make their comments more helpful.

Whatever the method, the object is to give students responses to their writing at an early stage before they consider it finished. This forces them to think of their papers in an objective way even if they don't pay attention to every bit of advice given. It also gives them a real audience and accustoms them to the idea that some-one besides the instructor is going to read the paper. One of the rewards of the activity comes when some student brings a really beautiful piece of writing: clear, sensitive, concrete, affecting. Students *always* know when that happens, and such moments become the most memorable and useful of the writing class. They rein-force every student's idea that she or he, too, can write well; they make the whole writing class seem more serious, more useful, more important.

For students the journey through this book is long and challenging, but they usually end knowing where they have come and why. In my syllabus I always tell students:

> I have no magic secret that will enable you to find the secret of writing. There is no secret except hard work. I cannot teach you to write easily—I can help you to make the process more productive and to make each succeeding draft better. I cannot promise that everyone in the class will be an excellent writer by the end of the semester. But I can promise that if you will stay in the class and do all the work, you will write better at the end of the semester than you do now.

Many students have commented at the end of the class that this promise has come true for them. That is the goal of this text.

Acknowledgments

I have incurred many debts to colleagues and students over the ten years this text has developed. It had its first concrete form in China, where I was a Fulbright lecturer, though some of the assignments had been developed in the Writing Workshop at the University of Hawaii. I thank my colleagues who encouraged this work, especially Professors Yuan Henan and Frank Deng. I owe a special debt of gratitude to the students in my writing classes in China. I worked there for two years when contact between our two countries was just beginning. I will ever be grateful for what the students there taught me and for their honesty and courage in writing about their experiences. Two student friends from those years deserve special mention: Ke Wang and Yanyan Zhang helped with typing, checking, proofreading, and general suggestions. Both first used the text as students in China, then used it for their own students in China and in the United States, where they are now working on degrees.

Since my return from China years ago, the old assignments have been readapted and new ones developed for the American classroom. Many people have contributed to the text. I thank most particularly my colleague Suzanne Jacobs, with whom I set up the Writing Workshop. She taught me more about how stu-dents learn, and thus what works in the classroom, than I could ever acknowledge.

Several other colleagues have contributed ideas for the text, notably Roger Whitlock, who graciously allowed me to use several exercises he developed. Elizabeth McCutcheon was particularly helpful when I began to rethink Chapter 4. Cristina Bacchilega, Joe Chadwick, and Barbara Gottfried have all used the text materials and encouraged me to continue to work with them. Larry G. Mapp of Middle Tennessee State University read the manuscript in two stages and has been a perceptive and helpful critic, as was Blake Smith, a student at Loyola-Marymount University. I could not possibly thank by name everyone at Mayfield Publishing Company who has contributed in one way or another, but I must express special thanks to Alden Paine, with whom I first discussed the project; Tom Broadbent, who sponsored the book and was my editor; Carol Zafiropoulos, who supervised copyediting, design, and production; Loralee Windsor, manuscript editor; and Jeanne Schreiber, art director.

Patient friends have read chapters and given me valuable suggestions: Nell Altizer, Tom Hilgers, Suzanne Jacobs, Rebecca Lee, Karma Lochrie, Todd Sammons, and Roger Whitlock. My mother, Wanda S. Petersen (whose several books have encouraged my writing); my sister, Myrna Olsen; and my friend Fay Hendricks helped with proofreading.

Concrete evidence of my students' contribution is the papers in the text. I have tried to retrace every paper to its author, but, unfortunately, when I first started collecting papers for use in class I thought I should make them anonymous, so I have lost the names of some authors. I would be very happy if former students would recognize their papers and remind me that they wrote them. I have obtained permission where possible, but even in some cases where I remembered the writers, I could not now find addresses for them. I would also be very happy to be in touch with those students again. To all of these writers, and to all of the others I have worked with, I give my heartfelt thanks. Their good writing, only a small portion of which I have been able to include, has been the main encouragement for this project.

One word of explanation needs to be given concerning the use of the materials about the island of Kaho'olawe. The Hawaiian language was written down and normalized by people who were not native speakers. It was also banned for years from the Islands in any public usage. Thus, some sounds not familiar to western ears were lost. The groups who are now trying to revive the language are making an attempt to represent its full complexity. The diacritical mark between the *o*'s in Kaho'olawe represents one such sound. This sound also occurs, for example, in Hawai'i, which is correctly written in that way. However, only lately have newspapers begun to recognize this spelling. Thus, the materials in the Research Materials appendix are inconsistent in this respect.

From this point on, I adopt the policy of using the correct spelling in my own text, but I reproduce the spelling in the appendix articles as it appeared in the original. Sometimes even the original articles are inconsistent. I appreciate the time Davianna McGregor of Ethnic Studies and Haunani-Kay Trask, Director of Hawaiian Studies, at the University of Hawaii spent explaining this to me, and ask their pardon where I have not been correct. I thank Professor McGregor also for talking to me at length about the controversy surrounding Kaho'olawe and for helping me to rewrite Chapter 7 in a clearer and more comprehensive way.

Contents

CHAPTER 2

A Scene to Reveal Character

CHAPTER 4

Illustrative Writing 111

PART TWO   Data-Based Writing

CHAPTER 5

Summary Writing

CHAPTER 6

Comparison and Contrast

CHAPTER 7

APPENDIX

Introduction: To the Student

One learns to write by writing, and even more, rewriting. I have often heard students say that they wish they "knew how" to write so that it would be easier, but unfortunately that is a mistaken notion. The best writers are those who work hardest at it. No writing teacher or text can give you a magic formula or shortcut to writing. What we can do is help you think more consciously and carefully about the *process* of writing by guiding you through it.

Process is the key word for this workshop approach. The text is divided into eight chapters, each of which helps you produce a piece of writing. Each chapter starts with exercises designed to help you collect ideas and material, leads you through a draft, helps you get feedback to encourage you to revise, and helps you edit and polish.

Drafting and revision are the keys to the process. The workshop method recognizes that writing is a way of thinking and that what a writer puts down on paper is not engraved in stone. A draft is a trial. It makes vague thoughts concrete and enables the writer to see what has to be done next. All professional writers draft and revise. Becoming more experienced at writing doesn't mean one learns to write perfectly on the first try. It means that one learns how to evaluate and "fix" one's drafts and how to use "prewriting" time to stimulate thought, which will make all the drafts more interesting. The activities and discussions in this text help you produce useful drafts and then evaluate them to turn out a paper you will like.

We do not mean to say that everyone will need to write the same number of drafts or even that one writer will go through the same process with each paper. Different writers work in different ways; different assignments call for different processes. We do mean to say that thinking of writing as a process that allows for thinking and rethinking, trying and rejecting, and trying again will make the task easier and more satisfying.

In all stages of the process your teacher and your peers will help you evaluate drafts and think through revisions. As a trained professional your teacher will be able to get to the problems in your draft quickly and make suggestions to improve them. But don't overlook the help you can get from peers. Your teacher is only one reader after all. When you write, you want to communicate your ideas, and the more readers who give you their responses, the better idea you'll have about whether you are communicating. Then, too, your peers are struggling with the same writing you are, and their problems and solutions may help you.

Ultimately, however, the writing, and the responsibility, is yours. The first question you must answer about any piece of writing is: Will it be interesting enough to hold the attention of the reader? You are the only one who can make sure that the answer is "yes," because your ideas will shape the paper and your experiences and knowledge will bring it to life, make your readers understand, and convince them that your paper was worth their time from the first.

The first step in the process is thinking and gathering material and ideas. Each assignment has a predrafting and planning section to help you with that. Sometimes that involves recalling; sometimes it requires reading and other kinds of data collection. Every writer uses this time differently. Some might want to start drafting much earlier than others. Some begin writing, but the writing is a form of thinking rather than a draft as such.

As you begin to write, the text discusses various aspects of writing to help you in your drafting. In addition, it furnishes a variety of samples to show you how other student writers have responded to the assignments. Once in a while examples from professional writers are included. These are not meant as models to copy. Rather they show you a range of responses, stimulate your thinking, and demonstrate that interesting writing can come from the assignments.

When you have finished a draft that you think merits consideration from others, your instructor will ask you to share it with other writers, who will also be sharing their drafts with you. As a member of such a group, your purpose is not to tell someone what is "wrong" with a paper, but to respond as an intelligent reader, telling where the paper works for you and where you are confused or lose interest or want to hear more. Sometimes you will be asked to respond to particular questions; at other times you will give unstructured responses. The purpose of writing groups is to give guidance for revisions. Sometimes response from group members will be the only reaction the writer will get before preparing a final copy, so you should try to be as helpful as possible.

Because different writers write differently, you should expect the drafts you see and hear in group sessions, and your own drafts for different assignments, to be in different stages of completion. Sometimes the draft you or a colleague brings to the group will be ready for final polish. Sometimes it will be in need of serious revision. But when you bring a draft for consideration by others, you should be at a point where you know you can profit from the reactions of a reader.

Often your instructor will read your drafts and talk to you about them. Again the purpose is to aid you in revision, not to tell you what is "wrong" with the paper. You should be ready to talk to the teacher, explaining what you are trying to do and asking for help where you have had difficulties, rather than just sitting passively while the teacher tells you what to do. The paper is *yours*. Ultimately its success depends on you.

When you have received feedback from your group and your teacher, you should prepare the next draft. Different drafts will require different kinds of work at this point. Some will require only polishing of the language. This we call editing. Often, however, a draft will require major work like reorganizing to make ideas clearer or rethinking to recall more details. This we call revision. Revision requires more than "fixing up" a few sentences. The word itself means "reseeing." If your paper is not communicating your idea or experience, you may need to "see it again" in terms of structure or content. The book gives advice to help you with this part of the process.

Once you have revised, you must edit, checking sentences for clarity, effectiveness, efficiency, and correctness. Some chapters have editing exercises to help you polish the paper. If you have trouble correcting grammar, spelling, or punctuation, you should consult a handbook and a dictionary or ask your teacher for help. A piece of writing can never be considered a final draft until you have paid attention to its sentences, and you should never hand in a paper until you have gone through it at least once doing nothing but that.

Writing well is hard work. It requires serious effort, but it gives serious returns. And the task is never finished. Each new piece of writing presents a new challenge. Don't be discouraged because your writing is not as good as someone else's. If you were an experienced writer already, you would not need this course. The idea is to start where you are and make progress from that point. No one can promise that after one semester you will have mastered the art of writing. But we can promise that if you will stick with the course and do the work required—not only by the teacher but also by your own sense of accomplishment and pride—you will be a better writer at the end of the course than you are now.

1 *A Scene from Life*

Statement of Assignment

The first assignment is to write a "scene." You know that in a movie a scene is one short sequence in which some action takes place. The piece of writing you are going to do is called a scene because you will write about an experience as if it were part of a movie. You will think back over some experience you have had and run it through your mind just as if your mind were a camera. You must "see" and "hear" again what happened, remember how things looked, felt, and smelled. To reproduce your scene, follow these three rules exactly:

1. Choose an experience that took fifteen minutes or less.
2. Write down *only* what you saw, heard, smelled, tasted, or felt (as in touched).
3. Write at least one page. (Your instructor may set more specific requirements.)

A scene can be any type of experience, whether sad, funny, or scary; it can be significant or commonplace. Below are four scenes that illustrate the possible variety. Read them through or, better yet, listen while someone reads them aloud. The first is an eyewitness account from Vietnam.

At the province hospital at Can Tho, patients were usually either very young or very old or women, and their wounds were often horrible. The more lightly wounded were being treated quickly in the hospital yard, and the more serious cases were simply placed in one of the corridors to die. There were just too many of them to treat, the doctors had worked without a break, and now . . . the Viet Cong began shelling the hospital.

One of the Vietnamese nurses handed me a cold can of beer and asked me to take it down the hall where one of the Army surgeons was operating. The door of the room was ajar, and I walked right in. I probably should have looked first. A little girl was lying on the table, looking with wide dry eyes at the wall.

Her left leg was gone, and a sharp piece of bone about six inches long extended from the exposed stump. The leg itself was on the floor, half wrapped in a piece of paper. The doctor was a major, and he'd been working alone. He could not have looked worse if he'd lain all night in a trough of blood. His hands were so slippery that I had to hold the can to his mouth for him and tip it up as his head went back. I couldn't look at the girl.

"Is it all right?" he said quietly.

"It's okay now. I expect I'll be sick as hell later on."

He placed his hand on the girl's forehead and said, "Hello, little darling." He thanked me for bringing the beer. He probably thought that he was smiling, but nothing changed anywhere in his face. He'd been working this way for nearly twenty hours.

Michael Herr, from Dispatches

The following scene presents a more mundane aspect of military life:

Noon in the Lejeune woods, chilly with autumn and the slowing drizzle, gooky red mud making sucking noises under our boots. Rain-laden pine branches brush across faces like cold hands. "S" Company is coming off the flame thrower range for chow. . . .

Steam rose from the field kitchen, the only warm thing in the entire world, and we held out messkits for the cooks to fill with savory glop. At 19 you're too dumb to know when you're uncomfortable. We were used to 3½ hours sleep, at ease with rifles and seven-eighty-two gear, beginning to feel like soldiers.

One blond kid with huge, round, blue eyes has lost his messkit. He takes chow in his canteen cup—stew, spinach, bread, canned peaches dumped on top, string beans. It all goes to the same place, he says. When you've been up and running since 4:30, you don't care what it looks like.

Sergeants bark at us, but act like we're human, which may or may not show good judgment on their part. I line up with the rest of these olive-drab warriors at chest-high log tables. We eat standing up in the soupy clay, gray clouds rolling and twisting overhead. Someone passes a rumor that we have declared war on Red China. Some believe it. Some always do.

There is no such thing as a recruit with enough to eat. Chow wasn't bad—not like at the chowhall where, when the cook scooped up the powdered eggs with an ice-cream scoop, green water filled the hole.

Along the log tables are jars of peanut butter and jelly for making Geigerburgers—two-pound sandwiches that keep you going through the training ranges of Lejeune's Camp Geiger. Huge wasps and yellow jackets crawl around in the jelly jars.

The man next to me eyes a hornet the size of a B-1 in his jar. The beast is obviously dangerous. On the other hand, the Marine wants a sandwich.

It doesn't pay to stand between a recruit and food. With a quick twist of his knife, he forces the hornet deep below the surface of the jelly and makes his sandwich with the top layers.

Others before him had done the same thing. I counted seven buried wasps, some still twitching.

Fred Reed, from "Tales from the Lejeune Woods"

Do you think you can write like that? True, professional writers wrote these samples, but students have written scenes just as compelling. The pair below show two possibilities. The first is a once-in-a-lifetime thrill; the other is simple and quiet.

Five Seconds to Go

The cacophony of the crowd rained down as we rose from the huddle. I saw the red 0:05 on the clock and prepared for one last spurt. We were down by one point in the fourth quarter, and this was our last chance for victory.

Each of us moved purposefully onto the court, knowing what we had to do. All the heat captured in the sweaty gym seemed to rush to my cheeks and to gather in drops on my hair and sides, soaking my green Jets shirt. As I took my place behind the blue-jerseyed Warrior at mid-court, my eyes methodically swept to the left and the right, trying to pick up any possible edge. My gaze met the eyes of another Jet, John Parker, who was destined to take the last shot of the game. I could see him blink slowly for a moment in fatigued vacancy, but his arms shook themselves in tense and knowing preparations.

When the whistle pierced the air, I knew that our chances were pretty slim. DJ took the ball from the ref out of bounds. He raised the ball over his head to a symphony of sneakers screeching for position. I gave a small shove to the blue-jerseyed hip before me, and pivoted to my right, creating a small passageway between DJ and myself. In a millisecond the hard, braillelike cover of the ball stung my hands. As I bounced it quickly forward, I saw one blue jersey cut me off ahead and another one slide to my direct left. The instant the ball hit my fingertips, I scooped it up and whipped it over my head.

As the brown sphere looped toward a splash of green, I saw an enemy player leap for my pass. My stomach tightened, but when I saw the ball beat his fingers by inches and fall into Parker's hands I breathed again. With a yell of rubber soles on wood, I raced for the basket, sweat stinging my eyes, insides churning, and heart pumping. As I crossed the paint about five feet from the basket I could see John beginning his jump. He pushed the ball toward the basket in an awkward thrust, a Warrior draped over him like a cloth.

I saw the ball arch upward for a few feet, then begin to descend.

"Too short!!" Taking a risk, I pulled in a rough breath and bent my legs for a last jump. My eyes on the ball, I uncoiled like a spring: knees first, then ankles, feet, toes. I saw the ball hit the rim, then as a forest of arms went up, I lost its flight. Frantically guessing its position, I tried to slap it back toward its goal. Arms flew around me in a windmill of motion, but I felt leather as I met the ball with a "whack."

The baritone buzzer thundered as I came back down on the far side of the basket. But I had time to look up and see the ball rip through the bottom of the net. I dropped to my knees on the slick court and felt the tenseness drain out. It was over. I knew that I had been lucky, but we had won.

David Sasdi

Morning

Wrapped in my sleeping bag, I could feel the penetrating cold air on my face. It was early in the morning and still dark outside. I leaned over and lit the candle by my bunk. Out the camper window I could see the moon, bright and strong even though only a quarter. Seeing that I was up, Sleepy, my grandparents' large, red dog, jumped up onto my bunk and sat directly in front of me wagging his tail and blocking my view. He dropped his head as I started to laugh. Unable to resist his pleading, I began slowly and gently to move my hand down over his smooth coat. As I brought my hand back up, it felt rough. When my hands grew tired and I stopped petting him, he lifted his paw and dropped it on my knee.

As I slid off my bunk onto the floor, the coldness came through my socks. I grabbed my shoes, slipping them on as I blew out the candle. I put on my Grandfather's jacket and stepped outside, holding the door open until Sleepy's long, slender body had finally passed through. Outside, he ran around the camper like a puppy, turning circles and jumping over rocks.

Laying my sleeping bag next to the fire, which had burned out early in the night, I gathered some firewood and a stack of old newspapers, piled them in a circle, found the matches in the pocket of Grandfather's jacket, and lit the newspaper on the bottom of the pile. The fire grew quickly. I stood for a while warming my hands and looking at the area around our camp.

I placed a small pan of water on the fire, watching the air around as it quivered with the heat. With the water I made hot chocolate and lay down in my sleeping bag to drink it. Resting on my elbows mesmerized, I stared out through the forest, growing tired. I threw the empty paper cup into the fire and turned over on my side. Sleepy, who had been lying at my feet, came over and curled up next to my stomach, placing his nose by my face. I fell asleep.

student paper

Getting Started

WRITING ACTIVITY: RECOLLECTION

This activity is most effective when a group of writers does it together. Your instructor may have you do it as a class or divided into smaller groups. Its purpose is to help you relive an experience to gather material for your scene. Begin by recalling a scene you have participated in. Close your eyes and replay that scene in your head, just as if your memory is a camcorder that can also smell and feel. Let your camera move and record what you recall as your instructor or a colleague asks you the following questions or others like them.

Where are you? Inside or outside? If outside, what do you see? Trees? What kind? How many? Flowers? Where? What kind? What colors? Do you see water? Is it a stream? A waterfall? The ocean? What do you see near you? In the distance? If you are inside, what does the room look like? What kind of furniture? Old? New? What is on the walls? On the floor? Now, wherever you are, can you smell anything? Is it a natural smell? Pleasant? Annoying? Sharp? Distant? Can you taste anything? Are you eating? What? What do you hear? Natural sounds? Traffic? Machinery? What about talking? Who is with you? Where are they in relation to you? Are the voices loud? Pleasant? Angry? Are you interacting with others or watching them?

As soon as the questions stop, open your eyes and begin writing to get the scene down. Don't worry about making a neat or coherent draft. Write quickly whatever you saw or heard, putting down sentences, words, phrases, and even drawings if that will help you get the scene down. Continue writing until the instructor or colleague tells you to stop. If there is time, share your scene with another student. Read what you have written, but don't hesitate to go beyond it if more pictures come to mind.

Writing a Draft: Elements to Use

You are now ready to write the first draft of your paper. If you liked the start you made in the recollection activity, go ahead on this scene. This activity often produces good material. If you want to use another experience, do this recollection exercise again, preferably with another writer.

Whether you decide to use this start or not, get your scene in mind now. The next section of the chapter talks about different elements that can go into a scene and includes several activities to help you think of material. These activities will be most useful to you if you can apply them to your draft as you write it. So begin the draft now, and write and rewrite it as you read this section. Let the activities help you in this process. Your instructor may ask you to do some of these in class or to do them elsewhere and bring them to class. The activities are to help make your draft effective. Use them any way that will serve that purpose.

Sensory Detail

What we know from the world around us we know because of our senses (sight, taste, smell, touch, sound). If you want your readers to experience your scene as you did, you must help them by helping their senses. Most narratives emphasize sight, because that is the easiest sense to write about, depending as it does on shape and color. But you can also use touch, which has to do with textures and with heat and cold. Think, for example, of a scene in the woods. Immediately green, blue, brown, trees, leaves, sky, flowers—sight images—come to mind. But think of the textures of these same objects: the smoothness of the green leaves, the rough bark on the trees, the soft green of the moss growing over the hard cold stone.

Don't stop with sight and touch. Even the quietest woods are filled with the sounds of birds, animals rustling the leaves, or water running over stones. And the woods smell of dirt and flowers. The sun warms your face; the wind blows your hair. All the time your senses are alive and working.

Read the following paper and note how the words and sentences bring your senses alive. As you read, mark passages that appeal to each of the different senses. Your instructor may ask you to point these out in class discussion. As you note details that describe sights, sounds, smells, tastes, and tactile feelings, think of places in your own scene where similar details might make it come more alive.

The Bus

As soon as the bus doors creaked open, I found myself in the midst of   1
the pushing crowd. It was around lunchtime, perhaps a little after twelve,
for the sun was blazing right above us. Perspiring people surrounded the
door and one by one thumped up three steps into the bus, clutching coins
in their sweaty palms. One girl, who held a dollar bill, frantically asked
her friend for change since the bus stop sign had instructed "Exact
change only." The coins clinked and rattled, piling on top of each other in
the tarnished metal box by the driver. Soon the forty-seven seats were
filled, and I was one of the many people who had to stand.

"Move to the rear of the bus!" the driver roared at us, and we all   2
shuffled a few inches down to let a few more people join us in the breathing furnace. I could feel the books of the guy next to me scratching my
arm, and the purse of the girl behind me jabbing my back.

I thought for sure the bus would burst. I guess the driver didn't   3
think so, for he shifted gears and the bus started off with a jerk and a
roar. It bumped noisily along its route, engine humming. Chatter
increased, competing with the occasional ringing of the bell and rattle of
the coins. Recklessly the bus sped around corners, causing riders to
swing and slide into each other. People calmly tried to keep their balance.
But one lady lost an apple from her grocery bag during an especially
abrupt stop, and to her dismay, she had to chase it down the aisle.

An occasional smooth part in the ride allowed the standing riders to   4
relax their grip on the poles and wipe their sweaty palms on their clothes.
Students shifted their books restlessly, and old ladies fanned themselves.
Then a guy next to me started moving to the exit door and managed to
step heavily on my foot.

"Thanks," I muttered under my breath, silently calculating how   5
much longer I would have to remain in the bus.

Looking above the people's heads, I saw colorful advertising signs on   6
the bus wall. People in the aisles with nothing better to do stared vacantly
at them. A little boy with glasses looked out from one ad, begging for
blood donations. A green outdoor scene tempted people to smoke KOOL
cigarettes. A yellow poster with cartoon characters drawn by Corky told
people to return their library books promptly.

Eyes wandered and eyes closed. A bald-headed man in the front seat   7
rustled his newspaper and turned the pages now and then. Two girls discussed the possibility that the heart announcing that Craig loved Cathy,
scribbled on the seat in front of them, was describing people they knew. A
student with books neatly sitting on his lap leaned his head on the window and fell asleep.

Though the windows were open as much as they could be—about half   8
way—the bus was unbearably hot and stuffy. The heat, combined with

the body odors, made breathing nauseating. Somebody's cheap "Strawberry Essence" perfume diffused through the bus made my stomach turn.

Finally my bus stop came into view. I rang the bell, elbowed my way   9
to the back door, and braced myself. The force of the stop nearly sent me to the front of the bus again. The green light above the door went on, and I pushed the door open. The blast of fresh air revived me enough to stagger the last block home.

Laurie Wong

As in most narratives, this one focuses heavily on sight, but notice also the many references to sound and touch. (For example, note the sounds in paragraphs 1 and 3, the references to touch in paragraph 2, and the smells in paragraph 8.) You have undoubtedly found many others.

Taste and smell are perhaps the hardest senses to write about, but these senses bring back memories as fully as the others. To help yourself think of language for these senses, think now of something you like to eat. Write a sentence or two that describe what that food tastes like. Share these sentences with other writers. As you listen to them read their sentences, note that taste is often described in terms of another sense: "The soft ice cream felt cold going down my throat" (touch). Note also that taste and smell are often described indirectly. This paragraph from a paper about a cookout handles smell and taste very well, mostly by suggestion rather than direct description:

Suddenly, I heard the sound made by hot iron and steaming water. I hurriedly uncovered the pot. Reddish pork, fried bean curd, green pepper, white onion, and cabbage all turned up and down. I watched, my mouth watering. A delicious smell permeated and vanished in the open air. The allurement was too much. I took a spoonful and burned my mouth. Still it satisfied me.

W R I T I N G   A C T I V I T Y

With the sensory words from "The Bus" in mind, take a paper and make a list of details from each of the senses (or as many as apply) in the scene you are writing. Start with sight images if that is easiest, but most likely you already have a lot of these that you remembered in the recollection activity on page 9. Move on to sound, then to touch. Then work on smell, and taste where it is relevant. Think back over your scene with each sense in mind. Write down a sound, such as cars going by in the street, and then think of words that you might use to describe the sound: bump of tires in the potholes, the engine's acceleration as the car finishes its turn at the corner, and so on.

The sample papers printed at the end of the chapter might help with this activity. Look at "Nature's Pure Energy" for exceptional sight details and at "Slow Train in China" for all of the senses.

Dialogue

Sometimes speech can be the most important "sound" in a scene. Generally a scene will not be composed entirely of dialogue, but if you remember people speaking, put down what they said. And put it down the way they said it. Don't pretty it up, or make it sound like an essay. The most important thing about writing dialogue is that it must sound like speech.

The following simple scene is not filled with speech, but the dialogue, as much as anything else, tells the story. The talk in the scene sounds right—that is, it sounds like something people would really say—and it is used just where it needs to be to make the action immediate and clear.

Farewell

Mike began to strum the guitar softly, and I sat down next to him on the hard yellow curb to wait for the shuttle bus to take us all to a cup of coffee at the airport coffeehouse. The lights illuminating the gate 14 area shone brightly behind us, and we could see the stars pretty clearly. Across the pavement from us Jan and Ronald looked over the rail at the rows and rows of blue lights that outlined the dark runways.

Behind me stood Barry, Jimmy, and Deborah. Jimmy and Debs were talking a little in hushed voices, but mostly they just stood there with blank expressions on their faces. Barry was a little bit apart from us, facing the other way, alone with his thoughts. He was crying.

Mike began to play the chords for ''Maile Lei.'' That's the song we had sung while each of us took our turn, one by one, in saying our personal goodbyes to mainland-bound Carrie with leis and kisses. Although she had been Barry's girl, I knew I would miss her, too.

Mike stopped playing. But I felt like singing. I felt like singing something beautiful, but I wasn't sure what. ''Let's try something.''

"What?"

"Anything."

Barry sat down on the other side of Mike and said, "Okay, what song?" His eyes were still red.

I said to Mike, "Do you know 'Summer Song'?"

"I don't know the chords."

"That's okay. Let's sing it without the guitar."

So we did. But we didn't know all the words, and after several minutes of trying to remember, we soon fell silent once again. I gazed at the broken yellow medial strip on the road in front of us, and I could hear a plane scream as it took off somewhere in the blue darkness.

The humid air of that late August night was even hotter in the crammed shuttle bus. Still we sang again very quietly the words we did know:

They say that all good things must end someday.
Autumn leaves must fall.
But don't you know that it hurts me so,
To say goodbye to you?

Later, sitting in the car, waiting for the congestion in the parking lot to clear up, we heard the roar of a 747.

And when the rain beats against my window pane,
I'll think of summer days again . . .
And dream of you.

Randall J. Ide

WRITING ACTIVITY

Look over the draft of your developing scene. Does anyone talk in it? Should anyone talk? Was conversation an important element in what happened? If so, someone should talk. Would conversation help the reader understand a character or the situation better? If so, someone should probably talk. Have you implied that someone was talking, that is, have you summarized someone's talk without actually detailing a dialogue? (I told my mother that I would be home soon and she said I shouldn't be late. I yelled at the coach that he just didn't understand me, and he yelled back that I didn't understand the game.) Such summaries sometimes work, but inexperienced writers tend to use too much summary. Often a dialogue can set up the action better for your reader. Let your readers hear as well as see. Look at the two drafts below:

Draft 1

Our friends were all there, some still had faint grins on their faces.
They began to cheer for us, and now they wanted us to go back up the ski
slope again; this time they would go too. Lynn and I exchanged glances
and said that we would never again venture to the top of a mountain.

Draft 2

We reached the bottom of the mountain to see our friends laughing
and cheering. "Let's all go again," they said. Lynn and I exchanged
glances. "Never again!" we said, pulling off our skis.

Find a place in your scene where people interact. Write four or five or more
sentences of talk back and forth. Do this especially if you have a *summarized* dialogue. Find another place and write another dialogue. Find yet another place if
you can. Maybe you won't want to use all these dialogues in the final paper, but
write them now just to hear your characters talk. If you write one or two dialogues, it will give you more material to work with as you write and revise your
scene.

Read your dialogues out loud to yourself, to another writer, or to a patient
friend. Ask them or yourself if what you have sounds like what the character, or
any real person, would have said. The paper "Airplane" at the end of this chapter
might help you with dialogue. It has an effective combination of actual and summarized speech.

Detailed Climax

Some papers that you write will be about exciting moments with a definite climax, like accidents or sporting events. When you write about such things, you
must remember clearly those very few moments when the accident actually
occurred or the final point was scored, and you must tell exactly what happened
around you at that time: what you saw; what you heard; and what you felt (not
internally, but physically), including pain, heat, and textures.

You cannot substitute phrases like "my stomach twisted," "I was scared," "my
heart beat faster," or "a thousand things ran through my mind" for the actual events
that went on around you. You might want to try one or two sentences that tell how
you reacted emotionally, but a little of that goes a long way. Your readers will be

able to visualize the scene *only* through remembered sensory details. You cannot hope to make your readers feel as you did simply by naming your feelings. You must tell your readers what happened and let the events, sights, sounds, and smells reproduce the experience for them.

The two following papers show how two writers detailed climactic moments. In "A Permanent Scar" not more than a few seconds could have passed from the time the writer touched the fence until she was knocked loose, yet she remembered the events exactly: the jerking head, the blood, the little brother running around. Likewise the writer of "The Relay" tells you what you see and do when you swim to win. Note the "sandpaper" starting block, the markings on the pool, the description of the turn, the sight of his opponent lunging desperately at the finish.

A Permanent Scar

Tommy and I sauntered along. Every now and then we stopped to gaze at the big holstein cows grazing in the distance. I whistled at Rex, our old collie, who bounded out of the garage and joined us in our carefree jaunt to the pasture. The canal turned a corner and led us to the bank of a branching irrigation ditch, which was wide at the mouth but narrowed as it slipped under a barbed wire fence. At the end of the ditch was the pasture we were gradually approaching. 1

"C'mon, Tommy," I urged. "Let's wade the rest of the way." I kicked off my Keds and began rolling up my Levis. 2

"Mommy said we weren't supposed to wade in the ditch, Sue, and Dad said so too. I'm not gonna do it. I'm gonna use the bridge like Daddy said," whined Tommy. 3

"Oh, Tommy, it'll be fun, and Mom and Dad won't even know. We can grab the fence here and follow it along so we won't fall. They just didn't want us getting wet." 4

I looked down at the swirling water as I slid one bare foot into the mud. It oozed between my toes and crept slowly along the top of my foot until it surrounded my ankle. "Oh, it feels neat," I shrieked, and I plunged my other foot into the murk beside the first one. Then with a skating motion, I eased my way forward until the almost icy water sucked into the mud depression, surrounding my toes first and forcing me to hesitate for a brief instant. The water, not so shockingly cold now, lapped at my foot and finally touched my ankles as my entire foot sank deeper in the mud and created a slight rush of water around it. As I approached the main current coming from the canal, I sensed a need for greater balance and edged my way carefully toward the barbed wire fence. 5

The fence within my grasp, I half lunged for it to steady myself as the water surged and gushed around my calves. As my hands clasped the 6 wire, I jerked in a convulsive reflex. Surging electrical current knocked me deep into the swirling water. My head whipped from side to side. My arms strained, pulling, struggling, trying desperately to break my grip on the wire. All the time this stream of electricity jumped and leaped inside my body, blinding my eyes and blocking thought out of my mind. I twisted and turned, tugging at my hands, trying to free myself. Holding me fast, the current merely clenched my fist tighter around the sharp barbs that were now ripping deep into the soft flesh of my hands. The electricity numbed the pain I had first felt, and in my struggle I tore and pierced my hands.

"Tommy," I screamed, "Get somebody. Help me! I can't let go. Get   7
somebody, please." Tommy, a sickly white with his two tiny hands clasped over his mouth, was half running, half stumbling in a dazed circle, unable to utter a sound.

Suddenly, inexplicably, I was free from the fence. I sat still, my matted   8
hair dripping with muddy water, and slowly placed one burned and bleeding hand on top of the other. I looked down and saw gashes in my skin oozing bright red blood around yellowish-white burned flesh. I slowly scooted myself forward, then backward, trying to raise my body from the now even muddier water. I finally gained my feet, but my tangled hair and clothes, dripping with both water and blood, evidenced the thrashing fight I'd had.

Tommy and I moved slowly toward the house. The sun was still warm.   9
As I held my dripping hands upward, part of the blood quickly dried on my arms, creating grotesque patterns for the heavier streams to follow as they ran down my arms and off my slightly bent elbows. Tommy, alongside, with frightened eyes, clutched my canvas Keds tightly to his chest.

student paper

A close look at "A Permanent Scar" can give you one hint about how writers create action. Reread paragraph 6, noting the verbs in each sentence: *lunged, surged, clasped, jerked, whipped, strained, jumped and leaped, twisted, clenched,* and so on. Each sentence in the paragraph has a verb that details an action. The abundance of such verbs coming so quickly increases the pace of the action and builds the tension almost unbearably. Suppose the paragraph had begun: "I reached for the fence as the water came around my calves. As I held the wire, I felt a convulsive reflex. The current pushed me deeper into the water. My head went from side to side. My arms pulled trying desperately to let go of the wire." The interesting details are still there, but the sentences have lost their punch.

Of course, the action here is tense and exciting. A quieter scene, like "Morning" at the beginning of the chapter, calls for quieter verbs:

Wrapped in my sleeping bag, I could <u>feel</u> the penetrating cold air on my face. It was early in the morning and still dark outside. I leaned over and lit the candle by my bunk. Out the camper window I could see the moon, bright and strong even though only a quarter. Seeing that I was up, Sleepy, my grandparents' large, red dog, jumped up onto my bunk and sat directly in front of me wagging his tail and blocking my view.

Look at the verbs in the sentences you have written so far for this scene. Are they interesting and vivid? Do they define and describe action? We will have more to say about using active verbs in the section on editing. For now just think about your verbs as you write the scene.

The Last Lap

As we sat down behind the starting block, we could hear the team cheering for us. Floyd, Conkling, and Wilfred all had serious faces as they paced around on the pool deck. If one guy blew it in this 400-yard freestyle relay, there went the championship. We'd lost last year to Kailua by only one tenth of a second; we wanted to redeem ourselves. We had to work together.

Floyd was up first, as I sat down on the cold cement. Wilfred stood behind Floyd, shaking his arms, loosening up, as if to shake the nervous-ness out. Floyd had a beautiful start and three solid turns, so he came in with a slight lead. Wilfred followed with his fastest second leg. As Conkling entered his second turn, I stood up and walked toward the block where Floyd and Wilfred were sitting catching their breath. "Come on, Glenn, you can do it," Floyd told me as I got up on the block and curled my toes over the sandpaper edge. As I leaned over slowly and followed Conkling in with my fingertips, I saw the Kailua swimmer at his knees. As my body fell, I swung my arms in a circlelike motion and pushed off as far as I could go.

The coldness of the water spread instantly over my whole body. With my legs kicking as hard as they could, I pulled my arms through the water. The dark tiles, forming a guideline in the center of the lane, passed quickly under me with every stroke I took. Out of the corner of my eye, I saw the Kailua swimmer as we crossed the middle of the pool. No longer could I hear the cheering and screaming, just the sound of my arms stroking and legs kicking in and out of the water.

About three feet from the turn, I started my flip. My legs felt cool air as they slapped out of the water and slapped back, and the tile of the pool felt slippery under my foot as I pushed off for my last lap. It was the best turn I had ever made, and we headed toward the finish.

My arms began tiring, but I took one last breath and, with all the strength I had left, put down my head and swam as fast as my arms could stroke. I could see and feel the waves created by other swimmers against my forehead as I looked toward the finish. The T on the pool wall seemed closer with every stroke I took, and it moved up quickly as I charged toward it. About two feet away, I took one last stroke and lunged at the wall with my right arm. At the very instant my fingers felt the cold tile, I turned my head toward lane 2 and saw the hand of the Kailua swimmer lunging in at the wall in a last, vain effort.

The championship plaque felt heavy as I carried it back to the team.

Glenn Inouye

The paper "Nature's Pure Energy," at the end of this chapter, has particularly good sensory details when the author begins to tell about the climax of his ride on a wave. The action in the third paragraph of that essay must have taken less than five minutes, but the author gives details of sight, feeling, and hearing, and uses active and interesting verbs.

WRITING ACTIVITY: RECOLLECTION

Pick the climactic five minutes (or three minutes, or even one minute) of your scene. Do a recollection activity like the one we started with on just that period of time. Ask yourself what you saw, heard, felt, smelled, and tasted. Your instructor might ask you to do this in class in pairs or in small groups. Or you could get a friend to help you. Push yourself and each other to remember every detail, every sound, every smell. Get more material than you could possibly use so that you can pick the best. Remember to write all these sensory memories down either as you remember them or immediately afterward so that they will be available for you when you write and rewrite that part of your paper. Then rewrite your climax making use of the freshly remembered details.

Beginnings and Endings

In writing a scene, you don't need to tell what happened the day before or detail any preparation or give any background information; just relate the scene. A writer once told me that after he had written the draft for a story, he always read through it until he came to the first paragraph where something really happened; then he threw everything before that away. Inexperienced writers often waste time at the beginning of a narrative giving information and introductions that are not really necessary. I call this clearing your throat or shuffling your feet. It is natural enough to do on a first draft, but, as you begin to rethink your draft, check the beginning of the scene to make sure it starts where the action really begins.

When he wrote the first draft for the paper "The Last Lap," Glenn started that morning:

> As I looked out of my window, I could see the sun's rays casting shadows and Diamond Head in the background. The sky was cloudless, and I thought to myself, "It's going to be a nice day to swim."

Glenn followed this with a short flashback to practice, went on to the meet, talked about several events, and finally put in the paragraph that now begins his essay. But by that time he didn't have time to detail his own swim, which was what he really wanted to emphasize. He tried again, eliminating the morning scene, the flashback, and even the other events in the meet. His next-to-last draft began:

> This was the event we had been practicing so hard for every day; the boys' 400-yard freestyle relay. We had lost last year to Kailua by a tenth of a second so it really meant something to us, this being the last time we would swim it. The pressure grew as the first swimmers went on the starting blocks. Floyd was up first and gave us a slight lead, but it was reduced when Wilfred came in just ahead of Kailua.
>
> Now it was all up to me. I could win it or lose it. Taking deep breaths as I curled my toes over the sandpaper-covered edge of the starting block, the nervousness grew inside me with every breath I took.

You can see by comparing this version with the one above that on the final draft, Glenn found out how to put the reader immediately into the scene and how to work the necessary information in after that. I might add that Glenn found his ending ("The championship plaque felt heavy as I carried it back to the team.") in the very first version of the paper and had sense enough to keep it for every subsequent version. He knew a good thing when he found it.

Following are two pairs of beginnings for scenes. In each pair, the first version wastes time, while the second begins where it should, right in the action. Pair A shows a slow beginning for the scene "Airplane," printed at the end of this chapter, followed by the actual beginning. The added information in the first version is simply not necessary.

Pair A

1. My father and I were flying together to Seattle. He had some business to do and I wanted to see old friends. When we got to the airport, we hurried to catch our plane. The waiting room was crowded, so it took a long time for everyone to board.

After we got all settled, the plane took off. When we were under-way, the stewardess served our lunch. While we were eating some workmen came and began to strip away a portion of the carpet.

2. I was sitting in the aisle seat, and my father, next to me, had been talking to an old woman from Dayton, Ohio, since we got into the air. She was telling my father about her nephews in Seattle while I lis-tened, eating my turkey sandwich.

   I noticed two of the crew members in the aisle had stripped away a section of carpeting. . . .

The first version in Pair B tells us more than we need to know about the cir-cumstances surrounding a card game, while the second just tells about playing cards.

Pair B

1. It was a nice day. All of my relatives had come over to our house. We all said hello and asked how everyone was. Mother had prepared a good meal, and we all ate chicken and rice and beans, and Mother had ice cream for dessert. Then we all sat around and talked about how everyone was doing in school. My aunt told us about my cousin who was going to get married, and another aunt told us about my cousin who was going east for school. Then, we wondered what to do, and since we always like to play cards, they said why don't we do that. My Aunt Emi always seemed to win these games, and everyone teased her, but soon my aunts and my mother sat down and the game began.

2. I sat forward, closely watching the game before me. I was hopeful that someone would ask me to take over their hand for them. Aunt Jane dealt out the cards in a brisk professional manner. Her wrists deftly flicked the cards out so that a little pile formed in front of each of the seven players. Some players would pick up and look at the cards as they fell. Some would arrange each arriving card in a neat pile before them. The rest just waited for all of their cards before collecting them.

   As the last card was dealt, everyone peered at their cards. No one asked me to play his hand, so I resigned myself to watching.

   Aunt Jane looked at her cards and stated, "It's for sale."

   This started feverish bidding among the players with poor cards.

One suggestion about beginnings might be useful to you: In your first sentence put a name (I and we are names) and an action. Look back at the first sentences of every scene we have read, and you will see that nearly all of them begin that way:

As soon as the bus doors creaked open, I found myself in the midst of the pushing crowd.

> Mike began to strum the guitar softly . . .
> I was sitting in the aisle seat, . . .
> I sat forward, closely watching the game before me.
> Tommy and I sauntered along.
> As we sat down behind the starting block . . .

What we have said for beginnings goes also for endings: Begin when the action begins, and end when the action ends. Don't tell what happened the next day, or even the next minute, unless it is vital for the understanding of the scene. You don't need to sum anything up for your readers. Let them figure out the implications for themselves. Leave them with a picture of some action that they can savor. Some of the scenes we have read had suggestive endings:

"Morning": I fell asleep.

"Farewell": Later, sitting in the car, waiting for the congestion in the parking lot to clear up, we heard the roar of a 747. [followed by the words to the song]

"A Permanent Scar": Tommy, alongside, with frightened eyes, clutched my canvas Keds tightly to his chest. [We don't really have to know what happened at the doctor's office, do we?]

On the other hand, two of the essays at the end of the chapter have more formal endings; one goes beyond the climax ("Airplane"), and one makes a pertinent comment ("Slow Train in China"). However, neither drags out the ending. The comment in the latter is really part of the scene because it names the emotion the writer was having as she lived through it.

WRITING ACTIVITY

Try an experiment with the scene you have written. Read your paragraphs and see whether your scene actually begins in paragraph 2 or later. Do the same with the ending: Does the scene end in the next-to-last paragraph or the one before that? If so, throw out the excess baggage.

Now look through your paper and see if you have a sentence somewhere else in your paper that is really your opening sentence or your closing sentence. Often writers write one really nice sentence and then bury it somewhere rather than putting it up front where the reader can really see it. If you like, ask someone else to read your paper and see if she can find a beginning sentence. Maybe you have not written your opening and closing yet. Think about it.

Reworking the Draft

You should have a draft of your scene by now. It may be very rough, just a sketch; it may be quite wonderful, almost finished. But a draft is just a draft. It is never carved in stone. That's the nice thing about going through the process of writing. You always have a second (and a third) chance to make your paper do what you want it to do. Once in a while you will be inspired as you begin to write, and what comes out the first time will require only minor editing. More often you will want to do more than fiddle with a word here and a sentence there.

Writers learn to write by writing and, sometimes even more, by rewriting. Scenes need to be revised for a number of reasons: to add details; to omit material that does not belong; to focus a narrative; to speed up the action, or to slow it down. We will talk about all of these here.

Begin your revision by checking your draft in this way. First go through it and try to eliminate every sentence or part of a sentence that does not reproduce something you heard, smelled, felt, saw, or tasted. Try to think of whether you have included enough sensory detail and dialogue that the reader can enter directly into the experience with you. Cut out comments and generalizations unless they are absolutely necessary. Be ruthless, but do not cut any of the experience. Think for a minute about your beginning. Have you entered directly into the story? Did you end when the experience ended? Don't drag out the scene with comment. Make sure that the details are given in a clear order so that the reader can follow the experience.

How are you doing? Did you cut your draft down below the minimum word limit specified by the instructor? Run the experience through your head again, making sure your recollection is complete. Go back to the writing activities you did and use more of the good material you produced. The following analyses will help you look at a draft to see where it needs work and how you can do the needed work.

Look at the excerpts below from the first paragraph of draft 1 and draft 2 of a paper on running. Cathy's first draft was too long, told too much, and did not focus on any part of the action. When the writer started draft 2, she decided to concentrate on the beginning and the end of the run. Note how she removed details from this paragraph to make her focus sharper.

Draft 1

"Boom," went the gun, and out of habit, my body leaned forward and I was off. My arms started pumping, and my legs began to move. I came around the first curve and I passed two runners and I knew we would scatter once we passed that line, but for now we had to stay in our lanes. As we came along the straightaway, one of the runners I had passed, passed me. It didn't bother me, so I started pumping my arms and started picking up my feet. As we passed the line, and scattered out, I somehow ended up in the back, placing me as the fifth runner. It really didn't bother me much because I knew we had three more full laps to go. Finishing the first lap and going into the second, I still maintained the fifth position, and I felt comfortable at the pace I was running. As I went into our third lap, I slowly picked up my pace, and I passed one runner. I could taste the salt in my perspiration and it stung my eyes, but I kept on running. I could hear the heavy breathing of the girl in front of me, and I could sense the girl in back of me picking up ground, so I ran even faster. I was exhausted and my body felt numb, but I kept on running.

Draft 2

"Boom" went the gun. I pushed off with my right foot, pumped my arms, and was off. My whole body was one moving machine, and it felt right. Everything seemed to fly by, and suddenly I was going into my second lap. Two runners passed me, and my competitive spirit boiled, but I ran smart. My strategy was to let them pass and use energy. I could then overtake them because I had preserved mine. In each lap, I could taste the salt in my perspiration and sometimes it stung my eyes. I heard the irregular breathing of the girl in front of me and the heavy pounding footsteps of the girls in back. I could sense they were picking up ground because their footsteps sounded close.

Since the writer wanted to focus on the beginning and the end, she removed material to deemphasize the middle laps, thus increasing the pace of the action. By contrast, the writer of the paper below made several changes that slow down the pace of the paper and build suspense. First he made three sentences out of the first one. This causes the reader to consider each action separately and thus slows the pace. Then, he substituted real detail for less concrete descriptions (for example, the actual words of the crowd for "cheered eagerly," and the batter striking his shoes for "the batter was very frustrated"). This allows the reader to get inside the action more completely and to savor each event, again building suspense more fully.

Draft 1

The first pitch I delivered was a ball and so was the next one, which caused me to panic. My body was soaked with sweat and the nervousness increased. The crowd cheered eagerly for our team. The third pitch was a strike, which made me feel just a bit relieved but still very nervous. The batter was very frustrated as he stepped up to the plate again.

Draft 2

The first pitch I delivered was a ball. So was the second. I began to panic. I heard the crowd yelling, "Come on, Scott." "Get control." "Strike him out." The third pitch was a strike. Relieved, but still nervous, I watched the batter return to the plate striking the bat against his shoes in frustration.

With these comments and examples in mind, look again at each part of your paper. Does any action move too slowly or too quickly? Does everything in your paper get exactly the same amount of emphasis so that there is no focus, no building of suspense?

WRITING ACTIVITY

Try an experiment now with one section (a paragraph or two) of your paper. Do one of the following to change the pacing (from slow to fast or vice versa) or the focus:

1. Eliminate some action while building some other action.
2. Change a summary of action and/or dialogue to real dialogue or a more detailed and exact account.
3. Lengthen and shorten sentences to make the reader pay attention to your action in a different way.

Do all of the above if you wish, and try more than one version of a paragraph. If you think it will help, work with another writer, giving and getting suggestions.

While you are thinking of getting help, you might consider one thing about revising. In order to revise effectively, you must decide what will work for your readers and what won't; what your readers need to know and how you can keep their interest. It is difficult to be your own reader, so the next section talks about getting someone who can be a reader for you. The final section talks about editing. Editing is the *last* step in writing a paper, so you should wait until after you have reactions from your peers to do the final revisions and editing.

Feedback from Other Writers

Your instructor will give you and your fellow students instructions for helping each other work on drafts. There are many ways to do this. For a short narrative paper like this perhaps the most common way is to have the writer read the draft out loud (twice if possible) to a small group of four or five other writers and let the group members respond individually in turn to what they have heard. Often the instructor or the class prepares questions to guide the response. Group members often give written responses to longer and more complex papers. Each chapter in this text will give some suggestions for responding to the kind of paper being discussed and give guidance about what you should look for. Your instructor may supplement these suggestions.

The process may seem intimidating if you have never actively sought help from readers. But remember three things:

1. This response is not a judgment on you as a person.
2. A draft is just a draft. It can be changed.
3. Ultimately your paper belongs to you. You want it to affect your readers, so hearing what readers have to say should help you see how successful you have been. If a number of readers respond in the same way, perhaps you ignore their response at your own peril. But if you want to ignore the advice, that is your prerogative. Your paper is yours.

Sometimes the most powerful experience in a responding group is not hearing what others have to say about *your* paper but hearing another paper in which the writer has really managed to bring the scene or the topic to life. Of course you would never merely imitate another paper, but sometimes hearing how another writer has handled the problem will give you ideas about your own. And don't ignore the fact that you can be extremely helpful to other writers, either as an example or as a responder.

Generally you help other writers most by telling them where the paper is most interesting and affecting and where it does not work for you. You can also tell where you might have been confused or lost track of the story or of the argument. You can often be very helpful to writers simply by telling them what you heard. You may well have heard something quite different from what they wrote, which would be a very good thing for a writer to know.

When you listen to responses to your paper, control the impulse to argue with the responder. Don't try to defend your work, even if the responses seem wrong-headed to you. Just listen to what the others have to say, take notes, and consider the suggestions later. You can, in fact should, ask the responders to clarify what they have said if you don't understand it. You may get more helpful responses if you ask your listeners to tell you about a particular part of the paper or to respond in a particular way. Remember: This is *your* paper.

Listen, consider, and then return to your paper and let what you have heard help you in your revisions. Did several of the listeners seem to miss the point of your scene or respond to some action or one of your characters in an unexpected way? If so, try to think why. Did several seem to indicate that they went to sleep at what you thought was the climax? That might spell trouble for you. Did they think your beginning or end was dull? You'd better look at it again.

As you listen to the drafts for this paper, keep in mind most particularly the second rule given at the beginning of this chapter: Put down only what you saw, heard, smelled, felt, or tasted. Your reactions might be summarized in two words: add and subtract. Where does the writer need to add more sensory details and action? Where does she need to subtract needless talk that does not bring the reader into the scene? Does the writer "clear his throat" for a sentence or two before he gets into the scene? Does she have a "hole" at the climax where you as a reader want to see, hear, and feel the action? Remember also to tell writers where they succeed. This not only gives the writers confidence but also reinforces their good judgment. Sometimes even if *you* think something is working, hearing someone else tell you that it does is very helpful.

Sentence-level Editing

If you have been careful to follow the three rules given at the beginning of this chapter, and if you have looked carefully at your paper yourself and listened to your colleagues, you should have a scene full of good sensory detail, interesting dialogue, and action. Now you are ready for editing. In this text the term *editing* means paying attention to sentence-level considerations, rather than to overall changes such as adding detail, moving material around, and adding and deleting ideas. Editing requires you to look carefully at your individual sentences. Sentences need to be efficient, even beautiful, as well as correct. We will concentrate here on the first two characteristics. We turn now to examples showing how writers have edited their texts, to some practice exercises for you, and to some suggestions about what you can look for in your own drafts.

Readers want your scenes to be full of detail but not necessarily full of words. In fact useless words get in the way of the narrative. In the passage below useless words have been removed, and sentences have been combined by the judicious addition of one or two words. As a result the action is clearer, and no detail has been omitted. This is an example of making sentences more efficient.

> ~~It was a very~~ hot ~~day~~ and ~~the track is dusty and dirty. There were~~
> *The*   *dusty*   *went through*
>
> mud puddles and sand hills, ~~It goes through trees~~ and ~~over~~ jumps.
> *over*
>
> The race was ready to begin. ~~Looking at the clock once more, I saw~~
> two minutes ~~remaining. Soon I felt~~ sweat ~~running through~~ my back
> *Only*   *ed*   *The*   *ran down*
>
> and onto my palms as I gripped my handlebar. I took a deep breath
> and ~~gave a last~~ look at the ~~opponent~~ next to me. The shot was fired
> *ed*   *biker*
>
> and we were off.

In the passage below, see if you can cut out unnecessary words and combine sentences as in the example above. Try to make a clearer, more efficient, and thus more effective narrative.

> There were just a few minutes left before the stores closed. There
> were so many people just roaming around the place while I was rush-
> ing. I had been rushing because I needed to buy my last Christmas
> gift. It was getting closer and closer to dark. I needed the gift badly.
> What was worse, I didn't even know what to shop for. Maybe my
> mind was a boggle because I had left a nice, fresh, air-conditioned
> office to catch the bus with the bad smell of body odor and children
> screaming, using obscene language. Maybe all these things made me
> feel boggled.

Did you notice that several words were repeated here? *There were* begins both the first two sentences. *Rushing* appears twice. *Boggle* and *boggled* both appear. Repetitions like this are the most obvious place to start cutting. The second and third sentences could probably be combined as " . . . while I was rushing to buy my last Christmas gift." In that same sentence, you could probably omit *the place*. You will find a lot of other places to cut.

Speaking of unneeded repetition, look at the following passage:

> I looked at the bar while I moved both of my feet parallel to it. I
> had them spread apart at shoulder width. I grabbed the bar with the
> tightest grip I ever used. I counted three, then I yelled with all my

breath and lifted with all my might. I did it; I had the weights above
my chest. I was holding for 10 seconds and during that time my face
was changing color. I was holding my breath while small grunts were
coming from my mouth. Then I dropped the weights and told myself,
"Yeah, I did it."

Have you ever written a passage like that? The passage has very good details, but it also has 101 words when it probably needs about 50 or fewer. It has eight sentences and probably needs only three or four. Working with a classmate or on your own, reduce the passage until it is not only detailed but also efficient. You will almost certainly have a clearer and better-paced description. Start by circling all the I's. There is nothing wrong with putting *I* in a scene, but overuse of the word can be boring, so eliminate as many as possible. For example, "I looked at the bar and moved my feet, spread apart at shoulder width, parallel to it." You can probably do even better than that.

One type of unnecessary repetition that often mars narrative is an overuse of the different forms of *to be*: *is, are, was, were*. Recall what was said above in connection with the paper "A Permanent Scar" about using active and interesting verbs. *To be* verbs do not show action, and thus do little to move your story. In narrative especially the verb is the backbone of the sentence. Much action, even sensory detail, can be expressed with a verb. If every sentence uses a *to be* verb, you slow your action and lose your punch.

The passage below, taken from a paper describing a first parachute jump, illustrates this problem. The writer remembered a lot of good sensory detail, but all the *was*'s and *were*'s flatten out the action. So do other repetitions, such as "the big moment was fast approaching," followed a few sentences later by "the big moment was now only seconds away." The *to be* verbs are circled to help you get started.

After about 10 minutes of flying time we (were) over the drop zone
and the big moment (was) fast approaching. There (was) a loud rushing
sound as the doors opened. The green light came on and the first
jumpers (were) put out. I (was) in the middle of the second stock of
jumpers, so after going around and coming over for the second pass,
we (were) on our feet. Then we saw the green light. The big moment (was)
now only seconds away. I did not really know what to expect the first
time out. I (was) now in the door. A tap on the back and out into the
wild blue yonder. I (was) counting, one thousand, two thousand, three

thousand, four thousand, and I looked up to a very comforting sight as I saw the chute billowed out full above me. It (was) a very exhilarating feeling as I drifted earthward. The points we (were) taught in jumping school kept going through my mind as I neared the ground. "Just do like you (were) taught and you won't get hurt: feet and knees together, toes pointed slightly downward, knees slightly bent, relax when you hit."

Obviously the first task in editing would be to replace the repetitive *to be* verbs. In the second sentence, for example, try taking the last verb, *opened*, and making it the main verb: "The doors opened with a loud rush." In the third sentence: "jumpers were put out" sounds like someone had pushed the jumpers out the door. Try an active verb like, "The green light came on and the first group jumped." That puts the action where it should be and, incidentally, gets rid of an unnecessary repetition of *jumpers*. And so on. The rest of the paragraph could also use some judicious cutting and revision. "The big moment was now only seconds away" doesn't add much; "I counted" would be more direct than "I was counting"; "Exhilarated, I drifted earthward" would make that sentence move; and so on.

Changing the sentence, "The green light came on and the first jumpers were put out," to "The green light came on and the first group jumped," illustrates a technique for editing that might be called unburying the verb. Sentences with a *to be* verb often have another word in the sentence that would make a more active verb. The changes in this paragraph illustrate this:

> Only one boy was in the water although ~~there could be heard the~~ *yelled and laughed* ~~yelling and laughter of~~ other boys ∧ at play. The swimming boy called repeatedly, "Come on, jump, jump." At first one boy jumped feet first into the water. Then, like a chain reaction, five other boys standing on the dirty concrete bridge followed. Now ~~there were~~ seven black heads and brown bodies splash*ed*ing ∧ around in the stream.

This passage has good material and generally good sentences. However, unburying better verbs improves the two edited sentences. Note that the words have to change from noun forms to verb forms: *Yelling* becomes *yelled*, for example, and *laughter* becomes *laughed*.

The following passage has good detail, but the verbs are not always effective. Try to unbury verbs in sentences that have weak *to be* verbs.

I was worried that the wind would make something crash through my window. Just when I made the decision that it wasn't blowing strongly enough, all of a sudden there was a big gust of wind. I jumped out of bed and went outside in a rush. The wind had blown our metal patio table into the pool. I saw some plants were uprooted and others were flat. Leaves were in the pool and the water was coming in big splashes onto the deck. Our back yard had the look of a disaster area.

WRITING ACTIVITY

The point of all this practice is to get you thinking about your own sentences. Read your draft now, looking for unnecessary repetition (particularly of *to be* verbs). Start by circling every *to be* verb in your draft. You don't have to eliminate them all, but circling them helps you concentrate your attention.

Pick out the longest and most important paragraph and circle repetitions of words, phrases, even ideas. Sometimes repetition can be effective, but circling repetitive elements will draw your attention to places that need work. Once you have finished this paragraph, go through the rest of the paper.

Be ruthless with yourself. Take out words; combine sentences; throw whole sentences out if they don't really add anything; or take out the one or two words that are useful and insert them into another sentence. Remember: This is not just an exercise to shorten sentences. Long sentences can be very effective as long as every word is needed. Make your action move. Make every sentence, every word, work for your reader.

Correcting Grammar, Spelling, and Punctuation

The last step in completing a paper is to reread it carefully, sentence by sentence, this time looking only for spelling, grammar, and punctuation errors. Your instructor may have you do some exercises and give you more hints about correcting grammar, spelling, and punctuation. You should also have a good dictionary and a standard grammar handbook to help you identify and correct various types of errors.

Sample Papers

Airplane

I was sitting in the aisle seat, and my father, next to me, had been talking to an old woman from Dayton, Ohio, since we got into the air. She was telling my father about her nephews in Seattle while I listened, eating my turkey sandwich.

I noticed two of the crew members in the aisle had stripped away a section of carpeting and were climbing down into the fuselage of the plane. I asked my father about it, and he said that they must be repairing something.

They remained inside the entrails of the plane for a long time. Meanwhile, the stewardesses were picking up empty trays and carefully evading all questions about the two men under the aisle. Then we all knew.

"Good afternoon, this is Captain Williams speaking. We have encountered some difficulty with our landing gear. The two crew members inside the fuselage now are inspecting the landing gear and repairing it. Please do not be alarmed. The situation will be remedied momentarily. Thank you."

After the announcement, everyone spoke a little more quietly, not wanting to let on that the announcement had bothered them. The stewardesses were trotting around with the same plastic grins asking people if there was anything that they would like. The old woman from Ohio told my father, "This is the first time I have ever flown in an airplane, and I was afraid something like this was going to happen." My father, smiling, replied, "I'm sure everything is going to be OK." Just then the captain came on again.

"We have inspected the landing gear and determined the problem. We have repaired it to the best of our abilities and think it will hold during landing. It is securely in place now, but there is a chance that it will not remain like that while we land. We are now flying circles over Seattle to use up the extra fuel that could possibly catch fire if we were to belly-land. I have notified the Seattle Airport, and they are clearing a runway for us. Thank you very much."

After that everyone was even quieter. Some whispered and others just looked around to express their nervous feelings. A man across the aisle ordered a double Scotch for his wife and himself. His wife was clutching a Kleenex in one hand and holding her husband's arm with the other. She was crying silently, and tears rolled down her cheeks and onto her plaid dress. Her husband was stroking her hair and telling her quietly that everything was going to be all right.

A stewardess stopped and asked me if there was anything that I would like. I said, "No." She smiled and moved on. I respected her for smiling at everyone while we were all in the midst of what could be a disaster.

I looked over at my father and was just going to ask him a question he couldn't answer when he looked me in the eyes, saying, "Don't be afraid." I was going to say something when the captain came on again.

"We will be landing in exactly ten minutes. Five minutes from now, we will be passing out pillows and blankets for those who would like them to cover their heads when in the emergency positions for landing. I repeat, please do not be frightened."

The woman by the window was looking at snapshots of her family, talking silently to each one as if reciting a poem. My father had his arm around my shoulders and was talking to me, his voice calm and measured, but I could see sweat standing out on his forehead.

"It is now five minutes to landing time. If you would like a pillow, press your hostess call button and a pillow will be brought to you. Please stay calm. Your cooperation is very important. Thank you."

My father's grip tightened on my shoulders, and I was glad that he was giving me strength. The husband and wife across the aisle were embracing and tears were gliding down her swollen, pink cheeks.

"Will everyone please get into their emergency positions. Be calm and please do as we say. There are now two and a half minutes until landing."

I pressed my chin on my knees and closed my eyes after looking toward my father and seeing the old woman beyond him praying. Eyes closed, I could hear the stewardesses walking in the aisle and the old woman's voice.

"One minute until landing."

The only sound was that of the plane gliding slowly down. Everyone waited silently . . .

"Thirty seconds, twenty, ten . . . "

I felt the plane touch down on the runway, lurch, then begin to roll in the usual jerking way. I got up from my position slowly and saw firetrucks and ambulances lining the sides of the runway. I wanted to laugh and cry at the same time. "We made it," my father said, his voice hoarse. The couple across the aisle kissed, and she laid her head on his shoulder.

The old woman from Dayton, Ohio, said, "I swear to God that I will never ride another airplane as long as I live." My father laughed and kissed her on the cheek.

Douglas Gardine

Slow Train in China

I had been told never to take the slow train, which was always terribly crowded, but this time I had to because I was going somewhere the express train would not stop. I shouldered my way through the crowds of people on the platform till I could move no further. On my right an old man with a wrinkled face stood beside a shoulder pole with two buckets tied at each end. On my left I saw a middle-aged woman with a basket of eggs hanging from her arm. Behind me a young man in a big fur hat and a black overcoat was tying two enormous blanket rolls together. In front of me a greasy green cotton-padded coat obstructed my view. So far as my eyes could reach, everyone I saw was a peasant.

The train pulled up. As the doors creaked open, all the passengers surged around in a fierce struggle to get onto the train. The clang of metal, the curse of a man who had been struck on the head, and the scream from a woman who lost something in the turmoil frightened me. As I made an effort to shrink, I felt something wet and sticky scratching my hand. I looked down and saw a blood-dripping pig head in a string bag carried by a stout man. Before I took out my handkerchief to dry my hand, I was pushed so hard from behind that I nearly fell down. I forgot all about my dirty hand and handkerchief and endeavored to keep my balance.

Fortunately the train had enough room to hold all the passengers, since I was among the last few to get onto the train. But the passenger cars were all full, and I had to stand in the passage between two cars. A tall conductor squeezed his way toward me to close the door as the whistle sounded piercingly. Just then, a middle-aged man came staggering up with a heavy burlap sack on his back. He got onto the first step, but he looked so worn-out and the burlap sack so heavy that his left leg didn't seem able to carry him onto the second step. Sweat trickled down his sallow cheeks, and his fingernails turned pale from grasping the handle too hard.

"Help!" he cried through clenched teeth as he raised his face to look desperately at us. The train was about to start. I stretched my arms, got hold of the string on the sack and pulled hard. But it was too heavy for me too. I looked round for help. To my surprise, I saw indifferent looks on expressionless faces. "Help!" I shouted at the haughty young conductor, who blushed, and, with a violent tug, hauled the poor man onto the train.

Closing the door, the conductor grumbled, "Why didn't you arrive earlier with such a heavy load?"

"Oh, thank you. Thank you . . . ," the poor man kept saying and managed a smile in which I saw only sadness. A smell of tobacco came from his ragged clothes. Obviously, he was a peasant.

"It's very heavy. What is in it?" I asked, pointing at the sack. Stroking the sack with his calloused hand, he said in a low voice, "Corn flour. I brought wheat flour to exchange it with townspeople for corn flour. One jin of wheat flour for two jin of corn flour."

"Why? Don't you have enough to eat?"

With a wry smile, he answered, "There was a failure in the crops last fall."

Instinctively, I put my hand into my pocket where there was ten yuan and some food coupons. I was about to pull them out and hand them to him when I saw, all around me, the same tattered, bent, and undernourished figures; the same gaunt, weary faces; and the same sad, hopeless eyes. I said to myself: "Do you save all the passengers on this train by giving this man a little money and a few coupons? Eighty percent of the Chinese population are leading a life more or less like this!" I shut my eyes to hold back the strong emotion aroused by this scene. The train rumbled on with a monotonous noise, and I wished it could take us someplace where there was no famine, no poverty, and no pain.

Wang Ke

Tornado Dance

Throughout the blistering day, the sky had been crystal clear blue. Being able to see for miles in any direction made the sky look even more clear and blue. The temperature had been in the lower 100s without even a trace of wind.

The wind had now kicked up almost instantly, and the temperature was in the lower 70s. The sky was blanketed with black, threatening clouds that looked like a floating tidal wave.

I was staying with my uncle in North Dakota. His small but functional house sat out in the middle of nowhere surrounded by a huge yard that was fenced in by a barbed wire fence. Beyond the barbed wire was a cow pasture. An oval dirt driveway made part of the yard look like a small football field. There were several small sheds scattered around the yard. Some were used for storing grain, some just to keep junk out of sight, and others made good shelters for gophers, rats, and barn swallows.

The tall, once-peaceful trees were now dancing wildly in the powerful wind, as if they were trying to say something. The cattle, instead of lying still trying to avoid the heat, were now in one huge group acting nervous, like something was wrong. They milled around, bumping into and stepping on one another. I asked my uncle what was wrong with them, but he didn't seem to hear me. He just stood looking out the window, staring at the sky. The look on his face was very intense. I was only 12, but I could see he was thinking very hard about something.

He must have stood in that one spot for at least five minutes, when he suddenly turned and went quickly into the storage room off the kitchen, where he picked up some newspapers off the floor, exposing a door. He raised this trapdoor and revealed an underground room. It was very simple looking, just dug out of the ground, with dirt walls, floor, and ceiling. A single unlighted light bulb hung from the ceiling. There was a box in the far corner and a flashlight. From the floor of the storage room, some homemade-looking stairs led to the floor of the storm shelter, but the rest of it was bare with the exception of a few roots that had found their way in.

The cattle had now gone wild, jumping over and running through the barbed wire fence, stampeding in all directions. Then I saw why. A tornado had just touched down in the pasture. It looked far away, but it was practically on top of us.

I just stood, mesmerized by that twisting cloud, rambling destructively toward us. Its shape changed with every turn; first it was tall and thin, then short and fat, then swaying in both directions destroying everything in its path. It completely destroyed one of the small sheds, scattering it and its contents as far as I could see, uprooting the fence, picking up everything within its grasp, and effortlessly flinging it aside.

Almost hypnotized by its strange beauty, I felt my uncle tugging forcefully on my arm, practically dragging me away from the window and down into the musty-smelling cellar. He closed the lid behind him as he came down the homemade stairs.

Together we sat and listened.

student paper

Nature's Pure Energy

A five-foot swell moved in slowly and steadily, its heavy thickness suddenly jacking up as it hit the inside reef. The lip was developing into a fine and even ridge. As it began to feather, the Kona wind blew the white spray back toward the blue Hawaiian sky. I lined myself up for the takeoff just as the lip of the wave began to curl over. I gave several hard pumps with my flippers. In a surge of adrenaline, I felt my body begin to slide over the ever-steepening wave, a wave that Mother Ocean had hurled down from a storm in the North Pacific, some 700 miles away.

Going to my right, I made a slight turn, putting my back to the wave, but still keeping my eye on the constantly changing hill of water. I put out my right arm to hold my body to its fluid face, and watched a rush of movement all around me. The water with its slight ripples, was jetting quickly upward toward the crest. Then, folding overhead, it passed behind me in a roar of foam below.

As the wave approached its inside section, it became more and more critical. I increased the pressure on my right hand to keep my body from slipping, which caused a blast of water in my face. The cool, heavy drops, sparkling yellow-white in the sun, burned my eyes. I shook my head, trying to get rid of the water, and sensed that the wave was too steep to hold with just one hand. Rolling onto my stomach, I put out my left arm as if to embrace the speeding water. On the glassy face of the wave, I could see a distorted reflection of the greenery along the North Shore. Below, through the crystal clear water, I saw the reef. Its gaping holes passed silently beneath me while its coral heads deflected billows of water caused by subsurface currents. By putting out both arms I had greatly reduced my speed, and the break began to overtake me. Slipping back into its hollow space, I saw the opening move farther and farther ahead and away from me, then suddenly close up altogether.

The last section of the wave was the most exciting, for the ride reached its climax. I was totally locked inside with no way out. Because of the transparent walls completely surrounding me, there was a sort of glowing blue-green light all around. The scene felt mystical. Totally tubed within this cylindrical room, I was surrounded by Mother Nature's pure energy!

Tim Murphy

2 *A Scene to Reveal Character*

Statement of Assignment

This assignment is similar to the last: You are to write a scene detailing one event that happened in a short period of time, perhaps an hour or less. You are to tell what you saw, heard, and so forth. But this assignment adds one requirement: You should write this scene in such a way that it tells you something about someone's character. Again the length will be set by your instructor—probably two or three typewritten pages.

Before you begin this assignment or pick your subject, look at the assignment in Chapter 3, since it is possible that you might want to combine the two. The assignment in Chapter 3 asks you to write a longer paper about someone with whom you have had a relationship. That paper will be developed largely through scenes that reveal character, so it is possible to choose to write about the same person in both assignments.

Getting Started

A good way to begin might be to do a recollection activity like the ones in Chapter 1. Do this with another writer, who will ask you questions about the scene. As soon as you have pictured the event in response to those questions, begin writing. Remember that this scene must characterize someone, so you need to picture that person: What did he do; what did she say?

Since this paper must characterize, not just any scene will do. If you cannot think of a good scene right away, try another tactic. Think of a trait that characterizes someone you know.

For example, asked to write down a word that characterized a friend, one writer wrote *bullheaded*. His instructor asked, "Why do you say that?"

"Because he always thinks he can do anything and do it his own way," answered the writer.

"Well," the teacher continued, "that must be true since he was bullheaded, but tell us *one time* when he did some bullheaded thing." In response, the writer wrote the following story:

Chris

That day after school, I went into the locker room to weigh myself and see how Chris was doing. The room buzzed with speculation as to whether he could lose weight by the five o'clock weigh-in for the wrestling match that afternoon.

I checked my weight, which was okay, then went over and asked Chris, "How much?" He was sitting on the bench putting on his sweat suit, which was wet because he had run laps during his lunch period and study hour. He was pale and his lips were badly chapped and split from dehydration. With a defiant expression on his face he replied slowly, "One and a half." He got up and went out into the gym to start running again.

I put my sweats on and followed him back out. Most of the team was there urging him on. He was already running laps when I got there, so I waited until he ran by and joined him. A couple of miles later I stopped, but he kept on running. In another couple of miles he too stopped and sat down next to me on the bleachers. "Do you think I can make it?"

I paused, contemplating the answer, then said quietly, "I think so, if you want to." After another long pause, he agreed.

He ran up and down the bleachers for a while, and when he finished, we walked over to the wrestling mats. I talked him through a set of cals and isos and then started him on a few wrestling drills. I could see the fatigue in his face. He took a badly needed break and rinsed his mouth out with water. The weight-losing sweat covered his body, but he was running out of energy and time.

At the coach's advice, we went into the large shower room and turned all twenty showers on as hot as they could go. Soon the room was steamy. His blue nylon sweat suit glistened as he did the cals on the tile floor of the shower room.

When he finished his workout, I filled the whirlpool with hot water. He was weak, and we had to help him take off his sweats. He stayed in for fifteen minutes while I read off each minute. The coach said to be careful and hold his head up if he passed out.

After fifteen minutes, we lifted him out of the whirlpool, his body red like a broiled crab, and carried him to the shower. The cool water revived him as I held him up, and in a while he was able to stand alone under the cool water.

The other team had arrived and the weigh-in was about to begin. Chris dried himself off and lay on the bench while I fanned him with a towel. If he made weight, he would have two hours to recover and regain his fluids. The coach said this would be sufficient since his opponent wasn't very good.

Finally his turn came to weigh in. He got up, went over to the toilet and shoved his finger down his throat, but nothing would come up. He walked over to the ref who checked his fingernails before allowing him on the scales.

Quietly he stepped on, and the ref slid the weight to 115 pounds. He was over. He stepped off; the ref checked the scales, and he stepped back on. Still over by one ounce. There was a soft groan from our team.

The excruciating pain of disappointment spread over his face as he stepped off the scales again. He had picked on something larger than himself. And, this time, he had lost.

Lyle Picard

The *whole story* about Chris, not the word *bullheaded*, adds up to his character. Try this approach. Write down a word that describes someone you think is interesting. Then think why that word describes the person. Remember the process the author of "Chris" went through:

Bullheaded

Thinks he can do whatever he wants to

Story of the weigh-in

Don't stop thinking until you get to the third level: a story, one particular time when you saw your person *do* or *say* something that illustrated the character trait you want to write about. For example, a writer might start by saying John is

	Unpredictable
because he	Always surprises me
I remember one time when	He told me he would not help me solicit funds for a candidate for our city council, but before I had knocked on three doors, there he was standing shamefacedly at my shoulder.

The third level is the story; that's where to start. Once you have the story in mind, you can do a recollection activity: Shut your eyes and picture the scene; see, hear, feel, and so forth. Remember what was said, who said it, and how it sounded (angry? condescending? loving? frightened?). Remember where everyone was and what the room, the forest, or the shopping center looked like. Then, with the exact picture in mind, begin to write.

Freewriting

If you are having trouble remembering a scene or recalling the details once you have the scene in mind, you might try a technique called freewriting. This is similar to the writing you did for recollection activities. However, here you don't start with a remembered scene but with an idea, such as, "I think I'll write about Susie." The point here is exactly that: to write about Susie. Sit down and give yourself a time limit, say five minutes. Begin writing, perhaps with the sentence "I think I'll write about Susie" or "What word could I use to describe Susie?" Then write for the whole five minutes, even if your sentences don't follow from each other or make coherent paragraphs.

This is not a draft. You are using writing to stimulate thinking. Some of what gets on paper might very well find its way into your paper, especially if you find yourself concentrating on one event. However, don't stop during this exercise to worry about whether what you are writing is coming together or making sense. Don't worry about writing complete sentences or about punctuation or spelling. There will be plenty of time for that later. For now, just write.

Go where your mind takes you. If your memory calls up one scene after another, get them out where you can think about them and "see" them later. If your memory wants to stay with one scene, fine. You may have found the nucleus for your paper.

What if your memory takes you nowhere? Try to free it and let it go. Move to another person. Think about when you first met, about yesterday, school, homework, or whatever. But keep writing.

What if you still go nowhere? Don't worry about it. This is a technique for searching your memory. It works wonderfully at times and not at all at other times. But it's a good tool to have. We'll be saying more about it as we move into other assignments.

Try one or all of these activities. The point is to get started thinking about a person and a single scene. Your instructor will probably have you do these or other activities in class. Doing them and then sharing the results and listening to what other writers come up with will help you get material for your scene.

Writing a Draft: Elements to Use

In writing this paper you should not use words such as *bullheaded, unpredictable, ornery,* or *loving.* Neither should you fill your paper with sentences like "He thinks he can do whatever he wants to," "She always surprises me," or "My teacher cares about his students." Instead, you should write the scene in such a way that your readers can say those words (or, more accurately, think them) as they read. Remember again that this is a scene. No one talks to you as you watch a movie telling you, "This is the good guy," "this guy is a punk"; what the characters say and do leads you to make such judgments.

We all make judgments, silently or out loud, about our friends, relatives, and acquaintances, but such judgments come from our experience. What we know about another person we know from seeing him do things or hearing her talk. Action, reaction, and dialogue are the keys to the scenes you will write. This section of the chapter will help you recall these things about the person who will be the subject of your paper. Decide *now* who that will be and what scene you want to use. The discussions and activities that follow will be much more valuable if you can apply them to a particular incident.

Sensory Detail and Personal Description

As in the first assignment, sensory details make the scene and hold the reader's attention. But here they must also reveal something about the central character. The first paper below illustrates one way of using sensory details in such a paper: to paint a setting. Setting can both characterize and set a mood. Here the rather somber setting heightens the melancholy of the little girl with her dark eyes beneath the palm leaf hat. The rain and dark emphasize her hopelessness; her calmness against this background makes her memorable.

The Leaf Hat

Clouds and drizzle had lasted for days without end. Over the vast river, the turbid water waved up and down dully. Sitting in the ferry, I shrank with cold in my raincoat, wondering whether I could reach the other bank before dark.

In such abominable weather, the ferry was usually quite empty. Tonight there were only three customers: an old peasant, a little girl, and me. I couldn't help asking myself what such a little girl was doing alone. Her small body curled at the stern under a big leaf hat. It was late autumn. The mixture of clouds and moisture made me shiver. But she wore only a thick coat that appeared much too large for her body. Her face was pale and her lips looked a little purple. Below her slender eyebrows, two lovely big eyes twinkled. As she realized I was noticing her, she shyly turned away. I felt uneasy and moved my eyes, looking into infinity over the water. I could judge she was not a girl brought up in the countryside. So, why was she here now? Who were her parents? Why was she out alone in such weather? Before I woke up from my meditation, I found that the ferry had stopped and she had already left it and disappeared into the moist darkness.

The path leading to the farm wriggled forward without an end. Nobody was in sight. I could see nothing under my feet, but felt my legs ploughing hard through the mud, sounding heavily with every step: "Wa-, Wa- . . . ''

Then I began to hear the same sound indistinctly ahead of me. Thinking it would be pleasant to walk with someone, I sped up. As I drew near the sound, a big leaf hat caught my eye. As I came nearer, the head in the leaf hat turned. It was she. She first looked at me curiously, and then her eyes sparkled as if I were her old friend. But she was still quite shy and greeted me without a single word.

Walking with her on this path, I realized she must live on the same farm as I. But I didn't want to believe it, for I hated to know that such a lovely little girl led a life that tasted bitter even to me. Even though the answer was quite obvious, I couldn't help asking her.

"Do you live on this farm?"

She answered, "Yes."

"But why have you been to town on such a rainy day alone?" I asked further.

"I have been to get some medicine for my mother. She has been ill for several days."

"Why hasn't your father been to town instead? Do you have any brothers or sisters?" I asked.

"My father—he died several years ago and . . . '' She stopped here and didn't give me more information.

No more questions were needed now. I surmised that she belonged to a family I had heard about. The father and mother had married without permission, and, though they were both over twenty-six, they were punished. The two little girls born to them were given no food coupons. In despair the father had taken to drinking. Once he won notoriety by drinking three bottles of wine at one time. After that his name was seldom mentioned until one day he had a traffic accident, and died young, leaving his widow and two little children. The poor mother cried almost to death at her loved husband's death.

In the darkness, the little girl and I dragged on abreast without a word. She appeared too shy to say anything, but I wanted to leave her little heart quiet. At a crossroad, she slowed her steps and said goodbye to me since her home was in sight. But I didn't let her go alone. Without a word, I took the fork with her and found myself standing before a small cottage. She told me her sister had been sent to neighbors and the mother was sleeping. The little girl asked me to step inside a while, but I told her I would come the next day.

I turned and went off into the dark. As I looked back, I found the little girl standing in the frame of the door looking after me, the big leaf hat in her hand.

Teng Wei

Though the scene you are now writing focuses on the character more than the setting, don't neglect to see the scene through your senses, just as you did the last one. Remember what you saw, heard, tasted, smelled, and felt.

One specific kind of sensory detail, *personal description*, will be especially important in this paper. The following paper illustrates this very well. Personal description here means more than description of Patrick's person. We see how he moves, what he wears, how he writes. All of these are the "facts" that place a person. Such facts are effective in this paper because they are specific to Patrick. They are not vague details (handsome, brown hair, nice build, and so forth) that could be applied to a dozen other people.

Think as you read how *two* characters come to life. The writer tells her readers about herself as she defines a friend.

Backpack Poet

I always have to start.

I pass him a sheet of notebook paper. On the front side is a carefully copied poem, with a note at the end asking for comments on the back.

Slouched deep in his chair, he reads my first real attempt at writing poetry. His hair is brown, shaggy, calls for no attention. His lips do not move as he reads, but his small, scrutinizing eyes travel steadily down the page. Extracting a pen from his baggy green backpack, he scribbles a third of a page, never pausing.

"Hello, Windy," the paragraph reads. "The first stanza of your poem I like very much. This says a lot since I don't like most published poetry I read. The second stanza is neither good nor bad, like old tofu. I don't like the third. In my opinion it's highly dangerous to use the word love—one has little chance of getting away with it (unless one is E.A. Poe). Other dangerous words: desperation, depths, despair, soul, chill, fear."

I glance at him. He is staring right through the head of a sleeping boy, at the teacher who is enthusiastically sketching the cosine graph in the distant front of the classroom.

"Hello, Patrick," I write back presently. "What do you think of my changes?" My handwriting is little-girl neat and round because I am paranoid of being misunderstood by Patrick; our communication is ambiguous enough. Patrick's writing begins on the first line available, wastes no space by margining or indenting. "I don't want to sound too harsh, but your improvements aren't. Don't pierce the subject's mind and extract a description, but instead show the details of a feeling's manifestation. I'm no poet, really. Occasionally I hit a good vein—usually copper. Oh well."

The period is over before I can reply. I turn to him hurriedly, but Patrick is already halfway down the aisle, baggy green backpack looped around his shoulder. He sees past people right out the door.

My poem and our notes are relegated to the last pocket of my red binder. Reminding myself that these things take time, I reread the first poem he ever offered me. ,

Windy Chien

WRITING ACTIVITY

Personal description, in the broad sense defined here, will be a key to your scene. Look over your developing draft and see how much you have. Use the questions below to help you remember more. As always, try to get out more material than you will use. Write from wealth not poverty.

1. Give a physical characteristic of the person. Another. Another. Another.
2. Write down something the person wears often. Something else. Something else.
3. What is something the person owns and is proud of?
4. Write down some habit the person has. Another. What is your response to the habits?

Share your list with another writer, if possible, and question one another to draw out even more facts.

Action

In the following paper details about the setting are as necessary to understanding the old man's character as the few bits of personal description. However, this paper depends heavily on *action*, which is another important characterizing element. The old man here says almost nothing other than what is necessary to get the boys started on their work. He just keeps on working. This action is what sets up his character. Pages of description will not bring a character to life for your readers as vividly as telling what the character did.

Hard Time

The path was muddy after the rain. Sun and I made our way to the threshing ground. When we got there, we saw Grandpa Niu, who was in charge of the threshing ground, squatting there and smoking a pipe. He was an old man with a furrowed face and stooped shoulders. When he saw us, he stood up, put away his pipe and said to us, "Come with me."

"What are we going to do?" asked Sun.

We followed Grandpa Niu to the barn, which was about 20 meters long and 10 meters wide. As we went inside, a new grain smell greeted us. Wheat lay deep on one-third of the floor. There was a winnower by the wheat.

"We are going to winnow the chaff from the wheat," Grandpa Niu told us.

"In here?" Sun asked doubtfully.

"We can't do it outside because the ground is wet." Then without giving us time to say any more, he started the machine and began to feed the winnower. We had no choice but to help him shovel the wheat into the winnower. In a minute, the barn was filled with clouds of dust, and we were completely covered.

My throat felt dry. "How much dust will we have to breathe?" I asked myself. Soon I couldn't bear it any longer, and I slid out of the barn. The air outside was so fresh that it caused me to sneeze. I breathed wholesome air greedily as if I had never breathed it before.

"Working in there will cut at least ten years off your life," said Sun as he came out.

I looked into the barn and I could vaguely see Grandpa Niu still working in there. Seeing this, I felt compelled to go inside. I breathed deeply, held my breath and ran into the barn.

I fed the winnower as quickly as I could. When I could no longer hold my breath, I leaped out. Then I breathed in the wholesome air, held my breath, and rushed into the barn again. Sun followed my example. I don't know how many times we had run into and out of the barn. At last when the machine stopped, Sun and I were exhausted. We leaned against the wall outside the barn gasping for breath. Grandpa Niu finally came out, looking as if he had just come up from out of the earth.

"It isn't comfortable to work in there, eh?" With these words still in the air, he left.

student paper

In some ways old Grandpa Niu was characterized as much by what he didn't do as by what he did. "Short Break," printed at the end of this chapter, is another paper that characterizes someone at work, this time definitely by what he does.

Reaction and Dialogue

Characters are revealed not only in their action, but in *their reactions to other people.* The next paper gives a striking glimpse of a young man on a bus. Most of his behavior is actually reaction to other people. Even his dialogue reacts; it makes this passing glimpse telling.

One element mentioned and illustrated in your first assignment takes on even more importance in a scene designed to characterize—that is, *dialogue.* A lot of what we know about people we know from hearing them talk and talking with them. Talk is a way of interacting with someone else. It is also a way of revealing ideas and feelings and, through them, character. The following paper shows a good use of dialogue. As you read this paper, remember the discussion on speech from Chapter 1. The same thing applies here: When you use dialogue, you must make what the character says sound like he really said it. The writer of this paper has done that. This paper depends heavily on talk since the writer knows almost nothing else about the subject. Thus the paper also shows how a perceptive writer can bring to life someone he knows only slightly.

Supply and Demand

I had just taken a seat next to a window in the bus when a tall boy sat down on my right. I identified him as Mike. I had seen him last year in one of my classes, but then he left school for about a semester and reappeared at the beginning of the new year.

"You're in my science class, huh?" he asked.

"Yeah, I think so."

"That teacher is such a drag, he thinks he's so cool."

"How come you weren't around school for a while?" I asked, trying to change the subject.

"I had to go live with my aunt in L.A. until my dad got back from this trip."

"Why? Did your mother go too?"

"My parents got divorced a long time ago." Mike looked out the window, his eyes were glassy, but his lips were pressed firmly together, grimly.

A Mercedes ripped past us, leaving the bus in the dust. Mike cursed the driver, calling her a "stuck-up bitch" who thought she was better than everyone else. I could see Mike's hand tighten against his knee.

Just then, Mike turned quickly and said, "I can't wait till I get home, man. I'm going to be in heaven."

With a puzzled look, I asked him, "Why?"

He pulled his backpack up to his lap and unzipped the pouch. Inside, he gave a tiny pull to a zip-loc bag, revealing a huge quantity of pot, probably worth a couple hundred bucks. In an instant, he shoved it back in and zipped it back up.

"Who did you get that from?" I asked.

"Hey man, I ain't no buyer; I'm a supplier. They come to me for this stuff. Even the football jocks gotta come to me." Mike's face beamed.

"It's my stop!" Mike yanked on the cord. He shoved my legs away and left the bus without a word, allowing the exit doors to slam on the person behind him. He started running to his next bus, which was just starting to leave the bus stop. Running full steam, he pushed a young boy aside, sending him into the mud. As my bus pulled away, I could see that Mike had missed his bus, and I saw him give a tremendous kick to the bus stop sign.

Alan Komeya

WRITING ACTIVITIES

Learning to write dialogue is excellent practice, because good dialogue requires insight into character. Below are three activities on dialogue. Your instructor may have you do some in or out of class, and you might like to try others on your own.

1. Suppose that Mike from the paper above was telling one of his friends about his conversation with the author. Write a short dialogue that might come from that scene. Be sure to take advantage of what went on in the scene, using bits of speech, action, and so forth. Did you learn anything about Mike from this exercise?

2. Now teach yourself something about your own character by writing some dialogues with him or her, even if the dialogues might not fit into your scene. You might, for example, have your character talking with a friend about *you*. Don't give all the dialogue to your character and make it a monologue. You might have your character tell another friend what happened just before your scene. Or you might have your character narrate the scene to someone else, such as a parent, a friend, or a stranger on a bus. Don't forget to have the other person respond, question, and so on. Work hard to make your character's voice right.

When you have played with your character's voice for a while, go back to the draft of your scene and see if you can hear her there. Should you? Where? If possible, let another writer look at the scene to see if it has dialogue where it needs it.

3. Now look at your scene (or have a colleague look at it) to see if you have dialogue where you don't need it; you can have too much dialogue as well as too little. The scene "Swimming Practice" at the end of this chapter uses bits of dialogue effectively. It does not reproduce complete lengthy dialogues, but selects pieces that really characterize Scott. Read that paper carefully, thinking about the dialogue that is not there and about how the author decided what to include. Your instructor might ask you to discuss the dialogue in class or in small groups.

With this in mind, write some rather lengthy dialogues (at least ten exchanges) that might go into your scene. Then decide where to cut. Maybe you will surprise yourself and leave it all in. Maybe you will not include any of these dialogues. Nevertheless, try to write them so they will give you insight into your character. Get someone else to help you look these over if you like.

Look back at Chapter 1 and review what was said there about beginnings and endings. Then study the beginnings and endings of the scenes in this chapter. Note that most scenes begin in the action—begin, indeed, with a name and an action—and ends simply and effectively as soon as the action is completed.

The scenes need no introductions or background. In the one scene where background is necessary, "The Leaf Hat," the explanations are worked into the story in a natural way. Even though your purpose is to bring someone to life, it is not necessary to give your reader long explanations or spend your time talking. Let the action, dialogue, and sensory details do the talking for you.

The following paper illustrates how all these elements work together. There is some excellent physical detail: W's eyes in paragraph 2; his clothes in paragraph 3. The central character emerges out of his actions and dialogue. Note his solicitude for the author's comfort at the beginning of the scene, and contrast it with his terrifying, yet carefully controlled anger when he works himself up later on. His dialogue reinforces what the action reveals. And, we might add, Wang's reaction to W. also points up some things about him. (Note the ending: "Is this the usually humble W. who used to pester me with silly grammar questions and a perpetual sweet smile?")

Maybe the most important thing is how fully the author lets the character come out through action, facts, and dialogue. She makes no comments, draws no conclusions. She just tells the scene.

The Gentle Voice

"Hullo, Wang." At the gentle calling, I raised my head and saw com-   1
rade W. joining me with his usual smile on his face. Side by side, we
walked toward the meeting room where I and several other students were
to be criticized as "an element of the capitalist restoration." W. would be a
criticizer. On the way, he greeted, in the same manner, several others,
some of whom were the same "element" as me. Having entered the room,
I looked round to see where the criticized sat and was ready to sit among
them. "No, here, it's very cold over there near the window." Saying this
in a low voice, W. sat on one of the chairs. I chose a seat a little distance
from him.

The meeting was called to order. One by one, the speakers took the   2
floor. They shouted and banged the desk to express their vehement opposition to the students like me and gave grotesque reasons for their opposition. Their violent speeches were accompanied by a constant whispering
and fidgeting of the audience. Among the humming audience W. sat
quietly, listening. He neither talked to his neighbors nor looked excited or
triumphant or anything else. Now and then his little eyes wandered here
and there, as if reading the minds of people around him. When my eyes
happened to meet his, my heart gave a start. I had never before noticed
the fire of hostility in those two eyes. Presently they turned away and the
fire died out. In a split second, they regained the mild and calm look.

When the last speaker had finished, the chairman asked subser-   3
viently if W. had anything to say. He rose and walked slowly to the desk.
Beside the stout and well-dressed chairman he appeared small and pitiful.
His blue coat was almost threadbare; his trousers were baggy; his hair
wanted cutting; and his face was pale.

"Comrades." The moment he opened his mouth, the room became   4
dead quiet. "I don't think I have very much to say. I only want to say one
thing. These students are our classmates, so we ought to be kind to
them . . . " His soft voice, meek demeanor and merciful words made a
sharp contrast to the previous speakers. For the moment, I thought that
my friends had wronged him by saying that he was the man pulling the
strings.

With his eyes sweeping across the audience, he went on: "But they   5
are trying to climb to the higher rung of the social ladder by following the
capitalist road. If they do achieve their object, what will happen?" His
voice was still low, but now it turned cold and piercing. Hatred shot from
his eyes and patches of red color appeared on his pallid cheeks. "Surely
they will lead us onto the capitalist road. Can we be so kind as to see them
climb up?" With a harsh stress on "climb," he raised his hands one above
the other as if to climb a ladder, and then all of a sudden, he let his hands

drop and recovered his composure. "By no means! We must criticize them every day so that they have no opportunity to climb up!"

His followers made such a roar that my ears were nearly deafened. 6
He motioned the group to stop and with an ironic tone, he concluded, "Well, listen, this is the answer from the revolutionary multitude." One by one, he looked at us. When I raised my eyes to meet his, he didn't make the least effort to avoid them. Two shafts of cold green light pierced my eyes. Stunned, I could only murmur to myself, "Is this the usually humble W. who used to pester me with silly grammar questions and a perpetual sweet smile?"

Wang Ke

A Professional Scene

Perhaps you would like to see how a master of the art uses all the elements we have discussed (dialogue, action, reaction) in a scene that builds *two* characters. In this scene Dot is expecting her husband Gerry to come in time for the birth of their child, even though he will have to break out of prison to do so. A friend narrates the scene, which takes place in a shack where she and Dot are hired to weigh trucks.

Dot was angry about having to go through it alone, and besides that, she loved Gerry with a deep and true love—that was clear. She knit his absences into thick little suits for the child, suits that would have stopped a truck on a dark road with their colors—Bazooka pink, bruise blue, the screaming orange flaggers wore.

The child was as restless a prisoner as its father, and grew more anxious and unruly as the time of release neared. As a place to spend a nine-month sentence in, Dot wasn't much. Her body was inhospitable. Her skin was loose, sallow, and draped like upholstery fabric over her short, boardlike bones. Like the shack we spent our days in, she seemed jerry-built, thrown into the world with loosely nailed limbs and lightly puttied joints. Some pregnant women's bellies look like they always have been there. But Dot's stomach was an odd shape, almost square, and had the tacked-on air of a new and unpainted bay window. The child was clearly ready for a break and not interested in earning its parole, for it kept her awake all night by pounding reasonlessly at her inner walls or beating against her bladder until she swore. "Kid wants out, bad," poor Dot would groan. "You think it might be premature?" From the outside, anyway, the child looked big enough to stand and walk and maybe even run straight out of the maternity ward the moment it was born.

The sun, at the time, rose around seven, and we got to the weigh shack while the frost was still thick on the gravel. Each morning I started the gas heater, turning the nozzle and standing back, flipping the match at it the way you would feed a fanged animal. Then one morning I saw the red bud through the window, lit already. But when I opened the door the shack was empty. There was, however, evidence of an overnight visitor—cigarette stubs, a few beer cans crushed to flat disks. I swept these things out and didn't say a word about them to Dot when she arrived.

She seemed to know something was in the air, however; her face lifted from time to time all that morning. She sniffed, and even I could smell the lingering odor of sweat like sour wheat, the faint reek of slept-in clothes and gasoline. Once, that morning, Dot looked at me and narrowed her long, hooded eyes. "I got pains," she said, "every so often. Like it's going to come sometime soon. Well, all I can say is he better drag ass to get here, that Gerry." She closed her eyes then and went to sleep.

Ed Rafferty, one of the drivers, pulled in with a load. It was overweight, and when I handed him the pink slip he grinned. There were two scales, you see, on the way to the cement plant, and if a driver got past the state-run scale early, before the state officials were there, the company would pay for whatever he got away with. But it was not illicit gravel that tipped the wedge past the red mark on the balance. When I walked back inside I saw the weight had gone down to just under the red. Ed drove off, still laughing, and I assumed that he had leaned on the arm of the scale, increasing the weight.

"That Ed," I said, "got me again."

But Dot stared past me, needles poised in her fist like a picador's lances. It gave me a start, to see her frozen in such a menacing pose. It was not the sort of pose to turn your back on, but I did turn, following her gaze to the door, which a man's body filled suddenly.

Gerry, of course it was Gerry. He'd tipped the weight up past the red and leapt down, cat-quick for all his mass, and silent. I hadn't heard his step. Gravel crushed, evidently, but did not roll beneath his tight, thin boots.

He was bigger than I remembered from the bar, or perhaps it was just that we'd been living in that dollhouse of a weigh shack so long that everything else looked huge. He was so big that he had to hunker one shoulder beneath the lintel and back his belly in, pushing the doorframe wider with his long, soft hands. It was the hands I watched as Gerry filled the shack. His plump fingers looked so graceful and artistic against his smooth mass. He used them prettily. Revolving agile wrists he reached across the few inches left between himself and Dot. Then his littlest fingers curled like a woman's at tea, and he disarmed his wife. He drew the needles out of Dot's fists, and examined the little garment that hung like a queer fruit beneath.

"S'very, very nice," he said, scrutinizing the tiny, even stitches. "S'for the kid?"

Dot nodded solemnly and dropped her eyes to her lap. It was an almost tender moment. The silence lasted so long that I got embarrassed and would have left had I not been wedged firmly behind his hip in one corner.

Gerry stood there, smoothing black hair behind his ears. Again, there was a queer delicacy about the way he did this. So many things Gerry did might remind you of the way that a beautiful courtesan, standing naked before a mirror, would touch herself—lovingly, conscious of her attractions. He nodded encouragingly. "Let's go then," said Dot.

Suave, grand, gigantic, they moved across the construction site and then, by mysterious means, slipped their bodies into Dot's compact car. I expected the car to belly down, thought the muffler would scrape the ground behind them. But instead they flew, raising a great spume of dust that hung in the air a long time after they were out of sight.

I went back into the weigh shack when the air behind them had settled. I was bored, dead bored. And since one thing meant about as much to me as another, I picked up her needles and began knitting, as well as I could anyway, jerking the yarn back after each stitch, becoming more and more absorbed in my work until, as it happened, I came suddenly to the end of the garment, snipped the yarn, and worked the loose ends back into the collar of the thick little suit.

Louise Erdrich, from *Love Medicine*

Reworking the Draft

When you have a draft that you think tells your scene fully and makes your character live, check it over carefully to see where it needs revision. Start with the beginning. Do you bring your reader right into the action, or do you "shuffle your feet" for a sentence or two? If you do that, mark those sentences out and begin your paper when something happens. Go through the rest of the paper making sure that something is happening in every sentence. At this point, you should be ready to show your paper to other writers to see how they respond to your character.

Feedback from Other Writers

When you have checked your draft, you would do well to have other writers respond to it. Your instructor may ask you to bring the draft to class and may give you further directions for response. As you hear other writers' papers, you may very well get ideas about how to make your own more effective.

Probably the most useful thing you and your colleagues can do for each other is to indicate whether the character in your scene comes through the way you want it to. As you listen to or read the drafts think of your own paper as you consider the following questions:

1. What one word could you use to describe the character you are hearing about?

2. What other words come to mind? Tell the other writers how you would respond to their characters. Imagine other scenes that might have involved that character.

3. Why do you think the writer chose this scene to reveal this character?

4. What part of the paper (what particular paragraph or detail of action, description, or dialogue) brings the character most clearly to life for you?

5. Are there any sentences or paragraphs in which the writer seems to be "talking" rather than narrating?

6. Where would you like to hear more?

7. What advice would you give the writer to improve the scene?

When the other writers respond to your paper, listen carefully to what they say and make notes so that you can consider their reactions as you revise. Their responses should let you know the impression they had of your character. Did they respond in the way that you wanted them to? Were they unsympathetic when you wanted sympathy, or sympathetic where you wanted judgment? If so, you might need to consider what in your paper called out such responses. Did they lose track of the main point? Get bored? Laugh in the wrong places or not laugh where you thought you were being clever? Try to determine why. As always, *you* are responsible for your scene. Think about both your scene and those of others. Listen, consider, and then revise.

Two Examples of Revision

Seeing revisions made by other writers can sometimes help you with your revisions. As you study these two papers, think where your own draft needs cutting, adding, and editing.

The following is the first draft of a paper with real potential. Nevertheless, it needs work. Read it through and write down the advice you would give the writer. Then read the discussion on revising it that follows. Your instructor may ask you to discuss the revisions in class.

Cop Car

I caught a glimpse of his green eyes before his nose wrinkled and   1
made both cheeks rise to cover half of them. James made this look of disgust because he found out he had a student rider that night. When he
turned, I noticed his waist was as broad as his shoulders and that it was
his short legs that made him look so stout. He looked bulletproof, like a
thick brick wall. It was then that I wondered if I should have settled for a
B in my class; for I took a shift with a cop to get an A in Streetlaw.

We got in the patrol car and he showed me the things that I could not   2
touch. "Don't touch this; it's loaded at all times. Don't touch that red button
unless you want every cop in Austin, Texas, surrounding you." I nodded
understandingly at the gadgets he pointed at. "You're pretty tough, uh?" I
said on first instinct and quickly regretted it until a moment later he cracked
a smile that led to a steady chuckle. Instantly, my shoulders became relaxed
and I sat Indian style in the car seat to become more comfortable.

Our constant conversation stopped with our sighting a D.W.I. (driving   3
while intoxicated). James put on his siren and flashed his lights from
high to low beam several times. The drunk screeched to a halt and stum-
bled out of his car. All this happening on a major six-lane highway made
James very uptight and violently angry. He threw open his car door,
looked behind him and ran over to the stopped truck. With the young
man's shirt tightly clenched in James's fist, and between many harsh
adjectives, I heard James threaten him with an expensive fine and even
jail. The young man rose to his toes so his shirt wouldn't rip and constantly nodded as James ordered him to exit and wait for him off the
highway. After directing traffic around the truck James walked back to
the car with his head slowly shaking left and right. I looked at him and
saw his mustache twitch as he produced quick, hard panting breaths of
disgust. I made an almost silent giggle and then began to laugh when I
heard his rare chuckle for the second time.

After acknowledging a call, we pulled up to a mangled white truck   4
molded into the rear of a blue Cressida, to find a large black man holding
a child and a woman and a blonde-headed man. All we heard was a big
blur of loud mumbling through the steel and glass of the patrol car. But
when we opened our doors the murmur turned into a distinct argument
about whose fault it was. Side by side we walked toward the cars examining the accident. "You take that one," he said, pointing toward the white
truck and screaming blonde. He looked at his watch, and walked away
saying: "Meet me back here in five minutes, and we'll get this story
straight." I lifted my chin and propped my shoulders back as I walked
toward the distressed couple. My eyebrows raised, and while rocking on
my toes then down to my heels, I asked with loads of importance, "OK,
let's hear what really happened."

When the calls started slowing down, James told me that he cried   5
once when telling a mother that her sixteen-year-old son died in a car
accident. And that he fired at a burglar before being fired at first. I told
him that I cried one day when my dad unexpectedly hugged me before
going to work. And in seventh grade I stole makeup from K-Mart. We both
laughed together as we looked back on our own remembrances.

When the shift ended, I stepped out of the car and turned around to   6
say goodbye. He rolled down the window and said, "You be careful out
there." "I'll try," I said and waved goodbye.

I knew that in that short period of time I had built a strong relation-   7
ship. And what I had discussed with him in that time is probably more
than what I will discuss with many in twelve years.

Elizabeth Hooper

A revision strategy for this paper might be: Add, then cut. The writer needs to add dialogue in a few key places and cut a lot of unnecessary explanation. Let's first consider what kind of dialogue might be added to make the scene more vivid.

Note the last paragraph of the paper. It consists of the kind of explanatory talk that should not be necessary in a scene, yet the writer seemingly felt compelled to add this final comment. Why? Isn't it possibly because the paper does not report what they said to each other but simply summarizes it? Look, for example, at the next-to-last paragraph. It gives an intriguing glimpse of the dialogue they must have had all during the shift, but it's a summary. Does it summarize one conversation, or several interspersed with the action? Wouldn't it be interesting to "hear" them as they talked? The few bits of James's conversation (paragraphs 2 and 4) give him a definite voice; hearing him describe his telling the mother about her son and firing at the burglar would bring him even more to life.

Summarizing rather than detailing dialogue is a common problem among inexperienced writers. Of course, no one wants to read every word of every conversation that occurred (unless, of course, you are trying to make your character boring or long-winded), but if conversation is part of the scene, it should be quoted, not summarized.

Look, for example, at paragraph 3: "With the young man's shirt tightly clenched in James's fist, and between many harsh adjectives, I heard James threaten him with an expensive fine and even jail." There's some good dialogue buried here. Maybe it went something like this:

Clutching the young man's shirt in his fist, James shouted, "You disgusting jerk; you trying to get someone killed? I could fine you a week's pay; a month's; maybe I should just let you stay in jail for that long."

> Standing on his toes so his shirt wouldn't rip, the young man nodded constantly as James continued, "Get off this highway at the next exit; I'm right behind you, so don't think you can lose me."

By contrast, paragraph 4 has all the dialogue it needs. We don't hear the argument between the cars' occupants, but we do hear the cop and the intern talking to each other, and they are the ones we are interested in. Their speeches show that they respond in similar ways and give a hint why they hit it off.

What can be eliminated? If the author added dialogue to show how the writer and the cop gradually opened up to one another, the last paragraph could go. Paragraph 6 has a better exit line anyway. The author could also edit each paragraph to tighten up sentences and make the action move. Compare the first paragraph of the draft to the edited version below:

> I caught a glimpse of green eyes before his nose wrinkled at me in disgust. When he turned his back, I saw a waist as broad as his shoulders and short legs that made him look stout, or rather bulletproof, like a thick brick wall. I wondered, "Should I have just settled for a B in Streetlaw rather than going for an A by taking a shift with a cop?" I knew the disgust was his reaction to a student rider.

This paper is not badly written, but several other spots could use work. Take one other paragraph in the paper and see whether you can add or subtract. Try doing a dialogue for paragraph 5, for example, or edit another paragraph. Then go through your own draft and see where you need to add or subtract.

In the following scene, note particularly the beginning and the end. The author had some really wonderful stuff, but in the first draft she felt impelled to begin with an explanation and end by dragging in extraneous material. Note, in the second version (which is actually a third draft) how beginning in the action and ending when the action is finished makes the scene more interesting.

Some of Carol's editing in the first draft is reproduced so you can see how thorough and effective she was. Look at paragraph 1, for example, where she begins to describe Eugene. The addition of the sentence, "How could I have not!" is inspired. Substituting "a sticky golf shirt" for "a clammy terrycloth shirt" gives a sharper picture. The first phrase in the next sentence, "What seemed to look like," is essentially foot shuffling on the part of the writer. That phrase is a waste of time. In the last sentence, the word *gigantic* might have been retained since *quite large* seems weaker, but editing is, in the last analysis, an individual matter. Certainly the work in this paper makes it clear that Carol knows what she is doing.

Eugene

Draft 1

The excitement of the first day in college is not easy to cope with.   1

Meeting new people and learning new faces are always interesting and

even mind boggling at times. It was the first day of Speech 151. We were

assigned to small groups of four. So one by one, we clustered together into

a corner exchanging smiles and Hellos in shy, but cheerful tones. It was

then that I noticed Eugene sitting across me. *from* "*How could I have*

not," I thought. ~~His glasses were thicker~~ *sticky*

~~than the listing of "Lee's" in the phone book.~~ He wore a ~~clammy,~~ terry-

golf *with a pair of*

~~cloth~~ shirt ~~and~~ "high water" pants. ~~What seemed to look like~~ an Army

that kept their hem from lapping

belt was the only thing ~~keeping his pants from touching~~ the ankles of ~~a~~

his *which made his feet look quite large.*

~~pair of~~ khaki hiking shoes, ~~covering gigantic feet!~~

I opened the discussion until a pause interrupted us. Eugene reached   2

a messy

in to ~~his large bulky~~ backpack and pulled out a pair of silver handcuffs.

The rest of us turned to him in curiosity. "Is that for real?" I asked.

A monotone voice replied,

"Um, . . . yes . . . I believe so." ~~Eugene replied in his hushed mono-~~   3

~~tone voice.~~

"Ahh," he told us, "they had a

Dean asked, "Where d'you get it from?" ~~"Job Lot. It was only $10,"~~   4

$10 sale at Job Lot." *gazed at him and*

~~he answered in his nasal tone.~~ We just smiled, ~~and said~~ nothing else.

Minutes later, *saying*

~~The discussion continued but this time a little later~~, Eugene was   5

holding a clear plastic mask that covered the nostrils and mouth area.

The green tinted piece that Eugene was holding against his face aroused

more curiosity. This time, Marci asked, "What's that for?" ~~Eugene now~~

He eagerly

~~eager to tell us,~~ replied, "Just in case someone faints in the class, I'll be

ready to give mouth-to-mouth recusitation through this hole at the top,"

pointing to the small tube near the center of the mask.

I believe our discussion was the most side-tracked out of the whole   6
class. Not only did we spend time observing Eugene, but individually
spent time thinking to ourselves about what this guy is about.

Around his sweaty collar hung a red stethoscope! Why? We decided   7
not to attempt to find out. I continued to read my assignment, but only
this time I could feel him staring at me. I raised my book to hide my face
to free me from this struggling relationship. Although Eugene was a
punctual, attentive student, often times he disguised it with his constantly shifting beady eyes or lack of neatness of dress. Eugene also emi-
nated a distinctive smell, like the kind one gets after running ten miles.

But Eugene rides a bicycle and usually prefers to take off his helmet,   8
mesh gloves, and velcro pants straps when he plops himself into a seat
near mine, exposing unique forms of odor from every piece of equipment.
His hair is always quite oily and unevenly cut. I prefer not to elaborate on
his fingernails.

Aside from his inadequacies, Eugene presented some good ideas for   9
our speech presentation and demonstrated a cassette tape of the theme
from "Mission Impossible." Of course, he would never forget his cassette
recorder at home.

I wonder what Eugene will bring next week. I can't wait!   10

Carol Komenaka

As you read Draft 3 below, you will see that the author omitted a lot of
explanatory material from the paper so that this version moves much more quickly
and focuses more clearly on Eugene. The last three paragraphs in the original version had some good ideas about Eugene, but they were not relevant to the scene
at hand, so they were omitted. The details about his bike gear are quite striking,
though, and might have been worked into the first paragraph, even if Eugene was
not wearing them the first time she saw him. You do not always have to stick to
absolute truth in a given scene; you can fictionalize enough to add colorful description about a character.

Eugene

Draft 3

It was the first day of speech class, and we were assigned to small   1
groups of four. One by one, we clustered together into a corner and
exchanged smiles or Hellos in shy, but cheerful tones. It was then that I
noticed him. "How could I have not!" I thought. He sat across from me,
wearing a sticky golf shirt with a pair of "high-water" pants. An army
belt was the only thing that kept its hem from lapping the ankles of his
hiking shoes, which in turn made his feet look large.

I opened a good discussion until a pause interrupted us. He reached   2
into a messy backpack and pulled out a pair of silver handcuffs. The rest
of us turned to him in curiosity.

"Is that for real?" I asked.   3

A monotone voice replied, "Ah. . . . Yes . . . I believe so."   4

Dean asked, "Where d'you get it from?"   5

"Ah . . . Job Lot," he told us; "they had an Under $10 Sale!" We just   6
gazed at him and smiled, saying nothing else.

Minutes later, he held up a clear mask that covered the nostrils and   7
mouth area. I was beginning to wonder if this guy was trying to be
humorous or was just plain crazy.

This time, Marci asked, "What's that for?"   8

He eagerly replied, "Just in case someone faints in class, I'll be ready   9
to give mouth-to-mouth resuscitation through this hole at the top," pointing to the small tube near the center of the mask. I was then out of words
to say, so I forced a smile to acknowledge him.

He then hung a red stethoscope around his sweaty collar. I decided   10
not to attempt to find out why. I continued to read my assignment, trying
desperately to concentrate on what I was reading. In the meantime, I
began to "feel" beady eyes peering straight at me through his thick
glasses. I raised my book to hide behind it and anticipated an interrup-
tion from the instructor.

Carol Komenaka

Remember, this last is a third draft. It has received additional editing between
the first and third drafts. Note particularly how much cleaner, sharper, and funnier
Carol has made the ending, even beyond cutting the unnecessary last paragraphs.
If you look carefully, you will also find several errors in spelling or grammar in the
first draft that Carol had corrected by the third draft. (How, for example, did she
spell *resuscitation* in the first draft?)

Note that a first draft that needs cutting can be a healthy sign. Too much is often better at an early stage than too little, because it indicates a wealth of material. On your first draft push to get action, facts, and dialogue on paper. You can always prune and shape later. The unseen wealth enriches what is actually given. That's what Hemingway meant when he said that a good story is like an iceberg: Only the top part shows.

Having said that, I must qualify it. Different writers work differently. For some, revision means adding; for others, it means subtracting; for some, it means both. You will discover your own needs as you write.

In this chapter you have done several activities, writing dialogues, adding facts, and so forth. So you should have a wealth of material. Read carefully through your draft now, noting where you might need to cut or shape to improve the focus or pacing. Is any dialogue too long? Do your descriptive passages go on too long and include pedestrian information that slows the action down without adding any insight? Are you taking too long to get into the action or to get out of it? Look at each paragraph. Stop at any sentence that is not either action or description. Ask yourself whether you need that sentence.

Ask another writer to read through the paper, while you read through his, and mark anything that seems to need cutting or shaping. Look at the suggestions and decide what, if anything, needs to be done.

Sentence-level Editing

Whatever else your draft needs in the way of addition or subtraction, it will always need editing—what Hemingway called "pencil work." Again *editing* in this sense denotes attention to sentences. After you have your draft in good shape—interesting material, good focus, appropriate pacing—you will always have to go over it again just to look at the sentences: Are they effective? efficient? beautiful? How about correct? Don't forget that.

The editing in the excerpt below reminds us to cut out unnecessary words that get in the way of the picture:

> The smell of their perfume and cologne ~~just~~ filled the ~~whole~~ room.
> *All were*
> ~~Everyone was~~ well dressed and looked as if they were ready for an
> exciting night ~~ahead of them.~~ The guys ~~looked real~~ classy ~~with their~~ *in*
> long sleeve shirts and ties ~~on as they strolled on past us.~~ The girls
> ~~looked~~ stunning in ~~their~~ strapless dresses as the lights ~~shined~~ *shone*
> brightly on them.

The next paragraph has more problems. It takes a long time to describe a simple dress, and it confuses the reader. Describing clothes can help fix a character, but unless the dress is important to the scene, it does not need this much attention. Work with a classmate to see if you can make the picture clearer and at the same time, radically shorter—one sentence, or two at most. As always, unnecessary repetition is a clue that editing might be necessary. Begin by circling the word *dress* at each occurrence just to highlight this problem. If you are confused about what the dress really looks like, try drawing a picture of it. Don't be afraid to shift material around.

> As I put on the dress, I can feel the heaviness of the dress and the softness of the material. The color of the dress is solid lavender with white, lacy ruffles about three inches in width that go from my left waist down diagonally toward my right leg. It stops about five inches from my ankles and goes around the dress twice. It's an off the shoulder dress with lavender ruffles, also three inches in width, that go around the very top of the gown.

Begin to make yourself a stickler for sentences and detail. Even a paper like the following, which is wonderfully detailed and generally well-paced, can use some fine tuning. I will present it paragraph-by-paragraph along with questions and suggestions. Try to act on these suggestions to put the finishing touches on the paper.

Racquetball

> Lou and I were in the locker room suiting up for our first match in racquetball. The loud chatter from around us and smell of sweat mixed with Ben Gay were unforgettable. We had often talked about our mutual love for the game but I could never feel challenged by playing against him. The rolls of fat surrounding his midriff quivered as I watched him quietly undress. I kept thinking he would be a "piece of cake." Quietly reaching in his old, smelly gym bag, Lou pulled out a pair of worn-out, hightop sneakers, baggy white woolen socks that had faded yellow from sweat, and a jock so dirty that it made me itch just looking at it. His sleeveless sweat shirt, ripped in the back and spotted with blood in front, made me wonder if he was dangerous on court. I mentally developed my strategy on how to play him. I thought playing to his backhand and running him from side to side would tire him rather quickly.

What is the point of the "were unforgettable" in the second sentence? If you get rid of that, you can take the nice details ("chatter" and "smell") and put them into the first sentence. Try using a word like *amid* to link the two sentences. The third sentence is confusing because it implies that the two characters have played against each other before. The verb form needs changing: I *had never* felt that playing him *would be* challenging. Don't the "rolls of fat" in the next sentence relate to the idea that Lou would be a "piece of cake"? How could you show this relationship? Try putting the last two sentences together by eliminating one of the forms of "play." Hint: Try putting a colon after *strategy* and letting the last sentence define that strategy.

> Dressed for action, we headed for Court 3. He didn't speak a word as he briskly walked pidgeon-toed in front of me, repeatedly squeezing the racquetball. Immediately inside the court, Lou began killing the ball against the front wall. The smashing sound echoed throughout the cold, brightly lit court. It was quite obvious that Lou was a very powerful player. I was a bit surprised at his agility as he chased the ball at will. A couple of minutes after warming up Lou looked at me half smiling and said, "Let's get it on." I offered the first serve to him, but he quickly tossed the ball back to me with a serious look on his face and said, "I don't want any favors, we'll lag for the serve". We did and I won.

This paragraph has some good sentences, especially at the beginning. It might be nice to "hear" the writer offer Lou the serve (dialogue, not summary). Can you find and correct some errors in punctuation?

> Unsmiling, he assumed his position and said, "Serve it up." I served low and hard to his backhand, normally the weak side, but he returned every serve. He consistently and swiftly beat me to the center of the court, which forced me to a running defense—a position I wanted him in. His witty manner of play was very surprising to me. I quickly became frustrated, realizing my error in judging him. Expressionless, he called the score aloud after each point. I sensed he was doing exactly what he had planned. He never quit. At times he even grunted out loud as he dove reaching for the ball. He left no doubt that he wanted to win more than me.

One question of clarity: The third sentence could be read to mean that the writer had Lou where he wanted him, though the opposite is true. Other than that, the paragraph could use work on the relationship of details and the order of the sentences. Each of the sentences starting from "His witty manner" is good in itself, but there seem to be so many. Combining some might make the action move faster. (Look at the "witty" one and the one just after it, for example; aren't they more closely related than they seem?) Do the next two sentences also relate, that is, is it Lou's expressionless scoring that makes the writer realize Lou was doing exactly what he wanted to? Likewise, the never quitting, the grunting, the wanting to win are all related. What could you do to show that? Three things happen here: The writer's plan of play is frustrated; he sees Lou's determination; and he realizes that Lou is in control of the game. I think that order of presenting the details might do more to build the action. (Try putting the sentence "I sensed he was doing exactly what he had planned" last.)

Ten minutes passed quickly and the game was over. He won. As I stared at his massive, sweat-drenched body, I couldn't help wondering how that had happened. I had been outplayed. Although depressed, I congratulated him and remarked about his game. He looked at me half smiling and softly said, "You took me too lightly; it's mind over matter."

Richard LaPorte

Great ending. The last sentence carries a good punch.

Sample Papers

We leave you with two irreverent characters from widely different locales.

Short Break

I picked up another green pineapple and threw it into a box that contained more green, rotten, or small pineapples. It must have been just one of the millions of pines that passed through my hands in a sequence that started with fresh and ended with canned pineapples. The smell of a pineapple is not too bad, until a million are bruised, smashed, chopped, and burned. Then they release a horrible aroma.

With my thick, bulky, yellow gloves, I slid pines onto the ginaca machine, at a rate of about ninety a minute. The ginaca was like a bicycle chain. It started with me, went to a cutting machine, returned underneath, and came back to its starting point. Just like a bicycle chain, it consisted of many links; each link had a spoke or arm that pushed a pine to the cutting machine. These arms were spaced so that a single pine had adequate space to fit.

"Move over!" yelled Joe. With the roaring noise from the generators, the klacking sound of the ginaca machine, not to mention the crashing of cans in the background, he had to yell just to be heard. "Ten minute break," he yelled again, and at the same time, motioned with his hand as he broke an imaginary object. Without breaking rhythm, I moved slightly to the left so that Joe was standing right beside me. He then proceeded to place the pineapples on the machine. I stopped and went around him on the other side. Joe's action showed he had more experience than I. With grace and ease, he placed the pines onto the ginaca without even thinking.

Joe then yelled, "If you get tired, just do this!" He quickly stuffed four pines into one link. I watched fascinated as the stuffed pines went toward the cutting machine. The crammed pineapples started to jam and plug the entrance of the machine, and, since the ginaca kept going, more and more pines were added to the crushing mess.

Quickly, the foreman, who was perched a floor above everyone else, noticed the jammed machine and yelled, "Stop number twenty-three." Just as quickly, a maintenance person with a grease gun in his hand ran over to the cutting machine and stopped it by pushing a red button. Using a thick, broomlike stick with a sharpened end, he began clearing the entrance to the machine by prying and jabbing into the mess. Joe and I sat back on a bench and watched in amusement. The maintenance person turned toward us, smiled and flipped the bird at Joe and at the same time yelled a filipino obscenity, which we could make out only by reading his lips because of the noise. Joe returned the routine. The machine was cleared quickly, and I returned to the ginaca. The cutting machine returned to normal, skinning the pine and coring it, leaving the pineapple looking like a giant Life Saver.

Joe finally yelled, "Don't do this all the time; they get really pissed off!" He smiled as he walked away.

Lance Maeda

Swimming Practice

Swimming the same lane with Scott on the first day of swim practice for the University of Missouri, best friends we were not. We had been rivals and enemies for four years of high school. As we warmed up, we watched each other closely. If he sped up, I would too. If I sped up, he would too. When we rested between the sets, the tension and silence were thick.

The last set of the day was supposed to be an easy 1000-yard freestyle with five-second breaks at each 100. It was my turn to lead, and I started out slow like the coach had instructed. On the second 100 I felt a hand tapping my feet. Scott wanted to pass me on a slow set. This is a sin in swim practice. I sped up and kicked harder. The tapping persisted. When we stopped at the wall for our five-second rest I asked, "What the hell do you want?"

"I want to lead," he answered.

"It's a slow set," I replied.

"You're barely moving."

"Sorry BUDDY, it's my turn to lead."

"I'm not your buddy, and it's a shame we're teammates because . . . "

"Hey," yelled coach. "You missed the interval. Is there a problem, Bechtold?"

I paused contemplating my possible answers.

"No sir," I replied as I pushed off the wall for my third 100.

This time he wasn't going to catch me. I pushed off the wall hard, and accelerated through the whole 100, passing the leaders in the other lanes who had left on time. I hit the wall in a rage, and watched the clock as my rest ticked away: five, four, three, two. Scott was just coming in, but instead of stopping he did a flip turn, and started his fourth 100.

"Damn!" I exclaimed as I pushed off beside him.

We took off at a dead sprint realizing we still had 700 yards to swim. Side by side we were like a runaway locomotive smashing the other swimmers out of our lane. There would be no more rest intervals for us.

We hit the 500 mark, then 600, still side by side. By 700 the other swimmers had stopped and were watching us. Coach was blowing his whistle, and waving his arms frantically as he ran down the lane beside us.

At 800 yards I was about to throw up. Scott was too. The team was now standing in the lanes bordering ours. The freshmen were cheering. The upperclassmen were laughing. The last 100 yards was like the fifteenth round of Rocky. We both were willing to die to win, yet we couldn't move our arms.

Heading toward the finish still side by side our eyes met as we took one last breath before the wall. We hit almost dead even. Our new coach was screaming hysterically at us for wrecking the set and disobeying him. The upperclassmen were choking from laughing so hard. Scott and I looked at each other, cracked smiles, rolled our eyes, and began to laugh.

As I was walking back to my dorm after practice, a car pulled up beside me. It was Scott.

"Can I buy you a beer?" he asked.

"Sure," I replied.

Some beers later we were rolling on the floor of his apartment laughing about our first swim practice.

"What the hell do you two think you're doing?" Scott mimicked.

"This isn't high school anymore," I chimed in.

"You guys have a lot to learn about Missouri swimming," we cried out together as we collapsed in laughter.

Joe Bechtold

3 *Making a Portrait in Words*

Statement of Assignment

This assignment builds on the scene-making skills you have developed in the last two papers. So far you have taken one short event and told it in detail. Here you will write about a series of events that occurred over a long period of time and add up to a portrait of someone with whom you share a relationship. You might think of this paper in terms of several large "chunks" of material, all related by a common idea or notion about the person. These "chunks" might be *scenes* like you have written before; they might be a series of shorter *miniscenes;* or they might be *facts* about the person. Each of these elements will be discussed later.

The whole portrait should be written so that readers will feel that they "know" the person about whom you are writing and can understand how you feel about that person. The following "rules" should guide your writing:

1. Write at least one scene involving the person. You may write more scenes if you wish.
2. The bulk of the rest of the paper must be summary scenes or facts about the person. There may be some comments, but only enough to help the reader understand your character and follow your ideas.
3. The paper should be considerably longer than the first two scenes—say about four or five pages. Your instructor may give you other instructions about length.

Getting Started

The subject of your portrait can be anyone whom you know well enough to draw on specific memories. The sample papers in this chapter tell about parents, grandparents, teachers, bosses, husbands, friends, and so on. As you do the recollection activities, you might find yourself thinking of first one person and then another. If unexpected ideas, pictures, or scenes of someone come strongly to your mind, feel free to switch subjects. However, try to decide as soon as possible whom you will write about. As always, the writing activities work best when they relate to an ongoing draft.

Some words of warning:

> Friends of the opposite sex with whom you have a strong attachment are hard to write about; infatuation sometimes makes it difficult to take a clear look at someone.

> Papers about parents, particularly mothers, are also difficult. They sometimes end up being more about the writer than about the parent. Separating oneself from a parent seems to be difficult. Grandparents, on the other hand, seem to be easy to deal with. Maybe they are just enough older to seem exotic.

But words of warning are only that: They are by no means prohibitions. Wonderful portraits sometimes come from these situations, as some of the papers in this chapter will show. Anyone who is interesting (and who isn't?) will make a good subject. The key to success is remembering and using an abundance of concrete memories. The exercises in this chapter should help, especially if you start them with someone in mind. You may have already chosen your character in Chapter 2. If so, you are ready to begin.

As usual, your first task is thinking. The paper is to be quite long, so collecting material may seem a forbidding task. However, the recollection activities, the discussions of types of material, and the samples in this chapter will stimulate your memory and you will soon find that you have more memories than you can ever use. The problem will be choosing and deciding in what form to use your material.

WRITING ACTIVITY: RECOLLECTIONS

A young man from Hawai'i, when asked to write down some things about his grandfather, came up with the following:

> When my grandfather came to this country, he took the name of the man he first lived with.

> His first job was working on the irrigation ditches. They dug them with hoes and shovels and built the mud walls with their own hands.

> Grandpa loves to have children around. Whenever our parents tried to punish us, he would say, "Let them go. I neva lick you when you was like that."

Grandpa used to get me up before daybreak to work in the yard. He wore old khaki pants and shirts and a World War I hat.

Grandpa worked as a supervisor on the plantation at Pakalo for twenty-five years. Now, as he works in the yard, all the men going to work greet him. He knows everyone in the town, and if anyone he doesn't know walks by his porch, he asks, "Who's that?" or "What they doing here?"

One time my cousins and I stripped all the leaves off his coconut trees to make a shack. When he came out and saw the trees, he just stopped, turned, and walked back into the house.

Now Grandpa's day starts with his special Kona coffee. All during the day he eats mangos or oranges. In the evening he listens for the plantation whistle, then goes on the porch again to greet the men returning home. Then, always before sunset, he has his bath and dinner.

Another such list of recollections was written by a young man in China about a former teacher:

My teacher Tang brought everyday, practical illustrations into our math class so that he held our interest even in the period when most schools were in utter chaos.

We affectionately named him "Our Old Tang."

During our march into the countryside he took our minds off our tiredness by singing and joking.

In the countryside Tang refused to take the most comfortable bed and beat me in an arm wrestling match to force us to give his place to a weaker boy.

Tang worked with us in the fields and shared his meager lunch with us, saying he was not hungry.

One night I saw him sipping water to fill his stomach.

If you look at the entries in these two lists, you can see that each item could be written out in detail, maybe even be made into a scene. The whole would then turn into an interesting paper. In fact, that has been done to the second list, as you'll see later in the chapter. A good way to begin your thinking for this paper, then, is to write down, in one or two sentences, as many such items as you can remember about the person you are working on. Don't try to connect them with one another or to arrange them in any order. And don't write them in detail. (You can do a more complete recollection on the items you want to turn into scenes later.) Just jot down a page full of these memories.

Once you have a lot of this raw material, you can begin to expand some of the ideas more fully. One way to do that is through interviews.

WRITING ACTIVITY: INTERVIEWS

A good way to find out about someone is an interview. Once you have recollected some things about your character by doing the exercise above, you and your colleagues might expand on that information by interviewing one another. Your instructor may ask you to do this in class. Choose a partner. Each of you will interview the other, asking questions that force the writer to think back over the relationship that is the subject for the paper. Some possible questions are:

When did you meet this person? Under what circumstances?

When was the last time you saw her?

What was the most important thing you ever saw him do or did with him? What was the funniest? The saddest? The stupidest?

What is one (more if you want) typical thing she always does? Did you ever see her do something completely nontypical?

What do you like best about this person? What do you like least?

Why are you writing about this person?

Think of other questions that require thought and memory to answer.

When you are being interviewed, don't just give one-word answers. When the interviewer asks you about something or some event, try to picture that event, and tell about it in some detail. When you are interviewing, give your partner time to think. Help with other questions if necessary, but don't be afraid to give thinking space. Write down the answers in some form so you can give your partner what you have written.

As you write your list of memories and as you are interviewed, remember that in this paper you want your reader to know how you feel about this person. Your impressions need not be only good or only bad. Ambivalence and confusion are real and interesting feelings. To see how effectively such mixed responses can structure a paper, look at "My Buddhist Grandma" and "My Karate Instructor," both of which are printed at the end of this chapter. Most people are complex; most reactions to other people are complex. Be sure you collect material that will make your portrait as complex as life is.

Writing a Draft: Elements to Use

Once you have gathered a lot of ideas and memories, you must start making a rough plan of the paper. Remember that part of the assignment is to make sure your readers know how you feel about the person you are writing about. As in the last paper, the most effective way to do this is not to use words like *kind, difficult,* or *conceited,* but to choose material that conveys such judgments to your reader. By the time you begin your draft, you should have a good idea of the general impression you want to give your readers. That impression, or feeling about your subject, will be your main guide when you begin to select material to use and emphasize.

In this section we will begin by talking about drafting parts: scenes and miniscenes. Later we will consider strategies for bringing the parts together. Don't feel that you must follow this procedure exactly. If your scenes begin to come together in a connected draft from the beginning, you are lucky. However, read and study each section of this chapter and try the activities. You may find alternate strategies to enrich your paper.

One way to build a draft is by building scenes. Obviously you will not have room to develop everything you have written down or thought about into a full scene. This is, after all, a sketch not a book. But there are other ways of working material into a paper. The following discussion will introduce you to some of the elements that can go into a paper like this. As you read through the next sections of this chapter, think of the lists of recollections you made and of the ideas generated during your interview. These sections will give you ideas about how to use them. Various activities are suggested during the discussion. Use these activities to help you get started on your draft or make it fuller and more interesting.

Narrated Scenes

By now you should know what a scene is. You will have at least one scene and maybe as many as three or four. They will be the largest blocks in your paper. Obviously you can write only a limited number because they will take up a lot of space in the paper, so you must choose them carefully. They need not be once-in-a-lifetime adventures, but they must reveal the person's character. The following extract illustrates this. Notice how all the elements of a good scene are here: sensory detail, action, and dialogue.

> "Wash your hands!" a voice from above demanded. It was Aunt Sarah, my mother's older sister. My little sister and I went back out. "BAM!" sounded the wooden spring door. We jumped to the faucet; cold water rushed through our hands, and in five seconds, "BAM!" went the door again.
>
> We knew as soon as we entered again we had committed a serious offense. She stood by the stove, her face stern, her eyes never moving from the two misfits whose chins barely reached over the kitchen table. The coffee started simmering. Her dark brown eyes flashed to it. Quickly and quietly we sat at the table. My front teeth dug deeply into my lower lip as I awaited our sentence.

Then she asked sweetly, "Would you like some coffee with me?" Our faces glowed with relief. We both nodded our heads in short, brisk, up-and-down motions. I got off my chair, grabbed one of the arms and dragged it across the room. Hanging onto the chair back I climbed on, and on tiptoe, I opened the glass door of the cabinet. In the cabinet she kept all kinds of cups and saucers. My hand reached in and paused by my favorite, which had a design of Tinkerbell, Jiminy Cricket, and castles painted all around it. One by one, bending and unbending my knees, I passed all three cups down to my sister's outstretched hands.

Stepping on my sister's shadow, I followed her all the way back to the table, then scooted up the chair, chin resting on the cold formica top. Aunt Sarah poured coffee in an orderly counterclockwise procedure, not spilling a drop. Placing the percolator down on the center of the table, she smiled and with a slight twist of the wrist, in went two tablespoons of sugar and lots of cream till the brown charcoal liquid turned to a delicate light caramel. She then picked up a silver teaspoon and stirred the mixture of coffee. Out from this potion curled and swirled fine lines of clouds in all directions, which then disappeared into Aunt Sarah's face. She placed one cup directly in front of me, one in front of my sister, and slid one in front of herself. I watched her intensely as she took a sip of her dark coffee and carefully put it down.

"Coffee is good, huh?" she said in a warm mellow voice.

"Yes," I answered. My sister was too busy blowing and slurping her coffee to notice what had been said.

The warmth between aunt and nieces is quite apparent in this simple scene. Note also how charmingly the viewpoint of a child is presented here. It's not easy to remember how the world looked and felt to a child, but that point of view can be very effective in telling some stories.

The next scene introduces a very different character. The minutely detailed action and the lack of comments make the scene very funny and make Baldy come to life.

The first time I saw him, I was at the butcher's. I was waiting in a queue to buy some meat when a little man of fifty or so came up. I was bewildered to see him grinning at me intimately, for I did not remember having ever met him. I was just about to ask if he had taken me for someone else when he suddenly turned round and sneakily squeezed into the line, planting himself squarely in front of me as if he had done nothing wrong. I expected an explanation from him for his boldness, but it never came. The little man never even bothered to turn his head around. Suddenly, I was irritated by the bald dome reflected in the overhead light in front of me.

The queue shortened. The bald man's turn came. It took him a good five minutes to examine the piece of meat placed on the counter. He kept making demands in a dissatisfied tone, until the butcher's assistant had put six or seven big pieces on the counter. Having carefully compared those pieces, Baldy finally chose a satisfactory one and, to my great surprise, he asked for only one ounce of meat. The butcher's assistant snorted contemptuously, and I could not help laughing under my breath. Totally ignoring us, he reached into his pocket and cautiously brought out a wallet made of colored magazine paper. He dipped two fingers into the precious paper wallet and took out a neatly folded two jiao note. On passing the note to the assistant, Baldy's face took on a serious look; his thin lips tightened, and his shifty eyes focused upon the small note as if he was full of regret to see it go. Then with one hand he tightly grabbed his one ounce of meat while stretching out the other to get his change. The assistant peered at him and purposely hesitated several seconds to give him his change. Yet Baldy did not feel humiliated at all, and his hand remained stretched straight out until several coins jingled into it. He slowly withdrew from the long queue, counting in the full glare of publicity, "One, two, three . . . ''

WRITING ACTIVITY

Look over the list you made for the first exercise and the material you recalled in the interview. Choose one remembered event that you think is important to your reader in understanding your character and your feelings toward her or him. Write a scene of at least one page. Make it like the scene you wrote for Chapter 2, filled with sensory detail, dialogue, and action. Share this scene with another writer or with a group. Respond to each other's scenes as you did in the first two chapters, that is, tell the writer how you would respond to the character; where you think the scene might need more, or less, detail; and whether you think this scene is important or revealing.

Don't necessarily stop with one scene. Pick two or three other items from your list and try to write scenes of them too. Remember that a paper may have several scenes but that the scenes must be important in helping your reader understand your character and how you feel about him or her. Perhaps not all the scenes you sketch out here will go into the final paper, but nothing will be wasted. Any thinking and writing will make your memories more concrete. Look at the next section for other ways to use the material you have gathered.

Miniscenes

As you begin to look over your materials and try to write some scenes, it will become obvious that you cannot develop every memory into a full scene. Yet you probably have much material that you would like to include in some manner in your paper. Writing what we might call miniscenes (or summary scenes) is an efficient way of using a lot of material in a small amount of space. Note how different events are used in this paper about a dog:

> There were many problems in growing up for Honi. (1) We set up a pan for her in the house. She watched as our kitten used it, carefully moving the dirt, then replacing it daintily. Honi, when she finally decided to use it, scratched until she kicked gravel all over the floor. At the time, we had cement floors, which were a hazard for Honi, who was trying to learn to walk. She was finally forced to develop a neat little wiggle in her walk which she still has to this day. (2) Honi later put the slick floor to good use. One night we had set her water bowl out in the middle of the floor. She spilled a little, and, on one of her journeys past it, slid. Hearing us laugh, Honi tried it again, in the process spilling more water. She sent us into hysterics that night running back and forth across the room and sliding for all she was worth.

This one paragraph has two miniscenes ((1) and (2)). Each has only one or two sentences, but gives a vivid picture. Together, they help characterize the dog. The next two small scenes explain a young boy's nickname.

> He lived in the next building in the same yard, but we seldom spoke to each other. He made himself famous for his fighting. People detested and feared him, and he earned the nickname, "Bad Egg." One day he conned some boys into digging a big hole in the yard. He put some thin sticks across the hole and covered it with a piece of paper. He then threw some earth on the paper and ordered one of the boys to take off his shoes. He carefully made some footprints with the shoes to make it seem like someone had passed the place. That afternoon poor old Aunt Li fell into the hole and sprained her ankle.
>
> Another time he met an old man selling watermelon. He bought one that was not quite ripe, so he said that the old man had cheated him. He threw the melon at the man's face, kicked his basket over, and then trampled all the melons.

These three scenes, short but vivid, talk about different aspects of a father's character.

> Father loved us and liked to play with us. As a little boy, every evening I would lean against his strong body and ask him to tell me a

story. He never disappointed me. Each time after he told a fairy tale, he would ask me what I had learned from it. When I told him, "A boy should be honest and never be greedy," he would lift me up and kiss me with his black prickly beard.

The Cultural Revolution brought our happy life to an end. One evening he came home with his head shaved. His face was pale and weary. Without any words, he lay down on his bed and began smoking one cigarette after another. I could see blood on the corner of his mouth. Shaking his arms, I asked him what had happened to him. He said nothing.

One afternoon, I was awakened by a banging on the door. I opened it. A group of men with cruel faces rushed in. I was frightened and tried to push them out. But I was knocked down. Lying on the floor, I cried. Suddenly, I felt two strong hands lifting me up. Opening my tearful eyes, I saw Father, who forced a smile and whispered, "Don't be afraid." I looked into his face. His moustache was black, but long. His face appeared thinner, but his eyes were still bright. I pressed my face upon his black prickly moustache. My home was looted and all the glass windows smashed.

Any of these three miniscenes could have been made into a fully narrated scene. But the author chose to tell them in this way to leave room for two longer scenes. The whole paper is printed at the end of this chapter ("Time Stolen Cannot Return"). In it you will see how these short scenes alternate with the longer ones to present a memorable character. Using a series of short scenes like this to introduce a longer scene is an effective way to get a lot of information and feeling into your paper.

The following summary scene vividly portrays an event that took place many times in the writer's childhood. Don't forget while writing your paper that such common scenes, which you may have witnessed dozens of times, make interesting reading and often reveal a person's character as much as more unusual experiences.

While I was three, the best thing in the world was to have Daddy come home from work. All day was full of fun and long hours of play. Suppertime came when I smelled meat and vegetables cooking, and the kitchen was all lighted up. Mom always built a fire in the fireplace and then began to cook. Sometimes I hung around her heels while she cooked, waiting for Daddy to come. While we waited, Mom gave us children tastes of raw meat or bits of salad-making. Then we could help set the table, or pour the milk. Soon we would hear a truck turn off the highway and drive slowly up the dirt road. Two lights would show through the white sheet curtains. Then as we listened, we could hear stomps and clomps of Daddy cleaning off his muddy boots on the lawn and terrace. Then the gold doorknob would turn and rattle; then the door would open, and a huge boot would enter. I'd run to his legs, hugging them, while Pam and Kristi hugged his thighs and jumped up and down. Then Mom would kiss him and we'd follow him playfully to the bathroom to wash our hands with him and to watch the black grease trickle down the side of the bowl all mixed up with soap.

Your miniscenes can be a sentence or two or a paragraph. They can be used several together or grouped around one of your longer scenes. They can come at the beginning, middle, or end of the paper. Make sure that every word, sentence, and part of a sentence gives something heard, seen, and so on. Miniscenes are short, but they follow the same rules as the longer ones.

WRITING ACTIVITY

Pick some items from your list that you don't want to develop into full scenes. Write two or three (or more) miniscenes from these items. You might make these scenes into a series of related stories. For example, look over the longer scenes you have written. Could you write a series of miniscenes that would build toward one of those? The paper "Time Stolen Cannot Return," discussed above, might serve as a model for you. Could you reduce one of the longer scenes to a miniscene and still have it carry your feelings about the character? Write at least one short scene that narrates something your character did often, like the scene above about welcoming Daddy home.

When you have several miniscenes, share them with other writers, asking them what impression they get from the scenes, and whether what you have written is in fact a scene and not just comments. Perhaps the other writers can tell you whether your miniscenes (grouped with a longer scene or alone) seem to work together.

Every week in *Parade* magazine James Brady writes a short sketch about some prominent person. Included in each of these is a sidebar called "Brady's Bits." These are, in fact, miniscenes, as you will see from this one about John Lennon and the Beatles.

I met his father once, met all the Beatles. This was in the American Hospital in Paris just before they flew here for the first time to appear on *Ed Sullivan*. They were getting their injections, nervous as we all are, their jokes corny and their Liverpool accents very thick. My daughter Susan, there to have a damaged finger repaired, toddled about the waiting room, talking 2-year-old talk with them. She didn't know who they were, these strange young men who played a new kind of music. All she knew was that each Beatle, in turn, graciously examined her sore finger and made a fuss. I will always remember that.

Facts

This final element of a relationship paper was introduced in the last chapter. Facts include physical description, you will recall, but involve much more. Think also of the little idiosyncrasies of movement, speech, and dress that characterize a person. Two things need to be said again about facts:

1. Usually a lot of facts can be worked into your scenes.
2. If for some reason you want to have a passage devoted only to facts, make sure they are facts peculiar to your character. If you write a passage of description that could fit any number of people you see, start over and concentrate on things that distinguish this particular person.

This scene does a good job of incorporating facts into the action. (The facts in this and the following examples are underlined for emphasis.)

> I was queuing up impatiently for fish when suddenly the people ahead in the queue began to stir. Like an electric current, the excitement passed on swiftly from person to person. The <u>taller</u> ones in the queue stretched their necks to see what had happened. The <u>timid</u> girl in front of me instinctively tightened her grip on her purse. A <u>long-haired, bell-bottomed lad</u> slyly took the chance to jump the queue.
>
> "You young people nowadays have no manners. Young man, you've got to apologize to this lady." Someone's <u>loud, shrieking warning</u> suddenly quieted everything down.
>
> "Mind your own business, eh!" <u>A note of cowardice</u> could be detected in the young man's voice.
>
> "It's everybody's business to teach you young people good manners."
>
> Oh, the voice, after 15 years I could still recognize it. It must be her!
>
> Forgetting my half hour's wait in the queue, I left it and hastened to the front. But I slowed down and hesitated when I saw in the crowd, shouting at the young man, a <u>middle-aged, stout woman.</u> The <u>beige woolen sweater and dark-blue pants she wore wrapped her up tightly.</u> Beside her stood a girl of about ten, clutching her mother's arm and entreating: "Oh, Mama, let's go home. I am afraid."
>
> Surely, it could not be her. A <u>slim figure, two dimples on her cheeks, a hearty, merry laugh</u>—those were what I remembered. But a second look at her made me burst out, "Butterfly, oh, Li Hua. It's you!" She turned around abruptly and gave me a big hug. "Hello, dear, we all look like old women now after so many years." Our dramatic chance meeting disappointed the spectators and dampened their interest. The <u>young man with whiskers</u> sneaked quietly away. My fellow shoppers went back to the queue one after another.

This scene reveals facts about a teacher:

> Sitting beside me, <u>breathing hard through his distorted nose,</u> <u>ruined in a car accident,</u> my teacher, Mr. Spencer, was looking over a rectifier circuit, a total mess with all sorts of electrical leads from a Simpson meter, an oscilloscope, and a power supply. Frustrated that he could not find the trouble, he began taking the leads and components apart, accidentally discharging a capacitor, which gave him a slight shock. His <u>husky body</u> jumped, almost causing him to fall off his stool. I began to laugh the way he laughed when one of us happened to get shocked.
>
> "Damnit," Spencer said. "I try to help you and you laugh at me." The whole class responded by laughing. Quickly he charged the capacitor with the power supply and threw it at me, giving me a shock. Spencer then <u>began to laugh with some short, fast "Heh, heh, heh's,"</u> <u>and ended with a deep, "Haw, haw, haw,"</u> causing everyone to start laughing again. Settling down quickly, we all returned to what we were originally doing, learning the characteristics of the rectifier circuit.

Besides all the action, which itself tells about Mr. Spencer, we here learn about his nose, his husky body, his speech patterns, and his strange laugh. Working facts into scenes helps the reader picture your character.

The following excerpts show how passages devoted largely to facts can be specific only to one person. The first paragraph presents facts about Uncle Yu's actions:

> He worked with my father for a good ten years, and they shared comfort and hardships alike. Wherever Father went he was at his side. <u>Never once did he go to bed before Father did.</u> When Father had some official papers to read over or some documents to write at night, <u>he would always sit beside him and wait, often far into the night.</u> At that time they were often hard up for food. In order to save food and let Father have enough to eat, <u>he often went out into the fields to find</u> <u>edible wild herbs or elm leaves to allay his hunger.</u> Many times he vowed that his stomach was full at the table, and <u>then he would be</u> <u>found eating wild plants outside.</u> After my eldest sister was born, he helped Mother look after the child. Mother remembered that when Sister was a year old, <u>he tied a rope to her waist and taught her to</u> <u>walk.</u> He took my family as his own family and my father took him as his own brother. They understood each other perfectly.

This miniscene characterizes by facts about Ables's art:

> I looked down the old stone walkway that ran along the antique building, outside the art classes. Ables stood straight at his easel looking out between two pillars that held up the roof of the lanai. He was posed at his work, with his serious face on. Using blues, greens, and other cool colors, he spread the paint across the canvas so that it looked like many beautiful webs.

This passage is made up entirely of physical facts. The details are carefully selected to tell the reader important information about the writer's father. A passage like this needs to be specific and to have a clear purpose. Can you tell why this writer devoted a whole paragraph to physical facts?

> Five foot four inches tall, his body is slowly wasting away. He has been losing weight steadily for about a year and now is only a hundred pounds. His eyes are a pale glassy gray. His nose gets bigger as his face becomes smaller. A dark tan hides the pale grayness of his face. The skin is pulled over his knotted hands and legs. Old age is creeping up on him.

This last passage of facts is used to introduce a longer scene:

> It was the first time I had seen my grandma lying in bed. Her white hair was chopped off, her gown was wrapped loosely around her body, and half of her face sort of sagged down. She was covered with a white sheet and a thin, light green blanket, which made her look much smaller than usual, as if she were being swallowed up by the bed. When I asked her what she had eaten for dinner, she bent her head to one side as if she were trying hard to remember, and then she replied she had forgotten. Grandma had never been like this.

By now you should have a good amount of material collected for your paper: facts and scenes of various lengths. Probably you have begun to think how these things will come together in a paper that will bring your character to life. We will talk about putting the paper together in the next section.

W R I T I N G   A C T I V I T Y

Do a few more activities to pull out even more detail, information, dialogue, and so forth. Here are some suggestions:

What was some habit that the person had? How did you feel about that habit?

What was something the person had and loved? What was something she did not have and wanted?

If the person didn't have something specific scheduled to do on a Saturday night, what would he be likely to do? Sunday morning?

Did this person ever give you advice? If so, what was it? (Make up some advice this person would give you if the person didn't actually give you any.)

What kind of clothes does she wear? Can you think of one outfit she especially likes?

What words can you use to describe his voice?

What is her most striking physical feature?

Can any of these things be worked into your scenes or form the basis for another scene or miniscene? Could some dialogue coming out of these recollections be worked in anywhere?

Bringing the Draft Together

By now you should have an abundance of material: one or more scenes, several miniscenes, facts, and notes of other events. You are ready to begin putting the paper together if you have not already begun to do so. Think first of the impression of your character you want to leave with your reader. Keep that foremost in mind as you begin to sort through your material to decide what to emphasize as a full scene, what to keep in another form, what to eliminate.

Following are two relationship papers developed with a combination of the elements we have been discussing. The first is made up almost entirely of six scenes. Some facts and transitional comments connect the scenes, but Uncle Len emerges overwhelmingly from action. By contrast the second paper has only two scenes (one in paragraphs 6, 7, and 8 and the other in paragraphs 13 and 14). The bulk of this portrait alternates miniscenes (paragraphs 3 and 9) with various kinds of facts (physical facts in paragraphs 1 and 2; facts about clothing in paragraph 4; and facts about mannerisms in paragraphs 5 and 11). As you read the two papers, try to think why the two authors chose such different combinations of elements. Note, too, how each paper, despite the differences, creates a real person.

Uncle Len

"Hey, Hart!"

"Yeah, what daya want now, Whitely?"

"Aren't you done yet?"

I was sitting down after spending the last two hours mowing my uncle's huge yard. I was almost done with the lawn, and there he was, standing on the back porch with his hands in his pockets laughing at me.

"What's so funny?" I asked wonderingly.

"You," Uncle Len said in the middle of his laugh. "You should see yourself. I think there is more grass on you than on the ground."

I didn't think that was so funny, so when he came down to inspect the job while I was finishing, I pointed the shower of grass at him. Now he had more grass on him than I had on me.

"All right, Moose," he shouted. "That's enough."

"Whatsa matter, Whitely," I said. "I thought it was funny."

"Okay. Okay. But don't be surprised if you find yourself sleeping in the pool tonight."

Uncle Len treated just about everything that way. He would either play it down somehow, or make a joke out of it.

One night when his wife (Aunt Lois) went to a movie with one of her friends, Uncle Len and I were going to have pizza for dinner. He gave me some money, and I went to get the pizza. Instead of taking my car, I took his for no reason, since I didn't even like his car. When I came back, I side-swiped the post between the parking slots in the garage. Uncle Len was sleeping in his easy chair, and he was snoring so loud that I was surprised he didn't wake himself up. After a few minutes, I worked up enough guts to wake him up and tell him what had happened, and prepared myself for the explosion. But all he said was, "Okay, let's eat that pizza."

I just stood there dazed by his reaction. "I wish you would chew me out or something. I would sure feel better if you did."

"Okay. You're chewed out. Now let's eat that pizza; I'm hungry."

Even though Uncle Len is rather well-to-do, he doesn't drive a big fancy car or have a yard man. He bought a Continental Mark IV for his wife for her birthday, but he drives a six-cylinder Mustang. On Saturdays, he goes to work about 6 a.m., comes home around noon, and spends the rest of the afternoon working in his yard.

I worked for him unloading 45-foot trucks of produce for two years. He owns a produce-distributing company that he bought for $10,000 when he could hardly afford $1,000, and he has turned it into a $250,000-a-year business. His office is above the warehouse where I unloaded, and every once in a while he would come down to see how things were coming along.

There were four of us unloading, but I was working on a truck of honeydews by myself, practically at a running pace. Uncle Len poked his head in the truck and yelled, "Faster, Hart, faster." I jumped and dumped over a stack of ten boxes, and he just laughed and walked away while I cussed a lot.

One of Uncle Len's and my "little projects" while I was staying with him was to stain the outside of his house. We were both constantly kicking or knocking over buckets of stain, and you hardly ever saw us when at least one of us wasn't half covered.

One day I was on the roof staining under some eaves while he was working on a post under me, when I kicked a bucket of stain off the edge. I looked over the edge to see where it landed, and just broke out laughing. Uncle Len was sitting on the ground in a pool of stain, covered from head to toe. Aunt Lois was in the kitchen making lunch, and she was laughing so loud I could hear her up on the roof. All Uncle Len said was, "Dammit, Moose. I told you if we don't quit spilling this we aren't going to have enough to finish." We both just sat there and laughed while he tried to wipe off some of the stain. His wire frame glasses were now so covered that he couldn't see, and his silver hair was brown. After about three weeks and a few paint-thinner baths he got most of it off.

Uncle Len and I also painted the kitchen while I was there. I guess he thought he might as well get as much out of me as he could. His wife wanted the kitchen painted an awful yellow color. After a long discussion (argument?) Uncle Len finally gave in. "You're the boss, Sam," he said. (Sam was his nickname for her.)

When we were painting he would edge around the corners and I used the roller and filled in everything else. When we got done, Uncle Len took one look at it and said, "Oh, my god; what have we done? It looks like somebody got violently ill." So optimistically I told him, "Maybe it will look better when it dries."

The next morning Uncle Len and I were watching a football game, and Aunt Lois was in the kitchen inspecting the walls and ceiling. I looked at Uncle Len and we both just shook our heads. Then came what we expected. "I don't like it," Aunt Lois said.

Without even taking his eyes off the football game, Uncle Len said, "Well, I can tell you one thing, Sam. This time you better be sure, because I'll paint that kitchen twice, but I won't paint it three times."

The next weekend, we painted it back to the original color. By the time we got done, I had backed into wet walls at least five times, and the seat of my pants was almost completely white, and Uncle Len's glasses were so splattered with paint that he could hardly see.

Uncle Len's first wife died when he was only about 25 years old, and he raised his son and took care of his mother who was very ill for over 20 years. So after all those years of hardship, now that he has it pretty good, he is kind of possessive—not stingy, though. He shows this in funny ways.

When the weather warmed up in Seattle, he bought 10-speed bikes for himself and Aunt Lois. But even when they started to ride regularly, he wouldn't let her go by herself. He just didn't want anything to happen to her and have to go through what he had before.

His house is his castle, almost literally, and he won't let anybody work in his yard except me. His yard is really beautiful and it is his pride and joy. The things he has are really his.

I think he wanted to do with me what he didn't have time to do with his son. He was always anxious to help me with everything. If I was working on my car and a good football game was on, he would always drag me away and say, "Come on, Moose, the Rams and 49ers are playing on the tube." So I'd come in and watch the game, and before the first quarter was over, we would be making popcorn or something else to munch on.

When I left Seattle in June to go back home, he took me to the airport. Naturally, after letting me stay with him for six months, I wanted to thank him and tell him how much I appreciated all that he had done. So, when I said, "Thank you," and started to tell him everything I appreciated, all he said was, "Thank you? Hell, I didn't do anything."

As I walked away, I turned to wave goodbye, and there were these cute girls behind me. So right in the middle of the airport checkin area, he yelled, "Hey, Moose! There are some cute girls to keep you busy on the flight!" So I yelled back, "Is that all you could get for me?" Those poor girls were really embarrassed, but Uncle Len and I both laughed aloud and walked away.

student paper

Bulldog

"Bulldog" was his name, that is, the name we used for our boss, Mr. Brown. A round, well-tanned face with saggy cheeks and a pug nose seemed to make that name fit just right. He even had a low rough voice and stout body to match. Originally we had thought up the name "Snow White," because his short, pin-cushion hair was silky white, but his rough mannerisms and cold masculinity soon made that name seem odd.   1

The ever-stern, unsmiling expression on Bulldog's face gave us quite a feeling of dismay on the first day that he showed up as the supervisor of our work party. Upon hearing his rough voice rumble through roll call, our first visual impressions of him were confirmed, and we dared not fool around for fear of getting chewed out, or worse yet, fired. Our first super-   2 visor had looked a lot friendlier than Bulldog, but even he had fired several people. We really thought we were in for it.

The first couple of weeks were spent trying to find out what kind of person Bulldog really was. That was hard because Bulldog wasn't very verbal and never expressed his opinion on anything. So untalkative was he that on his first day, he never even bothered to give us his name until we asked him for it. Thus, most of our impressions of him were from his actions and appearance, much of which conveyed a sense of eccentricity.

Bulldog was always wearing the same khaki-colored uniform with brown work boots. It seemed odd that he would always keep his boots clean, scraping the mud off with his weeder, against a curbing, or sometimes under a faucet, while not paying any attention to the mud that coated other parts of his clothing. A silver construction helmet covered his head most of the time, even though we were working in the open and not in any danger from falling objects. He persisted in wearing this helmet even when he got very hot. When the sun was shining, he was easy to spot from long distances by the bright reflection of his helmet.

Bulldog took slow, short steps with his body slumped forward, the total picture being like an imitation of Tim Conway's imitation of an old man. All the while, his face remained miserable and grouchy no matter what he was doing. It was this look on his face that always made it appear as if he were ready to chew anyone out who ever got out of line.

But Bulldog never lived up to this appearance for he never yelled at us. He got mad all right, but even when he did, the worst we ever got was a cold stare, or what might better be called a "stink-eye." I can remember once when we were assigned to pull weeds at a newly constructed townhouse-apartment project. Bulldog took us to a freshly planted area that fronted a canal and instructed us to pull the weeds from the slopes that bordered the length of the waterway. After doing so, he left us on our own and went to check something in another part of town.

Seeing his truck drive away, we felt sure that no one was watching us, for the buildings were yet to be inhabited. Soon, we were playing around and started to "bomb" things that floated by on the canal. Starting out with small rocks, we gradually got carried away until we were tossing, or more realistically, dropping, "miniboulders" into the stream. So involved were we that we failed to hear Bulldog's truck drive up behind the building in back of us. He was already halfway across the lawn when the first of us spotted him. One by one we took notice of him approaching and immediately dropped to the ground and tried to look busy. It wasn't until he was a mere ten feet away that the last of our bunch noticed him and started to work. From the tell-tale frown that covered his face, it was obvious that Bulldog had not liked what he had seen. Expecting a verbal blast at any moment, each of us crouched low to the ground, not looking up, while pretending that nothing had happened.

But that verbal blast never came, for when he spoke, his voice was in the same rough monotone that always characterized his speech. Not even mentioning what he had just seen, he just said that he had forgotten to tell us to weed another small area that needed extra attention. Then he drove off once more, not displaying any signs of second thoughts about leaving us alone. Shaken, but with a greater respect for this man, our group immediately got back to work.

In the months that followed, we got used to the looks on Bulldog's face and started noticing his good points. He was a very good teacher, explaining everything in complete detail while demonstrating at the same time. Even for such simple tasks as weeding, watering, or spraying herbicide, Bulldog always showed us the proper method to use. He would take the tool and actually start doing the work himself, all the while giving out pointers and repeatedly saying, "See, see how I do it? Like this, like this." Many times he would keep on going and do much of the work himself, while all we'd do was stand there and watch.

He was very lenient when it came to taking breaks, giving us one in the morning and an extra one in the afternoon. Our previous supervisor had the policy of "a little rain won't hurt you," but Bulldog really cared about our health and gave us "rain breaks" during the storms.

Eventually we did get to see Bulldog smile and even hear him laugh a few times. Though it wasn't often that laughter would come, you knew that when it did it was genuine, and that he was happy. It wasn't a very hearty laugh, nor was it a very long one, but soon you would find yourself laughing with him and you, too, would have a good feeling.

We often wondered how Bulldog felt about us personally, for he never started a conversation and he always appeared to be inhibited when talk turned to personal matters. It seemed as if he didn't want to become friends with us because he always tried to keep his distance.

Soon Christmas came around and we pondered the question of whether to get Bulldog a present or not. He had been good to us and treated us fairly, yet we didn't know if we had the bond of friendship that prompts the giving of a gift. After awhile, a decision was made to just give a small token of appreciation, and we chose a carton of cigarettes.

It was just after quitting time of the last working day before Christmas when we gathered around him just as he was about to climb into his truck and drive home. Bulldog was puzzled at first as I started to give a short "speech" of our appreciation. Then as we handed him the gift, a slight look of disbelief covered his face as he took a deep breath and hard swallow. His hand shook as he hesitatingly reached out for the colorfully wrapped present. His eyes turned glassy and his lips and cheeks trembled as he tried to find the right words to say. After a seemingly long interval, he thanked us and wished us a Merry Christmas with a warmth in his voice that we had never heard before. It was at that moment that we knew he was our friend.

student paper

These two papers illustrate the range of organizational strategies that can be used in characterization papers. Think of some of the differences in the way the two papers come together. We have mentioned before that the first relies almost entirely on scenes, while the second draws more on comment and fact. In addition, "Bulldog" moves chronologically with rather formal time transitions ("In the months that followed," "Eventually we did get to see Bulldog smile," "Soon Christmas came around") or idea transitions ("But Bulldog never lived up to his appearance"). "Uncle Len," on the other hand, is organized loosely by juxtaposition of one scene after another. Sometimes two scenes are related by association, like the painting of the kitchen following the staining of the house. Once, the author puts in a sort of organizing comment ("he is kind of possessive"), but mainly he relies on the piling up of scenes and pictures to carry the reader through the paper.

Can you make some judgments about why the two authors used such different strategies? You might note for example, that the author of "Uncle Len" knew his subject much more intimately than the author of "Bulldog" knew his. What about the different situation of the relationships: The writer of "Bulldog" was telling the story of a developing relationship, while the other writer was telling of an ongoing one. What effect might that have had on the time scheme of the two papers? Note the personalities of the two characters: Bulldog is rather formal, Len anything but. Could this have affected the organizational strategies of the papers? Discuss such questions with another writer or with a group. As you talk and listen to others, try to think of how the ideas relate to your own paper.

Remember that your organizational strategy must depend on your material and your purpose. Each writer will have to think such things through for him- or herself. As you can see from the two sample papers, the overall impression you are trying to convey will affect your organization.

As you begin to put your draft together, remember the things the first two chapters said about beginning a scene. When you write a scene, you want to start right in the action. When you write about a person, you can start in the action with a scene (note the beginning of "Uncle Len"), or you can start with a catching idea (as does the "Bulldog" paper). Whatever you choose to put first, bring your reader immediately in touch with your character.

In one way this paper differs from your scenes: Here you present events that occur over a period of time. How you handle time is up to you. You can, of course, start with the first meeting (see the paper "Love Is Patient" at the end of this chapter); you can start now and look back (see the paper called "Time Stolen Cannot Return"). However you choose to begin, remember that any necessary background can be worked into a scene quickly, so you do not need to clog your beginning with a lot of explanation. Don't explain more than is absolutely necessary. Name events; show action; build scenes. The sample papers printed at the end of this chapter show various ways to structure a paper. You might want to read them now, along with the short introduction, which points out some structuring devices.

W R I T I N G   A C T I V I T Y

Do you have your beginning and general chronology for the paper in mind? If you do and you are sure it is what you want, go ahead and write the draft. If you are still somewhat unsure, try an activity. Go through all your material (scenes, miniscenes, facts, and so forth). Choose the most unusual item you have and put that at the beginning of your paper. Does it work there? Does it give you ideas about what would follow?

Now try another beginning. Take the earliest memory you have and put that first. Take the latest and put that last. Do the other events, memories, and so on seem to arrange themselves between these two? Why or why not?

Try the opposite. Put the last thing you remember about your character at the beginning of the paper. Does something in that event call up memories from the past and suggest any organization?

Share all these ideas with a colleague or a group. Ask them if they have any preferences for your beginning. Or ask them to comment on one or more of the beginnings. Try reading the paper to another writer in two different chronologies and asking which works best.

Once you have decided on a beginning and on a rough plan for the paper, get the first draft in order. Even though this paper includes more than scenes, you should generally stick to things that you saw, heard, and felt. At various times in the paper, you may feel the need to talk about your person in more general or intangible terms as a way of tying your scenes together and keeping your reader aware of your purpose. For example, study how the authors handled their few comments about Uncle Len and Bulldog. They used only a few sentences, but they were pulling their papers together by putting their fingers on what seemed most important. Every paper will need a different amount and kind of comment. The important thing is that everything—comment, scenes, and facts—adds up to an impression about your person.

Reworking the Draft

When you have completed a draft, check it over for the first and most important criterion: Is it interesting? Events are interesting; life is interesting. A lot of vague generalization is not. You can check for a few specific things:

1. Check the amount of explanation, as opposed to scenes and visual detail. If more than a paragraph at a time is devoted to explanation, you may have too much. Maybe not, but look skeptically at long passages in which nothing is happening. The purpose here is to tell, to show, to let the material speak for itself.

2. Check your scenes. Are they concerned with what you saw, heard, and felt? Do you have good dialogue where it is needed? Your miniscenes won't be as detailed as your longer scenes, but they must be scenes. Again, strike out unnecessary explanations that do not reproduce the experience.

3. Are your facts and physical descriptions accurate? Are they specific to that person? If you have description that sounds as if it could apply to the next ten people you meet, drop it. Concentrate instead on your character's mannerisms, strange quirks, familiar expressions or movements, and idiosyncrasies of dress or appearance. Go through your paper ruthlessly. Omit information that isn't telling or graphic.

As always, your best aid in revising is reaction from readers. The next section gives you some suggestions for group response to your paper. Following this you will find some more specific suggestions about revision.

Feedback from Other Writers

When you have a completed draft, share it with a group of writers. Your instructor may have you do this in class. You could read this draft aloud as you did with your scenes, or you might read each other's papers and respond in writing. However you respond, keep in mind what was said in introducing the assignment: This paper should talk about a person in such a way that the reader will know the person and know how the writer feels about that person, whether the feeling is favorable, unfavorable, or ambivalent. The paper should be as interesting and complex as the person it is written about.

Here are some questions you might use as the basis for your response. You or your instructor will probably think of others. As you listen to or read the papers, apply these questions to your own paper as well.

1. What feeling do you get about the person who is the subject of the paper? Write a sentence or two describing it.

2. What scenes or details in the paper give you the clearest feeling for the character?

3. Where, if anywhere, do you think the writer tells too much—that is, where are you bored or restless in your reading?

4. Where, if anywhere, do you want the writer to tell you more?

5. Which paragraph in the paper do you think is most interesting?
6. Which do you think is least interesting?
7. Do any of the paragraphs need editing? Which ones?
8. If you were going to give the author any advice for making the paper better, what would it be?

Make notes of your peers' comments, and use them later when you revise. Remember, the response from other readers is only a guide. The paper is yours, and only you can make decisions about revision. Nevertheless, it can be helpful to find out where others are confused, restless, or, hopefully, entertained.

Examples for Revision

You might get some specific ideas for revision by looking at these drafts and parts of drafts, and by considering the discussions about them.

> There are times when I believe that Greg is the only person who really cares about me. After dinner one night, I decided to go running so I could burn off some of the anger that had built up in me against Laine. It was night already and though everyone was "concerned" about my safety, only Greg would run with me. After I let out some steam, Greg stopped suddenly and asked, "What's bugging you?"
>
> I yelled that I wanted Laine dead for all the anguish he caused Terry, my best friend. As we talked, he skillfully discovered that I was also having family problems. Anger quickly turned to tears, and I cried for what seemed an eternity. Greg provided the strong shoulder, the comforting words, and the advice I so badly needed. I now understand that no family is perfect.

The passage starts nicely, and we get a good piece of information about Greg when we see him run with her. But after his question, the dialogue disappears, and we get nothing more except tears and generalizations. Scenes like this are hard to write successfully, because the effect depends on dialogue, but reproducing everything that was said would be boring. For example, here we probably do not need to hear about the writer's family problems in detail. But Greg's advice would be very relevant; certainly hearing his voice as he responds to her would tell us a lot about him.

The paper has much the same problem in a later passage:

> One day I received a letter from Malia. During the last few years of high school she and I were like sisters. When I finished reading the letter, I was confused and crying wholeheartedly. I ran to Greg's room looking for the one person who could help me. I plopped myself behind Greg who was lying on his bed and buried my head in his blanket.

Greg took a look at me, then said to Kip and Laine, "Why don't you guys leave?" He then turned over and faced me. "What's wrong, Carrie? What happened?"

I couldn't answer Greg because I was crying so I could hardly breathe. "Everything will be all right, Carrie, just let it all out."

When I calmed down, Greg asked solemnly, "What's wrong?" I gave him Malia's letter to read. When he finished, he said, "You really miss her, yeah?"

"It is like a part of me is gone. I feel betrayed and very lonely."

As Greg continued to talk, I found it hard to hold back tears. I missed my friend dearly. I leaned against him and cried while he gently held my head and slowly patted my back like a mother would a child.

"Everything will be all right. Go see her off on the twentieth. I'll catch the bus with you if your sister can't take you."

We continued to talk about Malia. At the end of our conversation, I was smiling and laughing about Malia. I was genuinely happy that I had become friends with her, and my feelings about betrayal had disappeared. I finally understood that friendships never die. They only grow stronger.

Carrie Matsumoto

The same thing that we saw in the other scene also happens here. We get a few tantalizing glimpses (Greg sending his friends away; Greg patting her back and offering to go with her on the bus), but dialogue is sketchy at best. Again, he helps her to a resolution of a real problem, and again we don't get to "hear" it happen. Greg doesn't become a flesh-and-blood young man; he's an abstraction—sort of the answer to every prayer. Because of too many passages like these, the writer was never able to make this paper work.

A few things might have helped. First, the paper had too many scenes like this; too much of it was too much alike. A better strategy might have been to avoid a lot of truncated scenes like this, and instead choose one and put the reader really inside the action. Greg must have been a very wise young man who could say the right thing when a serious occasion demanded. That is a rare quality. So, first and foremost we need to *hear* him. We need to hear some of those good things he says; once will be enough, but we need that once. And that one time, the writer should get to the serious conversation more quickly. The writer could then tell us quickly (perhaps in a series of miniscenes) that such things happened often. The rest of the paper could then show other parts of Greg's life that were hinted at but not developed: He was a bright engineering student; he kept a messy room; he was handsome. The paper has much potential. It needs cutting in some places and expansion in others.

W R I T I N G A C T I V I T Y

Check your draft to see if it needs cutting or expansion. Try the following checks:

1. Are there any important ideas about your character that are hinted at but not really developed? Do they need to be? How could you develop them? By dialogue? By miniscenes? The reactions you got from your group might be especially helpful in looking for such things.

2. Do two or three of your scenes do the same thing? That is, do they all develop only one side of the character as the scenes in the paper about Greg did? Can one of them be omitted and other memories about different aspects of the character substituted?

3. Do you need to expand a miniscene to bring out some important idea about your character? Or can you reduce a larger scene that repeats something you have already developed? Can you put in a *series* of miniscenes to develop some idea about the character?

The following is a complex paper about a mother-daughter relationship. Each scene is understandable, but the comments and transitions don't seem to add up. Further, all the material used in the paper is not of equal quality. By reading the paper and the comments given after it, you can see how one student might have done an overall revision. The comments here relate to shaping a paper and making it reveal the character.

What Counts

"Janey, it doesn't just matter how things are, but how people think they are." I'll never forget those words, because it was the first time my mother ever said anything I thought was wrong. I've disagreed with my mother about silly things: clothes, getting grounded, cleanliness, but before this moment I had agreed with my mom on everything.

It was a Sunday afternoon, and I'd come back to my parents' room to talk to my mom. She was wearing a T-shirt and shorts, drinking a Coke and reading the paper, which was spread out over the unmade bed. I pushed the paper out of the way and climbed on the bed. The bed felt soft and cool, I always loved the feel of my parents' bed more than mine.

"Hi, Mom."

"What's up?"

"Kevin and I had a disagreement last night."

"Oh? What happened?"

"He doesn't like me going out with Carl and Dan."

"Well, Janey, that is understandable."

"But they're my best friends."

"Try to see it from Kevin's point of view, Janey."

"I'm trying, but I'm not going to stop going out with Dan and Carl."

"You're going to have to choose who's more important to you. If Kevin's more important, you'll stop seeing other guys."

"But they're just my friends—nothing's going on!"

"But that's not how it appears. Just last weekend you went on a date with Carl to the drive-in."

"It wasn't a date!"

"Janey, it doesn't just matter how things are, but how people think they are."

I remember dressing a few summers ago for a trip with my family. I had decided to wear a pair of new crisp white pants and a brightly colored shirt. "Janey, I can't believe you're going to wear white pants to travel in," my mother said exasperated. I didn't even reply, just finished last minute packing. On the plane, the stewardess passed out small containers of fruit punch. I punctured the plastic covering with a straw and red juice sprayed out . . . all over my white pants. I spent the rest of the flight in the ladies' room trying to scrub the stain out. My mother didn't have to say anything. I was telling myself I should have listened to her. To me, it simply reinforced what I'd known forever: Mom was always right.

The most recent argument my mom and I have gotten into was last spring before my senior prom. I'd met my mom to shop for shoes for the prom. Kevin didn't want to look like everybody else at the prom, so Kevin and I had gone to a costume shop to look for something original for him to wear. I'd liked him better in an old-fashioned tuxedo, but he liked the mobster suit better, so that's what we chose. I knew Kevin didn't really want to go to the prom at all, so it was a small sacrifice for me to make compared to his. As Kevin was filling out the necessary forms, a quick thought, "What will Mom say?" flashed through my mind but I didn't worry about it. I was in no way prepared for her reaction.

When I first told her, she was still working and was forced to conceal her irritation with a plastic smile. It was walking through the mall that I realized how upset she really was.

"We might as well not even buy shoes. You might as well go barefoot. No matter how nice you look you'll look stupid because you'll be with him."

"I can't believe this, Mom! Why are you so upset?"

"Because he's going to ruin your prom for you."

"No, Mom, he's not going to ruin my prom. I don't care <u>what</u> he wears. I'm going with him, not his clothing. Why are <u>you</u> getting so upset? It's my prom not yours."

"You're my daughter, and it will reflect badly on me."

"What? I doubt I'll run into any of your friends at my prom, Mom."

"What about your grandparents? I won't be able to send them pictures and they'll be very hurt."

"Mom, I don't care what anyone else thinks. It is <u>my</u> prom, not yours or Grandma and Grandpa's. I am <u>going</u> to have fun. I think a lot of people lose sight of the fact that a prom is supposed to be fun, because they get so lost in all the preparations. But I am going to have fun and I don't care if Kevin goes in shorts and a T-shirt."

My mother still didn't see my point. To get her to help me pick out a pair of shoes I had to stand in the doorway of the store with high heels on and yell, "Mom, Mom!" until she came in and helped me. I guess I still thought she'd be right about what shoes to get. She apologized, and although she wouldn't say that Kevin looked nice when he came to pick me up for the prom, she didn't say anything more about it.

I realized after this experience that my mom cares a lot about what people think about her. There's nothing really wrong with that, but I feel differently. I believe in doing what you want with who you want and if people misunderstand you, then it's their misfortune. So my mom is no longer omniscient in my eyes. She is a person, a friend. Just as I accept differences of opinion that I have with my friends, I can now accept differences of opinion with my mother. I am growing up to be Janey, not a replica of my mother. Now that I see her as a friend I think the love I feel is more special. It is a love that accepts faults and flaws, not just an instinctive love. And I do love her—and will hug her and tell her, no matter what my friends say. So isn't she lucky that I don't care what people think of me?

student paper

The major problem in this paper is that the central impression the writer is trying to give about her mother is fuzzy in places. She seems to be saying something like: My mother cares about appearances, but I don't. The first scene shows this rather well; her mother even states it when she says, "Janey, it doesn't just matter how things are, but how people think they are." However, the flashback scene in which Janey ruins her white pants on the plane seems to contradict this, especially when she comments, "Mom was always right." Of course, this is another level of rightness—one of the "silly things" mentioned in the first paragraph. But the purpose of this memory is not very clear. The last scene, about the prom, seems to go back to the first idea in a straightforward way, and the paper ends with a restatement of it: "So isn't she lucky that I don't care what people think of me?"

Either that one flashback scene doesn't fit in this paper, or the writer needs to be clearer about how she is using it. Is this an example of ambivalence? Does she mean that sometimes her mother is right, but not on important matters? Or simply that sometimes her mother is right?

Could this be cleared up by making a transitional statement that would help place the flashback? Or would the paper be stronger without it and with something else? The paper has good potential. It does have the revealing dialogue that was lacking in the paper about Greg. In order to make the paper as good as it could be, something needs to be done about the middle.

The revisions we have discussed in the two preceding examples have to do with the whole paper. However, a thorough revision requires that you look carefully at particular sections of the paper as well. These two versions of the same scene, the first from a first draft and the second from a final draft, will show you how one student improved his paper by going back and remembering action and facts more accurately.

Draft 1

Some students were playing around while working with the test equipment. Getting carried away, they accidentally shorted some leads, which blew the power supply, causing sparks to fly all over the place. Watching everything that went on, Spencer ran over and pulled out the plug from the wall socket immediately and began yelling at the two students. Not concerned about the burned out equipment, Spencer was upset about the carelessness of the two, which could have seriously injured themselves and others around. Never had I seen the redness in his face, the coldness of his stare at students before. So scared, the two students could only hide in their shame. Spencer regained his composure and clearly pointed out the lesson which no one in the class would ever forget: ''Never fool around with high voltage.'' And with this memory, we never saw Spencer in that situation again.

Final Draft

Two students were playing around while working with test equipment. Getting carried away, they accidentally shorted some leads, which blew the power supply, causing sparks to fly all over. Spencer ran over, pulled the plug out of the wall socket, and immediately began yelling, ''You damn fools wanna kill yourselves?''

The two guys just sat looking at the burned out equipment, avoiding the blazing stare and red face of Spencer. "Never mind the power supply. Damn it, you're lucky you didn't burn yourself and the whole class. Now clean this stuff up, put everything away, and just sit there."

Then, regaining his composure, Spencer clearly pointed out the lesson, which no one in the class will ever forget: "Never fool around with high voltage."

Note how the second version uses dialogue where the original summarized what the teacher said. Note how the red face and blazing stare get worked into the action. Note finally how omitting the last sentence adds punch to the end.

Sample Papers

A Professional Portrait

Printed below is a portrait written by journalist Roger Simon, whose columns are reprinted widely in newspapers throughout the country. You will see he wrote it as a tribute to his grandfather. Note that it is filled with the very elements we have been discussing: miniscenes and facts in abundance. Note also how he uses dialogue in the scenes to point up the character. Pay particular attention to how Mr. Simon unifies this piece by reference to his grandfather's hands. That's a strategy that you might consider as you put your paper together.

Missing a Grandfather

Mostly, I remember his hands. How large they were, how the big, blunted fingers would wrap around my own. When I was little, I would hold my palms up against his, feeling his hard calluses and measuring how far up his hands reached my own.

My grandfather's hands were a working man's hands, a carpenter's hands. He would tell me how, when he was very young, it was decreed that he should become a blacksmith because that was what his village needed.

He would work over the forge, the heat and smoke blackening his young features, until one day he could stand it no longer and ran away. It was an act of unheard-of rebellion, shocking the entire community. But he won in the end and was allowed to become what he wanted to become, a carpenter.

"But why did they try to make you do something you didn't want to?" I would ask him. He would laugh, knowing the hopelessness of explaining 19th-century village life in Russia to a child of America.

He came over by boat to Canada with his young bride. This, too, is something that barely can be understood now. It was an arranged marriage. I think my grandfather once told me he never had seen my grandmother before their wedding day. And yet he loved her and cared for her with a single-minded devotion that lasted beyond her own death a few years ago.

They settled in the ghetto of Montreal, and he built wooden railway cars for the Canadian Pacific. They paid him 13 cents an hour. He reared two sons and a daughter, my mother, and then came south to the land of unlimited promise, where he became an American citizen.

In Chicago he built homes and stores. Nothing famous, no landmarks. Just places where people lived and worked. He would carry his toolbox from job to job, from contractor to contractor, going wherever there was work.

For years I think he harbored the hope that one of his grandsons would become a carpenter too. It was something he used to joke about, and I really do not know if there was seriousness behind the joking.

When I first became a reporter, he sat me down and asked me to explain just what I did for a living. "I talk to people, Grampa," I said. "Then I take what they say and I put it in the paper."

He just looked at me for a while.

"Tell me something," he said, with the beginning of a smile, "for this they pay you?"

The only picture of my grandfather and me was taken at my wedding a few months ago. In the picture, his hands are wrapped around mine, dwarfing them, like they did when I was a child. What astounds me is that in the picture I am taller than he, something that must have happened over the years without my realizing it. And now, looking at it, I still prefer to think that it is a trick of the camera, an optical illusion.

Two weeks ago, at age 91, my grandfather had a heart attack. He recovered well, drawing his strength from a life of hard, physical labor. When I visited him in the hospital, he was sitting up and eating a large lunch. I showed him the picture of him and me, which he had not seen yet.

"I would say very handsome," he said, holding it. "Very handsome." I told him that he looked handsome too. "I was talking about me," he said, smiling.

Two days ago he died. I am writing this a few hours before his funeral. I always have hated stories like this one. It always has seemed to me that they glorify more the writer than the man written about. People admire the fine phrases and fine sentiments, which is merely a knack that writers learn over the years.

But I understand now why they are written. At some point, after spending your life building word upon word, you find that you really cannot feel anymore except through them. And those words haunt you until you put them upon a page.

My grandfather does not need these words for his memorial. His memorial is to be found in the homes of his city, homes that still stand, homes in which people still live.

When I was 10, my family decided to move to California for a while. We broke the news to my grandfather, who sat weeping at our kitchen table, sure that he never would see us again. I still remember seeing him wipe his eyes with the backs of those huge hands. I tugged at his jacket and asked him why he was crying. "Your grampa will miss you," he said, wrapping me in his arms. "He will miss you."

Today, I miss him.

Roger Simon

Student Papers

Following are a number of additional examples, several of which have been quoted or referred to earlier in this chapter. Taken together, they illustrate a variety of strategies for using the different elements we have talked about and for organizing those elements into effective papers. For example, the first paper is interesting because the author works flashbacks, in the form of miniscenes, into a longer scene. The second paper combines summary scenes with two longer scenes. The paper "My Buddhist Grandma" uses the idea of the writer's grandmother's appearance and religion as an organizing theme similar to Simon's use of his grandfather's hands. "Our Old Tang" uses the teacher's pipe in a similar manner. Read all the papers, noting their special techniques and noting how each develops the character through action, carefully chosen descriptive facts, and dialogue.

Love Is Patient

"Hey you wanna go to a party with me tonight?"

"The nerve of this guy yelling across the snack bar in front of everyone in his egotistical manner," I thought to myself. "No, thank you," I said in a very matter-of-fact tone.

Bo shrugged, smiled, and went back to the swimming pool where he worked as a lifeguard.

Every day he would wear a wide-brimmed, woven straw hat and colorful shorts that hung loosely around his hips. With his flashing smile, he would flirt with and flatter all the ladies as he sat up in his stand watching over the pool. The old women as well as the younger ones would talk with him for hours. He was always having a home-cooked meal at the home of one of his admirers.

One day one of the girls that I worked with said to me, as we cleaned up the snack bar for the evening, "Nona, isn't Bo nice. He is always so happy and friendly to everyone!"

I just smiled but didn't say anything, because I felt that he was definitely one to be wary of. So with my defenses up, I managed to turn down several of his invitations for dates in spite of his electrifying charm and flirtatious ways.

However, as the weeks went by, I noticed another part of him that was very touching. Bo always talked and played with the kids. I would glance out the window of the snack bar as I worked and see at least five little boys flocked around him. Practically every morning before the pool opened, little kids would peek through the holes in the fence and yell inside, "Bobo, Bobo, let us in. We will help you clean."

Smiling and then whacking their bottoms one at a time as they scrambled through the gate, he would open the pool a half hour early. He put them all to work scrubbing the tiles on the sides of the pool, playing of course as they worked. Afterward he would treat them to sodas and ice cream, while they all sat under the big banyan tree next to the pool joking and laughing with one another. I started to change my first impression of him after I watched his kind and gentle manner with the children.

By the end of the summer, I had accepted a date with him. We went to a wedding of one of Bo's friends. I loved watching him in action! He was the life of the party. He struck up conversations with absolute strangers and totally enjoyed himself visiting with his old as well as his new friends. I felt good being with him.

One year later we married.

Several years had passed when I received a phone call from a community college in another city accepting me into their nursing career-ladder program. Bo and I sat down that evening at our dining room table and began to discuss the opportunity and what it would mean to our relationship. We sat in silence for several minutes. Bo, who had barely touched his dinner, randomly moved his vegetables to one side of his plate with his fork. He often lost his appetite when we would have a heavy discussion over an issue. He looked up and said, "You know I can't go with you, don't you?"

"Yes, I know. How do you feel about that?" I asked.

"I feel stuck. There is nothing I can really do about it. My job is here.

I'll feel abandoned for a year, but I would never do anything to stop you from going, if that's what you want to do.''

He chose the words he spoke carefully. I had never seen him more serious. The fun-loving, carefree spirit I had known for years was not present. He placed his fork from one hand to the other at least a hundred times and then shoved his plate aside. He grabbed my hands from across the table, looked at me, and said, ''Change is growth, Nona. This next year will be a time for growth for both of us.''

Three months later, I walked down the yellow-carpeted stairway that leads to the living room. Bo sat on our brown corduroy sofa with his curly head bowed. I looked around the room and focused on the collection of knickknacks placed on the television set in the corner. Bo had bought me the statue of the little boy and girl bent over facing one another with their eyes closed and lips puckered for our first Christmas together. The egg-shaped terrarium containing a tiny ceramic bunny was an Easter gift.

As I looked at other objects, I remembered an awful fight. It left me in tears while my husband stormed out of the house. He returned a few hours later with that small square glass etching. ''Love,'' carved in grace-ful script decorated its upper right corner, while a rose was etched on the opposite corner. Carved in the center was:

Love is patient and kind;
Love is not jealous or conceited;
Love is not proud or selfish;
Love is not happy with evil;
Love is happy with the truth;
Love never gives up;
Its faith, hope, and patience never fail.

''Bo, it's time to go now,'' I said in a soft tone. He raised his head and looked at me with his penetrating eyes and said, ''I'm sure going to miss you, you little squirt.''

He stood, moved toward me, and wrapped his arms around my shoul-ders, holding me tight but gently. More than once I have felt his strong arms around me. I remember when we bought a new Volkswagen and I managed to wreck it completely six months later. While I was standing at the police station hysterical and crying, he held me in his arms and told me, ''Cars are replaceable, honey; you're not.'' Again, when I came home from work one day, saddened and very upset by the death of a dear patient, he held me. The security of his embrace comforted me.

As we walked toward the door hand in hand, I glanced quickly over one shoulder at my house and then at Bo who still had a tear in his eye. I would miss him, too!

Nona Irvine

Time Stolen Cannot Return

In a small room at the corner of a hospital yard, we stood silently and motionlessly beside a bed in which my father was lying. Covered with a white quilt, he looked calm and seemed to have fallen asleep. The usual deep wrinkles on his forehead and around his eyes had disappeared. Apart from a small cluster of grey hair on the top, his head had become bald.

Unable to believe the stern fact, I several times put my hand on his heart, but I could feel only his cold body. He was only 58 years old and yet he could never talk to us any longer! I pressed my head upon his. Tears covered my eyes.

Back home, we sat silent in Father's study. The room was surrounded by shelves packed with all kinds of books that had survived the cultural revolution. Beside the simple bed was a writing table on which lay a pile of letters and a copy of his newly published book that he had received just a few days before.

Father was a writer who wrote hundreds of articles for the newspapers and published several books. His talent and originality had been recognized. But for thirteen years, since the cultural revolution, he had been tortured and deprived of the right of publication. A few days before, when he got his newly published book, he stroked the corner of it and said happily, "From now on, I can get my books published again." He told us he only expected to live another ten years. His plan was to finish another ten books. Pointing to the pile of letters he said, "I'm now pressed for time. They are all asking me to write something for them." A few days later, his heart failed him.

Father loved us and liked to play with us. As a little boy, every evening I would lean against his strong body and ask him to tell me a story. He never disappointed me. Each time after he told me a fairy tale, he would ask me what I had learned from it. When I told him, "A boy should be honest and never be greedy," he would lift me up and kiss me with his black prickly beard.

The cultural revolution brought our happy life to an end. One evening he came home with his head shaved. His face was pale and weary. Without any words, he lay down on his bed and began smoking one cigarette after another. I could see blood on the corner of his mouth. Shaking his arms, I asked him what had happened to him. He said nothing. Soon I learned from Mother that Father was accused of being a capitalist roader and a reactionary scholar. Soon he was not allowed to come home.

One afternoon, I was awakened by a banging on the door. I opened it. A group of men with cruel faces rushed in. I was frightened and tried to push them out. But I was knocked down. Lying on the floor, I cried. Suddenly, I felt two strong hands lifting me up. Opening my tearful eyes, I saw Father, who forced a smile and whispered, "Don't be afraid." I looked into his face. His moustache was black, but long. His face appeared thinner but his eyes were still bright. I pressed my face upon his black prickly moustache. My home was looted and all the glass windows smashed.

Six years later, in a small hut, far away from the living quarters of the so-called May 7th Cadre's School, I sat beside my father. Flies and mosquitoes buzzed restlessly, and the terrible smell coming from the pigsties forced its way into my nose. Swaying now and then, the small candle on the broken table gave out its dim light. My father was lying in bed. The mental and physical torture had made him very ill from liver and lung diseases. And only three weeks before he had a serious heart attack and almost lost his life.

"Let's go back home, Pa," I said.

Stroking my hair, he answered, "We can't."

"Why?" I asked.

"They will not allow me to go back unless I admit being a counterrevolutionary."

A short silence. "Are you a counterrevolutionary?" finally I asked.

His face twitched, but immediately he smiled, "Pa is not."

Groping in the shabby bag beside his pillow, he took out a big envelope. Slowly he picked out several pieces of old yellowish paper. "There are some of the articles opposing the KMT I wrote before liberation. I joined the revolutionary organization and did what I could for the revolutionary cause. Once during the revolution a guerilla was to carry a transceiver to the liberated area; I helped him to get a passport. Later I was almost arrested . . . " Father got very excited. Looking at these papers, I believed him. He had always told us that a man should be honest.

It was not until thirteen years after the cultural revolution, that was one year before he died, that the false charges against him were completely removed.

Dai Xing

Our Old Tang

I saw Tang for the first time after I had been in high school for about a month. As was the common phenomenon in school at that time, the classroom was full of noises; some students were reading novels, some were chatting, and some were even humming. Then the door opened and he entered. Most of the students just gave him a glance and went on with their own affairs. But I, interested in the sample thermometer in his hand, looked at him a bit longer. He looked above 50, not tall, his face wrinkled and his hair grey. A pair of glasses and a used grey uniform made him look like a typical high school teacher. He walked to the platform and put down the thermometer.

"Comrades," his sonorous voice hushed the noises. "My name is Tang Hong-kai. Today, we are going to take up the concepts of positive numbers and negative numbers." The noises rose again. I took up the novel I was reading.

"Did any of you last evening go to watch the ice hockey match in the gymnasium?"

The noises became even louder. Some boys cried, "Yes!"

"Then do you know why there was ice on such a hot summer evening?" I put aside my novel. "Who knows?" He looked around at us, and we looked back at him. "Nobody? Well, surely you know ammonia . . . "

He then began to tell us how people used liquid ammonia to get ice. It sounded interesting. I never knew this stinking compound had such an important use. "When the match was going on, the temperature below the knees of the athletes was minus five degrees C. Does any of you know what is minus five degrees C?"

He looked around at us again. Some shook their heads. "Why! It's such a simple question. Minus five just means five degrees below zero." We all laughed. "Then do you know what zero degrees means?"

"Zero degrees means no degree," one said.

"Well, you are . . . " he stopped. "Right," another person said . . . "Wrong!" he then cried.

All of us burst into more laughter. He took up the thermometer and explained that sometimes zero didn't necessarily mean nothing. He talked about the concepts of negative and positive numbers, and how people used the concepts in math and in daily life. As he was speaking, I felt something strange. Suddenly I realized that the room was quiet; all the students were listening attentively to Tang, whose voice was loud and clear.

After the first class, all the students took to him. In his class no one wanted to make noise. Even if someone did, Tang didn't pay any attention to him, for the other students never failed to silence the offender.

After class, Tang made fun of us, and we did the same to him. Behind his back, we called him "Our Old Tang." With Tang as our math teacher, we made progress very rapidly. The more progress we made, the more we respected him.

Time flew. The second summer came, and we students were sent to help peasants in the countryside. Tang was assigned to be the teacher responsible for our class.

The summer night was quiet and chilly. Stars studded the sky disorderly. Street lamps passed us one by one. Although there were many of us, except for footsteps little could be heard, a contrast to how it had been when we started. We had walked for hours. The pack on my back seemed unbearably heavy, and my clothes under it were already wet through, in spite of the chilly winds. Tang, with his own pack on his back, walked among us. "Kon Hai-bin," he called a girl's name, "Sing us a song!"

There was no response. But the troop buzzed for a minute. Then someone said, "One, two." At the two, the students ahead shouted in one voice, "Teacher Tang, sing us a song! Teacher Tang, sing us a song!" Our Old Tang couldn't resist so many enemies. He sang us a song of Chairman Mao's quotations. The old voice was very funny. We responded with applause and laughter. The light air came back. We chatted, told stories, and proposed riddles as we walked along. Tang took out his pipe, filled it, and puffed contentedly.

We boys were to live with Tang in a classroom in the school in the village. There were some desks in the room. Tang led us arranging the desks side by side. Then he told those who were weak to make their beds on the desks. He himself and the rest spread their plastic cloths over the ground. The boys on desks managed to save a space. They asked Tang to put his quilts there.

Tang turned and pointed to the weakest one on the ground, "Tan, fill in the space." We wouldn't have it. Someone took up Tang's quilts and put them in the place.

"I'm the teacher," Tang pretended to be angry. "I have the final say!" We just ignored him and began to make the bed for him. "OK, boys," Tang had to compromise. "Let's settle it this way. We will have hand wrestling. If I lose, you choose who takes the desk. If I win, I choose." We agreed.

I was the strongest in the class, so I took the challenge. We clasped each other's hands on a desk. The students stood around. A fellow said, "One, two," and the contest began. I had the upper hand. His hand was tilted, and I felt it trembling. I looked at him victoriously, and got a start. His face was red, the veins bulged; almost invisible, tiny sweat drops covered his forehead. I thought of my father, about the same age, the same grey hair, the same wrinkles. When I was thinking, I felt the back of my hand touch the desk. Tang stood up and laughed triumphantly, "Well, boys, you are too young. Now go to your places."

Tang went to the fields with us every day. After several days, the work became unbearable to us. Every morning, right after the work began, we started to expect lunch. The lunchtime came in due course. We boys devoured our meal—three steamed buns—in about five minutes. For the rest of the time, we complained about the pitiful ration over bowls of water. Tang ate with us and hadn't yet finished his share. Having heard our complaints, he pointed to the two buns in his bowl and went away without a word. Soon he came back with several steamed buns in his hand. He put them into bowls and put the bowls, including his, before us.

"The girls need your help. Finish them," he told us.

We held out our hands. One person, with a bun in hand, remembered and asked Tang, "What about you? You haven't eaten up your ration."

Tang eyed him critically. "Don't be so considerate. If I had your good appetite, I wouldn't be so modest."

There was no need to persuade us further. Smoking his pipe, Tang looked at us eating. I could sense a smile in the corners of his eyes. After that day, Tang gave us extra buns at every meal.

It was a hot summer noon. After the whole morning's heavy work, and the half-satisfactory lunch, the students lay on their beds and slept soundly. I went to bed later than the others. When I was about to doze off, I heard the sound of a mug. I opened my eyes and saw the profile of Tang. He sat a few beds away from me with a biscuit and a mug in his hands. He chewed the dry biscuit over and swallowed it with a sip of water. I could see clearly the Adam's apple move up and down. It took me a little while to understand that he was drinking the water to put something in his stomach. I shut my eyes again, but I didn't want to sleep. Something hot was turning in my chest.

Besides the physical labor, Tang had also to take care of the class work. Each night, when we were already in bed, he sat under a lamp smoking and putting notes in his notebook.

On the eve of returning to our homes, we students were both happy and troubled, for though it meant hearty meals and the end of the hard labor, it also meant being awakened at midnight to struggle all the way back. Maybe I was too excited. I couldn't sleep steadily. Each time I awoke, I saw Tang smoking. In the darkness, the fire in his pipe was like a little red star. It dimmed down, glowed, dimmed down, and glowed again. I saw his glasses and wrinkled face in the twinkling. I could just hear the sounds from the pipe when he drew in the smoke. I had the fancy that the red star would thus burn itself out soon. But it just went on twinkling at intervals, to keep time with the steady breathing of the young men, once, twice, again.

I haven't seen Tang for at least seven years, and I don't know whether he has retired or has gone to teach elsewhere. But I am sure of one thing: No matter what he is doing, his heart is beating for the young generation.

Cha Xiao-hu

My Karate Instructor

"Shigemoto, what do you think you're doing?" snapped my karate instructor from across the large polished wooden studio. "That's not a back kick!"

I was standing at a ballet bar before a mirrored wall, watching my right leg lift up at the knee, swing down, and kick back rapidly as he had instructed us to do. Confused, I put down my leg and looked across the mirrored wall at the rest of the students. In their white gis, they raised their legs by the knee and kicked backward easily. Wasn't I doing the same thing? My husky instructor, in white sweat pants and yellow-striped sweatshirt, passed behind them and stopped next to me, petite in my white gi pants and dark blue T-shirt.

"Kick like this!" he said impatiently, looking down at me through his black-rimmed glasses. He pulled his long leg up by the knee and kicked backward easily.

I still could not see what I was doing wrong, but I raised my leg by the knee and almost strained my knee as I kicked backward.

"That's a little better. Practice that. You have only three months of classes left, you know, Shigemoto. Karate is discipline and patience." He turned and walked away.

I shrugged my shoulders and sighed. I'm always on his hit list, I thought. Will I ever get off it? During the first week of class, my instructor had always smiled at me and called me by my first name. But when I couldn't catch on easily to the punches and kicks, he started frowning down at me and calling me by my last name.

Now, the corners of my mouth going down in the mirror, I sighed again. Only three months left. How could I learn anything well? "Shigemoto! Are you daydreaming down there?" I shook my head without looking at my instructor and began practicing my back kicks.

A month later, my instructor brought in his brown-belt student from his club and had him demonstrate the basic kata for us. He never demonstrated anything fully, but always picked a student he liked to give the instructions. Once he had made a student balance on her left leg and kick front, side, and back with her right leg. After she had done this easily, he had told us, "This is how to balance. It's been a long time since I did this. I don't think I could do it now. But you need to learn to balance. Eh, Shigemoto, don't be clumsy." I shrugged my shoulders, knowing I would be clumsy.

As the brown-belt student whirled, pivoted, punched, and kiaied in demonstration, my instructor sat on a counter against a wall, tapping a long wooden pole on the polished floor and swinging it sometimes from side to side. When the student was finished, he raised his head and told the sweating student to run us through the kata a few times. Then he continued tapping the pole on the floor, not watching us. After the student was finished, he leaped off the counter and walked over to him. Patting him on the back, he turned to us and told us, "I hope you took great interest in this kata. It's the first step to defense. Did you hear that, Shigemoto? I hope you caught on." I mustered a smile, already forgetting the first half of the kata.

During the next class, my instructor ran us through the kata without demonstrating it again. After the fifth time, he told us that if we did it perfectly the sixth time, we could go home. Halfway through it, I pivoted to my right instead of my left. "Shigemoto made a mistake!" he shouted. "You all have to do it over again!" Everyone groaned. Oh great, I thought. Now I'm on everybody's hit list. "Hey, Shigemoto," he added, "how do you expect to defend yourself? You have only two months of classes left, you know." I sighed. Would I ever learn anything well?

Because my instructor never offered any suggestions on how to improve myself, I had begun practicing at home with my three-pound hand weights and ankle weights, since exercising with weights makes a person move faster after they are removed. A month later, I stood at the ballet bar practicing my back kicks. In the mirror, my right leg lifted up by the knee quickly and shot back easily. My instructor appeared suddenly behind me. I sighed. Here we go again, I thought. However, he was not frowning. His eyes were wide and his mouth was agape.

"Wow!" he exclaimed. "That's good, Shigemoto. Punch for me."

I turned to him, made a fist with my right hand, pulled it back to my waist, and thrust it forward quickly, feeling the air rush over my fist and arm.

"Wow!" he repeated. "That's perfect. How'd you get to be so good? What happened to you? Your name is Anne, isn't it? You're going to be my next black belt!"

I turned to the bar to practice my back kicks. The corners of my mouth went up in the mirror as my instructor retreated to a corner. I'm off his hit list, I thought. Only one more month to go.

Anne Shigemoto

My Buddhist Grandma

When I was a little girl, I liked to compare my grandma to the plaster statue of Buddha that she always kept beside her pillow. Indeed, Grandma resembled the smiling, corpulent Buddha, except that she seldom showed such an appealing smile, and she had a pair of 4-inch feet that could barely support her overweight body. When I once told her so, she tweaked my ear so hard that I immediately cried out, "Dear Grandma!" Nevertheless, behind her back, I continued to call her "Buddha Grandma."

The first time I saw Grandma was at my home in Peking, the year I was eight years old. Awakened one morning by half-suppressed babbling, I found an old lady sitting erect in the armchair, her face fat and smooth, her hair snow white. Hearing my mother call her "Mother," I perceived that she must be my grandma, who, as mother had told me, was to live with us for some time.

With an ill-proportioned, 200-pound body, Grandma seldom moved around. She spent most of the day in the armchair, supervising and commanding everybody and everything. I could always see her small, bright eyes and hear her harsh, rough voice, "Mind your manners!" "Be lady-like!" "Eat slowly!" "Walk gently!" "Speak softly!" and so on, and so forth. Once I spilt some soup at the dinner table. Grandma shot me a sharp glare, and remarked sharply, "If you go on behaving like that, no one will want to marry you!"

As time went on, I noticed that Grandma had some secret from me. Many times I saw her hide something in bed hurriedly, while my two-year-old brother sat on her lap, eating, so finally I determined to find the secret out. One morning after getting up, I went directly to her bed, pretending to help her make it. "Keep off it, do you hear?" Grandma shouted immediately in such a startling tone that I instinctively loosed my hands. Grandma, doing morning exercises a few paces away, began to maneuver her huge body slowly but forcefully toward me, but her small feet allowed her to move only inches at a time. Seeing this, I grasped the quilt again. Grandma stopped. She snatched a wooden ruler, banged it on the table, and then pointed it squarely at me, snapping, "Come here!" At the thought that she was going to beat me, or tweak my ear, I grabbed a pillow at once and put it on my head. Just then a bottle full of chocolates rattled out. "You little imp!" was all Grandma said.

Grandma could be very kind, though. When no one else was around to carry out her orders, she would turn to me, handing me in one hand a broom or an empty soy bottle, tossing into the other one a one fen coin or a candy. With threads of wrinkles emerging round her eyes, she would smile sweetly and say, "Take this, and do this, my nice child." She also appeared amiable when she worshipped the Buddha statue. Then her eyes were closed, her hands before her breast, her mouth trembling slightly with a stream of words trickling out; "God, let me live forever! Please!" was the only thing I could understand.

Eight months later, Grandma left Peking.

Ten years passed before I saw her again in her attic in Shanghai, the year she was 80 years old. Entirely paralyzed, she lay in bed, the Buddha beside her. Her once strong fleshy body was now sagging, sloping, falling away in every direction. One of her eyes was blind. The other saw me dimly and tried to trace out my appearance, my clothes, my hair, even my ears that she had twisted so many times in anger. All the time she kept saying, with a catch in her throat, "I can't see you clearly, my child."

The last time I went to see her was to bid her farewell. Having felt all over me, she motioned me to remove the Buddha. Then sliding her head slightly aside, she asked me to get out her small bag beneath the pillow.

Hands trembling, she uncovered the string round the bag and took out a leather purse from which she drew out a ten-yuan note. "Take it, and buy yourself a new dress."

At this, I recalled what happened on the morning of one Spring Festival. Traditionally my grandma, the oldest of the family, would hand out some money to the young. She gave each grandchild five yuan and each great grandchild two yuan. A few minutes later, she sent her maid over to say that she had given two yuan more than she intended and demanded it back. We all became uneasy and handed back the money. The maid counted it and then went back. Soon she came again, saying that Grandma insisted on two more yuan. Seeing that there was no way out, I handed over the amount demanded.

Hesitantly I told Grandma that I had bought enough clothes and that she'd better keep the money for her own use. Her dim eyes became moist. A tear rolled along her wrinkles, "My dear child, I probably can never see you again. Please don't refuse me." So sincere was she that I held her hands tightly in mine and accepted the offer. She smiled, happily, with a tear glistening on her cheek.

Zhang Yanyin

4 *Illustrative Writing*

Statement of Assignment

Illustrative writing makes a transition from the three narrative papers you have completed to the writing you will do in subsequent chapters. This type of writing calls for an explicitly stated thesis or guiding idea, rather than the implied idea you worked with in Chapter 3. This paper fits into the category of expository writing, since in it you will explain your thesis and make it clear and convincing to your reader. However, the paper will also be narrative since supporting data will be in the form of scenes and miniscenes.

An illustrative paper should do three things: (1) state a clear and interesting guiding thesis; (2) narrate incidents (examples) that illustrate and develop that thesis; and (3) explain how the narratives relate to the thesis. Since these tasks are not simple ones, this paper needs to be as substantial as your last one, perhaps four or five pages. Your instructor may give you more specific guidelines on length and content.

Illustrative writing is common in magazines, books, and newspapers. It sometimes takes a simple form: a statement followed by a series of simple narrative examples with a few words of explanation to move the reader from example to example. At other times, illustrative material is more complex, building from a statement in the beginning through examples to an enhanced restatement at the end. The essay "Childhood Innocence," printed below, will acquaint you with the form. It uses the illustrative form reduced to its simplest terms, but the paper is not simple. The next example is an excerpt from the *Autobiography of Mark Twain*, which shows a more complex illustrative form. The first paper presents an idea and illustrates it with a variety of narratives; so does the second. But the second uses the narratives and the ironic commentary to undercut the idea and show finally how absurd it is. Illustrative papers can do either.

Childhood Innocence

Many people regard the innocence of childhood as a wonderful thing to see, but being the victim of it can be anything but wonderful.

One summer my friend and I volunteered with the summer fun program in our neighborhood. One day all of the kids were running around in the gym when all of a sudden I heard this little boy about eight years old say, "You fatta bulla," then laugh. I looked at the girl he had been teasing and saw that she was on the verge of crying but all she said was, "Be quiet." I looked back at the boy and told him not to say that anymore and he kept asking me why. Then I thought to myself, "How can he practically make someone cry and ask why, like there was nothing wrong with it!" Later he even made fun of me. He would say, "You're fat yeah?" as casually as if he were asking me if I liked pizza or something! I just ignored him but at the same time couldn't help feeling hurt, self-conscious and "fat." Other episodes such as this occurred frequently between the kids, and I could see that it was as natural as running and playing.

Besides helping with summer fun I also helped with the second grade Sunday school class. In each of the four years I've helped, there has been one boy (usually) who is noted for being the troublemaker. One such boy was making fun of a girl's drawing of a horse. The girl ignored him and that was fine, but then the rest of the boys and girls began to laugh at the funny things he was saying about it, and she began to cry. It wasn't really the direct insults of the one boy but the innocent laughter of the others that had made her cry.

Once when I was in elementary school I had asked this girl, "How come your hair is frizzy?" I meant it strictly out of curiosity but all of a sudden she began to cry! I didn't know what to do. I couldn't understand why she was fine one minute and the next was crying. In later years I realized why she was crying and what I had done.

As one of our Keywanettes projects we would go to Haili church to babysit. One night two girls who had been sticking to each other like glue and were so called "best friends," were playing nicely until the last ten minutes of the hour. One of the girls came crying to me and said, "I don't like Julie."

"I thought she was your best friend."

"No!"

"Why not? What happened?"

"She said that my picture looked like a monster!"

"Well, what's wrong with that?"

"It's supposed to be a girl!"

"Oh, well I'll talk to her, ok?"

"Ok."

I went over to the other girl and tried to patch this thing up.

"What happened with you and Susie?"

"I don't know, all I said was that her picture looked like a monster and then she got mad at me."

"Well, I think she felt hurt because you called her drawing a monster; it's supposed to be a girl."

"Oh! I didn't know, I'm sorry."

I saw that she had drawn a picture too and inquired, "Is this your picture?"

"Yes."

"It's a picture of a monster!"

"Yeah, I saw hers and thought it was neat so I wanted to make one too."

Julie had made an innocent admiring remark about Susie's drawing, but she had taken it the wrong way and felt insulted.

All of these experiences have helped me to see and understand children a little more. Some of their innocent remarks could be considered "cute," as many people think they are, yet others can really hurt.

Sandy Haraguchi

But a boy's life is not all comedy; much of the tragic enters into it. The drunken tramp who was burned up in the village jail lay upon my conscience a hundred nights afterward and filled them with hideous dreams—dreams in which I saw his appealing face as I had seen it in the pathetic reality, pressed against the window bars, with the red hell glowing behind him—a face which seemed to say to me, "If you had not given me the matches this would not have happened; you are responsible for my death." I was *not* responsible for it, for I had meant him no harm but only good, when I let him have the matches; but no matter, mine was a trained Presbyterian conscience and knew but the one duty—to hunt and harry its slave upon all pretexts and on all occasions, particularly when there was no sense nor reason in it. The tramp—who was to blame—suffered ten minutes; I, who was not to blame, suffered three months.

The shooting down of poor old Smarr in the main street at noonday supplied me with some more dreams; and in them I always saw again the grotesque closing picture—the great family Bible spread open on the profane old man's breast by some thoughtful idiot and rising and sinking to the labored breathings and adding the torture of its leaden weight to the dying struggles. We are curiously made. In all the throng of gaping and sympathetic onlookers there was not one with common sense enough to perceive that an anvil would have been in better taste there than the Bible, less open to sarcastic criticism and swifter in its atrocious work. In my nightmares I gasped and struggled for breath under the crush of that vast book for many a night.

All within the space of a couple of years we had two or three other tragedies and I had the ill luck to be too near by on each occasion. There was the slave man who was struck down with a chunk of slag for some small offense; I saw him die. And the young Californian emigrant who was stabbed with a bowie knife by a drunken comrade; I saw the red life gush from his breast. And the case of the rowdy young brothers and their harmless old uncle; one of them held the old man down with his knees on his breast while the other one tried repeatedly to kill him with an Allen revolver which wouldn't go off. I happened along just then, of course.

Then there was the case of the young Californian emigrant who got drunk and proposed to raid the "Welshman's house" all alone one dark and threatening night. This house stood halfway up Holliday's Hill and its sole occupants were a poor but quite respectable widow and her blameless daughter. The invading ruffian woke the whole village with his ribald yells and coarse challenges and obscenities. I went up there with a comrade—John Briggs, I think—to look and listen. The figure of the man was dimly visible; the women were on their porch, not visible in the deep shadow of its roof, but we heard the elder woman's voice. She had loaded an old musket with slugs and she warned the man that if he stayed where he was while she counted ten it would cost him his life. She began to count, slowly; he began to laugh. He stopped laughing at "six"; then through the deep stillness, in a steady voice, followed the rest of the tale: "Seven . . . eight . . . nine"—a long pause, we holding our breaths—"ten!" A red spout of flame gushed out into the night and the man dropped with his breast riddled to rags. Then the rain and the thunder burst loose and the waiting town swarmed up the hill in the glare of the lightning like an invasion of ants. Those people saw the rest; I had had my share and was satisfied. I went home to dream and was not disappointed.

My teaching and training enabled me to see deeper into these tragedies than an ignorant person could have done. I knew what they were for. I tried to disguise it from myself but down in the secret deeps of my troubled heart I knew—and I *knew* I knew. They were inventions of Providence to beguile me to a better life. It sounds curiously innocent and conceited now, but to me there was nothing strange about it; it was quite in accordance with the thoughtful and judicious ways of Providence as I understood them. It would not have surprised me nor even overflattered me if Providence had killed off that whole community in trying to save an asset like me. Educated as I had been, it would have seemed just the thing and well worth the expense. *Why* Providence should take such an anxious interest in such a property, that idea never entered my head, and there was no one in that simple hamlet who would have dreamed of putting it there. For one thing, no one was equipped with it.

Mark Twain, from *Autobiography of Mark Twain*

Getting Started

Each of the papers above had a guiding thesis. Sandy was illustrating how children's innocent remarks can cause pain to those around them; Mark Twain was illustrating how his Presbyterian conscience caused him to believe naively and insensitively that the violence and tragedy around him were for the purpose of saving his soul. As you read the sample papers in this chapter, you will find some familiar guiding ideas (You should never drink and drive. Children need to learn how to do things on their own.) and some unfamiliar, even controversial ones (People like winning too much ever to accept defeat graciously.).

You will need such a guiding thesis for your paper. Perhaps one has already come to you from your own experience. If that is the case, you have passed the first hurdle for this assignment. Now you need to collect material. Take a pencil and write your idea at the top of a page. Now make a list similar to the one with which you began the relationship paper. List a series of events that illustrate that idea. Be sure you have listed events. Mark Twain's list might have looked like this:

The death of the drunk in the jail because of matches I gave him

Shooting of Smarr

Slave man struck down

Death of the young man stabbed by a bowie knife

The young brothers trying to kill their uncle

The invasion of the "Welshman's house" and the death of the assailant

When you have your list, talk to another writer, sketching the events and explaining how they illustrate the point you want to make. Your instructor may have you bring the list to class and work in pairs or groups.

If you do not have your idea in mind, you will need to begin your thinking in another way. Perhaps one or all of the activities described below will help you. They are all based on the technique of freewriting that was introduced in Chapter 2. You might like to go back and review that section.

WRITING ACTIVITY

Start thinking of an experience or experiences that seem significant to you or that simply come readily to your mind. Write about these for five or ten minutes. Begin by retelling the experience if you like or by "thinking on paper" about the experience. Go where your writing takes you. Don't worry about making a coherent paper (much less about sentences, grammar, or spelling). Just write. If you begin to think about another experience, go with it.

When you have written for a while, stop and reread what you have said. Can you see an idea emerging? If so, write it down. Begin to write again with that idea in mind. Ask yourself if any other experiences come to mind as you think of the one (or ones) you have been writing about.

Share this writing with another writer and talk about the thoughts that came to you as you wrote.

WRITING ACTIVITY

Look at the following statements, or parts of statements. They are given not as sample thesis statements, but as triggers to get you thinking. Choose one that seems interesting, and begin freewriting as above, keeping the statement loosely in mind. If your writing leads you from your original idea to another, follow that one, even if it is not on your list. Keep on writing for about 10 minutes. Then stop and read what you have said. Is there an idea emerging? Write it down and continue to freewrite. Again, after one or two tries, stop and discuss your writing (and your ideas) with a colleague.

Last year I was . . . ; this year I am . . .

I play a dozen different roles.

When I am a student, I . . . ; but when I am not, I . . .

People think I am . . . ; but I really am . . .

One common idea that I think is wrong is . . .

One old tried and true idea I believe is . . .

One thing I have learned even though I did not want to learn it is . . .

One thing I know that a lot of people don't seem to is . . .

The last statement really helped one writer come up with his idea. He had been struggling along trying to work with a tired idea about how much we need education, but he didn't really want to write about that. Maybe he thought he should write about it, but nothing interesting was coming. He came in despair to his instructor who asked him a simple question, "What do you really know a lot about?"

"Swimming."

"Do you know something about swimming that most people don't know?"

The answer was immediate and clear: "Training hard is important in winning races, but not as important as training to swim smart." As soon as the sentence was out, he began to talk about times when he had proved that to himself, and his paper was under way. The result, "Swimming Smart," appears later in this chapter.

When you have an idea in mind, or one that is beginning to surface, go back to the first exercise in this chapter, and make a list of events or scenes that you can use as examples in the paper. At this point you will be ready to begin your draft.

Writing a Draft

As you begin to write your paper, you need to consider several factors: How will you use the material you have collected? What order will you present it in? How and where will you present your thesis? How much explanation will you need to convince your readers of the truth of your thesis? We will take up each of these questions in this section.

You should now have a general idea in mind for your topic. You may modify it as you go along, but the following discussion and the accompanying activities will be useful to you only if you have an idea in mind.

How Will You Use Your Material?

The illustrative paper is like the relationship paper in that it is made up largely of scenes, which can be fully narrated scenes or miniscenes. However, as we will see later, sometimes your narratives will go beyond the strict time limit we observed in the first three papers.

Like a relationship paper, an illustrative paper can make very good use of a series of short scenes. Mark Twain illustrated that, as does the excerpt below from a paper on motorcycling. Here there are four miniscenes in the second paragraph (indicated by parenthetical numbers). Each is only one or two sentences in length, but each has sensory detail and action, just like a longer scene.

Death or Delight

Last summer I spent many of my extra hours on the thick black seat of my Honda 300 flashing along the highways of Indiana and Kentucky. In doing so I found myself a member of a fraternity of rugged road cyclists. I also found that I was lumped in a group that contributes greatly to reports of traffic fatalities. Although highway cycling is dangerous, to me it was always fascinating and often exciting.

More than once I saw the bleeding body and twisted hump of steel that sits as the temporary monument to a careless cycler. And more than once I came close to erecting my own. (1) As I slowed down to maneuver through the congestion of red-crowned Highway Patrol cars and bag-burdened vehicles of curious travelers, I sickened to see a flesh-scraped whimpering man being carried out of the ditch at the side of the road where his cycle lay. (2) That night, fooled by the vague illumination of dim headlights, I misjudged a curve and found myself hurtling toward a guard rail. Panic wouldn't have helped. I just gravely faced the realization that if I didn't pull out of it, the tragedy of the afternoon might be reenacted. (3) Weeks later when I tried to slow down for a long blind curve, wet with an afternoon rain, the cycle's wheels began to slide from under me. Again, as I wrestled the cycle for control, I found myself in that suspended state waiting to see if the machine would carry me away from the approaching threat of an oncoming car. (4) My face grew grim when I was greeted by blinking blue ambulance lights on the outskirts of Richmond, and I saw the torn, battered body of a boy who almost made it home lying in a pool the color of his gnarled red cycle. Dangerous, yes cycling is dangerous.

"Death or Delight" shows the effective use of miniscenes. However, as with the relationship paper, an illustrative paper might use longer scenes, and the narratives used might go beyond the narrow limits of time we have set for scenes in the past. Many times an illustrative paper presents a connected narrative that goes on for a day or several days. The following paper has some scenes, but it presents a narrative quite a bit longer than one scene.

Don't

Just after my older brother had gotten his driver's license, my mother and father sat us both down for a talk. "You guys can drink," they said, "and now you can drive. But don't you ever, ever do both at the same time." I respect my parents, and I listened to them very closely when they said this. Still, I was your typical headstrong teenager, so I had to find out about drinking and driving for myself.

I got my own driver's license soon after my talk with Mom and Dad, and I promptly forgot about what they had said. Alcohol was already a great socializing tool among most of my friends, and we lived for fast cars and faster cars. I began driving to most of the parties that I attended, and didn't really think too much about having a few beers and then driving home at the end of the night. Sure, a couple of times I bumped a curb or two, or missed seeing a sign, but weren't there a lot of sober drivers who did things worse than that? There were a few occasions when I forgot things behind the wheel after a party, and times when I probably shouldn't have driven. Still, I knew my limits and nothing bad had happened to me. I was drinking and driving and doing fine.

I was not alone in drinking and then driving afterward. My best friend Adrean was also a car fanatic. Most of his spare time was spent under the hood of his 1970 Plymouth Barracuda tinkering with this or adjusting that. A countless number of our nights together we both worked on the car in his garage accompanied by the mandatory radio and case of beer. On one such night, after repairing a damaged fuel pump and going through all but two beers, Adrean proposed that we "test the new pump out with a quick drive around town." I quickly seconded the motion, anxious to get out of the musty and grimy garage. Adrean and I both staggered into the 'Cuda, and off we went into the night.

In no time we were flying down the Mass Turnpike, weaving in and out of traffic as if we were characters in some penny arcade video game. As we approached the Copley exit I asked Adrean if he wanted to stop off and get something to eat. He nodded vigorously and the car whipped onto the off ramp so hard that I almost fell into Adrean's lap.

"Slow down a little!" I yelled, pulling myself again into a sitting position.

"Why, you afraid of a little speed?" Adrean challengingly slurred.

"No! I just don't want to get killed tonight, that's all."

Sensing the uncertainty in my voice, Adrean swung quickly back toward the highway. We plunged down the on ramp at incredible speed. I glanced warily out of my left eye and saw a huge tractor-trailer rig approaching the car. I was confident that even with a couple of beers in him, Adrean would slow down and let the trailer pass. The rig kept on coming, and Adrean didn't let up on the gas. I stared at him. He was leaning against his seat heavily, his eyes lidded and red. The rig was now only about five feet away from us, and I screamed at Adrean to stop. He suddenly snapped upright and slammed on the brakes automatically. The screech of rubber on asphalt filled my ears as I hung onto my seat. The 'Cuda slid onto the highway, slipping past the back of the rig by no more than a foot.

On the way home neither of us said a word, but I could hear my heart pound. I didn't want to believe that Adrean's drinking had almost killed us both, and ran several other excuses through my mind. Still, deep down I knew that alcohol was the cause of the near miss, and I was afraid.

Each time that you get behind the wheel of a car, even if you're sober, you are taking the chance that you'll never make it back home alive. Alcohol just makes these odds that much longer. Adrean and I were challenging the odds and had been fantastically lucky. Unfortunately I know another person who wasn't.

During the summer of my senior year in high school I joined a pickup softball team. I spent many a summer day swatting big, round softballs and tilting back as many beers as I could "to stop dehydration." Edwin "Chip" Guiney was our shortstop, and had been an all-state baseball player in high school. Chip was going to enter Boston College in the fall on a scholarship to play for the varsity team there.

Chip and I hit it off immediately and became inseparable. Every Sunday I'd meet him at the ballpark for a game and then go out and party with him afterward. Many nights we'd "cruise the streets of Newton" in search of "excitement, adventure, and a good serious party." Usually at these parties we'd drink, and then I'd race him in his car. Again I was pushing my luck, and it seemed that soon the odds would catch up with me.

One Saturday night Chip called me, asking if I wanted to go to a friend's house to see some videos. No, I replied, I had a date with my girlfriend. The next morning I was startled awake by the staccato ring of the telephone at the foot of my bed. It was my friend Bob, who also happened to be Chip's neighbor.

"What's the deal with calling so early," I moaned into the receiver, seeing that it was still only seven o'clock.

"I'm at Newton-Wellesley Hospital," Bob tensely replied. "Chipper was in a car accident last night, and he's hurt pretty badly. You better come down here real soon."

Still numb from the news, I was able to quickly dash out of bed, throw on some clothes and speed the mile-and-a-half to Newton-Wellesley. I met Bob in the main emergency area and he filled me in on the details. It turned out that Chip had been drinking with two others in his Camaro, driving around and looking for some action. They said that he suddenly began to pick up speed and steer the car very erratically. He whizzed through several streets until the Camaro spun out, glanced off of a light pole and was stopped when it slammed into a stone wall. The police had estimated the impact speed at almost 65 mph. Blood tests had showed Chip's alcohol level to be over twice the amount needed to be legally drunk. One of his passengers was lying in a room upstairs with critical injuries. The other had been pronounced dead.

I wasn't able to see Chip for several days, but that gave me some time to think about what exactly had happened to him. Chip had been a definite pro baseball prospect, and a fun, easy-going, carefree guy. Now he was hanging on in a hospital room for his life with two broken legs, a shattered arm, and a fractured neck. He was being sued by the parents of the boy who had died in the crash, and a possible homicide charge was pending against him.

Luckily, Chip's story was not a totally tragic one. After many weeks of intensive therapy he was released from the hospital, and most of the charges and suits against him were dropped. Still, Chip did not win. Chip will have to live with the fact that he will never play sports again, but even more tragically, he will have to live with the fact that he was respon-sible for another person's death. That is going to haunt him forever.

While Chip was in the hospital, I often thought long and hard about what had happened to him. I could have very easily been the one who had died in the Camaro that night, or for that matter been the one who had been driving it. It was at this point that I finally realized how downright stupid I had been. Any night when I had been drinking and driving could have been my last. That night with Adrean on the turnpike should've been except for the fact that we were amazingly lucky. Drinking and driving was no "macho" thing to do. It's simply a plain idiotic way to push your luck and ask for death.

I still drink at parties. I still often use the car to get where I want to go. But I am also much wiser now. You can't fool around with alcohol and cars. Cars are dangerous enough by themselves, and introducing alcohol into the picture just makes things that much worse. Life is too precious a thing to throw away in such an imbecilic, careless, and preventable way.

David Sasdi

WRITING ACTIVITY

Begin now to write the scenes that will illustrate your thesis. Go to the list of events you made earlier in this chapter. Is one more important than any of the others? Probably you have noted that some of these papers have fewer long scenes than the relationship paper. However, one or two substantial scenes can sometimes be effective. If you do have one example in mind that needs to be written in detail, do so now. If not, choose two or three items from your list and develop them as miniscenes. Do you have an example that needs to be narrated over a longer period? Look again at "Don't," to see how David handled the part about Chip. Then try a longer, connected narrative like that one.

When you have written your narratives, read them to another writer or to a group without giving them any interpretative comments. Ask them to tell you what they think your point might be. Have them tell, also, whether the narrative is effective and compelling.

In What Order Will You Present Your Material?

By the time you have written a few scenes, you will almost certainly have begun to think about putting them together into a paper. If the paper is emerging naturally as the scenes take shape (it might happen!), you are very lucky. Just keep on writing. However, if you are still searching for a structure, the following discussion will help you.

The most obvious way to present a series of experiences is simple chronology, the method used in "Don't." However, it is not always the most effective. It works in "Don't," because the purpose there is to follow the development of David's education about drinking and driving. At first, he mildly believed that the two did not mix, but gradually, through experience, he became wholly converted to the idea.

Not all illustrative essays need this chronological movement. Another strategy, equally simple, might be called the string of beads. Here the writer presents the central idea and then simply narrates a series of illustrative events, usually equal in importance and drawn randomly from experience. The simplicity of the form can be a strength, as in "Childhood Innocence," where simplicity is part of the point of the essay. But this kind of essay can also be simpleminded, even boring. If you adopt this strategy, you need interesting material, and you need to make it clear why each of your beads is strung into this paper. In the paper below each event illustrates part of the point the writer is making about competitive swimming. Note, however, that the writer has divided his examples into two categories that illustrate two different strategies for swimming.

Swimming Smart

As in any sport, training for competitive swimming involves various strategies. Training long and hard, putting in the necessary sweat, is one important strategy, but, strangely enough, it is often not the most important element in a successful performance. Of course, one needs the basic strength and stamina, and needs them in abundance, but knowing exactly how to swim a race and being able to apply that knowledge to a given situation is often more important.

Any experienced swimmer will tell you that a good start, efficient turns, and the right finish will make the difference between first and second in a tight race. One important race quickly gave me experience in that area.

It was an invitational swim meet, one of the biggest held annually in the state. I was to swim the 200-meter butterfly. I had practiced long and hard, and I knew I was in shape. As I heard the prerace call, I got up on block number five and shook my arms to release the tension. I looked around nervously trying to size up the other players. Then, the starting gun went off, and I jumped—too deep. I came up behind the other swimmers and began a desperate struggle to catch up.

I am naturally a very strong swimmer, and as we approached the turn, I had passed several weaker swimmers and was closing in on the leader. Unfortunately, my attention was on him, not on my swim. I charged the turn, but misjudged the wall and slipped. I was again several swimmers behind.

I swam the remaining two lengths with great intensity. My long hours of hard training served me well—as did my mistakes so far in this race. In the next two turns I streamlined my approach and gained, rather than lost time. I gradually advanced myself to a tie for first place.

I stayed even with the other swimmer coming down the last lap. I knew that our finish would decide the winner. Nervous and inexperienced, I did not know whether to take the half stroke into the wall which was a strong, but risky way to finish. I decided not to take it, but my competitor did. That made the difference: I lost the race by one one-hundredth of a second.

As I got out of the water, I knew that I won the race on strength but lost it because I had no strategy for beginning, turning, and ending. I learned fast. My next event was the 100-meter fly. I determined before I hit the water exactly how I would start, turn, and finish. The results were outstanding. I won the race and broke the record by half a second.

I have had other hard lessons in swimming. I always felt like I should swim all out in every event. This can be a good strategy sometimes, and it always shows determination and a desire to win. However, one important key to winning a race is learning how to pace. I mastered this strategy the hard way very early.

At the National Age Group Championship held in California, I stood next to my starting block thinking back over how hard I had worked over the last year to get this chance. I heard a whistle shrill over the cheers, and I stepped up on the block to swim the event I had come for: the 400-meter mixed. I was psyched. I jumped eagerly to the buzz of the electric starter. My start was fast as I plunged into the heated pool. But I was too excited. I swam as fast as I could from the beginning, and had used most of my energy by the time I completed the first 100-meter butterfly.

As I changed to the backstroke, I felt the first pain. At the end of this section, I had already dropped from first to third. Even swimming my most powerful breaststroke in the next section didn't help. I fell to fifth place. Down to the last 100 meters of freestyle, my body was too exhausted to sprint. I finished last in the event.

These two events, and others, have taught me the importance of strategy in racing. I continue to practice hard and long. I continue to swim all out whenever I need to. But I think through a race before I get into the water. I think: beginning, end, turning. First, last, and always, I think: pacing.

Scott Kolona

Scott's paper is essentially a string of beads. Each story makes the same point: A swimmer needs strategy. Of course, he illustrates different strategies, but the simple beginning idea is still there at the end. Scott has an interesting writing strategy here, however. He narrates failures, not successes. His pacing is also good. The one success is told quickly so that he can give more attention to how he learned through another failure. It's a simple paper, but not simplistic.

Another way of ordering an illustrative paper might be called a pyramid. Instead of putting relatively equal examples on a simple string, this strategy builds toward an ending that is not at once obvious from the beginning. The writer, of course, always has a guiding idea in mind and keeps it in front of the reader. But each example deepens, maybe even alters, the thesis subtly until by the end the idea is richer than it was at the beginning. The string of beads is a stroll in which the writer points out things to note; the pyramid is a dance in which the writer uses each movement to build to a preordained, but maybe not obvious conclusion. The following paper shows a simple pyramid; in it the writer moves from the first idea that women's lives have improved to the realization that they still carry unnecessary burdens.

Women in a Shanxi Village

Probably you have never lived in or even seen a cave dwelling. But I have. About fifteen years ago, when I worked in a small town in Shanxi Province, I lived in a peasant's cave for about nine months. I was horrified on hearing that I would live in a cave, which I associated with darkness, dampness, rats, spiders, and scorpions. But I came to like it gradually and love it immensely in the end. I even shed tears when I had to leave it. I loved the cave for its own sake; it was warm and cosy in winter, cool and nice in summer. I loved it more for all the women and girls I got acquainted with there.

I had read a lot about women in the countryside before I actually ever had a person-to-person contact with them. I knew that women from the poor families suffered untold miseries in the old days. But those stories had always seemed remote, even sensational to me because of my comfortable life. In Shanxi I heard them from women who had experienced them. I also witnessed in person that they did not all happen in the past.

My hostess was forty-five. But wearing her hair in a coil, with weather-beaten, wrinkled, thin face, she appeared to me an old woman of fifty-five. She had a teenage daughter named Feng-xien with whom I shared the cave room. One evening after my hostess finished her washing up, I casually asked, "Aunty, you are from Honan, aren't you?"

"Yes, I was born and brought up there. That was a poor place, you know."

"But how did you come to Shanxi?" I pursued.

Calmly and expressionlessly, she told her story:

"During the great famine in 1939, I was only eighteen and newly married. My parents and parents-in-law all starved to death. People in our village began eating earth after they stripped all the leaves and bark off the trees. My husband and I followed the stream of refugees to Shanxi Province. We begged all our way here. People got so hungry that they even resorted to eating each other."

I could not believe my ears.

"Yes. I saw that with my own eyes."

With the same calmness, she continued, "Our baby son died on the way. When we came to this village in Shanxi, we became so weak that we could move no further. My husband lay on the path dying when a man came and talked him into selling me."

"Selling you?" I could not help crying out.

"Yes, it was a common practice in the famine. To save both, parents sold their children, and men sold their wives."

That was how she came to settle down here. She married this man Zhang who had been too poor to get a wife until thirty. With a smile on her lips, my hostess added, "We now live in paradise."

As time went on, I heard stories similar to our hostess's. One woman became a child bride at the age of six and never had warm clothes to wear in winter. She now suffered from serious arthritis and had to wear cotton padded trousers even in summer. Showing the mark left from a whipping by her father-in-law, she said contentedly, "Now our life is a world better."

When I observed the present life of my hostess, I came to understand the word paradise better. The family now had two cave rooms and a store-house. They had electric lights, a radio, and two bicycles, as well as layers of warm quilts and surplus grain in the storehouse.

I often heard women say, "The old society was like an abyss, at the bottom of which lay the women," and the words sounded meaningful to me as I listened to such stories and compared them with the relative affluence I saw in their homes now. Their contentment with the present life was well justified. However, as I began to pay more and more attention to the women, I found out that their emancipation was far from thorough. It was true that women had broken some fetters, but others remained.

I noticed most of the burdens of house drudgery fell on women. In the field, women and men worked equally. But as soon as the wife got home, she would lose no time in doing all sorts of household chores: cooking, sewing, mending, feeding pigs, while the man sat in the shade under a tree smoking a pipe. The aunty living next door had five children, and very often she had to make shoes for them until the small hours of the night. But the next day she would rise at five o'clock, cook breakfast and feed pigs before she started off for field work. Men were not lazy, but they simply thought rearing children, cooking, and sewing belonged to women.

Women suffered in other ways. One day a woman named Hiu Hua came running wildly in the street crying, "Save my baby! Save my baby!" It so happened that her baby son rolled over from the bed and fell into a big boiling pot. The poor thing got so badly burnt that he died on the way to the county hospital. That tragic story broke everybody's heart. But the tragedy occurred because of the conditions in the household. Hiu Hua had three baby sons, and each was one year older than the last. Whenever she went to the fields, she left all the three at home with nobody looking after them. Can you imagine Hiu Hua was only nineteen by then?

Marrying young caused part of women's sufferings. But women in the village did not seem to be aware of it. Girls in the village became engaged at the age of fifteen or sixteen. They got married when they reached seventeen or eighteen. As soon as they got married, they had children, one after another, the more the better. I made an attempt to persuade some of them to postpone their marriages. But I stopped doing it when I overheard their gossip about me: "She is twenty-six and not married? What has happened to her?" "She is not bad looking. How is it that nobody wants to marry her?" "She will have a hard time giving birth to a baby when she is that old."

These events took place about fifteen years ago. But to this day, I still miss the women and girls in Shanxi. I still miss the cave dwelling I shared with Feng-xien, who must by now have become a mother of four or five children. The state of women in the village still bothers me. Do they still carry alone all the irksome housekeeping burdens? Have the girls come to see the harm caused by early marriage and having too many kids? Have they come to see how they could still better their lives?

Tu Pei

The following paper might also be called a pyramid. At its center is the rather commonplace, yet important, idea that no one, especially in this case the mentally ill, should be judged without knowledge. However, as the author leads us through her experiences, we get more than this; we get an exploration of one person's fears of herself and of the unknown, then a gradual ability to accept not only former patients who are now well but even those who are still unable to control their behavior. Only with this final acceptance can she control her own fears.

Mental Illness

That evening I walked the six blocks home from school debating with myself whether I should tell Mom about Jeanie. By the time I reached the back steps I had pretty much made up my mind to keep quiet, but when Mom greeted me with, "Hi, how was school?" the only thing on my mind tumbled out.

"Jeanie's sick! She tried to kill herself last night and took a bottle full of pills." My voice quivered as the tears welled under my lids.

"Stupid girl! She should have known better than to run from her problems. It wouldn't have happened if she had an ounce of sense in her head!" Mom retorted and continued cutting out the cookies.

I hadn't expected sympathy from Mom, but her answer shook me. A part of me cried for Jeanie; a part of me was afraid—I wasn't sure why. Finally I resolved the fear by declaring that Jeanie's action was irresponsible and could not be excused. Jeanie survived, but no one forgot that she had "a problem" and could not be trusted.

From that time on I avoided anything having to do with mental illness. In my thinking I relegated the mentally ill to a place nearer criminals than the sick. Lectures, articles, or books on mental illness never seemed worth my attention so I avoided facing and working out my feelings.

Some time after I graduated from high school a former classmate, Laura Johnson, called me. Her mother had to return to the state mental hospital and there was no one to cook meals for the family and care for the two youngsters during the day. Could I please help? She and her sister were both involved in summer school at a distant university and could only return weekends.

"Oh no!" I thought. "I could never do anything like that. What would the home be like? How would I act with the children knowing where their mother is?" I felt uncomfortable around Laura and the rest of the family.

When it became evident that either I help them out or Laura and her sister quit school, I reluctantly agreed to go. Kathy and Lisa, the two youngsters, were delighted to have me there. We spent our mornings busy with housekeeping. They both helped by sweeping the floors, wiping dishes, and carrying the laundry. We talked about their mother. They knew where she was and accepted the fact. They also said she would get well and would return soon. The home seemed like any other home.

During my time there I discovered that Mrs. Johnson had lost two children in accidents, was raising a mentally retarded son, and was recovering from a disfiguring accident when she had her breakdown. For the first time I began to realize that there could be understandable reasons for mental breakdowns and that someone who had one could be in all other respects like anyone else.

When Mrs. Johnson came home, Mom and I invited her and the girls over for punch and cookies. The woman I met when I answered the door that day was plainly dressed in a grey cotton print and had her hair carefully combed back and pinned. The shadow of a scar on her left cheek ran from her upper lip to just below her eye. Heavy stockings covered her scarred legs and I noticed a slight limp when she walked.

"Hi, come on in!" My bold invitation disguised my lingering hesitancy. But soon the visit seemed commonplace.

"Hello. Kathy and Lisa have been so anxious to come. I really appreciate your invitation."

I showed them into the living room. Kathy and Lisa made themselves at home playing with our grey cat and their mom sat quietly on the edge of the sofa. The talk was hesitant but normal.

"Are the girls anxious for school to start?"

"Kathy isn't, but Lisa can hardly wait to start kindergarten."

The cat left so the girls began looking through the books in the corner rack. When I felt we had talked enough I suggested we have some cookies.

"Yea!" The girls jumped up and raced to the table. Their mom followed.

"What nice cookies. Did you make them? Lisa, don't take so many!"

"Yes I did, do you enjoy cooking?"

"Sometimes, but I don't have much time."

Between bites we chatted about more nothings. When the cookies were gone they excused themselves and left. I have no idea what bizarre behavior I expected, but all had gone well and I relaxed with relief.

As I reflected on my relationship with the Johnsons, I realized how cruel people have been to avoid this woman. She badly needs a friend. How wrong I was to judge her before I knew the circumstances.

This experience began to change my mind about mental illness and I resolved to learn more about it. Finally, when I went to the university, I enrolled in a psychiatric nursing course. We studied causes, treatments, and cures of mental illness and spent two days a week working in a clinical setting.

My introduction to the patients almost reinforced my old prejudices. They were not at all like Mrs. Johnson. I was met by Florence who demanded, "You want this rake in your face?" Then, "Get away. We hate you!" she growled when I approached her. I decided I had better stay away from her.

Sitting by herself in the corner Alice looked docile with her head lowered and her hands folded in her lap. "All she needs is a friend to talk to and she should come out of her shell," I decided, so I charged over, sat down, and began chattering away nervously. After a minute she eased herself away from me and turned her back. I continued to chatter away with no response from her. Realizing I had come on pretty strong, I excused myself and promised to return in ten minutes. When I did she had moved to the opposite corner in an attempt to avoid me.

"I'm back, Alice. You don't have to talk to me if you don't want to, but may I please sit by you? I'd like to know you better."

As I sat quietly beside her I could sense her increasing agitation. She began to wring her hands and breathe deeper and quicker. Then with one loud sigh she jumped up and fled to the other side of the room.

"Maybe my old fears are justified," I thought to myself at the end of the first day. "From what I've experienced, they don't want to be helped." I guess I had expected these people to be like Mrs. Johnson, "normal" and easy to talk to. I had been able to overcome fears of the mentally ill—but only so long as they acted like I did. I had not yet learned to see beyond their behavior to the humanity beneath it.

With each encounter with the "clients" at the clinic I slowly reformed my thinking about the mentally ill. The other students and I cooked, sang, worked, arranged flowers, and played games with these people, and I began to see that their strange behavior was only a protection for them, not their essence. I no longer have fear or contempt for them. Some will recover. Some may not, but I've found that they all can be helped.

I have spent a lot of time with Florence. I have come to see that she fantasizes a lot, and talks to people whether they are beside her, just passing, or across the room involved with another patient. Most of her delusions put her in a benevolent position where she can do things for people.

"You come live in my boarding home. O.K.? You can come for only $200. I have a maid and cook. I'll go to my store and bring you all the things you need, for free. O.K.?" She offered on one occasion.

To ask her reality questions about the "here and now" can often bring on hostility, but I discovered quite by accident that distraction helped. I once noticed her trying to trim her nails, so I offered to give her a manicure. As we sat there, I asked her a few questions about herself: What time does she go home? How does she get home? What does she do on weekends? She answered them all normally without going into her fantasy life. Between answers she sat there amazingly quiet. After that my best times with Florence have been while working puzzles, arranging flowers, or similar distracting activities.

After my overwhelming approach with Alice the first day we avoided each other most of the time. Linda, a classmate, did work with her and though many times Alice fled outdoors, the last week she began talking to the rest of us. In fact the last day she even greeted me with a smile and, "Hi," as I walked in the door.

These insecure people who have coped with life in unusual ways are not to be feared or hated. They deserve the love, concern, and acceptance of others so they can learn new and better ways to deal with life. Now that my fear is gone, I can begin to help them and myself toward better mental health.

Annette Wicklund

WRITING ACTIVITY

Perhaps by now you will have begun to put all your material together. If not, these activities might help. Take your outline of possible material, and the scenes you have written, and try some of them.

First write a working introduction for your paper. This should be a statement, more for yourself than for your readers, of just what you want your paper to "mean." Very likely this paragraph will have to be rewritten, maybe even discarded entirely, when you revise the paper. But write it now as a guide for yourself.

Now try arranging your examples (scenes) in a strictly chronological order. Does that make any sense? Does the chronology help clarify your paper or help it build to an interesting conclusion?

If you are not satisfied with a chronological presentation, try to think of other arrangements. Does your idea break down into subideas like Scott's swimming paper? (Recall that he talked first about learning to pay attention to the beginning, turns, and end in a race, then he talked about pacing.) If you can think of a breakdown like this, try arranging your examples according to that.

If breaking your idea down into subideas doesn't work for you, try to think whether your central idea builds and alters as the paper goes, as did Annette's. (Recall she first talked about fears of mental illness, which were assuaged when she discovered that the former patient was as "normal" as she was; then she later had to learn that even beneath seemingly bizarre behavior, mental patients had the same needs as she.) Does your idea have stages of complexity?

Share the organization you think will work with another writer or with a group. If you have a draft, let them read it. If not, relate the draft out loud, telling them the strategy you are contemplating and how the examples will fit into it. Let them tell you where they are confused, enthralled, or bored. Ask them to tell your idea back to you so you can see whether you are communicating successfully.

How and Where Do You Put Your Thesis and Explanations?

As in the portrait, the amount and placement of comment in an illustrative paper depends on the strategy you use, which, in turn, depends on your material.

Striking a balance between narrative and comment is always a challenge. In this paper you may need more comment than you used in the last paper since here you are presenting an explicit thesis.

The effectiveness of this paper depends on the judicious interrelationship between short and long scenes and comment that makes the scenes meaningful. You must have comment, but it must never substitute for the action. Probably you will have one or two sentences that state your main idea explicitly. Maybe you will have comments throughout the paper that add up to your feeling.

The following paper handles scenes and comments well. A young woman thinks back over the goals she has reached and those she has not. She gradually discovers that the goal is the journey itself. You might be hard put to find any one sentence that you could call the thesis of this essay. Since some of the narratives are extended beyond single scenes, the paper does not have the simple string-of-beads form. The idea develops and deepens with each experience. After each of the narratives, the author has placed a sentence—maybe half a sentence—of comment. At the end she devotes two whole paragraphs to summarizing what the experience has meant. In this instance that is not too much. It is just right. Clearly, the ideas in the two paragraphs *come from the experience.* She has *earned* the right to talk because the experience has prepared her readers to listen.

Journey of a Thousand Steps

Goals are something we live with every day. Sometimes they are easily attained, sometimes not. Sometimes they're destroyed before we ever reach them. And sometimes we reach them only to find that they weren't what we expected them to be. So why do we have goals at all? Are they worth all the effort we put into them?

I began one important experience with a great deal of hope and commitment, but nearly ended in frustration before I reached my goal. My job when I worked on a farm was taking care of pine tree seedlings in an attempt to grow a little forest. Every day I went out into the hot sun with my hoe and hose to dig up weeds and water each tree individually. After a year and a half, the trees that had survived the deer, the summer drought, the insects, and disease seemed well on their way to maturity.

One day I went out to work as usual and was shocked to see a big, black patch of burnt trees. A careless worker had tossed a lighted cigarette from his jeep as he rode through the fields. A lot of my labor had literally gone up in smoke. When I saw the extent of the damage, I was so angry and frustrated, thinking of all the hours I had worked to keep those trees alive and growing for nothing, I just wanted to give up and walk away. But I looked at the trees that had had the luck to survive and I thought to myself that there was still something worth saving. So I put my hoe to the ground and attacked the weeds again.

When I left the farm a couple of years later, that job had passed on to others, but my old boss told me as I was leaving that he was going to name our trees "Darlaine's Woods."

Goals that we set for ourselves sometimes do fall short of becoming reality; other times they are more than we ever expected.

A couple of years ago I was traveling in a relatively modern Asian country. After a few weeks of unsuccessfully avoiding the tourist crowds, we decided to head off into some unknown area. A single sentence in a book about some cave drawings near an obscure village aroused our curiosity, so we made our way in that direction.

Nearing the area of the drawings, we found ourselves walking along a pleasant deserted road. Unexpectedly, we came upon an ancient temple, its colors fading in the tropical sun. Monks in saffron-colored robes walked serenely among the ruins. They told us that the drawings we were seeking could be found by following the path through the forest. The beautiful temple was already more than we had expected, but even more was to come.

After a short walk, we came to some strange rock formations, and there unfolded before us a whole community of prehistoric dwellings. Gigantic stone caves had served as homes and places of worship for people who had lived there 5,000 years ago. Some were like giant beehives and could only be entered by climbing a ladder. Others had benches cut to such a degree of perfection that even a modern engineer could appreciate them. At the farthest corner, a later civilization had carved out a giant seated Buddha who, judging by the fresh flowers laid in his open palms, continued to attract worshipers. In the end we found the extraordinary drawings, but that goal had become almost a by-product. We had unexpectedly discovered something that far surpassed our expectations.

High expectations are what led me to make the most demanding journey of my life—trying to reach Mount Everest base camp in Nepal. We had a choice of possible treks, but when we got to Kathmandu, we knew that it had to be Everest. I had mixed feelings about it; it seemed so commonplace to attempt something that had become a cliché. After all, it wasn't the most beautiful mountain, and there were many more treks that would have taken us through more magnificent scenery. Still, we felt compelled to test ourselves against this symbol.

So we set off, vaguely conscious that the journey we were going to make, although it would be measured in physical terms, was actually a test of spirit.

The first day was sunny and warm and we took our time, resting as often as we wanted and stopping for tea at every Sherpa house. But then the valleys and the passes became more extreme, and every day we'd end up going higher than the day before, only to then descend lower.

On the fourth day, we reached a windy, snowy pass, and, cooled by the freezing wind, my sweat-drenched clothes turned into sheets of ice, and my body temperature plunged. That night I became very ill and developed a high fever. Determined to conquer my fever, I insisted on continuing our journey, mostly because I felt guilty for slowing my companion down. But at the end of the day my fever would be raging, and I would end up shivering in my sleeping bag again. One day I virtually crawled into a village and sat down on a stone wall, unable to go any further. I had to give up the smaller goal of continuing steadily on to reach the larger one: Everest.

A few days later, with the help of antibiotics, I recovered and we were on our way again. But where we were going nature was no friend. As we trudged along day after day over rough terrain, I often wondered why I was doing it. All day I struggled to reach a goal that in the end came down to a plate of potatoes and a meager fire.

Then before we knew it, we were almost to our first goal. We had one more high mountain to cross, then a long valley, a frozen river to ford, and finally our first <u>view</u> of Everest. For some, this was achievement enough, close enough. But when we got there, it didn't feel like anything. We stood on a peak, looking at the Black Mountain, feeling physically exhausted and spiritually empty. What was it all for? We didn't really know. Maybe it would be better to leave it as an ideal rather than face further disillusionment.

After much arguing, we decided to turn back. But in the morning, the first thing I said to my companion when I woke was, "I'm going to the end, with or without you," not knowing why, just that after coming so far, I <u>had</u> to. We argued again as I had expected, but then quite suddenly he seemed to understand exactly what I was feeling, and, his face lit up by renewed faith, he joined me and we both headed toward our common goal.

Looking back, that goal often seemed immense and insurmountable, but as the old Asian proverb goes, every journey of a thousand miles begins with the first step. I have often not reached my goals, and probably have missed many adventures that way, but we eventually did reach the mountain that we had set our minds and our bodies to, and with it, an indescribable feeling of accomplishment. The journey itself hadn't been all good or all bad. For one month we walked—walked when we felt like it, walked when we didn't feel like it, walked in sun, snow, rain, hail, cold, heat; walked when we were fresh and rested, walked when our feet and back were aching, and we were dying to stop and rest.

As a friend in those days said to me, "It's the journey there that's important." I've also learned that it is having a goal that you believe in that <u>creates</u> the journey. Sometimes that journey begins in one direction but leads to another. Sometimes it leads to disappointment and disillusionment. And sometimes it begins without a clear direction. But by taking that first of a thousand steps, you often discover not only that your dreams can come true, but that you are already living them.

Darlaine Dudoit

WRITING ACTIVITY

The papers considered so far have shown that the amount and placement of comments can vary considerably in an illustrative paper. To demonstrate this to yourself again, pick another paper in this chapter (either one presented before now or later on). Mark every piece of comment you find. Begin by underlining the thesis statement, or several sentences that might act as a thesis. (Don't always expect to find it at the beginning of the paper, by the way.) About how much of that paper is comment? Ten percent? More? Less? Is that about right for this paper? Now find another paper that has significantly more, or less, comment. What makes the difference? Your teacher may ask you to discuss this in class.

Often it is difficult to know where you have too little or too much comment or whether your thesis is sufficient and clear until you have a draft. In the revision section that follows, we will discuss this question again by considering revisions in two papers we have already read.

Reworking the Draft

Below is printed the first draft of Annette Wicklund's paper, "Mental Illness." Compare it with the final draft of the paper given above, and then read the commentary.

Mental Illness

That evening I walked the six blocks home from school debating with myself whether I should tell Mom about Jeanie. By the time I reached the back steps I had pretty much made up my mind to keep quiet, but when Mom greeted me with, "Hi, how was school?" the only thing on my mind tumbled out.

"Jeanie's sick! She tried to kill herself last night and took a bottle full of pills." My voice quivered as the tears welled under my lids.

"Stupid girl! She should have known better than to run from her problems. It wouldn't have happened if she had an ounce of sense in her head!" Mom retorted and continued cutting out the cookies.

I hadn't expected sympathy from Mom, but her answer shook me. A part of me cried for Jeanie, but another part declared that such irresponsible action could not be excused. Jeanie survived, but no one forgot that she had "a problem" and could not be trusted.

From that time on I avoided anything having to do with mental illness. In my thinking I relegated the mentally ill to a place nearer criminals than the sick. Lectures, articles, or books on mental illness never seemed worth my attention so I avoided facing and working out my feelings.

Some time after I graduated from high school a former classmate, Laura Johnson, called me. Her mother had to return to the state mental hospital and there was no one to cook meals for the family and care for the two youngsters during the day. Could I please help? She and her sister were both involved in summer school at a distant university and could only return weekends to help.

"Oh no!" I thought. "I could never do anything like that. What would the home be like? How would I act with the children knowing where their mother is?" Because of where their mother was I was repelled from the whole situation. I felt uncomfortable around Laura and the rest of the family.

When it became evident that either I helped them out or Laura and her sister quit school I reluctantly agreed to go. Kathy and Lisa, the two youngsters, were delighted to have me there. We spent our mornings busy with housekeeping. They both helped by sweeping the floors, wiping dishes, and carrying the laundry to and from the laundry. Kathy even took the responsibility for making the boys' beds and picking up their room. Afternoons we played or went out. We talked about their mother. They knew where she was and accepted the fact. They also said she would get well and would return soon. During my time there I discovered that she had lost two children in accidents, was raising a mentally retarded son, and was recovering from a disfiguring accident when she had her breakdown. I found nothing threatening about the situation.

When Mrs. Johnson came home, Mom and I invited her and the girls over for punch and cookies. The woman I met when I answered the door that day was plainly dressed in a grey cotton print and had her hair carefully combed back and pinned. The shadow of a scar on her left cheek ran from her upper lip to just below her eye. Heavy stockings covered her scarred legs, and I noticed a slight limp when she walked.

"Hi, come on in!" My bold invitation disguised hesitancy.

"Hello, Kathy and Lisa have been so anxious to come. I really appreciate your invitation."

I showed them into the living room and disappeared to tell Mom they had arrived. Kathy and Lisa made themselves at home playing with our grey cat and their mom sat quietly on the edge of the sofa. The talk was small. "Are the girls anxious for school to start?"

"Kathy isn't, but Lisa can hardly wait to start kindergarten."

"It was fun taking care of them. Are you glad to be home?"

"Yes."

"That was quite a storm we had last night. Did it do any damage at your place?"

"Just a couple of fallen limbs."

The cat left so the girls began looking through the books in the corner rack. When I felt we had talked enough I suggested we have some cookies.

"Yea!" The girls jumped up and raced to the table. Their mom followed.

"What nice cookies. Did you make them? Lisa, don't take so many!"

"Yes I did, do you enjoy cooking?"

"Sometimes, but I don't have much time."

Between bites we chatted about more nothings. When the cookies were gone they excused themselves and left. I have no idea what bizarre behavior I expected, but all had gone well and I relaxed with relief.

As I reflected on my relationship with the Johnsons, I realized how cruel people have been to avoid this woman. She badly needs a friend. How wrong I was to judge her before I knew the circumstances.

During the past seven weeks I have been involved in a psychiatric nursing course. We studied causes, treatments, and cures of mental illness and spent two days a week working in a clinical setting. I was surprised to learn that the trend is to control illness with drugs and therapy and then place patients in day hospital settings within the community. With the recent development of psychotherapeutic drugs many symptoms can be reduced or removed, enabling the patients to deal more directly with their problems and function in a much more normal fashion. With each encounter with the "clients" at the clinic I slowly reformed my thinking about the mentally ill.

"You want this rake in your face?" demanded Florence when introduced to Arnold.

"Get away. We hate you!" she growled when I approached her. We then decided we had better stay away from Florence.

Sitting by herself in the corner Alice looked docile with her head lowered and her hands folded in her lap.

"All she needs is a friend to talk to and she should come out of her shell," I decided, so I charged over, sat down, and began chattering away nervously. After a minute she eased herself away from me and turned her back. I continued to chatter away with no response from her. Realizing I had come on pretty strong I excused myself and promised to return in ten minutes. When I did she had moved to the opposite corner in an attempt to avoid me.

"I'm back, Alice. You don't have to talk to me if you don't want to, but may I please sit by you? I'd like to know you better."

As I sat quietly beside her I could sense her increasing agitation. She began to wring her hands and breathe deeper and quicker. Then with one loud sigh she jumped up and fled to the other side of the room.

"Maybe my fears are justified," I thought to myself at the end of the first day. "From what I've experienced, they don't want to be helped."

These seven weeks we've cooked, sung, worked, arranged flowers, and played games with these people, and I no longer have a fear or contempt for them. Some will recover. Some may not, but I've found that they all can be helped.

Florence sat beside me one day during current events discussion.

"You know, you so lucky I take care of you. If anyone tries to hurt you just tell me and I'll box 'em up! O.K.?" Florence spends a great deal of time fantasizing and talking to people whether they are beside her, just passing, or across the room involved with another patient. Most of her delusions put her in a benevolent position where she can do things for people. Money is very important to her.

"You come live in my boarding home. O.K.? You can come for only $200. I have a maid and cook. I'll go to my store and bring you all the things you need, for free. O.K.?" She offered on one occasion.

To ask her reality questions about the "here and now" would often break her mood and bring on hostility, but I discovered quite by accident that distraction helped. I once noticed her trying to trim her nails, so I offered to give her a manicure. As we sat there, I asked her a few questions about herself: What time does she go home? How does she get home? What does she do on weekends? She answered them all well without going into her fantasy life. Between answers she sat there amazingly quiet. After that our best times with Florence have been while working puzzles, arranging flowers, or similar activities.

After my overwhelming approach with Alice the first day we avoided each other most of the time. Linda, a classmate, did work with her and though many times Alice fled outdoors, the last week she began talking to the rest of us. In fact the last day she even greeted me with a smile and, "Hi," as I walked in the door.

These insecure people who have coped with life in unusual ways are not to be feared or hated. They deserve the love, concern, and acceptance of others so they can learn new and better ways to deal with life. Now that my fear is gone, I can begin to help them and myself toward better mental health.

Annette Wicklund

Most of the major revisions Annette made in her final draft had to do with the relative weight of narrative and comment. Interestingly, she often *reduced* scenes and strengthened comments. She cut the scene with Mrs. Johnson and the girls, because a long scene was not needed to make the point that the interaction with this recovered patient was as commonplace as an interaction with anyone else. Some of the scenes with Florence have also been cut.

On the other hand, note how many comments have been expanded so that Annette's growing awareness about the mentally ill becomes clearer. Only in one place were comments cut, and these general comments about the treatment of mental illness did not seem to relate to the subject at hand even though they were interesting. All in all, the changes in this paper were not extensive, but they made the point of the paper sharper and showed the writer's development more clearly.

WRITING ACTIVITY

Printed below is the first draft of the paper, "Swimming Smart." Compare it with the final draft given above. You will see that it differs mainly in the commentary: introduction, transitions, and so on. Read the two versions and try to decide why the author deleted and added what he did. Do you find any passages that you would have treated differently? Be prepared to discuss the changes, justifying deletions and additions. If you think some parts were better left alone, justify your belief. If you would make other changes, decide why. Your instructor may ask you to discuss this in class.

Swimming Smart

A lot of people don't realize that swimming a race has several strategies. Training hard for a race is an important strategy, but it isn't as important as knowing exactly how to swim a race. I've had several experiences where a start, turn, and finish have made the difference in winning and losing. Another important key in swimming that spectators don't realize is learning how to pace.

It all happened at the Invitational Swim Meet, one of the biggest held annually in the state. I was to swim the 200-meter butterfly. As I heard the prerace call, I got up on block number five and shook my arms to release the tension. The starter sounded the gun and the competition began. My dive unfortunately was too deep. I came up behind the other swimmers and began a desperate struggle to catch up. This was because I concentrated more on the other swimmers and not on myself.

While I charged the turn I misjudged the wall and slipped. I panicked and tried to catch up in the next lengths. I swam the remaining two lengths with great intensity. In the next two turns I streamlined my approach and gained, rather than lost time. I gradually advanced myself to a tie for first place.

I stayed even with the other swimmer coming down the last lap. I knew that our finish would decide the winner. Nervous and inexperienced, I did not know whether to take the half stroke into the wall which was a strong, but risky way to finish. I decided not to take it, but my competitor did. That made the difference: I lost the race by one one-hundredth of a second.

From that moment on I learned the importance of a start, turn, and a finish. My next event was the 100-meter fly and I made sure that I knew exactly how I would start, turn, and finish. The results were outstanding. I won the race and broke the record by half a second.

Swimming a race all out is great. It shows your determination and a desire to win. However, one important key to winning a race is learning how to pace. I learned this strategy faster than any other in my past five years.

This incident happened at the National Age Group Championship held in California. I stood next to my starting block thinking back over how hard I had worked over the last year to get this chance. I heard a whistle shrill over the cheers, and I stepped up on the block to swim the event I had come for: the 400-meter mixed. I was psyched. I jumped eagerly to the buzz of the electric starter. My start was fast as I plunged into the heated pool. But I was too excited. I swam as fast as I could from the beginning, and had used most of my energy for the 100-meter fly.

As I changed to the backstroke, I felt the first pain. At the end of this section, I had already dropped from first to third. Even swimming my most powerful breaststroke in the next section didn't help. I fell to fifth place. Down to the last 100 meters of freestyle, my body was too exhausted to sprint. I finished last in the event.

From then on I realized that pacing plays an important role in competitive swimming. I hope that through what I have just written you've gained more of a knowledge of strategies and how pacing, starts, turns, and finishes can make the difference in competitive swimming.

Scott Kolona

Feedback from Other Writers

As always, getting response from other writers can be helpful once you have a good draft. Here you should tell each other whether the narratives are effective, but you also need to talk about something else: Is the idea you have in mind being communicated clearly, and is it convincing? You should keep this in mind as you read or listen to the papers of other writers. Written below are some questions to consider as you read (or maybe listen to) the papers:

1. What is the main idea of the paper? Write it in one or two sentences.
2. What scenes or details show this idea most clearly?
3. How much of the paper is narration? Is that enough?
4. Where does the paper need more narration?
5. How much of the paper is comment? Is that enough? Too much?
6. Where does the paper need more comment or less?
7. Is there any place in the paper where you do not follow the idea or do not see how the scenes relate to what is going on?
8. Is there any place in the paper where you lose interest or get impatient?
9. Which paragraph or paragraphs need editing?
10. What advice would you give the writer?

You can respond to these questions in writing and give the response to the writer, or you can tell them your responses. You or your instructor may also have other questions.

Sample Papers

Professional Essay

We said at the beginning of the chapter that illustrative writing is a common form in professional contexts. This long, complex, beautifully written illustrative paper draws on the experience of a park ranger in Arches National Park in Utah. You will see that it uses a very complex pyramid structure. Note as you read how the narratives build to the controlling idea, which is not given explicitly until the end of the paper. Following this are two sample essays written by students.

The Serpents of Paradise

Perhaps this is the loveliest hour of the day, though it's hard to choose. Much depends on the season. In mid-summer the sweetest hour begins at sundown, after the awful heat of the afternoon. But now, in April, we'll take the opposite, that hour beginning with sunrise. The birds, returning from wherever they go in winter, seem inclined to agree. The pinyon jays are whirling in garrulous, gregarious flocks from one stunted tree to the next and back again, erratic exuberant games without any apparent practical function. A few big ravens hang around and croak harsh clanking statements of smug satisfaction from the rimrock, lifting their greasy wings now and then to probe for lice. I can hear but seldom see the canyon wrens singing their distinctive song from somewhere up on the cliffs: a flutelike descent—never ascent—of the whole-tone scale. Staking out new nesting claims, I understand. Also invisible but invariably present at some indefinable distance are the mourning doves, whose plaintive call suggests irresistibly a kind of seeking-out, the attempt by a separated soul to restore a lost communion:

Hello . . . they seem to cry, *who . . . are . . . you?*

And the reply from a different quarter. *Hello* . . . (pause) *where . . . are . . . you?*

No doubt this line of analogy must be rejected. It's foolish and unfair to impute to the doves, with serious concerns of their own, an interest in questions more appropriate to their human kin. Yet their song, if not a mating call or a warning, must be what it sounds like, a brooding meditation on space, on solitude. . . .

As mentioned before, I share the housetrailer with a number of mice. I don't know how many but apparently only a few, perhaps a single family. They don't disturb me and are welcome to my crumbs and leavings. Where they came from, how they got into the trailer, how they survived before my arrival (for the trailer had been locked up for six months), these are puzzling matters I am not prepared to resolve. My only reservation concerning the mice is that they do attract rattlesnakes.

I'm sitting on my doorstep early one morning, facing the sun as usual, drinking coffee, when I happen to look down and see almost between my bare feet, only a couple of inches to the rear of my heels, the very thing I had in mind. No mistaking that wedgelike head, that tip of horny segmented tail peeping out of the coils. He's under the doorstep and in the shade where the ground and air remain very cold. In his sluggish condition he's not likely to strike unless I rouse him by some careless move of my own. . . .

What to do. I drink some more coffee and study the dormant reptile at my heels. . . . Am I to be compelled to put on boots or shoes every time I wish to step outside? The scorpions, tarantulas, centipedes, and black widows are nuisance enough.

I finish my coffee, lean back and swing my feet up and inside the doorway of the trailer. At once there is a buzzing sound from below and the rattler lifts his head from his coils, eyes brightening, and extends his narrow black tongue to test the air.

After thawing out my boots over the gas flame I pull them on and come back to the doorway. My visitor is still waiting beneath the doorstep, basking in the sun, fully alert. The trailerhouse has two doors. I leave by the other and get a long-handled spade out of the bed of the government pickup. With this tool I scoop the snake into the open. He strikes; I can hear the click of the fangs against steel, see the stain of venom. He wants to stand and fight, but I am patient; I insist on herding him well away from the trailer. On guard, head aloft—that evil slit-eyed weaving head shaped like the ace of spades—tail whirring, the rattler slithers sideways, retreating slowly before me until he reaches the shelter of a sandstone slab. He backs under it.

You better stay there, cousin, I warn him; if I catch you around the trailer again I'll chop your head off.

A week later he comes back. If not him, his twin brother. I spot him one morning under the trailer near the kitchen drain, waiting for a mouse. I have to keep my promise.

This won't do. If there are midget rattlers in the area there may be diamondbacks too—five, six or seven feet long, thick as a man's wrist, dangerous. I don't want *them* camping under my home. It looks as though I'll have to trap the mice.

However, before being forced to take that step I am lucky enough to capture a gopher snake. . . . The gopher snake, *Drymarchon corais couperi*, or bull snake, has a reputation as the enemy of rattlesnakes, destroying or driving them away whenever encountered.

Hoping to domesticate this sleek, handsome and docile reptile, I release him inside the trailerhouse and keep him there for several days. Should I attempt to feed him? I decide against it—let him eat mice. What little water he may need can also be extracted from the flesh of his prey.

The gopher snake and I get along nicely. During the day he curls up like a cat in the warm corner behind the heater and at night he goes about his business. The mice, singularly quiet for a change, make themselves scarce. The snake is passive, apparently contented, and makes no resistance when I pick him up with my hands and drape him over an arm or around my neck. When I take him outside into the wind and sunshine his favorite place seems to be inside my shirt, where he wraps himself around my waist and rests on my belt. . . .

We are compatible. From my point of view, friends. After a week of close association I turn him loose on the warm sandstone at my doorstep and leave for patrol of the park. At noon when I return he is gone. I search everywhere beneath, nearby and inside the trailerhouse, but my companion has disappeared. Has he left the area entirely or is he hiding somewhere close by? At any rate I am troubled no more by rattlesnakes under the door.

The snake story is not yet ended.

In the middle of May, about a month after the gopher snake's disappearance, in the evening of a very hot day, with all the rosy desert cooling like a griddle with the fire turned off, he reappears. This time with a mate.

I'm in the stifling heat of the trailer opening a can of beer, barefooted, about to go outside and relax after a hard day watching cloud formations. I happen to glance out the little window near the refrigerator and see two gopher snakes on my verandah engaged in what seems to be a kind of ritual dance. Like a living caduceus they wind and unwind about each other in undulant, graceful, perpetual motion, moving slowly across a dome of sandstone. Invisible but tangible as music is the passion which joins them—sexual? combative? both? A shameless *voyeur,* I stare at the lovers, and then to get a closer view run outside and around the trailer to the back. There I get down on hands and knees and creep toward the dancing snakes, not wanting to frighten or disturb them. I crawl to within six feet of them and stop, flat on my belly, watching from the snake's-eye level. Obsessed with their ballet, the serpents seem unaware of my presence.

The two gopher snakes are nearly identical in length and coloring; I cannot be certain that either is actually my former household pet. I cannot even be sure that they are male and female, though their performance resembles so strongly a *pas de deux* by formal lovers. They intertwine and separate, glide side by side in perfect congruence, turn like mirror images of each other and glide back again, wind and unwind again. This is the basic pattern but there is a variation: at regular intervals, the snakes elevate their heads, facing one another, as high as they can go, as if each is trying to outreach or overawe the other. Their heads and bodies rise, higher and higher, then topple together and the rite goes on.

I crawl after them, determined to see the whole thing. Suddenly and simultaneously they discover me, prone on my belly a few feet away. The dance stops. After a moment's pause the two snakes come straight toward me, still in flawless unison, straight toward my face, the forked tongues flickering, their intense wild yellow eyes staring directly into my eyes. For an instant I am paralyzed by wonder; then, stung by a fear too ancient and powerful to overcome I scramble back, rising to my knees. The snakes veer and turn and race away from me in parallel motion, their lean and elegant bodies making a soft hissing noise as they slide over the sand and stone. I follow them for a short distance, still plagued by curiosity, before remembering my place and the requirements of common courtesy. For godsake let them go in peace, I tell myself. Wish them luck and (if lovers) innumerable offspring, a life of happily ever after. Not for their sake alone but for your own.

In the long hot days and cool evenings to come I will not see the gopher snakes again. Nevertheless I will feel their presence watching over me like totemic deities, keeping the rattlesnakes far back in the brush where I like them best, cropping off the surplus mouse population, maintaining useful connections with the primeval. Sympathy, mutual aid, symbiosis, continuity.

How can I descend to such anthropomorphism? Easily—but is it, in this case, entirely false? Perhaps not. I am not attributing human motives to my snake and bird acquaintances. I recognize that when and where they serve purposes of mine they do so for beautifully selfish reasons of their own. Which is exactly the way it should be. I suggest, however, that it's a foolish, simple-minded rationalism which denies any form of emotion to all animals but man and his dog. This is no more justified than the Moslems are in denying souls to women. It seems to me possible, even probable, that many of the nonhuman undomesticated animals experience emotions unknown to us. What do the coyotes mean when they yodel at the moon? What are the dolphins trying so patiently to tell us? Precisely what did those two enraptured gopher snakes have in mind when they came gliding toward my eyes over the naked sandstone? If I had been as capable of trust as I am susceptible to fear I might have learned something new or some truth so very old we have all forgotten it. . . .

All men are brothers, we like to say, half-wishing sometimes in secret it were not true. But perhaps it is true. And is the evolutionary line from protozoan to Spinoza any less certain? That also may be true. We are obliged, therefore, to spread the news, painful and bitter though it may be for some to hear, that all living things on earth are kindred.

Edward Abbey, from *Desert Solitaire*

Student Papers

Winning

The runners mingle on the field beside the synthetic track. They seem friendly, each girl hugging another.

"Have you seen Jane? I'm worried about her; if she doesn't show soon, she'll miss the race."

"No, but I'm sure that she'll show. If I were the state champion, I wouldn't miss defending my title. I hope she shows."

Good sportsmanship at its best, or so it seems. Yet each of those girls was probably hoping that the state champ wouldn't show, so that she would have a chance at the title. I know, I have often felt the same way.

How many times have I pushed a little harder against a weaker opponent? There have been too many times to try to remember them all. Oh, it's not nice, but when you've trained for weeks, you're going to use all of the other team's weaknesses to your advantage. As my volleyball coach said, "A good serve is one that is hard to return. To make a good serve a great one, you must hit it to the weak player. Every serve, every spike must be aimed at that player, because after she has missed a couple of times, she will be feeling unsure and will keep making mistakes."

It's hard to believe that this was the same coach who became furious when it was hinted that she had taken a player out of a game because the girl had made a mistake. At that time she had said, "My team plays for the sake of playing. Every one of my girls plays in every game. I took her out because she had played two straight sets, and it was someone else's turn."

Personally I found this hard to believe. The girl was terrible, and we were all glad that she was benched. We all comforted her, however, saying, "Don't worry! Cheer up, it wasn't your fault that we lost the point, actually, it was mine. I should have been covering you." Then, when she was off the court, we would all say to ourselves (at least I did), "O.K., now we can start playing some real volleyball."

When you lose, you put on a smile and congratulate the other team, all the while saying to yourself, "Next time, we'll cream them!" One of my basketball coaches was a master at this. He was always the first one to congratulate our opponents on a victory. Yet long after the last spectator had left the gym, my team would still be running out punishment laps, one lap for every point that we had lost by. At the next practice session following a lost game, he would refresh the techniques of shoving or hitting an opponent without being caught and awarded a foul. This resulted in our team winning the tournament.

It's human nature. No one likes to lose. Even those who say that they wouldn't mind losing to the world champion, that it would be an honor, wish that they could win. Losing to a friend is hardest of all. No matter what people say, there are hostilities. The student who comforts a friend on a "just missed A" paper is secretly happy that she got the higher grade. Although she says that her friend's paper was better anyway, she doesn't really believe so. Our naturally competitive instincts tell us that it is not right to lose. Society hates losers, but most of all, our egos hate losing.

In the sixth grade my teacher awarded a yellow strip of paper for each good deed and a green one for each bad deed that a child committed. All of the tickets were kept in open envelopes bearing, in large print, the child's name. These envelopes were kept on display, tacked to a wall. At the end of each week, the tickets would be tallied up, with each yellow strip being worth a "brownie point."

I hoarded those bright bits of paper, counting them with trembling fingers at least twice a day. My heart used to pound with joy whenever I found that I had more than anyone else, but being a "good sport," I always replied to my classmates' inevitable question of, "How many?" with, "Not much." How I used to preen when they found out exactly how many were in my fortune!

Thus, from an early age I understood the necessity of seeming humble. I became a master at it, doing exactly the right thing for that point or a particular grade, yet seeming surprised when I received the reward for my efforts. So how can the idealistic values of good sportsmanship be truly practiced when, from childhood, we are taught the importance of winning?

Perhaps this is a pessimistic view of human nature. After all, the record books abound with examples of athletes who have, in their honesty, challenged decisions that favored them because they knew that the official's decision was wrong. Yet it is hard for me to forget the shameful examples of how to behave in defeat provided by athletes such as John McEnroe, Mary Decker Slaney, or Larry Holmes. Perhaps the extent of true sportsmanlike conduct varies with the individual. I personally believe that people like winning too much ever to be able to accept defeat graciously.

student paper

Parents and Children

I'm the father of two sons, the elder one a junior middle school student. Yet, with so many years of experience of being a father behind me, I still find it by no means easy to be a good father. I used to think that I knew more than my children in anything and everything and that they should always listen to me. But my experience has proved that children have their own ideas and enjoy finding and discovering things for themselves.

Once my two sons wanted to make a kite. They had seen kites fly in the sky but had no idea how to make one. So they came to me for help. I explained the procedures to them: how to split bamboo slips, how to arrange and bind the frame, how to cut and paste the paper. But when they tried their hand at the job, everything was in chaos. The bamboo sticks were either too long or too short or crooked; the thread got all tangled up; the paper crumpled. I taught them several times by showing them the handwork. But they just couldn't reach my standard. I was soon out of patience and took everything over. I told the two brothers to stand aside and watch me do it. I worked for two hours and made a very beautiful butterfly kite. The kids said it was beautiful and marveled at my skill. Then I hung the kite carefully in their room.

Over breakfast next Sunday, I overheard them murmuring something about kite flying and asked, ''Are you going to fly the kite today?'' My younger son just stared at me without answering my question. My elder son said, ''Yes. We have both finished our homework.'' I told them to be careful and soon put the matter out of my head.

I went to their room at about ten o'clock to look for a pair of scissors. To my surprise I found the butterfly kite was still hanging on their wall. My curiosity was aroused, and I went down to have a look. There on the playground the two brothers were flying a kite. They were running and laughing merrily. I looked up. The kite they were flying was just a plain, ugly-looking, so-called Tile kite—and there was a big patch on it. But the kids were really enjoying themselves.

The reason was obvious: That kite was of their own making.

I remember another similar experience. Just as the frisbee came to Peking and became popular, I bought one for my two kids. They jumped with joy when they saw the bright pink frisbee I brought home and wanted to play with it right then. I persuaded them to be patient and promised to play with them after supper. I was really enthusiastic to teach them and thus arranged an early supper. Then I took them down to the playground. There were the three of us spread out into a triangle and I gave out orders: my elder son was to pass the frisbee to my younger son, my younger son was then to pass it to me, and in turn I would pass it back to my elder son. The order was never broken. Meanwhile I gave them a lecture on frisbee throwing: the right postures, proper throwing angles, taking aim and measuring strength, and so on and so forth. They didn't seem to be enthusiastic, and before twenty minutes passed they said that they hadn't finished their homework yet, and we came back without much progress.

After that I asked them several times if they wanted me to practice frisbee with them. They replied that I was too busy and they didn't want to waste my precious time. A week or so later I happened to see them playing with the frisbee with their playmates. I was amazed that they could fly it in many fancy ways I had never thought of. I was sure that if they had been practicing with me all the time they would not have learned half as much as they had.

The lesson I learned: I should give them some freedom to develop their own talent.

Last summer my elder son was admitted into a middle school. Since his school was some distance away, I decided to teach him to ride a bike. He was somewhat shy and timid. For many early mornings my wife and I had to help him hold the bike by turns. My younger son envied his brother very much and pleaded with us to teach him as well. I told him he had to wait for some time as the bike was still too tall for him. He knew too well that it was useless to argue with me, so he didn't insist.

However, when two weeks or so later, one of my colleagues remarked to me, "Chen, it's really marvelous that your younger son can ride a bike at so early an age," I told him it must have been my older son. "No," he said. "I know them too well to take one for the other."

That evening I asked my younger son, "Can you ride a bike?" "Yes," he replied somewhat timidly, but not without some pride in his tone. Then he told me how he had learned it: For two weeks, as soon as I got back he would take my bike key and slip out to practice riding the bike. He dared not let us know it, so he had to learn it all by himself. Too short to get on the seat, he simply thrust his right leg through the frame of the bike and rode the bike in a sort of standing position. And he learned it. I remembered once or twice during those two weeks he had come home limping. I had found some bruises on his legs and he had said that he had a fall. Now I knew how he hurt himself. But do you think I could blame him?

Children do need advice and guidance from their parents. But they don't like to be ordered about all the time. They have their own pride and dignity, which grown-ups should give due respect.

I have always wanted my kids to be punctual. I want them to value time and form good habits. For some time I used to remind them almost every day: "It is time to have supper," or "You must go to bed now." They had invariably obeyed me, but their resentment was obvious. Later I changed my tactics. I had a talk with them one evening and told them a story about how Lenin had arranged and made full use of his time. Then I suggested they make a timetable of their own. They soon worked out a very good one. Since then they have been very conscious in observing their own timetable. And they were no longer reprimanded for not keeping good time.

Some people say between parents and children is a generation gap that cannot be bridged. I remember when I was a child I often resented my parents because they seemed to be always reminding me to do this or not to do that, for example, to keep clean, to sit straight, to mind table manners, to be punctual, not to climb trees, not to play dangerous games, not to speak with strangers—the list was almost endless. I knew they meant well and those were points we should pay attention to. But I always felt that they should trust me to be my own master. I had decided that when I should have my own children I would be easy with them and give them more freedom. But when I did become a father I slipped into that old rut without realizing it. Some conflicts with my children made me think I would never understand the kids. But after careful thinking and reflection I came to see some light. That kind of gap can be bridged. The key lies in the parents' attitude toward their children. Parents should trust and respect their children and be on equal footing with them. If they want their children to do something, they should explain and discuss with them instead of ordering them about. The result would be much more satisfying.

Chen Teh-Chang

5 *Summary Writing*

Introduction to Summary Writing

This chapter teaches you summary writing, a skill basic to exposition because it is a tool used to report on and react to books and articles in a given field, answer essay examinations, and gather and use material in term papers. When you summarize, you read carefully, making sure you understand what an author has said, and then you put the ideas in your own words.

Though summaries are used in many college assignments, a summary is more apt to appear as part of a larger paper than as an assignment by itself. The simple summary you will write here and the comparison/contrast summary you will write in Chapter 6 are presented as preparatory exercises leading to the longer papers in the last two chapters. At the end of this chapter you will find some shorter summary exercises that will also prove useful to you in your college work.

Definitions

As we will define it, a *summary* consists of the following parts:

1. A statement of the author's *stand* (guiding idea or thesis) about the *issue*.
2. An explanatory statement of each *reason* for the author's stand. The explanatory statements might include subreasons and evidence.

Suppose you read an editorial in your local newspaper arguing that there should be a stoplight at a certain intersection. The *issue* is whether that intersection needs a stoplight. Suppose the editorial then says that the stoplight *is needed* because (1) two busy streets intersect there and (2) three accidents have occurred there during the last month. The writer's *stand* is that a stoplight is needed. The major *reasons* for the stand would be (1) and (2) above.

If the next day someone writes a letter to the editor objecting that the stoplight is not needed, the issue would be the same (whether the stoplight is needed), but the stand would be different (no need for the stoplight). If the letter objected to the stoplight because (1) the number of accidents was small compared to elsewhere and (2) it would cost too much money, the major reasons for this negative stand would be (1) and (2).

In addition to stating their stands and their major reasons, both writers would normally include subreasons and evidence for their stand. The whole (issue, stand, reasons, subreasons, and evidence) can be called the author's *argument*.

In this chapter you will be asked to summarize the author's argument rather than his article. That is, you will not write what is said paragraph by paragraph in the article. Instead, you will first read the whole selection carefully to determine the author's stand (thesis), the reasons, and the support for each reason. Your summary will then reproduce this information clearly and completely enough so that *someone who has not read the article will be able to understand the author's argument*.

Following is a short editorial from the *Honolulu Star Bulletin* concerning an after-school day-care program. Read it carefully, and decide what are the issue, the stand, and the major reasons for the stand. Discuss this with another writer to make sure you both understand these terms.

> The state's A+ after-school care program is beginning to look like the new kid being bullied on the playground and also hassled in class by the teachers. The quick-starting pilot program is less than two months old and appears to be doing well, despite attempts of so many to make life difficult for the nation's first statewide effort of this kind.
>
> Legislators, school board members, the teachers' union and various budget-crunchers have either been sniping at the program or trying to complicate its finances. Somehow, it is succeeding, as the responses of some 15,000 youngsters indicate. . . .
>
> As supporters of the A+ concept, with early reservations about its details, we are encouraged by the program's first weeks. We think A+ should have time to operate, and room to breathe, before the financial tinkerers in the Legislature or the state Board of Education try to make a good thing more complex.
>
> The present arrangement of having all parents pay a flat rate, with those qualifying as needy paying nothing, seems workable to us. . . . Arguments continue about imposing a graduated payment rate so upper-income working parents would pay more. An income-based fee structure now would add immeasurably to the work and costs, no matter how simply its proponents say it could be done. And it would put the school system further into an income-policing function than it should be.
>
> If the A+ experience after a full school year shows the need for an income-related fee schedule, the school board can consider it, but for now, let's see how the program works. . . .

The Issue

The summary you will write for this chapter, plus the writing in the next two chapters, will be based on a collection of material (newspaper articles, pamphlets, and histories) relating to the island of Kaho'olawe in the Hawaiian chain. Kaho'olawe is an uninhabited island. Since the Second World War, it has been used by the United States Navy as a bombing target area for training pilots. More than ten years ago various groups of citizens in Hawai'i began protesting that the island should not be used in this way, but should be returned to the state or to the Hawaiian people for civilian use.

After several years of protest, the imprisonment of some activists for trespassing on the island, and the death at sea of two others, the navy and Protect Kaho'olawe 'Ohana (the major protesting group) came to an uneasy truce, which allowed limited use by the 'Ohana (a Hawaiian term signifying extended family). Both sides are still unhappy with the current state of affairs.

Thus the overall issue for these papers is: What should be done with Kaho'olawe? Two possible opposing stands on the issue are:

- The navy should continue to use the island.
- The navy should return the island to the state.

As you read the material, you will find that some writers present other more complex stands. You will also see that all of the articles, no matter what their stand, give major reasons for the stand, including the military need for the island, its developmental potential, and its cultural and historical value.

Writing Outlines and Summaries

Here is the procedure to follow in writing a summary:

1. Read the selection under consideration, carefully noting the main idea the author tries to get across (the stand). You must read the entire piece through first. A summary is not a sentence-by-sentence paraphrase, written as you read. Furthermore you will not always find the author's stand in the beginning of the article.
2. Write in one or two sentences the issue and the author's stand.
3. Determine the major reasons, subreasons, and evidence given for the stand.
4. Complete the summary by writing at least one paragraph for each major reason.

Remember that in a summary you do not make a judgment. You will not put personal opinions or reactions in your summaries even though you may disagree with the author's idea. Later assignments will give you ample opportunity to respond to the ideas in the material and to advance your own ideas. Here we are concerned with learning to read accurately and convey ideas carefully.

This chapter and the next will give you suggestions for outlining as a preparation for writing your summaries. The discussion of outlines will use standard level markers: Roman numerals (I, II, III) followed by letters (A, B, C). An outline is a way of helping you think through the structure of both your own summary and that of the articles you are summarizing. However, the form used in outlining is not crucial. An outline is only a shorthand way of planning organizational strategies before you begin to write. Other methods of thinking might work well also: a series of sentences, other visual sketches, and so on.

In Chapter 8 you will find a discussion of other methods of planning organization and getting ready to write. If you have developed methods of your own, feel free to use them instead. Your instructor may give you further instructions in this area.

PRACTICE SUMMARY

The following practice exercise will lead you through the process of making a summary. Your instructor may have you do this together in class or in small groups.

STEP 1 Read Article 8 in the Appendix: "Kahoolawe from the Beginning," by Frank F. Midkiff. As you read, ask yourself the following questions: What is the issue under discussion? What is the author's stand on the issue? What are the reasons for his stand? You will be asked to respond to these questions in writing after you have finished, so read the article carefully.

STEP 2 Now that you have read the article, write one sentence stating Midkiff's stand on the issue as you understand it. Don't make this too difficult. Simply write down the biggest, most basic idea. You now have the opening sentence for a summary.

STEP 3 Now begin to plan the remainder of your summary. First, write down the major reasons Midkiff gives to support his stand. There are two. Label them I and II.

STEP 4 You now have determined the author's stand and the major reasons for his stand; in short, you have outlined his argument in its most basic terms. Now go back to the article and determine Midkiff's subreasons for I and II. You need to be careful here that you are really understanding Midkiff's argument. Find two subreasons for both I and II. Write them under the appropriate headings and label them A and B.

As you finish each step, compare your answers with those of other writers to see if you all agree about the parts of Midkiff's argument. Different writers will use different language, but you should all have the same major ideas. If not, go back to the article and try to reconcile your differences.

You now have the bare bones of a summary that you can flesh out to almost any length. A summary can be three or four sentences, or it can be almost as long as the article itself, depending on how much detail you want or need to include. If you merely want to indicate the main ideas in the article, you might simply turn your outline into sentences and paragraphs. If you want to indicate details about the argument and evidence, you would write more.

Your instructor may have you write a summary from this outline or use it only as the basis for discussion with other class members. At the end of this chapter you will find a two-level outline like the one you have written and a sample summary of Midkiff's article written from the outline. Use this summary and outline in connection with the following discussion on the aspects of a good summary.

First note that the first sentence of the summary gives Midkiff's stand on the issue. This sentence functions like a thesis or guiding statement.

The remaining two paragraphs of the summary each develop *one and only one* of the major reasons for the stand that Midkiff gives in his article. These correspond to I and II on the outline you made. The subideas you wrote under I and II are also developed in the respective paragraphs.

The most important characteristic of a summary is clarity. You are writing so that someone who has not read the article will understand what is in it. Part of this responsibility is helping your reader move from point to point. Thus the sample summary has transitional words that help the reader keep up with the ideas and see how they all work together. These words are underlined in the sample.

One further note on clarity. Midkiff quotes from another source, a book by S. M. Kamakau, to back up his contention that Kaho'olawe cannot support permanent habitation. The sample summary makes it clear that Midkiff is quoting and that he agrees with the source he quotes. When you summarize an article that cites another source, you must always make it clear when the author is quoting and whether she agrees or disagrees with the source quoted. We will have a good deal to say about this aspect of summary writing later on.

The sample summary ends with actual words from Midkiff's article. Note that these words are placed inside quotation marks. As you begin to write assignments that draw on material written by others, the question of plagiarism arises. Plagiarism is the use of another person's words or ideas as if they were your own, that is, not giving credit where credit is due. Most of your summary should be written in your own words. However, you may want to use a sentence or part of a sentence from the original text to emphasize some point. Whenever you use *any* language taken from the original article (even including one word, if that word is a key one), you must put the words quoted in quotation marks. Whenever you write a summary, you should check it against the original to make sure you have used quotation marks whenever you quote.

You must be extremely careful to indicate quoted material. Not doing so could cause you to get a failing grade on a paper or even an entire course. Even unintentional plagiarism is unacceptable. *Do not let sentences or parts of sentences from the original articles creep into your summaries without quotation marks.* Your instructor will certainly check you on this point. Chapter 7 has a detailed discussion about using borrowed material carefully and accurately. But begin to develop careful habits now.

Statement of Assignment

For this assignment you will make a summary of the article "Kahoolawe in the Raw" by Harold T. Stearns. This is Article 7 in the Appendix. Read the article carefully and then summarize it as you did the practice article. Think again of writing the summary in parts: a statement of the author's stand on the issue (in the first sentence or sentences), and a statement of each reason for the stand (usually one to a paragraph), along with supporting details for each reason. Proceed as you did in the exercise. Write the statement of the stand first, outline the reasons and support, and then write the summary. The next two sections will help you with this process.

Remember to think of yourself as writing for someone who has not read the article. Make your summary clear enough so that such a person will understand it. Your instructor will give you specific instructions about the length of the summary. The length will determine how much detail you can include.

Getting Started

"Kahoolawe in the Raw" is more complex than "Kahoolawe from the Beginning." Midkiff's main idea and stand were made clear in the middle of his article. The Stearns article does not give the main stand as clearly. Furthermore Stearns discusses several issues, presenting opposing views on some of them. Here, even more than in the practice exercise, you must read the entire article and make sure you have digested the discussion before you begin your summary. Do not attempt to summarize by going paragraph by paragraph. Follow the steps used in the practice exercise.

After reading the article carefully, begin by writing one sentence that gives Stearns's stand. Don't try to go into great detail. Just state the biggest, most important idea. Be sure to mention Stearns's name in this sentence.

Next determine the major reasons for the stand and list them. How many reasons did you find? Label them I, II, and so forth. This process will not be as easy as it was for Midkiff's article. It is quite possible that you may see the structure of the argument somewhat differently from other students. But write down the reasons as you understand them.

Now go back to the article and see what subreasons Stearns gives for each major reason you have found. Make a two-level outline or plan that shows Stearns's argument as you understand it. Hint: You may not find all the material on a reason in any one paragraph of the article. Go through the entire article and list supporting material for each of the reasons (I, II, and so forth) you found.

One section of this article might give you particular trouble as you analyze the parts of the argument. In both Midkiff's and Stearns's articles the authors have referred to material from other sources: Midkiff quotes a book by S. M. Kamakau, and Stearns summarizes the Marinco Report. You will recall that Midkiff agrees with Kamakau and uses his ideas to support the contention that Kahoʻolawe could not be used for development.

Look now at the first half of Stearns's article, where he deals with the Marinco Report. Does he agree with this source the way Midkiff agreed with Kamakau? Why is he talking about this report anyway? You need to be careful when you read this section of the article and even more careful when you summarize it.

The activity below should help you figure out Stearns's attitude toward the Marinco Report, and it will help you generally as you begin to think about what Stearns is saying and about how you will summarize it. Your instructor may ask you to do it yourself, or she might have you do it with a classmate.

WRITING ACTIVITY

1. Summarize in two or three sentences just what the Marinco Report advocates for Kahoʻolawe (not what Stearns advocates).

2. Summarize in two or three sentences what Stearns thinks of the Marinco Report. (Hint: How many reasons does he give for his analysis of the report?) You must be very careful here to distinguish between what the report is saying and what Stearns is saying.

3. Write in one sentence the real purpose of the report according to Stearns. Write in such a way that you make it clear that you are reporting on Stearns's ideas.

It may be useful for you to compare your answers with those of other writers. If you find disagreements, go back to the text together and reread the relevant paragraphs. Discuss these until you are able to resolve your differences. You need not use the same language, but you should have the same interpretation of what the Marinco Report says and what Stearns says about it.

When you have done these three things, decide how this information will be worked into your summary. Remember, your purpose is to summarize Stearns's overall argument in the article. The information on the Marinco Report is part of that argument. Where on the outline you are preparing will you put the sentences you have written about the report? Will they all go in the same place? Do Stearns's ideas about this report relate to more than one of the major reasons in his argument?

You may also need to go through this process with other sections of the article. Once you have determined the stand and the major reasons, you will need to figure out how everything in the article would fit under those reasons. Because of your word limit you will probably not use all the details of the article in your summary, but you need to know where everything fits.

Writing a Draft

When you have outlined the material for your summary and decided where you will put all the ideas, you are ready to write the summary. Begin with your statement of the issue and the stand. That will be the first paragraph.

Next consider your outline. Take the major reasons (I, II, etc.) on your outline and write at least one paragraph about each.

When you are writing expository essays, paragraphs are important units. A paragraph is more than a random group of sentences. Each paragraph plays an important part in the argument. In these summaries paragraphs are closely related to your outline, since each major part of your outline presents one important part of Stearns's argument. You should begin your second paragraph with a statement that defines the first major reason in Stearns's argument. You complete the paragraph by filling in the support for that reason.

Look, for example, at the sample summary of the Midkiff article. Recall that Midkiff had two reasons for his stand that Kaho'olawe should be used by the military:

I. Kaho'olawe is not suitable for development.
II. The military needs the island.

Note that the second paragraph in that sample summary begins with a statement about Kaho'olawe's lack of potential and that the third paragraph begins with a statement about its use to the military (the first paragraph, of course, is devoted to Midkiff's stand). Each paragraph then fills in the details for that reason.

That is exactly the way to proceed with this summary. After you have written your first introductory paragraph, start the second paragraph with a statement that defines Stearns's first major reason for his stand. Then write about the supporting ideas and evidence for that reason. When you have finished with this reason (I on your outline), go to the second and do the same thing: Write a statement that defines the reason, and then write about the supporting ideas and evidence. Continue until you have completed your summary.

Since this article is more complex than Midkiff's, and since you are writing a longer summary, you might have more than one paragraph for each major reason. Look at the second paragraph in the Midkiff summary. Note how the first reason for his stand (Kaho'olawe is not suitable for habitation) is broken down into two parts that correspond to A and B on the sample outline. A longer summary of Midkiff's article might have used one paragraph for A and another for B.

The most important quality of a good summary is clarity. Remember that you are writing for someone who has not read the original article, and you want them to be able to understand what that article said. You must write so that your reader can follow from point to point and understand what Stearns was arguing at all times. Look at the sample summary of Midkiff's article again. Note particularly the underlined words and phrases. These are for the purpose of letting the reader know what idea is being discussed at that point. Don't forget your reader as you write.

As you write, remember to use your own words almost exclusively. When you want to use a key phrase from the article, put it in quotation marks. Check yourself on this from the very beginning. Get another writer who is familiar with the article to read your draft to make sure that you have not allowed Stearns's words to slip unmarked into your text.

Reworking the Draft

Feedback from Other Writers

Because you are all working with the same material, you and your colleagues can be especially helpful to each other on this paper. You can help each other decide whether you have understood the article and presented your understanding clearly. Since the only purpose of the summary is to present Stearns's ideas clearly and accurately, your responses to other papers should concentrate on these two issues.

Always keep in mind the following criterion: You should write your summary in such a way that someone who has not read the material could understand from it what Stearns's argument was. As you listen to or read the drafts, you should try to be that reader who has not read the article. This will not be easy to do, but work at it so that you can tell other writers where they need to improve their clarity.

You might try this activity with a colleague or with a group. As one writer reads his paper, listen and attempt to make a two-level outline of his argument. You don't need to include all the details. Just see if you can show the major structure of the summary you are hearing. If you are working in a group, have each member make such an outline and then have several listeners put the outlines on the board or share them in some way.

Can you see the purpose for this activity? If a listener can outline the argument, or if several listeners can come up with essentially the same outline, the paper is probably clearly structured. If not, the writer may need to go back and see where her summary has not made the issue, the stand, the major reasons, or the subreasons clear.

It is quite possible that the drafts written by you or by your colleagues will need major revision. Some writers might not have recognized the structure of Stearns's argument. In that case the most fruitful use of time in the group is to discuss the article itself, not the drafts. You might want to go back and reread the article as a group, discussing sections that are not clear. You might even try to work together to outline the argument.

Students sometimes need to abandon a first draft of this paper. Summary writing appears to be simple, but it is not. However, the effort put into such a draft is not wasted. Writers often must begin to write before they can understand and digest material. Don't be frustrated if your colleagues question your ideas or tell you that your summary is unclear. Get them to help you clarify the ideas, and then go back and rewrite the parts where they had trouble following your organization or your train of thought. The discussions in the section below should help you as you make needed changes.

Examples of Revisions

As you begin to revise the summary, keep in mind that it must be clear enough that someone who has not read Stearns's article will be able to follow the summary. It must reproduce the argument accurately so that a reader will not get a mistaken idea about what Stearns has said. And you must use the material honestly, making sure that your sentences are your own words or that you indicate Stearns's words with quotation marks. The discussions in this section will concentrate on these three characteristics: clarity, accuracy, and honesty.

Following are the first two paragraphs of a draft of this summary. Certain phrases are underlined to emphasize inaccuracies that we will discuss later.

> Harold T. Stearns in his article, "Kahoolawe in the Raw," is in favor of a compromise between the state of Hawai'i and the <u>naval forces posted on the island of Kaho'olawe.</u> He suggests that the target

areas be kept by the navy, while the safe sites are opened to the public.

Stearns <u>faults the navy</u> for its Marinco Report. He refers to it as a "snow job." He feels the navy composed the report "to exaggerate the difficulty, danger, and cost of cleaning up the island in order to justify the continued use for a bombing practice range." The use of remote-controlled <u>robots</u> to rid the land of unexploded bombs is mentioned in the report. Stearns cites past events such as World War II. The catastrophic damage done in Europe was cleared through conventional means, not through expensive landscaping. He adds that if the soil were dug up as suggested in the report, the land would erode away within twenty-five years. However, while he feels that the Marinco Report is flawed, he feels, through personal observations on the stagnating growth of plant life, that the land is not suitable for farming due to the lack of available ground water.

As you read through these paragraphs, you might have been annoyed by some of the sentences, but you were probably able to follow the ideas. However, return and try to read the summary from the point of view of someone who had never read the original article or even heard of Kaho'olawe. The first paragraph gives minimal information, but it might pass (except for the inaccuracies we will note later). But the first sentence in the second paragraph is too abrupt. Surely a reader unfamiliar with the whole issue needs to be told that the Marinco Report relates to the question of how this island, which has been bombarded for so long, can be cleaned up for civilian use.

The next two sentences, which summarize Stearns's reaction to the report, are quite good. However, the four following sentences, which summarize Stearns's two objections to the report, would probably puzzle a reader unfamiliar with the issue. The sentence about World War II following a sentence about robots would be confusing, as would the fourth sentence, which introduces material about erosion. These sentences require some introduction, which would define Stearns's objections to the report—something like "Stearns objects to the report on the grounds that the means it suggests for removing dangerous ordnance from the island are (1) too elaborate, and (2) actually harmful to the island."

Another serious fault of this second paragraph is the hasty addition of the last sentence, which inadequately and unclearly summarizes one of the important points in Stearns's argument: Kaho'olawe is not really capable of being developed. This point needs a paragraph of its own.

Reread the second paragraph of the excerpt above, leaving out the last sentence. What is that paragraph about? The Marinco Report. True enough, but how does it relate to Stearns's stand that there should be a compromise on the use of Kaho'olawe? That stand has two parts: The navy can use the island and the civilians can use the island. Under which of these two ideas does the information about the cleanup of the island logically fit?

Remember that your purpose in writing the summary is to show a reader how Stearns's argument works, not merely to write down ideas that occurred in the article. Each paragraph that you write must explain part of that argument. Thus, even if this account of Stearns's analysis of the Marinco Report is made clearer and more accurate, it still needs to be put into a paragraph that shows how it relates to either military or civilian use. The same is true of the underdeveloped material about farming. It needs to be made more complete, and it needs to be put into a paragraph that explains how it relates to Stearns's stand. Thus this summary is deficient in the first and most important characteristic: It is not clear.

Now let's talk about accuracy. Three phrases in the draft are underlined. Each is inaccurate in reporting on something in Stearns's article. For example, take the word *robots*. Did Stearns say the Marinco Report advocated the use of robots? Or did he say "remote controlled bulldozers"? Is *robot* a good paraphrase for this? Look at the other two underlined sections. What is wrong with the information in each?

Below are three additional sentences taken from drafts for this summary. Each has a problem with accuracy. Can you see why?

> The one-year project attempts to clear the island by removing $4^{1}/_{2}$ feet of the ground.
> If the soil were dug up, Kaho'olawe would disappear in approximately twenty-five years.
> They [the navy] would be able to use the western tip of the island and could give guided tours to tourists on the days they weren't bombing.

Go back and read the article again if you cannot spot the inaccuracies. Such inaccuracies can find their way into your paper because of faulty understanding of what you have read. They can also work their way in because of careless wording. Either way, you should read your draft carefully and have a colleague read it to make sure that what you are saying is accurate in its details.

This next paragraph does a more accurate job of connecting Stearns's ideas about the Marinco Report with his overall stand on the issue. Thanks to some editing, it also presents his argument clearly. The phrases in brackets were not in the first draft. They were added later in response to a colleague's suggestion that the paragraph would not be understandable to someone who had not read the original article. Do you see how the additions clarify the relationship of ideas in the paragraph?

> Although Stearns feels that Kaho'olawe is an important asset to the navy and that the island can't be developed, he claims there are some parts that can be used by civilians. For example, Smuggler's Cove, located on the western tip of the island, could be "released to the public for picnicking, fishing, and camping." But the Marinco

Report recommends that [before any civilian use of the island is possible] some parts of Kaho'olawe [would need to] be bulldozed to remove unexploded bombs. Stearns [however, disagrees with the idea that such extensive work would be necessary. He] maintains that the Marinco Report was written to convince the state of the "difficulty, danger and cost of cleaning up" Kaho'olawe so that the navy might have use of the island. [Stearns feels that the parts of the island he recommends for civilian use could be cleaned up much more easily than the report indicates.]

Note how the writer we have just read has incorporated small quotations from the original article into his sentences and has enclosed them in quotation marks. By contrast, note how carelessly borrowed material has been used in the following paragraphs. Compare them to the original article if you cannot spot the careless parts by yourself. These paragraphs show problems with what we will call honesty. (Careless use of quoted material might come from just that, carelessness, rather than from conscious dishonesty, but the result is still a problem in the honest use of sources.) Several quotations are included without the benefit of quotation marks. The first two have been marked by brackets; can you find others? Note the last sentence, which the author has placed in quotation marks. Is this an exact quotation? Compare it to the original article and see.

Lastly, Kaho'olawe cannot be used for development. In the Marinco Report it says if the state uses bulldozers and other equipment to remove the shrapnel and unexploded ordnance in the ground, it would be useful for farming and establishing golf courses. Stearns points out that this is false because there is [no developable ground water] and [the cost of desalinating sea water is prohibitive for farming or golf courses]. The navy did an experiment by growing different kinds of trees on the island, but they grew poorly due to thin soil, strong winds, and very little rain. Thus, the island cannot be wholly used for civilians.

In summary, Stearns believes that the cooperation between the civilians and navy should be instituted because of the facts presented. He states, "If those parts of Kahoolawe which are safe, were released by the navy, civilian resentment against the navy would disappear."

A Professional Use of a Summary

At the beginning of this chapter we indicated that most often summaries are not articles by themselves, but are incorporated into larger studies. The following summary by a professional writer illustrates this use. In her book *The Creation of Patriarchy*, Gerda Lerner discusses the Babylonian marriage system by considering different interpretations of its significance. The excerpt shows one way you could use summaries in the paper you will write in Chapter 8. Summarizing the views of Paul Koschaker, Lerner says:

The contrasting view, held by Paul Koschaker and by most European Assyriologists, is that Babylonian marriage was marriage by purchase, and that the bride price was in fact an actual payment by the groom — or his family — for the bride. Koschaker calls attention to the existence of two forms of marriage in the Mesopotamian region. The older form, which survived for a long time, is marriage without joint residence. The wife remains in her father's (or her mother's) house; the husband resides with her as either an occasional or permanent visitor. There are reflections of the existence of such marriage forms in the Code of Hammurabi and in the Biblical record, where it is called *beena* marriage. It is a form of marriage which allows the woman greater autonomy and which makes divorce easier for her. Koschaker thinks that CH and MAL formalized the other form, patriarchal marriage, which gradually [became] predominant. In this marriage system the wife resides in the husband's house and is entirely dependent on his support. Divorce is, for the wife, virtually unobtainable. Koschaker thinks that this marriage system began initially as marriage by purchase, but that it developed, approximately at the time of Gudea of Lagash (ca. 1205 B.C.), into marriage by written contract. This development was characteristic of Sumerian society; but Semitic societies retained the earlier form of patriarchal marriage. Both concepts are represented in Hammurabi's law codes. . . .

Thus Koschaker seeks to explain the contradictions in Hammurabic law, to which we have called attention. He also cautions against a vulgarized reading of his hypothesis, which would interpret it as meaning that the wife was owned as a slave. He agrees with Driver and Miles that the bride price was not the economic equivalent for the wife. But it was, he points out, its judicial equivalent. "The marriage is a marriage by purchase even when the juridic relationship resulting from it is not ownership of the wife but legal power of the husband over the wife." The distinction is highly suggestive from our point of view precisely because it defines a new sort of power relationship between husband and wife, for which there was no equivalent in earlier society.

Modern anthropological evidence seems to support Koschaker's reconstruction of a historic development from marriage without joint residence to patrilocal patriarchal marriage. The former is more characteristic of nomadic and hunting and gathering tribes, while the latter occurs in connection with plow agriculture. Neither Driver and Miles nor Koschaker explain adequately the origin of marriage by purchase; they simply assume its existence and show how it devolved. An understanding of this development is only possible if we consider class as a factor. Marriage by purchase was a class phenomenon, and it did not apply equally to women of all classes.

Additional Summary Exercises

In college writing summaries are placed in the context of a larger paper sometimes as factual explanation or background, sometimes as support for the writer's thesis, and sometimes as ideas to be refuted or modified. Often only part of an article will be used, and only a partial summary need be made. Suppose, for example, that you were writing a paper on the history of Kaho'olawe. You might want to use the first part of Midkiff's article, "Kahoolawe from the Beginning" (Article 8 in the Appendix), where he uses the quotation from Kamakau's book concerning the use of Kaho'olawe as a penal colony to prove his point that the island has never supported a permanent population. Suppose that you wanted to agree with Midkiff on this point. You might use an abbreviated summary of this part of his article like this:

> Certainly the facts suggest that Kaho'olawe has never supported a permanent or numerous population. Frank Midkiff uses these facts to support his contention that Kaho'olawe should remain under the control of the military. He cites the book Ruling Chiefs of Hawaii by S. M. Kamakau, which refers to Kaho'olawe as a penal colony and indicates that even though prisoners were given food, they suffered from starvation. Midkiff rightly, I think, contends that since all the other islands were heavily populated even "to the extent of interisland and intervalley warfare for food," such a use for Kaho'olawe, coupled with the inability of the prisoners to support themselves there, indicates that permanent use of the island was not possible.

By contrast, suppose you wanted to claim that Kaho'olawe's history was quite different and that Midkiff's use of Kamakau was not convincing. You might write paragraphs incorporating a summary of the same part of Midkiff's article like this:

> Arguments that hold that Kaho'olawe's past includes no important or permanent habitation make too much use of certain written sources and not enough of physical evidence such as Heiaus and temples. For example, Frank F. Midkiff bases his entire argument against important historical use of Kaho'olawe on a passage from S. M. Kamakau's book Ruling Chiefs of Hawaii, which describes the use of

the island as a penal colony. Kamakau indicated that prisoners were given food but still "suffered with hunger and some died of starvation." From this, Midkiff concludes, prematurely I think, that "although all the other islands . . . were occupied and capable of producing crops and food, Kahoolawe never had any permanent inhabitants." He goes on to speculate that surely the Hawaiians made "conscientious and even desperate efforts to convert Kahoolawe into a place of human habitation," but that the efforts "never were successful." He says that the ruins of Heiaus and temples found on Kaho'olawe were the results of "short periods, when the first settlers landed in Kahoolawe."

Mr. Midkiff's conclusions seem to be based on a huge leap from the one passage cited. First, does Kamakau's book indicate that Kaho'olawe was always a penal colony? If not, what were the conditions at the time of such use that caused starvation? Second, the relation of the prisoners and the settlers who erected the Heiaus during the "short periods" of their first arrival is not at all clear. That seems to be a fabrication based only on Midkiff's prior assumption that no settlements were permanent or successful.

As practice in using summaries in a context, take some small part of Stearns's article (a paragraph or two) and write a summary of it to show how it might fit into a larger paper. You need to write only one or two paragraphs. For example:

1. You might be writing an article in which you are defending the findings of the Marinco Report. Write a summary of Stearns's ideas about the report and indicate how you would disagree with him.

2. You might be agreeing with Stearns about the possibility of development on Kaho'olawe. Summarize his arguments about this question to show your approval.

3. You might be refuting Stearns's major contention that the military and civilians could safely share the island.

Remember to concentrate only on the parts of the article that relate to your purpose and to write into your summary sentences of your own that let a reader know what your purpose will be.

When you have completed this exercise, compare your results with those of another writer. Your instructor will probably not ask you to revise these exercises since they are meant for practice only. He or she may ask you to do more than one of them. Some of these summaries might serve you well in Chapter 7.

Sample Summary

Two-level Outline of Midkiff's Article,
"Kahoolawe from the Beginning"

Thesis: The military should retain control of Kaho'olawe.
I. Kaho'olawe is not capable of any development.
    A. Historically, no permanent settlements have been possible.
    B. Because of its position, little rain falls there.
II. The military needs Kaho'olawe.
    A. They need a place to train personnel.
    B. We need to keep strong defenses in the Pacific against Russian expansion.

Summary of Midkiff's Article

Frank F. Midkiff, in his article "Kahoolawe from the Beginning," says that the military should keep control of Kaho'olawe. He bases this on <u>two</u> major arguments.

<u>First</u>, he says that Kaho'olawe is not suitable for habitation or development. He argues <u>first</u> on historical grounds, citing Kamakau's book to say that, <u>though</u> in the past there were inhabitants of the island, they were mainly convicts who could not live on its resources, but that permanent settlements were never made. He <u>then</u> asserts that no permanent habitation is possible in the future since Kaho'olawe lies in the lee of Mount Haleakala and <u>thus</u> has no water to support farming.

<u>Since</u> the island is not fit for other use, Midkiff says that its value lies in supplying a training ground for pilots. He argues <u>first</u> that we must keep our defenses strong and that strong defenses rely on a trained military. <u>To emphasize</u> the need for a military presence, he cites the buildup of Russian naval forces in the Pacific waters. He <u>adds in summary</u> that we should "not jeopardize the Navy's use of Kahoolawe to train our forces for national defense until an adequate alternative site is established."

6 *Comparison and Contrast*

Statement of Assignment

This chapter introduces a more complex form of summary writing. Not only will it give you another chance to write a summary, but it will also teach you about a common writing strategy, comparison and contrast. You will write a summary of the two articles you have already read: "Kahoolawe from the Beginning," and "Kahoolawe in the Raw." The summary will require you to consider the ideas of two authors, telling where they agree and where they disagree. The aim is the same as in the last chapter: to make a summary clear enough that someone who has not read either article can understand what the two authors said.

Your instructor will tell you how many words you should have in your summary, which will probably be about the same as in the summary you wrote of Stearns's article alone. You will not be able to include as much detail, but the summary will still present the issue, the stand, and the major reasons and subreasons for the stand of each article. The following exercise will prepare you to write this summary. The procedure is essentially the same as for the simple summary, but you must take into account two arguments. Your instructor may ask you to do this exercise in class or with other writers.

W R I T I N G   A C T I V I T Y

Two of the articles in the Appendix have eyewitness accounts of Kahoʻolawe: Harold T. Stearns's "Kahoolawe in the Raw," and Bunky Bakutis's "The Two Faces of Kahoolawe" (No. 9). If you were going to write a short comparison/contrast summary of these two views, you might begin by answering the following questions.

1. What is Stearns's overall impression of Kahoʻolawe? What is Bakutis's overall impression? Is one more favorable than the other?

2. Do the two authors agree on any facts about the appearance of the island? What agreements do you find?

3. Does Bakutis talk about an aspect of the island's appearance that Stearns does not?

4. Both writers talk about one specific fact about Kaho'olawe's ability to support vegetation. What is this fact? Do they see this "evidence" in the same way?

Using the information collected in the answers to these questions, write a four- or five-sentence summary of the two views of the island, including the following:

S T E P 1   Define the overall difference in the two authors' impressions of the island (one sentence).

S T E P 2   Tell what they saw that was the same.

S T E P 3   Write a sentence or two about their disagreement about vegetation on the island and mention how this relates to their overall impressions.

S T E P 4   Write about the aspect of this island that Bakutis mentions and Stearns does not, and tell how that relates to Bakutis's impression of the island.

This simple exercise has led you through the process for making a comparison/contrast summary. First, read the two articles, noting differences and similarities. Then make a plan or outline for noting the differences. Then write about them. The following section will help you with the planning stages for the summary which you will write. Be sure you have read both articles carefully before you begin.

Getting Started

The process for writing this paper is essentially the same as for the last. Here, too, you will be summarizing the argument of the articles. In order to do this you will have to read both carefully, deciding the issue and stand, the major and subreasons for the stand, and the evidence for all of these. Since you have dealt with both of these articles before, this part will be a review.

Issue and Stand

Clearly, the issue for both articles is the same: What should be done with Kaho'olawe? Recall that Midkiff's and Stearns's stands are not the same. In what way do they differ? Write one sentence in which you define how these two stands differ. Use the form "Frank F. Midkiff, in his article, 'Kahoolawe from the Beginning,' thinks . . . , while Harold T. Stearns in his article, 'Kahoolawe in the Raw,' holds that . . . ." Don't try to summarize the whole article in one sentence. Simply write the main idea of each author. This will be the first sentence, and the thesis, of your summary.

Outlining the Major Reasons for the Stand

Just as in the simple summary, here you need to determine what major reasons Midkiff and Stearns give for their stands. Look at the outline that was included with the sample summary of the Midkiff article in the last chapter, and consult the outline you made for your summary of Stearns's article. Recall that the major reasons are stated as I, II, III, and so on on the outlines. Although the two authors have different stands on the main issue, they both present two major reasons that are the same. What are these two reasons? Does either of the two articles present a major reason that the other does not?

It might help at this point to make a chart like this:

Midkiff	*Stearns*
Thesis:	Thesis:
I. Reason 1	I. Reason 1
II. Reason 2	II. Reason 2

Which side of the chart needs a III?

Subreasons

If you look again at the outlines of Midkiff's and Stearns's arguments from the last chapter, you will recall that on a two-level outline such as those, the subreasons were labeled A, B, and so on and placed under the appropriate major reasons. You should now fill in your chart with this level of the argument. For example, the Midkiff half of the chart would start like this:

Thesis: Kahoʻolawe should be used by the military.
I. K. is not suitable for development.
    A. Historically there were no permanent habitants.
    B. There is not enough rainfall.

Complete the chart for both Midkiff and Stearns.

Planning the Organization

When you had completed your outline of the Stearns article in the last chapter, you were ready to write the draft for the simple summary merely by following that outline. However, the chart you have prepared here is like a double outline.

Organizing a comparison/contrast summary is a more complex task, because you have to decide how to work in all the information on both sides of the chart.

If you look at your chart, you will see that you have two elements to consider in organizing a comparison/contrast essay: (1) the things being compared—in this case Midkiff's and Stearns's articles—and (2) the bases for comparing the two things—in this case the major reasons for the stands. It should be obvious that either of the two elements can serve as the basis for organizing. That is, you can have two basic types of organization for a comparison/contrast essay:

Type 1, where you discuss all of the first subject, then all of the second subject, is called alternating comparison.

Type 2, where you use the bases for comparison as the main parts of the essay, is called direct comparison.

Type 1	*Type 2*
Thesis:	Thesis:
I. Midkiff	I. Reason 1
Reason 1	Midkiff
Reason 2	Stearns
II. Stearns	II. Reason 2
Reason 1	Midkiff
Reason 2	Stearns
Reason 3	III. Reason 3
	Stearns

Let's take another example to make this clear. Suppose you wanted to write an essay comparing Chinese and American students, and you decided to compare them according to study habits, motivation, and background. You could use one of the following outlines:

Type 1	*Type 2*
Thesis:	Thesis:
I. Chinese students	I. Study habits
A. Study habits	A. Chinese students
B. Motivation	B. American students
C. Background	II. Motivation
II. American students	A. Chinese students
A. Study habits	B. American students
B. Motivation	III. Background
C. Background	A. Chinese students
	B. American students

These organizing principles are basic to comparison/contrast writing, but the two types of organization need not be followed rigidly. In a long and complex essay you might even combine the two types in various ways. We will discuss variations in subsequent chapters.

The essay you are writing now might also be organized in a third way. Since you are comparing the two essays to see where the authors agree and where they disagree, you might use the following organization.

Type 3

Thesis:

I. Points of agreement
II. Points of disagreement

The type of organization you choose will depend on which seems clearer according to your own conception of the paper. Once you have read the articles and decided on the major reasons and subreasons for each article, choose how you want to organize your essay. Then make a two-level outline, using the type of organization you have chosen.

When you have completed your outline, you might share it with another writer to see whether you agree on the major reasons and subreasons for each of the two authors' arguments. If you do not agree, discuss the two articles and resolve your differences. You do not need to have the same organization or use the same words to summarize the reasons and subreasons. However, you should both see the overall structure of the two articles in essentially the same way.

Writing a Draft

In writing any expository paper, it is usually a good idea to begin your draft with what might be called a working introduction. This will almost certainly be rewritten later. An introduction presents the issue, giving whatever background information would be necessary for a reader new to the subject and a statement of the thesis or stand. For this paper, write in two or three sentences a summary of the issue (What is happening on Kaho'olawe? How do people feel about that?), and then give your statement of the stand. This will be your first paragraph.

Next, begin to write your paper using the two-level outline you developed earlier in this chapter as a rough guide. Generally you will need at least one paragraph on each major section (I, II, etc.) of the outline. Begin your discussion on each of the major reasons with a sentence that defines the reason for your reader.

For example, if you are using organization type 1, and the first major reason you are dealing with is military need, you might say at the beginning of the second paragraph, "Both Midkiff and Stearns believe that Kaho'olawe is important to the military." You will then write in this paragraph about the subreasons that each author gives for military need. It is possible that you will use two paragraphs for this part of the paper if each author has quite a bit to say on the subject.

When you have finished writing about this first reason, begin your next paragraph with another statement about the second reason ("Both authors also agree on the possibility of developing Kaho'olawe," for example), and continue in that way. Develop each paragraph to tell your reader what the authors say about the reason under consideration. Don't forget to use transitional language to help your reader follow your organization: "the second point is," "on that same issue," "On the other hand, Midkiff says," and so on.

As you write, remember to be honest and careful in your use of the ideas and words of Midkiff and Stearns. Write most of the summary in your own words. If you do want to quote some sentences or parts of sentences, do so accurately (don't change a single word), and place all the quoted words in quotation marks.

Reworking the Draft

Feedback from Other Writers

As in Chapter 5, you and your colleagues can be particularly helpful to each other in responding to drafts of this summary. Look again for clarity, accuracy, and honesty. The same exercise suggested in Chapter 5 would be helpful here: Listen to or read each other's drafts and see if you can make a two-level outline of the paper.

Think of the following questions as you listen or read:

1. Is there any place in the paper where you lose track of the two authors' arguments? In other words, where, if anywhere, does the organization of this paper seem unclear?
2. Is the summary an accurate statement of Midkiff's and Stearns's arguments?
3. Is there any sentence in the paper where the writer might have been careless with quoted material?
4. What advice would you give this writer?

Examples of Revision

The revision of this paper is guided by the three characteristics of a good summary mentioned in the "Examples of Revisions" section in Chapter 5: clarity, accuracy, and honesty. You already have some good advice to help as you begin to do the final draft of this paper. The following discussion of excerpts from drafts will also help.

Following are the first two paragraphs of a draft. Look at them first for clarity.

> Frank F. Midkiff thinks that Kaho'olawe should be used solely for military purposes, while Harold T. Stearns holds that Kaho'olawe should be shared by the military and civilians.
>
> High winds that deprive the island of moisture and a lack of "ground water" make the island unproductive for agricultural or commercial purposes. Midkiff attributes Kaho'olawe's lack of water to the island's location. Because it is located "in the lee of Mount Haleakala, winds flow by and over Haleakala and thereby lose the water they have picked up from the trough of the trade winds and the Japan Current." Stearns, through personal observation, noticed a "lack of change there during the last 37 years," and mentioned that trees planted by the state were growing no higher than eight feet because of thin soil, strong winds, and very little rain, so he agrees with Midkiff that the island is unsuitable for "permanent" human habitation.

The introduction states the thesis for the summary clearly enough, but gives no other information. It needs a sentence or two to introduce the issue to the readers.

The second paragraph starts with a lot of specifics and does not get around to defining the major idea under discussion until the last half of the last sentence. This might be confusing to someone who was not familiar with the two articles. Such a reader might not see how all these particulars relate to the thesis. How could this paragraph be made clearer?

This paragraph also has problems with accuracy and honesty. The first sentence of the second paragraph mixes a paraphrase from Midkiff (is it accurate?) with a quote ("ground water") from Stearns. That is perhaps a bit dishonest, or at least misleading, in its use of borrowed material. There is also an unacknowledged quotation. Can you spot it? Are the other quotations exact?

The next three paragraphs, taken from another paper, give an interesting direct comparison between Stearns and Midkiff. However, they also have some problems.

> Midkiff and Stearns also believe that Kaho'olawe is a "wonderful place to train aviators and other types of troops," for bombing practice, because it is located near Pearl Harbor. However, both say that an alternative site may be established. This is where their differences begin.
>
> Because Midkiff was once the high commissioner of the Trust Territory of the Pacific Islands, he may be looking at the situation from a "defense only" point of view. Because the Soviets have been steadily "increasing the number of ships of their navy and planes of

their air force," he feels it is of the utmost importance to keep our military strength equal to that of the Soviets. "To become number 2 in strength would invite possible disaster." And since Kaho'olawe serves no other purpose, Midkiff feels it should be used only by the military until an alternative site is found.

Because Stearns was once a district geologist with the U.S. Geological Survey and is now a consulting engineer-geologist, he may be looking at it from a "land use" point of view. Stearns contends that because only part of the island is used for target practice, the other parts that the military doesn't use should be given up by the navy for civilian use. He mentions Ahupu Bay, Smugglers' Cove, and Waikahalulu Bay as possible civilian recreational areas. He opposes the Marinco Report, a report which in his opinion, exaggerates "the difficulty, danger and cost of cleaning up the island in order to justify continued use for a bombing practice range." According to Stearns, cleaning these areas of unexploded bombs could be done easily and at a small cost. He states further that sharing the island would help to ease tension between the navy and civilians.

The first paragraph begins with a direct comparison between the two authors' ideas and is thus clearer than the preceding paragraphs. But, the sentence "However, both say that an alternative site may be established," gives a false impression. This idea was merely mentioned in passing by Midkiff and was not one of his major arguments. Does Stearns mention it at all? Remember that you must be accurate. You must not make either writer seem to say something he does not say.

The second paragraph is quite good, as is the beginning of the third. However, read the discussion of the Marinco Report. Would this discussion be clear to someone who had never heard of this report and thus did not know that it related to removing dangerous ordnance from the island? How might you make this discussion clearer?

Discuss all these excerpts with other writers. They have strengths but need help in clarity, accuracy, and honesty. Go through your own draft paragraph by paragraph trying to see where it might need this kind of work.

A Professional Comparison/Contrast Summary

Adrienne Rich, feminist and poet, summarizes what four other feminists have to say (or don't say) about lesbian experience as a way of showing that a commitment to heterosexuality blinds writers to any other experience. Her comparison/contrast summary illustrates for you one of the major skills you will need to learn in college writing.

My organizing impulse is the belief that it is not enough for feminist thought that specifically lesbian texts exist. Any theory or cultural/political creation that treats lesbian existence as a marginal or less "natural" phenomenon, as mere "sexual preference," or as the mirror image of either heterosexual or male homosexual relations is profoundly weakened thereby, whatever its other contributions. Feminist theory can no longer afford merely to voice a toleration of "lesbianism" as an "alternative life style" or make token allusion to lesbians. A feminist critique of compulsory heterosexual orientation for women is long overdue. In this exploratory paper, I shall try to show why.

I will begin by way of examples, briefly discussing four books that have appeared in the last few years, written from different viewpoints and political orientations, but all presenting themselves, and favorably reviewed, as feminist. All take as a basic assumption that the social relations of the sexes are disordered and extremely problematic, if not disabling, for women; all seek paths toward change. I have learned more from some of these books than from others, but on this I am clear: each one might have been more accurate, more powerful, more truly a force for change had the author dealt with lesbian existence as a reality and as a source of knowledge and power available to women, or with the institution of heterosexuality itself as a beachhead of male dominance. In none of them is the question ever raised as to whether, in a different context or other things being equal, women would *choose* heterosexual coupling and marriage; heterosexuality is presumed the "sexual preference" of "most women," either implicitly or explicitly. In none of these books, which concern themselves with mothering, sex roles, relationships, and societal prescriptions for women, is compulsory heterosexuality ever examined as an institution powerfully affecting all these, or the idea of "preference" or "innate orientation" even indirectly questioned.

In *For Her Own Good: 150 Years of the Experts' Advice to Women* by Barbara Ehrenreich and Deirdre English, the authors' superb pamphlets *Witches, Midwives and Nurses: A History of Women Healers* and *Complaints and Disorders: The Sexual Politics of Sickness* are developed into a provocative and complex study. Their thesis in this book is that the advice given to American women by male health professionals, particularly in the areas of marital sex, maternity, and child care, has echoed the dictates of the economic marketplace and the role capitalism has needed women to play in production and/or reproduction. Women have become the consumer victims of various cures, therapies, and normative judgments in different periods (including the prescription to middle-class women to embody and preserve the sacredness of the home—the "scientific" romanticization of the home itself). None of the "experts'" advice has been either particularly scientific or women-oriented; it has reflected male needs, male fantasies about women, and male interest in controlling women—

particularly in the realms of sexuality and motherhood—fused with the requirements of industrial capitalism. So much of this book is so devastatingly informative and is written with such lucid feminist wit, that I kept waiting as I read for the basic proscription against lesbianism to be examined. It never was.

This can hardly be for lack of information. Jonathan Katz's *Gay American History* tells us that as early as 1656 the New Haven Colony prescribed the death penalty for lesbians. Katz provides many suggestive and informative documents on the "treatment" (or torture) of lesbians by the medical profession in the nineteenth and twentieth centuries. Recent work by the historian Nancy Sahli documents the crackdown on intense female friendships among college women at the turn of the present century. The ironic title *For Her Own Good* might have referred first and foremost to the economic imperative to heterosexuality and marriage and to the sanctions imposed against single women and widows—both of whom have been and still are viewed as deviant. Yet, in this often enlightening Marxist-feminist overview of male prescriptions for female sanity and health, the economics of prescriptive heterosexuality go unexamined.

Of the three psychoanalytically based books, one, Jean Baker Miller's *Toward a New Psychology of Women,* is written as if lesbians simply do not exist, even as marginal beings. Given Miller's title, I find this astonishing. However, the favorable reviews the book has received in feminist journals, including *Signs* and *Spokeswoman,* suggest that Miller's heterocentric assumptions are widely shared. In *The Mermaid and the Minotaur: Sexual Arrangements and the Human Malaise,* Dorothy Dinnerstein makes an impassioned argument for the sharing of parenting between women and men and for an end to what she perceives as the male/female symbiosis of "gender arrangements," which she feels are leading the species further and further into violence and self-extinction. Apart from other problems that I have with this book (including her silence on the institutional and random terrorism men have practiced on women—and children—throughout history, and her obsession with psychology to the neglect of economic and other material realities that help to create psychological reality), I find Dinnerstein's view of the relations between women and men as "a collaboration to keep history mad" utterly ahistorical. She means by this a collaboration to perpetuate social relations which are hostile, exploitative, and destructive to life itself. She sees women and men as equal partners in the making of "sexual arrangements," seemingly unaware of the repeated struggles of women to resist oppression (their own and that of others) and to change their condition. She ignores, specifically, the history of women who—as witches, *femmes seules,* marriage resisters, spinsters, autonomous widows, and/or lesbians—have managed on varying levels *not* to collaborate. It is this history, precisely, from which feminists have so much to learn and on which there is overall such blanketing silence. Dinnerstein acknowledges at the end of her book that "female separatism," though "on a large scale and in the long run wildly impractical," has something to teach us: "Separate, women could in principle set out to learn from scratch—undeflected by the opportunities to evade this task that men's presence has so far offered—what intact self-creative humanness is." Phrases like "intact self-creative humanness" obscure the question of what the many forms of female separatism have actually been addressing. The fact is that women in every culture and throughout history *have* undertaken the task of independent, nonheterosexual, woman-connected existence, to the extent made possible by their context, often in the belief that they were the "only ones" ever to have done so. They have undertaken it even though few women have been in an economic position to resist marriage altogether, and even though attacks against unmarried women have ranged from aspersion and mockery to deliberate gynocide, including the burning and torturing of millions of widows and spinsters during the witch persecutions of the fifteenth, sixteenth, and seventeenth centuries in Europe.

Nancy Chodorow does come close to the edge of an acknowledgment of lesbian existence. Like Dinnerstein, Chodorow believes that the fact that women, and women only, are responsible for child care in the sexual division of labor has led to an entire social organization of gender inequality, and that men as well as women must become primary carers for children if that inequality is to change. In the process of examining, from a psychoanalytic perspective, how mothering by women affects the psychological development of girl and boy children, she offers documentation that men are "emotionally secondary" in women's lives, that "women have a richer, ongoing inner world to fall back on . . . men do not become as emotionally important to women as women do to men." This would carry into the late twentieth century Smith-Rosenberg's findings about eighteenth- and nineteenth-century women's emotional focus on women. "Emotionally important" can, of course, refer to anger as well as to love, or to that intense mixture of the two often found in women's relationships with women—one aspect of what I have come to call the "double life of women". . . . Chodorow concludes that because women have women as mothers, "the mother remains a primary internal object [*sic*] to the girl, so that heterosexual relationships are on the model of a nonexclusive, second relationship for her, whereas for the boy they re-create an exclusive, primary relationship." According to Chodorow, women "have learned to deny the limitations of masculine lovers for both psychological and practical reasons."

But the practical reasons (like witch burnings, male control of law, theology, and science, or economic nonviability within the sexual division of labor) are glossed over. Chodorow's account barely glances at the constraints and sanctions which historically have enforced or ensured the coupling of women with men and obstructed or penalized women's coupling or allying in independent groups with other women. She dismisses lesbian existence with the comment that "lesbian relationships do tend to re-create mother-daughter emotions and connections, but most women are heterosexual" (implied: more mature, having developed beyond the mother-daughter connection?). She then adds: "This heterosexual preference and taboos on homosexuality, in addition to objective economic dependence on men, make the option of primary sexual bonds with other women unlikely—though more prevalent in recent years."

Adrienne Rich, from "Compulsory Heterosexuality and Lesbian Existence"

A Note on Taking Essay Exams

Writing essays in examinations will present a direct application for the skills you have learned in Chapters 5 and 6. In essence, an essay question asks you to make sense out of a large body of material you have read and heard and to summarize it (often though not always in a comparison/contrast format) according to an answer that you must formulate.

You might think of the procedure for answering an essay question as much the same as that for writing a summary. First you must have read and understood the material assigned. Then you must understand the issue presented by the examination question, take some stand on the issue, and then present your major reasons for the stand in an orderly fashion, along with subideas and evidence.

For example, suppose you were asked the following question in a world history exam: "Compare the American Civil War with the English Civil War with respect to causes."

Your first task here (and in any examination situation) is to analyze the question to make sure you understand exactly what is asked. One major problem in essay examinations is the failure to answer the question asked. Often students simply write down all the information they can think of about the subject and let it go at that. But an essay question asks you to write an argument essay that answers the question asked.

The issue in this question is the causes of the two wars. Your stand, therefore, must make an assertion about the causes of both the wars. Since you are usually under time pressure in an examination, a good rule of thumb is to start with your stand, or your thesis. Your first sentence, therefore, should be a straightforward generalization that you think answers the question. Since this is a comparison/contrast essay, you should use words that show sameness or difference, such as *more*, *less*, *both*, and *neither*. Your first sentence (stand or thesis) might be:

The causes of the American Civil War were <u>different</u> from those of the English Civil War.

or

> The political causes of the American Civil War were <u>different</u> from those of the English Civil War, but the economic causes were <u>similar</u>.

or

> Economic interests were <u>more</u> important in causing the American Civil War than in causing the English Civil War, where religious interests were primary; however, economic antagonisms were crucial to both.

When you have determined your thesis, make a plan outlining your major reasons for this stand, and showing how you will draw on sources (reading, lecture notes, etc.) to support each of your major reasons. For example, if you choose the third thesis suggested above, economic reasons were more important in the American Civil War, you might divide your answer into I. The American Civil War, and II. The English Civil War. Under each heading you would list three or four causes of the war in question, highlighting the economic basis for those under I. and the religious basis for those under II.

Another plan might be to make the causes the basis of the organization: I. economic causes, II. other causes. You would then highlight the American Civil War under I. and the English Civil War under II. The second plan would work better if you wanted to stress that economics played an important role in each war but that other causes were more vital in England. You can always think of alternate strategies for writing any essay. Your strategy comes from your thesis and material, and from the emphasis you give different material.

In making your plan be sure to keep your thesis sentence in mind. Don't include in this outline everything you have ever heard about the wars. Don't give a history of the battle plans or a detailed account of the events that led up to the wars, unless those events clearly show the causes. Don't tell what happened as a result of the wars; your subject is causes. Forget the organization of the textbook or of the professor's lectures, just as you had to leave the organization of Midkiff's and Stearns's articles to make your summaries.

When you have made a short plan (remember the time constraints of an exam), begin to write. Start with your thesis and a very short introduction, then follow your outline, devoting one paragraph to each major section. Begin every paragraph with a clear statement of that part of your argument (of the particular cause for the war in our example), present your proof, and move on to the next part of your outline. Make what you write clear and readable English. In the few moments you have for writing it is best to concentrate on the clarity of the message. Keep thinking: "I have to persuade my instructor that sentence 1 is a valid claim."

Consider another example, drawn from biology, to help you see the thinking needed. Suppose you were given the following question: "What is one important property of the DNA molecule? Support your answer." You recall from your lectures that the professor stressed, among other ideas, that DNA was built to store information. So you take your stand: "DNA is a good molecule to store hereditary data."

Immediately a welter of information about DNA comes to mind. You must sort through what you know about the molecule and decide on three or four characteristics of DNA that make it good for storing hereditary information. Pick out three ideas from those given below that would make good major reasons (I, II, III) for your stand.

DNA is made up of a combination of three parts that make up two complementary strands.

DNA has good storing capacities.

DNA has unusual stability

DNA is often seen as a ladderlike network.

DNA has a unique processing capability that can correct mistakes

Do you see that the items here that merely talk about the structure of the material do not show that DNA stores information? Some of this information about structure may be used later to show, for example, why DNA has unusual stability, but it is not the information you want to draw on when you are deciding on major reasons for your stand.

Suppose that you decided to use the third idea above, stability, as I. on your outline. What would you write as the first sentence in your second paragraph (after the introduction with its statement of your thesis)? What kind of information about DNA would you use to follow this sentence?

The following steps will help you answer an essay examination question:

1. Read the question and decide what it asks you to do.

2. Formulate an answer to the question (in one sentence if possible, or two or three). This is your stand, or thesis.

3. Write a quick sketch plan of two to four statements that are the major reasons for your stand. Jot in some supporting data for each.

4. Begin by writing your thesis/answer and a short introduction, and then follow your plan, writing one paragraph for each part of your outline. Start each paragraph with a clear statement of the reason under consideration.

5. Leave out everything that does not pertain to the thesis you have chosen.

7 *Argument*

In this chapter you will write a con/pro argument paper about the controversy surrounding the military's use of Kahoʻolawe, taking into consideration all the articles in the Appendix. Since everyone will be using the same issue and the same reading material, this chapter presents good opportunities to work collaboratively with other writers, most obviously in the planning stages, but also in the drafting and revision stages.

An argument paper is one written to defend or support a stand relating to a controversial topic. The paper presents a thesis statement defining the author's stand and provides analysis and evidence to support the stand. Obviously both of the articles we considered in the comparison/contrast summary, "Kahoolawe in the Raw" and "Kahoolawe from the Beginning," were argument papers.

The con/pro paper is a special type of argument in which the author supports or argues one idea or stand but considers the evidence and arguments for all sides of the controversy under discussion. The name "con/pro" comes from debating. In argument or debate, the stand a given person supports is the "pro," while the side that person argues against is the "con." Although you may be used to seeing these terms in the other order (i.e., *pros and cons*), we use con/pro because well-written papers frequently place arguments in favor of (pro) the thesis last. This follows the tenet (also derived from debating) that the argument heard or read last has the most force.

The following sample papers present examples of con/pro papers and illustrate two possible structures. We will discuss their organization in detail later, but for now read them through to get an idea how a con/pro paper works.

Reverse Osmosis in Desalting Water

The abundance of undrinkable seawater and the relative scarcity of fresh water for drinking and agriculture in many areas have encouraged experimentation in methods for desalinizing water. So far no method has proven to be efficient enough or cheap enough for widespread practical use.

One method for producing fresh water from salt water that has received much attention is ultrafiltration or reverse osmosis. Basically the process is the reverse of osmosis. First, in osmosis you have a diffusion of a substance from an area of a higher concentration, through a semipermeable membrane, to an area of a lower concentration of that substance. If we have a tank divided by a semipermeable membrane, with salt water on one side and fresh water on the other, the high concentration of fresh water would diffuse through the membrane to the salt water until an equilibrium is reached. However, in reverse osmosis you would apply pressure to the salt water, causing water, fresh desalinated water, to diffuse through the membrane to the fresh water side. Although this reverse osmosis method has distinct advantages, I feel that it still has several economic and technical problems to be solved.

There are several reasons why the reverse osmosis project seems to be a good solution to this problem. It uses a portable unit that can be easily carried or stored in small spaces. This makes it ideal for both astronauts and sailors, to whom space and water supply are very important. Comparatively little energy is needed to run the unit: just enough to produce the pressure on the salt water. The process needs no excessive heat, chemical treatment, or phase changes from a liquid to a vapor, as in distillation, or from a liquid to a solid, as in freezing. The process also runs at ordinary room temperatures, thus avoiding corrosion and sealing problems.

Even so, several problems remain with this process. The major problem is the short membrane life. This causes an acute financial burden in producing more membranes and requires labor for producing and installing them. Present membranes are capable of producing 1,500 to 2,500 gallons of fresh water per square foot of membrane. The result is that their life expectancy is only a few weeks. Minor punctures and tears are, to a major degree, self-healing, but these build up and cause the breakdown of the membrane.

Flux, another problem, is related to the semipermeable membrane. The reduction of the dense, thick cellulose diacetate layer on the membrane causes the membrane to be useless. The several techniques to increase the thickness of cellulose diacetate have all proved failures. The only remedy is to develop a new polymer that will have the properties of cellulose diacetate but not be able to be reduced in thickness.

Lastly there is the problem of salt rejection. The present membranes are not up to perfect standards. Under ideal laboratory conditions the membranes produce 96.5 percent salt rejection, but 98.6 percent salt rejection is necessary for potable water.

As we can see, reverse osmosis has a great potential in the effort to desalinate water, but it still has many years of research ahead before it can be put to use on a large scale.

Teacher's Job, Good or Bad?

To work as a teacher is considered admirable and respectable in most countries. But in China nowadays, many young people, especially students in our Foreign Languages Institute, are not willing to become teachers after graduation because they see a lot of disadvantages in doing this job. I strongly feel that a teacher's job is at any time not only important but also very interesting.

One of my classmates expressed to me the thought that a teacher is just like a candle that lights others' way while burning itself out. In other words, he thinks that a teacher gives his knowledge to the students, but gets nothing in return.

Anyone who has the experience of teaching will probably disagree with this idea. In teaching one always finds himself learning something. A teacher is by no means an encyclopedia; his knowledge and way of thinking are limited. Sometimes he's consciously or unconsciously enlightened by students' brilliant ideas and questions. On the other hand, the students' desire for knowledge is never limited. Their ever-increasing desire for knowledge requires the teacher to keep learning and to redouble his efforts. According to my cousin, who taught in Futan University, when one works at a school, he never feels himself alienated from study. With so many erudite professors, qualified teachers, and good facilities around, one furthers his study very conveniently and gets help whenever he needs it. "Thanks to the two years of continued hard work at the university after graduation, I succeeded in the exams for the interpreters of U.N.," my cousin told me in his letter. "Had I not been kept in the school to work as a teacher, I would not have made progress in my study so rapidly."

Li, my roommate, told me the other day, pointing out the example of many of the teachers in this institute, that one of the disadvantages of a teacher's job lies in the fact that to teach more or less the same thing all the time is too monotonous and one can easily get tired of it. Some of our fellows often say, "We are young, we want to come into contact with all kinds of knowledge, so that we can broaden our minds."

However, one of the advantages of being a teacher is that one has many chances to enrich his mind and life. First of all, a responsible teacher can never stick to his own professional knowledge. He needs to learn other things concerning his work, psychology, methods of teaching, and the like. This is both necessary and interesting. Secondly, according to my observation teachers are actually not bound by teaching. They get chances to go abroad either for further study or to work as teachers for a period of time. Furthermore, the relative abundance of free time makes it possible for them to do whatever they are interested in, such as translation work, research work, compiling books, and working as interpreters. Meanwhile, the two long vacations assure teachers enough time to enjoy themselves, making their lives meaningful.

Still another objection to the teacher's job is that generally speaking teachers' salaries are not high. They don't get bonuses no matter how hard they work and they can't pick up a few crumbs out of their work. As this is the most practical problem, many people don't want to become teachers and some even look down upon the job.

Although this is an obvious disadvantage, it can be clearly seen that recently our government has taken this problem into consideration. Most teachers have already gotten raises in their salaries. Teachers also get extra money or profit by working in their spare time. The father of one of my classmates, whose pronunciation and intonation are very excellent, was invited to give English lessons over the radio, and he gets as much as 50 yuan in a month, which is much higher than a worker's bonus. One more advantage that I see is that in schools teachers have several promotions. Everyone is impelled to gain professional proficiency and make good, for one can get a higher salary if he achieves the promotion.

All in all, the job of teaching is not as bad as some young people think. Instead, one can benefit a lot from it in many ways.

Statement of Assignment

The two papers you have just read provide models for the paper you will write next. First you will read and digest all the articles about Kahoʻolawe in the Appendix and decide what *you* think should be done with the island. Then you will write a paper in which you take a stand and support it with your own reasons and evidence drawn from the articles, while you also consider arguments for other viewpoints. The paper will teach you to read and analyze material, to come to a conclusion, and to write your conclusion in a coherent paper using evidence from written sources. This paper will be fairly substantial, probably three or four typewritten pages. Your instructor will give you specific directions about length. She may also give you specific instructions about collaborative work at several stages in the process.

The issue concerning Kahoʻolawe is whether the military should continue to use the island for training or return it to the state of Hawaiʻi for the use of the

Hawaiian people. Perhaps the best way for you to get an overview of the issue is to read Articles 1, 25, and 27 in the Appendix. The first article sketches the history of the island to about 1972. Articles 25 and 27 give more current history, and detail the activities of the Protect Kaho'olawe 'Ohana, which has played the leading role in protesting military use of Kaho'olawe.

As is so often the case with political issues, this involves a basic conflict of values. As Davianna McGregor, member of the 'Ohana, said, "It is so clear that there is a distinct split: The navy wants the island to train for war; we need the island to rebuild our future as a people." As American citizens, we are all familiar with the arguments for military preparedness. The beliefs of Native Hawaiians regarding their land may not be so familiar. Along with the various articles written by 'Ohana members, the following quotation from George Helm, who disappeared during a visit to Kaho'olawe in the days when such visits were not permitted, gives these ideas in graphic form:

> I have my thoughts, you have your thoughts, simple for me, difficult for you. Simply . . . the reason is . . . I am a Hawaiian and I've inherited the soul of my *kupuna*. It is my moral responsibility to attempt an ending to this desecration of our sacred *'āina, Kohe Malamalamama o Kanaloa*, for each bomb dropped adds further injury to an already wounded soul. The truth is, there is man and there is environment. One does not supercede the other. The breath in man is the breath of *Papa* (the earth). Man is merely the caretaker of the land that maintains his life and nourishes his soul. Therefore, *'āina* is sacred. The church of life is not in a building, it is the open sky, the surrounding ocean, the beautiful soil. My duty is to protect Mother Earth, who gives me life. And to give thanks with humility as well as ask forgiveness for the arrogance and insensitivity of man.
>
> What is national defense when what is being destroyed is the very thing the military is entrusted to defend, the sacred land of (*Hawai'i*) America. The spirit of pride is left uncultivated, without truth and without meaning for the *keiki o ka 'āina* [children of the land] cut off from the land as a fetus is cut off from his mother. National defense is indefensible in terms of the loss of pride for many of the citizens of *Hawai'i-nei*.

This is the issue you will be asked to deal with. The articles in the Appendix detail history, opinions, events, and other "facts" relating to the issue. You should begin to read these selections thoroughly and thoughtfully, since you will eventually need to take a stand, that is, write a thesis, for your paper.

The two most obvious stands that could be taken on this issue are familiar to you: (1) The military should continue to use the island, and (2) the military should return the island to the state or to the Hawaiian people. However, we have already seen that Stearns supported a third alternative: (3) The military and the state should work out a compromise. As you read the articles, you will see that this is what has actually happened in the past few years, since the 'Ohana has been given limited access to the island. Other possible stands are (4) Both the military and the state should leave the island alone and return it to the Native Hawaiian people for religious and cultural uses; (5) The island should be used as a laboratory for agricultural production (see Article 18 in the Appendix). You may think of another possibility. Your stand on the issue need not be original or complex. It does need to be one you can support with the available material.

Getting Started

Reading and Analyzing Sources

Before you take your stand, you should read all the articles carefully. The activities below will help you analyze the material in the articles so that you will begin to see how you can use it in your own paper. Doing these activities with other writers will make them easier, and will give you other points of view on the materials. Your instructor may have you do them in class.

WRITING ACTIVITY: CON/PRO OUTLINE

The first activity is based on the article, "Kahoolawe Tug-of-War Cost Navy $572,000" (Article 17). Though not clearly organized, this is a con/pro article because it presents evidence for both sides of one subissue in the Kaho'olawe controversy: whether the military really needs the island. It is an interview conducted with Lt. Commander Scott Stone of the U.S. Navy, which seeks to get his reaction to a report by Ian Lind, a pacifist who has written a special report saying that the navy does not need the island. Scott, in turn, asserts that Kaho'olawe is necessary for navy training.

Work with other writers and outline the material (opinions, facts, etc.) you find in this article that could be used to support military use of the island and the material that could be used to oppose it. Since Lind's report is the basis for the article, it might be best to begin your analysis of the article by listing his three points, as outlined in the sixth paragraph of the article. Set them up in a chart like the following:

Antimilitary (Lind)   *Promilitary (Stone)*
Argument 1: No navy search for
    alternative

Argument 2: K. not important to
   military
Argument 3: Superior facilities
   elsewhere

Read through the article again and note all of Stone's responses to Lind's arguments. You will find refutations for all three points, but they will not be treated in the same order and might be scattered throughout the article. Begin by making a list of every point that Stone makes.

When you have Stone's ideas, match them against Lind's like this:

Antimilitary (Lind)	*Promilitary (Stone)*
1. No navy search for alternative	1. Looked at several sites Kaula Rock Barking Sands

Continue to fill in the chart showing how Stone refutes, or attempts to refute, each of Lind's points.

When all this information is put on the chart, you will have a con/pro outline of the usable arguments and evidence in the article. In the next activity you and your colleagues will work with all the articles in the packet, seeing what arguments and evidence are available and sorting that information into usable categories.

WRITING ACTIVITY

The article "Kahoolawe Tug-of-War" discussed only one of the subissues relating to Kaho'olawe: military need. As you read all the articles, however, you will find that they also discuss two other subissues: the importance of the island to Native Hawaiian culture and the subject discussed by both Stearns and Midkiff—the physical characteristics of the island and its resources and limitations. If you now read all the articles and make a con/pro outline for each issue, drawing on everything you have read, you will have done the basic preparation for your con/pro paper.

This reading and outlining can be made easier by cooperation, so in this exercise, your instructor might ask you to work in groups and assign each group one of the subissues named above. You should still read all the articles, drawing from them any material relating to the issue you have been assigned. From all the material you collect, construct a rough con/pro outline.

For example, take the question of the alleged desolate nature of the island. We have mentioned before that both Stearns and Midkiff argue that the lack of water limits the use of the island. As you read, you will find others who dispute this, notably McGregor and Lyman, whose views are reported in Articles 26 and 18 and who argue that the lack of water might be overcome by building rubber-lined reservoirs (an expedient currently practiced on Moloka'i, another island in the Hawaiian chain). You might also consider the testimony of Inez McPhee Ashdown (Article 22), whose father had a ranch on Kaho'olawe. She says that the island was once described as a "forest land." Several other articles discuss this issue.

If you were outlining the issue of development, you might start like this:

Kaho'olawe Desolate	*Kaho'olawe Can Be Restored*

1. Lack of water
     Midkiff
     Stearns
	1. Water resources
	     Possible reservoir (Lyman)
	     Rainfall (McGregor)
	     Once forest (Ashdown)

2. Destruction by goats, etc.	

3. Midkiff: No permanent
     inhabitation
	3. Historical evidence
	     Ashdown
	     Article 25 on past inhabitation

Read through all the articles, noting historical evidence, present-day conditions, and so on, and list your evidence, matching cons and pros whenever possible. Note that you will not necessarily have a con for every pro or a pro for every con.

You will also find varied evidence and opinion on the other two issues. We have already seen cons and pros for military use in the "Tug-of-War" article. You will find another detailed statement of the military side in Article 19, which gives reasons other than the ones we have seen. McGregor (Article 26) refutes some of these. In addition, the 'Ohana members argue against the military on the grounds that it is destroying important remnants of their culture (Articles 13 and 25). We have read Midkiff's claim that the island has no real historical importance. This is disputed by several articles detailing important archaeological finds (Articles 5, 11, and 25, for example). These are only hints. As you read, you will find many more ideas for your outline.

Compare your outline with those made by other writers, if you have worked alone. In collaboration with your colleagues, prepare a master outline of each of the three subissues. When you have completed this task, the outline will serve as source material for your paper.

The purpose of these two activities has been to teach you to read and analyze material. When you write an argument paper of your own, you might not need to outline your sources in such detail. You will, however, need to learn to read sources carefully to see what they are saying on your topic and to see how they will fit into your argument. We will talk more about this in the next chapter.

Analyzing Arguments

The following paragraphs discuss types of evidence used to support a given stand and talk about subjectivity, objectivity, and emotion.

Recall the article, "Kahoolawe from the Beginning," which you summarized in Chapter 6. The author of the article presented the stand that Kaho'olawe should be retained by the military for bombing practice. His two major reasons to support this were that (I) the island is incapable of supporting development, and (II) the military needs the island. His two subreasons were that (A) the island has never in the past supported permanent inhabitants and (B) does not have enough water to do so now. His evidence for subreason A is the quote from Kamakau's book, which says that lawbreakers who were sent to the island suffered from starvation. The quote states the historical facts that Kaho'olawe was used as a prison and prisoners stole food. Fact is one major type of evidence. Another major type is opinion. Thus, based on the facts from Kamakau's book, Midkiff gives his opinion that the Hawaiians must have tried and failed to grow food on Kaho'olawe.

A fact, then, is a statement about objective reality (although facts are not always easy to establish, and you may find people disagreeing even about facts). An opinion is someone's subjective analysis of a fact. Both opinions and facts are legitimate evidence, but opinion clearly has a different status from fact. If someone is an expert or is well-informed on a situation, and if she obviously bases her opinion on fact, that opinion can be very valuable. Your thesis, for example, will be an informed opinion.

Note the terms *subjective* and *objective* used above. We have said that a fact is a statement about objective reality, while opinion is someone's subjective analysis. However, making an exact dividing line between the two is difficult if not impossible. We use the terms here merely to suggest the difference between use of what "happens" and use of what someone makes of the event. Again, the subjectivity of an opinion does not necessarily discredit it.

Objective is often contrasted with *emotional*, but this is not always an accurate contrast. Being objective about a subject does not mean either that you must be neutral on it or that you can never argue for your stand with strong feeling. Objectivity does not rule out emotion. It does, however, require that you back up your stand with more than emotion.

Every article that you read will not be equally useful. As we mentioned above, even "factual" information can be disputed, and an opinion is not automatically valid because the author cites facts to back it up. Facts can be irrelevant or interpreted in a biased way.

While opinions of various writers will make up the bulk of what you read, some opinions are more useful than others for several reasons:

1. One person expressing an opinion might be more qualified than another.
2. The quality of the opinions, as well as the facts and analysis that back them up, may differ widely.
3. The conclusions drawn from an opinion may or may not be warranted.

Many arguments based on opinion have a strong emotional content. This does not disqualify them as long as the emotion is not the only reason for the argument. As a reader you must be able to determine whether the argument you are reading is as strong as the emotion the author is evoking. You must see whether the facts and analysis really support the conclusion and whether the action advocated will have desirable consequences.

Following are analyses of three letters written to discuss whether the military really needs Kaho'olawe. The first is in favor of the military's need, and the other two dispute that need. The discussion should help you with your critical thinking by pointing out some questions to think about in assessing particular articles.

First read the article (actually a letter to the editor) written by Dick Daugherty who is a major in the Marine Corps (Article 14, "Isle Needed for Training Says Marine"). Daugherty begins reasonably: He says that the opinion expressed by a Mr. Greenstein—that we do not need training on Kaho'olawe because we are not now at war—is wrong. He compares the training of combat pilots to that of plumbers, making the point (presenting the fact) that plumbers and pilots need training before an emergency demands that they put the training into practice. He ends by saying that we were "not at war on the early morning of December 7, 1941," when Pearl Harbor was attacked. Daugherty is clearly edging toward an emotional appeal based on the Pearl Harbor attack—which is permissible. But the next paragraph in the article needs to be looked at skeptically for a number of reasons. Daugherty says:

> If some day in the future a young Hawaiian mother should approach you, seriously wounded herself and with her dead babe in her arms, the result of an attack by an enemy such as on December 7, 1941 and ask you, "Why? Why did this happen? You were part of a driving force which resulted in our military having no place to adequately train, to prepare to defend us against an enemy. Why?" What would be your answer to this young Hawaiian mother?

Aside from his dramatic use of emotion, Daugherty here makes no attempt to establish, either by fact or by opinion based on fact, that Kaho'olawe really is the only place where the military can "adequately train." Thus, the reasonable line of argument that plumbers and pilots need training is not followed by an equally reasonable attempt to show that pilots need training *on Kaho'olawe*. Instead Daugherty evokes an emotional picture of a wounded mother and child, and that seems to be the end of his argument. After this, all the opponents of training on

Kaho'olawe are dismissed as dangerous pacifists. Some of the writers who argue that the military should give up Kaho'olawe are antimilitary, but some of them are not. They simply say that this island is not necessary for training. Daugherty's argument, then, sidesteps the issue of how much the military really needs Kaho'olawe.

In the article (again a letter to the editor) "Reply to Daugherty" (Article 16), Charles Kim makes the two points that (1) Hawai'i is threatened by military attack, rather than protected by it, because of the military presence, and (2) the type of practice done on Kaho'olawe cannot help defend Hawai'i. Both of these have some merit. It's pretty hard to argue against the first one. However, the second point, though it is not a bad refutation of Daugherty, does not refute the argument that the military needs Kaho'olawe for training any more than Daugherty's established that need.

Kim says: "I have never heard of a Phantom jet shooting down an ICBM Missile," and thus, "training on Kahoolawe cannot help defend Hawaii against modern weapons." However, the military does not justify training on Kaho'olawe as a means of protecting Hawai'i as much as it does on the general assumption that military pilots need practice. They are concerned with general military readiness, not the protection of Hawai'i as such. Thus, valid as Kim's argument may be from the Hawaiian viewpoint, it does not speak to the immediate issue of using Kaho'olawe. If Kim wanted to argue for the larger proposition that the military should leave Hawai'i totally and go somewhere else, not only to practice but also to live and work, his argument might have more force.

Kim's two arguments point up the difficulty of distinguishing absolutely between fact and opinion. They both seem to be facts because they relate to an "objective" situation, the presence of the military on Hawai'i. However, consider his first argument, that Hawai'i is threatened by attack only because the military is here. That seems to be a reasonable idea; the military's presence was certainly the cause of the attack on Pearl Harbor. However, it is not inconceivable that an enemy might attack a nonmilitary outpost, especially one as isolated as Hawai'i would be if the military were not there. This is not to argue that Kim's point is invalid or that military presence in Hawai'i is necessary but simply to show that the line between fact and opinion can be blurry.

Richard Hamasaki (Article 15), also writing in reply to Daugherty, defends with much emotion the right of Hawaiian activists to protest the destruction of their heritage. He says that "ever since the Hawaiians lost control of their own land and heritage," the greedy hunt for profit has destroyed "the cultural roots that were the basis for the Hawaiians' rich and healthy civilization." He goes on to say that bombing Kaho'olawe "is a direct insult to the native Hawaiians" and that "Kahoolawe is sacred as are so many land areas and religious sites in Western and Far Eastern culture."

If one reads the information about legends of Hawai'i given in the pamphlet put out by the Protect Kaho'olawe 'Ohana (Article 25), it is clear that this argument has merit. (Check also the sentiments expressed in the interview "Behind Bars," Article 21.) Perhaps people with a Western heritage, who are used to thinking of "important" religious sites as being those associated with "world" religions (e.g., Christianity, Buddhism, Judaism, and Islam), may resist such an argument. But one does not have to belong to a religion with ten million believers to feel strongly about sacred places.

Again, such emotion does not disqualify this as a legitimate issue. It is not Daugherty's emotion that makes his argument specious but his using emotion to sidestep the real issue. For Hamasaki, the real issue is destruction of a sacred spot, and it is a legitimate issue. Some writers, particularly Midkiff, as we have seen before, simply say that Kaho'olawe is not an important site in Hawaiian culture or history. If that argument could be established, it would undermine the Hawaiian argument. However, several articles introduce archaeological evidence for ancient establishments on Kaho'olawe.

One of your tasks will be to assess the arguments for and against the historical and cultural value of Kaho'olawe. We have said before that the value of an opinion depends partly on the knowledge and qualification of the person expressing it. Obviously the people who belong to a given culture are the most knowledgeable and qualified spokespersons for it. They will also have the most stake in its being considered legitimate. You will have to keep all of this in mind. In assessing the validity of the cultural question, you will also have to assess whether national defense takes precedence over cultural claims.

As you read each article, try to understand what the author is arguing, but also look at *how* the argument is made. This should help you assess the arguments and also make you more careful as you begin writing your own arguments.

Thesis and Tasks

Having completed the exercises in analyzing the articles, you should now have an idea of the arguments and evidence available for your paper. You will not, of course, use everything in the articles. What you do use will be determined largely by your thesis. A thesis is simply a statement of your stand. Look again at the five possible stands enumerated in the section "Statement of Assignment." These are all stated in the form of theses. You can select one of these theses if you like, or you can write another like them.

Once you have your thesis, you will use it as the basis for organizing the paper and selecting material. Every thesis will present certain tasks that the writer must perform in his paper. For example, recall the possible theses discussed at the beginning of this chapter. Consider the first thesis, that the military should continue to use the island. To establish this, you must do the following tasks:

1. Show that the military does need the island (pro) and that those arguments saying it does not (con) are not valid or not sufficiently strong
2. Show that the arguments for using the island in some other way (con) are not compelling or feasible (pro)
3. Show that the bombing is not destroying valuable historical or cultural treasures (pro) and that arguments to this effect (con) are not valid, or, that at any rate, the military need outweighs cultural arguments (pro)

Analyzing the tasks demanded by a thesis is not the same as making an organization. You could, of course, write this paper in the order of this analysis, but you might not want to do so. You might, for example, want to refute the claims for civilian use, including the cultural claims, before you begin to establish military need. That is essentially the strategy used in Midkiff's article. Or you might want to establish the military need and then use it to refute any other civilian claims.

The second thesis is that the navy should return the island to the Hawaiian people for religious and cultural uses. Here you would have to:

1. Refute the arguments that Kaho'olawe is necessary to the military
2. Refute the ideas that its physical characteristics make it a barren, useless "rock"
3. Strongly support the ideas of religious and cultural use

Suppose you wanted to support a thesis like Lyman's, that Kaho'olawe should be used as a site for agricultural experimentation. What tasks would you have to perform in order to support that thesis? Discuss this with another writer.

Choosing a thesis commits you to certain tasks; your thesis and the material you use to support it help you design an organizational strategy for your paper. The next section discusses organization.

Planning the Organization

Having thought through your thesis and the tasks that it requires you to do, you are ready to begin planning an organizational strategy that will work for your thesis and the material you want to use to support it.

In organization a con/pro paper is like a comparison paper. That is, you have two sets of variables: (1) the con arguments and the pro arguments, and (2) the two or three issues you have decided to write about. Like the comparison paper, the con/pro paper has two basic types of organization. The following chart simplifies this:

Type 1

I. The con arguments
   Physical nature of K.
   Military need
   Cultural arguments
II. The pro arguments
   Nature of K.
   Military need
   Cultural arguments

Type 2

I. Physical nature of K.
   Con
   Pro
II. Military need
   Con
   Pro
III. Cultural arguments
   Con
   Pro

If you look back at the two sample papers given at the beginning of this lesson, you will see that "Reverse Osmosis" is an example of a type 1 paper and "Teacher's Job" is an example of type 2.

A two-level outline of "Reverse Osmosis" would look like this:

Type 1

Thesis: Reverse osmosis is not yet satisfactory

I. Con (arguments showing the advantages of the process)
   A. Portable
   B. Uses little energy
   C. Operates at ordinary room temperatures
II. Pro (arguments showing its drawbacks)
   A. Short membrane life
   B. Flux
   C. Salt rejection

If you look back at "Reverse Osmosis," you will see that it begins with an introductory paragraph giving needed background information and then states the thesis (the last sentence in the first paragraph). Its second paragraph presents the three con arguments (i.e., the reasons for thinking the process is satisfactory): portability, low energy use, and operation at ordinary temperatures. The third paragraph begins with a transition to the pro side ("Even so, several problems remain with this process") and then develops the first problem, the short membrane life. Each of the next two paragraphs discusses one other disadvantage of the process: flux and salt rejection. The final short paragraph acts as a summary and restatement of the thesis.

The essay, "Teacher's Job, Good or Bad?" shows the other organization. Its outline would look like this:

Type 2

Thesis: A teacher's job is important and interesting

I. Is a teacher's job rewarding?
    Con: no
    Pro: yes
II. Is a teacher's job interesting?
    Con: no
    Pro: yes
III. Can a teacher earn a decent living?
    Con: no
    Pro: yes

The paper begins again with an introduction that states the thesis: "I strongly feel that a teacher's job is . . . not only important but also very interesting." The second paragraph introduces issue I: Does a teacher get anything in return for his work? This paragraph presents the con (he does not), and the next paragraph presents the pro (he does). The fourth paragraph begins issue II: Is the teacher's job interesting? This paragraph develops the con (it is not), and the next develops the pro (it is). The sixth paragraph discusses issue III: Can the teacher earn a good living? It details the con, and the next paragraph gives the pro (conditions are improving). The paper ends with a conclusion that reaffirms the thesis.

If you compare these two outlines, you will see one reason why the first essay uses type 1 and the second type 2 organization. Note that the essay about teaching presents the con and the pro of the same major reasons or issues: rewards, interest, and salary of teaching. Therefore the paper lends itself to a direct comparison of cons and pros. However, the major reasons given for the con argument in the paper about reverse osmosis (portability, energy, temperature) are not the same as those given for the pro side (membrane life, flux, salt rejection). It would be difficult here to match con reasons against pro reasons.

Another way of thinking about this is to note that in "Teacher's Job, Good or Bad?" the pro reasons are direct refutations of the con reasons. That is, they present evidence that contradicts or disproves the con. In "Reverse Osmosis" the con reasons are not refuted, but the pro reasons are thought to be equally or more important. Thus, in the teaching paper the writer handles the con reasons by refuting them; in the reverse osmosis paper the writer deals with the con reasons by conceding them and going on to present stronger arguments for (pro) the thesis.

These two types of organization are only the most obvious patterns. You may want to vary or combine the patterns in some other way. In Chapter 8 you will see examples of a variety of organizational strategies. Whatever organization you use, your thesis and materials will determine the ultimate structure of your paper.

Notice on all the sample outlines that the con arguments are given before the pro ones. As we said earlier, this paper is called a con/pro paper because it is usually more effective to present the opposing arguments first and end with your own side. The ending of a paper is a strong position, because readers will often remember the ideas and arguments they read last. However, keep in mind that such "rules" are only guidelines. In the next chapter we will see that good writers can ignore or alter these guidelines for particular purposes.

WRITING ACTIVITY

With another writer, discuss one of the theses given above, or, better still, the thesis you have decided to support. Talk about the advantages of various organizational strategies. There is no one correct way to organize any paper. In fact thinking through several strategies will help you get started on your paper.

Since this paper is a preliminary argument paper meant to illustrate basic ideas about structure, the discussion on thesis and organization has been rather simple and mechanical. When you write a con/pro paper of your own, the process will be generally the same but much more complex and probably a lot less tidy. You will have to struggle to make sense of your own reading and to decide what your own thesis is and how it will be broken down into subarguments. Furthermore, once you have a plan or rough outline, you may not have solved all your organizational problems. As you write, you may alter your plan as you think of new ideas and ways of presenting evidence. Different people write in different ways. Some writers will want to make a more complete plan before they start, while others may prefer to begin writing at an earlier stage. The discussion and advice here about thesis and organization are meant to teach you about a way of thinking, not to detail a rigid plan for writing.

Having read and outlined the material for this paper and thought about several theses and organizational possibilities, you should now be ready to write your own thesis and make an organizational plan. Perhaps you did so as you went through the exercises above. If not, write your thesis now. Decide what tasks the thesis commits you to and what organization might work best for you. Keep in mind that you may alter your plans as you begin to write. Your instructor may have you continue to work collaboratively in the drafting stage of the paper as you did when you analyzed the material. However, whether you work alone or with others on your paper, the following section will give suggestions for making that process manageable.

Writing a Draft: Elements of the Paper

Introduction

An argument paper starts with an introduction; one paragraph will probably be enough for this paper. Most people find that writing a rough introduction helps define the task of the paper. However, you may want to rewrite this introduction, sometimes several times, particularly after the rest of the paper is complete. For now begin your draft by writing a working introduction. Remember that an introduction needs to (1) define the basic issue, (2) present enough background information for your reader to understand the issue, and (3) give a statement of your thesis.

WRITING ACTIVITY

Write a working introduction for yourself. Share this with another writer, or with several. Have them pretend that they know nothing about the subject, and ask them whether your introduction would get them ready to read your paper.

Once you have a working introduction, think of writing the draft in sections, guided by your outline or plan. That is, think about each major part of your outline as a distinct section of your paper that will tell your readers one reason they should consider your thesis. You need to keep your mind on the part of your paper you are writing, but you must also keep your mind (and your reader's mind) on the overall stand of your paper to make it clear at any point what is being argued. The sections below will help you make your emerging paper clear and complete.

Paragraphing

Recall that in Chapter 5 we talked about the importance of paragraphs in an expository paper. Each paragraph in your paper will contribute some specific idea to your argument. It might present a reason to support your stand; it might present a con reason that you will refute; or it might discuss an important bit of evidence. Whatever a paragraph does, it must do *something*, and do it clearly.

Each major point on your outline must have at least one paragraph. Recall how the discussion of the papers "Reverse Osmosis" and "Teacher's Job" showed how the paragraphs in these papers are closely linked to their outlines. In more complex papers each major part of the outline might require several paragraphs. But each paragraph has a purpose that must be made clear to the reader.

A paragraph, then, is not just a random collection of sentences but a coherent unit of the paper that develops one part of the thesis. It is almost like a small paper in itself; it has a thesis, whatever analysis or explanation is necessary, and some evidence to back up the thesis.

However, a good paragraph must be more than a statement and some sentences relating to it. It must come together in a logical way and move from sentence to sentence clearly. The following paragraph illustrates a common problem. It contains a lot of good information about why the military needs the island of Kaho'olawe, but it has no logical structure. It is just a series of sentences, all of which relate to the general question, but none of which follows logically from the others. The effect is a jumble:

> There are several reasons cited for letting the military retain control of Kaho'olawe. First, Weisner stresses the importance of the island as a means to maintain combat readiness. Frank Midkiff suggests that the Soviets have been making great effort on the military buildup and establishing fleet bases in the Pacific. To cope with the increasing threat of war, the navy has to have pilots well trained. Admiral Maurice Weisner also says that Kaho'olawe has the advantage of lying near Pearl Harbor. The navy has tried to find a place with a location as good as Kaho'olawe's but has failed. The third reason is, as Stone says, Kaho'olawe's value is that it costs only about $10,000 a year. Alternative training sites would involve much more expense. Furthermore, as Bunky Bakutis points out, the visibility of the island makes it an ideal bombing target. There is another important thing that should be mentioned. Admiral T. B. Hayward, Pacific fleet commander, points out that Kaho'olawe is the only place within any reasonable range where the military can do training with combined forces (ground, sea, air). The only other possible site for this is San Clemente Island in California, and even there training is restricted by "environmental restrictions." Also Stone points out that Lind included Air Force and Air Guard flying time that is unrelated to Kaho'olawe when he said that total target training time was not large. That is obviously wrong.

This paragraph dumps together every military argument the writer can think of but gives no context to explain how they relate to each other. Someone who was not already familiar with the material you have read would not be able to make sense out of all these arguments. For example, the reference to Lind and Air Force flying time would be a complete mystery to the average reader. A paragraph must do more than spew out facts. It builds a context in which the facts and opinions make sense and lead toward a clear conclusion.

The following paragraph illustrates an argument that is built up carefully with bits of evidence that come together into a unified whole.

> Frank F. Midkiff paints a bleak picture of Kaho'olawe's potential, relying heavily on one passage from Kamakau's book, <u>Ruling Chiefs of Hawaii.</u> This passage states that the island was a penal colony and that prisoners sent there had to swim to other islands to steal food. However, this passage says nothing about the history of the island before or after this time. MacDonald's history indicates that this period lasted only from 1830 to 1843. The pamphlet <u>Aloha 'Aina</u> states

that Kaho'olawe "was continuously inhabited from approximately 1000 A.D. to 1941" and indicates that even while convicts were living there, "local residents refused to leave" the island. Further, the same source says that "Hawaiians fished, farmed and lived in coastal and interior settlements across the entire island." In more recent times, Inez McPhee Ashdown, whose father started a ranch on Kaho'olawe in 1917, states: "The hundreds of pounds of Australian salt bush, pili and maninia grass and red-top seeds we planted thrived wonderfully," and adds, "I could show photos to prove that the island was . . . covered with verdure . . . ." The inhabitability of the island is certainly attested to by the multitude of archaeological sites found in 1977 by a state historical site study team, one of whose members said, "For a little island we weren't expecting to find much on, it's completely flabbergasted us" (Bakutis, "Little Island"). This expedition and other surveys have led to the island being placed on the National Register of Historic Places. Clearly Midkiff's conclusion from the Kamakau quote is hasty and unfounded.

WRITING ACTIVITY

You have written a working introduction for your paper. Now, working from your outline, try to write the second paragraph. Remember, this must begin to develop the first major reason for your stand. Begin by writing a sentence that lets your reader know what you are doing. Then, using the orthodox strategy, write about the first con argument for this first major part of your paper. Will you now attempt to refute this con, or move on to another argument? Will this require another paragraph? More?

Now try to write another version of the beginning of your paper. Vary it. You might experiment with presenting the pro arguments for your first reason before the con, or you could try using a different organization. How would you have to change the first sentence of your paragraph? Share these two paragraphs with another writer and discuss the strengths and weaknesses of each.

Read the information given next about coherence and about using borrowed material and apply it to the paragraphs you have written. Then continue to follow your outline, writing your draft a paragraph at a time.

Coherence

Coherence means "holding together." In expository writing we use *coherent* to describe the kind of writing that makes it easy for a reader to move from paragraph to paragraph and from one major idea to another, always knowing what the author is doing. *Coherence* does not necessarily imply simplicity. A complex idea can be argued coherently, and a simple idea can be presented in a totally incoherent manner.

As you begin to write the paragraphs for your paper, and especially when you check your draft, keep in mind that you are writing the paper for someone who has not read the articles. You must not only make your ideas and arguments clear, you must also help your reader follow the thread of your argument. Even someone who has read the articles will not be familiar with your way of using them, so you need to help the reader move with you from paragraph to paragraph and from point to point.

Coherence in your paper begins with a clear statement of the issue and of your thesis in the introduction. After that coherence will depend on clear statements of the major reason in each paragraph and good transitions from one major reason to the next.

One particular problem with clarity and coherence in a con/pro paper is that you are presenting con ideas that you will then either refute or discount. Your reader must be able to distinguish between your ideas and other people's ideas, so that you can later agree with, refute, or modify them. As you begin to analyze the pros and cons of each reason for your stand, write a sentence or two that will keep the reader straight. If you are not careful to let your readers know what you think and when you are refuting someone else's ideas, they will simply think you don't know what you are talking about.

The key to clarity and coherence comes in writing transitional sentences. We have said that each paragraph has a statement, something like a minithesis. Often the statement also acts as a transitional sentence. At other times you might need both a transitional sentence and a statement to introduce the main idea of the paragraph.

Transition sentences often contain certain words that are transitional markers. These might be divided into two types: reverse and forward. The latter type tells the reader that the author is simply moving from one point to another, and the former tells the reader that the author is switching from one idea to another, probably contradictory, idea. In this case, of course, reverse transitions indicate the switch from con to pro arguments.

For example, in the osmosis paper the author uses mainly forward transitions: In the third paragraph, for example, "There are *several* reasons," introduces the con arguments. In the fifth and sixth paragraphs "*another* problem" and "*lastly*" move the reader from point to point. Since this paper follows the type 1 organization, there is only one switch from con to pro and only one reverse transition. This is the first sentence in the fourth paragraph: "Even so, several problems remain with this method." The underlined phrase is an obvious reverse transition; it tells the reader that the author is now ready to present an opposite viewpoint.

Let's see what sort of transitional sentences you might use to help your reader move from point to point in a paper written for the thesis: "The military and the state should both give up Kaho'olawe and return it to the Hawaiian people for religious or cultural uses." Suppose the major points on your outline look something like this:

I. The military use of the island is (A) not necessary and is (B) destructive of Hawaiian cultural values.
II. Far from being a useless rock, Kaho'olawe is and has been an important place in Hawaiian history.
III. Thus the most important use of the island is to protect and enhance its cultural and historical heritage.

Suppose you have written your introduction with its statement of thesis. You are now ready to write about your first reason. Using the most orthodox strategy, you begin by presenting con arguments for IA. You might begin your second paragraph like this:

> I would not argue that using Kaho'olawe as a bombing range should cease if I felt that this would materially affect our national defense. However, despite the navy's arguments to the contrary, I am not convinced that the practice on Kaho'olawe is vital. Perhaps the strongest most detailed argument for the navy is given in a letter to Senator Inouye from Admiral T. B. Hayward. (You would now give a summary of the navy's arguments.)

When you have finished this con presentation, you would be ready to present your own side, showing that the military's arguments are not convincing and that the bombing is destructive. You might begin the next paragraph, where you switch to the pro (still IA) something like this:

> I find the arguments of Hayward and other proponents of the bombing to be self-serving and weak. The truth is that Kaho'olawe is bombed mainly because it is convenient and cheap. (You would now give your evidence for this idea.)

Having completed your arguments that the navy doesn't really need the island, you might switch to your further argument (IB) that the bombing is destructive. This part of your paper might be introduced like this:

> Perhaps the strongest argument of the 'Ohana against military use of Kaho'olawe is that the bombing destroys Hawaiian history and culture. Certainly, the navy claims to protect such sites, but the evidence against their claims is strong. (You would then discuss the evidence pro and con on this issue; this might require one or two paragraphs, depending on your material.)

When you had completed this part of the paper, you would be ready to switch to point II on your outline, that Kaho'olawe is not a minor, barren island. Here you would begin with another transitional sentence. Try to write a sentence or two that would make that transition and give a statement for the next part of the paper.

When you completed the discussion of Kaho'olawe's history (II), you could move to point III (protecting Hawaiian culture) with a sentence something like this:

> Building on the history of Kaho'olawe, and on their knowledge of their own culture, the 'Ohana is already showing that it is quite possible to repossess the island as a place to study and further the Hawaiian heritage.

You would then present the 'Ohana's arguments for their use of the island and whatever you wanted to about their activities.

All of these transitional sentences and statements remind you that both you and your reader should always be aware of what issue you are arguing and why you are presenting this particular discussion and evidence. That is what coherence means.

WRITING ACTIVITY

With another writer, or in a group, look at the first sentence of every paragraph you have written so far. Decide whether that sentence would let your reader know (1) what part of your argument (i.e., what part of your outline) you were working on, and (2) how this paragraph relates to what has gone before. You might read the sentence to another writer and ask her if she could tell you what issue you were writing about and what your stand would be.

Using Borrowed Materials

The foregoing discussion has given you ideas about how to make your paragraphs clear and how to handle the statements and transitions. But paragraphs must do more than present ideas clearly. They must also be convincing. In the first part of this text, writing from concrete details was stressed as the most important element of narrative. Concreteness here is equally important, and it comes from making sure that your reader knows why you argue for the thesis you are presenting. You cannot expect your reader to be convinced or even impressed by your argument if you do not present facts and outside opinions to back up your thesis.

Since you are not personally acquainted with the island of Kaho'olawe, the evidence you use to support your thesis will have to come from other sources. You will be expected to acknowledge the sources of evidence and to use quotation marks whenever you quote. The next section will show you how to do this.

The distinction between borrowed and original material is a tricky one. Obviously it would be absurd to acknowledge every bit of information you have about Kaho'olawe, even though everything you now know about the island was received originally from some source. A rule of thumb might be the following: If the evidence or idea you want to use in your paper is general knowledge and can be found in many sources, you need not acknowledge it. Clearly Kaho'olawe does not have much rain; it has too many goats; it has been used as a target area by the navy since World War II. Such things are general knowledge. However, if you want to use a particular piece of evidence (such as the information from Lt. Commander Scott Stone that Kaho'olawe was used for bombing 285 days and 123 nights in 1979) or a particular suggestion or theory (such as Lyman's suggestion of building a rubber-lined reservoir on the island), you had better acknowledge the source. And it should go without saying, that you never use passages, sentences, or even key words and phrases from *any* author without putting them in quotations. To do so is plagiarism, and plagiarism, whether conscious or unconscious, is a violation of honest scholarship.

The best way to avoid the careless or dishonest use of borrowed material is to be aware of ways in which you can use other people's ideas and words honestly and carefully. Basically, there are three methods:

1. *Direct quotation.* It is not a good idea to fill your entire paper with quotations, but sometimes you will want to quote a passage—maybe a sentence or two; maybe a whole paragraph—to back up a key point. When you quote directly, you must observe this important rule: A quote must be exact, word for word. You may not change anything, add anything (without enclosing it in brackets ([ ]), which indicate that the material is not in the original), or subtract anything (without using the ellipsis (. . .), which is a universal symbol indicating omission). Following is a direct quotation from Midkiff's article:

> The important reference from Kamakau . . . shows that although all the other islands except Kahoolawe and parts of Lanai were occupied and capable of producing crops and food, Kahoolawe never had any permanent inhabitants. The fact that all the other islands were heavily populated, often to the extent of interisland and intervalley warfare for food, indicates that the Hawaiians must have made conscientious and even desperate efforts to convert Kahoolawe into a place of human habitation.
>
> However, it's clear that these efforts never were successful. It is probable that during short periods, when the first settlers landed in Kahoolawe, they may have erected their temples or heiaus. Ruins of these would still be found in a few places on Kahoolawe. Ruins of the fishing heiaus are found

in various places, but this makes no substantial comparison of Kahoolawe with the islands that were capable of sustaining human population.

Note that the quotation is indented and single-spaced and does not have quotation marks around it. This is the rule for a quotation that would take up more than three lines in the text. If a quotation is less than three lines, it is enclosed in quotation marks and incorporated right into the sentences of the article. It is not set off in a block, but it must also be introduced so that the reader knows its source.

A direct quotation has the advantage of using the author's exact words and thus making his idea unmistakably clear. However, it has the disadvantage of being long and perhaps including some material that is irrelevant for your purposes. If you want to give only a rough idea of an author's thoughts in a short space, you might want to use the next method of presenting borrowed material.

2. *Complete paraphrase.* As its name implies, you put the author's ideas *entirely* into your own words. You do not use any of his sentences, phrases, etc. The following is a complete paraphrase of Midkiff's quotation:

> Quoting from Kamakau's book, Mr. Midkiff shows that, although attempts were made to inhabit Kahoʻolawe, none were ever permanently successful. He further states that since the pressure of population was heavy throughout ancient Hawaiʻi, such efforts must have been made. He indicates that the ruins that remain are remnants of such efforts.

The obvious advantage of the complete paraphrase is its brevity. Note that it gives Midkiff credit for his ideas and does not carelessly mix Midkiff's words and the writer's.

3. *Partial paraphrase.* The third method of using borrowed material is a compromise between the other two and has some of the advantages of each. It is shorter than the original quotation, because it paraphrases or omits ideas that are not relevant, but it retains important words and phrases from the original quote. Compare the partial paraphrase of Midkiff's passage, given below, with the original quotation:

> According to Midkiff, the quote from Kamakau's book proves that "Kahoolawe never had any permanent inhabitants." Midkiff states that the other Hawaiian islands were "heavily populated, often to the extent of interisland and intervalley warfare for food," and concludes that the Hawaiians probably "made conscientious and even desperate efforts" to settle Kahoʻolawe. He says that the ruins found on the island today are the results of

these efforts, "but this makes no substantial comparison of Kahoolawe" with the other inhabitable islands.

The partial paraphrase is perhaps the most useful tool for using borrowed material because of its flexibility. If you observe the following rule, you will be assured that you are using your material effectively and honestly: In a partial paraphrase, *when you paraphrase, do so completely; when you quote, do so exactly, and enclose the quoted words in quotation marks.*

As a final warning against the careless use of borrowed material, I include a passage that might be called the lazy writer's paraphrase. *Never use any borrowed material in this way.* Note how Midkiff's words are thrown into the writer's paragraph with no indication of where they came from, and no attention to accuracy. The whole passage is a careless muddle that adds up to plagiarism. Compare the passage with the original quotation.

> The important reference from Kamakau shows that all the other islands were occupied and could produce crops and food, but Kaho'olawe alone never had any permanent inhabitants, even though population pressure was such in old Hawai'i that the Hawaiians fought interisland and intervalley wars over food. This must surely show that they made conscious and desperate efforts to convert Kaho'olawe into a place for human habitation. Thus the ruins that are still found on Kaho'olawe come from these efforts, but we should not, thus, make substantial comparison of Kaho'olawe with the other islands in Hawai'i that were capable of sustaining human settlements.

One final word on quoting and paraphrasing: When you omit words from quotations, or paraphrase completely or partially, be scrupulously careful to retain the author's ideas and attitudes intact. In other words, *never make anyone seem to be saying something that he or she did not say.*

WRITING ACTIVITY

The following three examples show ways in which inexperienced writers sometimes become careless in using borrowed material. Study them carefully, correcting them where appropriate.

The first example shows careless quoting and paraphrasing. Following it is a reference to the original source, an analysis of what is incorrect, and a corrected version that shows how the material might have been handled more carefully. Turn to the article from which the passage is taken and compare it first with the careless, and then with the correct, passage. Your instructor may have you do this with another writer or in a group.

Example A

> Richard Lyman, Jr., who first made lava produce crops, agrees
> that parts of Kaho'olawe can be used agriculturally. "Old fashioned
> methods of farming should be used," he continued. "You can't just
> plant a tree, walk away, and expect it to grow big and healthy. That
> will never happen. They must be tended to like children."

This passage is taken from Altonn's interview with Richard Lyman (Article 18).
It first refers to the first paragraph of the article and then cites ideas from the 18th
paragraph. The problem is that the so-called "quote" in the last sentence is primarily a careless paraphrase and not Lyman's words at all. The material should have
been handled like this:

> Richard Lyman, Jr., who first made lava produce crops, agrees
> that parts of Kaho'olawe can be used agriculturally if "old-fashioned"
> farming methods are used. He contends that certain trees could grow
> on the island, but that "they must be tended like children."

Example B

> One member of the team says that though the navy did establish a
> conservation area on the summit of the island and the summit does
> have the most rainfall, it also is the "hottest place on the island. If the
> Navy had planted trees in the ravines where most of the vegetation
> grew, they would find that parts of Kahoolawe take well to agriculture
> despite the natural forces against it."

This material is taken from Bakutis' article (Article 9). Again, the problem is
careless quoting. In the first place, the ideas come from Bakutis himself, the author
of the article, so why not simply cite him instead of "one member of the team"? Secondly, the long "quote" is again partially a quote and partially a paraphrase. Bakutis
never really said that the trees would have grown well if planted in the ravines, he
merely implied that. It is well to make such distinctions clear. Write a version of
this paragraph that clears up these problems and creates a more honest representa-
tion of the idea. Work with another writer if you like, or compare your version
with hers.

Example C

> "One member of a state study team said that the waters surrounding
> Kaho'olawe are in pristine condition: water and reef areas are crystal
> clear with ocean colors varying from deep blue to light green in the
> shallows—just like what existed in the days of old Hawaii."

Find this "quotation" in the Bakutis article and define what is wrong with this
use of the material. Did one person say all of this? Where is the material found in

the article? Write a more exact version of the material. Work with other writers on this.

The following paragraph shows a careful and clear handling of borrowed material from a paragraph in a student paper. Obviously this paragraph is part of the discussion of military need. The material, which presents the con and pro of some key arguments, is taken from three different articles but is integrated into the structure of the student's paper and is handled correctly. Quotation marks are put where they are needed and quotes are exact. Everything is introduced so that it is clear whose material is whose, and sources are given where necessary.

> Ian Lind charges that the military "made no serious search for an alternative to Kahoolawe, that the Island plays a small role in the total military training picture, and that superior training facilities are available" in Nevada, Arizona, and California, where they use "multi-million-dollar sophisticated electronic warfare test ranges" (Nelson). However, Admiral Maurice Weisner, commander of the American military in the Pacific, refutes all of these claims. He indicates that Kahoolawe is vital "as a means to maintain combat readiness of the military." He also says that the military has searched for alternatives and cannot find any, and that the Island's importance for military practice is shown in the fact that it is used "almost on a daily basis" for target practice (Tong). Admiral T. B. Hayward, Pacific Fleet Commander, adds even stronger refutation when he indicated that "131 islands in the Pacific have been examined and rejected as possible alternative sites." He also indicated that Kaho'olawe's real importance in training is in "Marines' combined arms training," and that it "is the only place in the mid-Pacific area where surface ships can practice naval gunfire support." Admiral Hayward indicated that transferring such training operations outside the mid-Pacific region would be costly (Kakesako).

Giving Credit for Borrowed Material

Note that the last sample paragraph enclosed in parentheses (following the evidence cited) the last name of the author of the article in which the evidence appeared. This practice is called "parenthetical citation," and it is how you will be expected to give credit for the evidence you use in your paper. Parenthetical citations take the place of the traditional footnotes or end notes in much current scholarship. To use this type of citation, you simply put the author's last name and a page number in parentheses after the quotation, partial paraphrase, or complete paraphrase. The page number is not given in the samples above, but you should do so—for example (Midkiff, p. 322)—using the pages on which the material occurs in the Appendix of this text. Of course, many of the newspaper articles you will use in this paper do not have an author's name. In this case, you put in the parentheses a short form of the title, such as ("Bomb Ban" 316) for Article 4.

At the end of your paper, you include a page titled List of Sources Cited, on which you list all the sources you have cited in alphabetical order according to the author's last name, or the first word of the title where there is no author. After the number of each of the articles in the Appendix you will find a citation giving author, title, place of publication (usually a newspaper), date, and page number. These entries show you how to list the items in your list of sources. Be sure you copy these citations exactly as you find them.

In Chapter 8 we will discuss this method of giving credit for sources in a paper in more detail. For now simply use the form given here unless your instructor tells you otherwise.

Keeping in mind everything that we have discussed—the need of your reader for clarity and the need of your argument for support—continue to write your paper from your outline or plan until you have a complete first draft. Then begin your revision as usual. Your instructor may have you share the draft at this point with other writers—always a good thing to do at this stage whether it is required or not. If you have been collaborating with another writer or a group, you might like to share now with other writers. Some suggestions for getting peer response are given after the next section.

Reworking the Draft

Since a con/pro paper depends both on an overall argument and on small arguments within each paragraph, a good revision strategy is to look at overall structure first and then examine each paragraph. This section shows you how to do both.

When you have finished your draft, read through it carefully. As you read your paper, keep in mind that you are writing for a reader who has not read your source material and who is probably not familiar with the situation on Kaho'olawe, certainly not as familiar as you are. Thus you cannot merely cite random facts and ideas. You must tell your reader what the facts show and how the ideas are related. As has been indicated in the sections on organization and paragraphing, you must have a logical order to your discussion, and your "voice" must lead the reader from point to point in the paper. Your paragraphs are the key to clarity in your argument, and the transitions and statements for the paragraphs are keys to clarity of the paragraph.

Stage One

You can give your paper a first rough test for clarity in the following way: Go through it (or have someone else go through it) by reading only the introduction, the first sentence or two of each paragraph, and the conclusion. Would it be possible for a reader who is not familiar with your material to get a good idea of your thesis and your main arguments from such a reading? If not, the paper may have basic structural problems. Look, for example, at the following paper. Try going through it first in the way we have just suggested: Read the introduction (paragraph 1), the first sentence or two of each paragraph, and the conclusion (paragraph 8).

Kahoʻolawe is an island located in the Pacific Ocean which is part of the Hawaiian Chain. For many years this island has been used primarily by the military for training purposes. But for a few years there has been some controversy among Hawaiʻi residents and the military over the use of Kahoʻolawe. I think that the military and the state should make a compromise over the island so that both sides will benefit from it. 1

According to Harold T. Stearns "no developable ground water exists in Kahoolawe." Because of the lack of water supply there, no development or habitation of any kind can be possible. As evidence, the navy and state experimented by fencing an area and planting trees. But as a result, the trees have either died or grown very poorly. The navy has tried to keep the goats from multiplying but despite their efforts, the goats are uncontrollable. But Bunky Bakutis, an <u>Advertiser</u> staff writer, says that the military can put fences around the planted trees to keep goats out and plant trees in areas with the most rainfall. Another suggestion made by Richard Lyman, Jr., president of Bishop Estate Board of Trustees, says that we could rehabilitate the land for lab use. These undeveloped and uninhabited areas therefore are excellent for the military to use for training purposes. But the military doesn't use the whole island and they don't use it very often. David Tong, an <u>Advertiser</u> staff writer, says that they bomb the island only 285 days and 123 nights in a year. 2

Stearns points out that to clean up the island to make certain areas safe will not cost much. 3

On Kahoʻolawe is Smugglers Cove, which is an ideal place for civilians to engage in recreational activities such as "picnicking, fishing and camping." 4

Because of its location Stearns says that it is an advantage to the military that it is close to Pearl Harbor until another convenient location can be found. Since the location is so convenient, Lt. Cmdr. Scott Stone of the US Third Fleet says that the pilots can practice daily, and Midkiff says 5 that we need the security against the Soviets. But Lind says that the military haven't looked for any other sites and that they could find a better place elsewhere.

According to Noa Emmett Aluli, a member of the Protect Kaho'olawe 'Ohana, there is evidence indicating historical sites where the military have been bombing, such as fishing heiaus and temples. Evidence includes basaltic glass tools, shells used to prepare seafood, and cave dwellings. There is also other evidence that there was a population as dense as the island of Lanai and that sweet potatoes once grew there.   6

Despite these possibilities, it's impossible to grow crops there because of the lack of water mentioned earlier. There were no permanent inhabitants because long ago when prisoners were sent to this island, they starved to death.   7

Although it is very clear that both the military and the state can use the island, it would be senseless for the island to be used strictly for the military or for the civilians. Instead, both parties should make a compromise in sharing Kaho'olawe so that both will benefit from it.   8

The introduction here is sketchy and does not set up the gist of the issue for the reader, although it does give a thesis in the last sentence: The two parties contending for control of the island should come to a compromise. The first two sentences of paragraph 2 state the first reason for the stand: lack of possibilities for development because of lack of water. This is still reasonably clear, though putting the second sentence first might help.

Paragraph 3 is only one sentence and would be incomprehensible to someone who had not read the Stearns article. Moreover, it does not seem to relate in any way to the introduction. Paragraph 4 makes another seemingly unrelated comment about a bay. Paragraph 5 introduces the military, paragraph 6 introduces the historic sites, and paragraph 7 goes back to the lack of water. None of the first sentences in these paragraphs really tells how any of this relates to the thesis.

Paragraph 8 restates the thesis, which seems to have been lost in the other paragraphs. It seems that the paragraphs in between the first and the last belong to another discussion. Thus, even a quick scanning of the beginning of each paragraph in this paper shows that it has serious problems.

By contrast the following sketch of the paper favoring the 'Ohana's arguments, which we outlined in the coherence section, lets you know exactly what the argument is even though it includes only the introduction (paragraph 1) and conclusion (paragraph 7) and the first sentence or two of each paragraph. From reading only this much of the paper, you could reconstruct the organization.

When most people think of Hawai'i, they picture white sand beaches   1
covered with suntanning visitors set against high-rise hotels. However,
the island of Kaho'olawe, though it is one of the eight main islands of the
chain, presents an entirely different picture. Instead of manicured lawns,
there is barren lava; instead of swimming pools, the island is marked
with craters caused by bombing. Since World War II, this island has been
the site of target and bombing practice and has been under the control of
the United States Navy. For many native Hawaiians, whose beliefs hold
that all the Hawaiian land is sacred, this situation is intolerable. Since the
early seventies a group known as the Protect Kaho'olawe 'Ohana has been
trying to get the military to return the island. They have met with some
success, since they are now allowed access to the island for certain periods each year. Because of this access, they have come to realize that
Kaho'olawe is full of religious and historical sites in better shape than
almost anywhere else on the islands. Thus, for them, the island has
become a key to rebuilding the future of their people. The military is
reluctant to return the island to the state, citing their need for a training
ground for troops stationed at Pearl Harbor and other bases on Oahu.
However, I feel that the arguments of the Native Hawaiians are more compelling than those of the navy—that their need is greater. I thus favor the
ultimate return of the island, not to the state of Hawai'i, except perhaps
temporarily, but to the Hawaiian people.

I would not argue that using Kaho'olawe as a bombing range should   2
cease if I felt that this would materially affect our national defense. However, despite the navy arguments to the contrary, I am not convinced that
the practice on Kaho'olawe is vital. Perhaps the strongest most detailed
argument for the navy is given in a letter to Senator Inouye from Admiral
T. B. Hayward.

I find the arguments of Hayward and other proponents of the bomb-   3
ing to be self-serving and weak. The truth is that Kaho'olawe is bombed
mainly because it is convenient and cheap.

Perhaps the strongest argument of the 'Ohana against military use of   4
Kaho'olawe is that the bombing destroys Hawaiian history and culture.
Certainly, the navy claims to protect such sites, but the evidence against
their claims is strong.

More important than any specific destruction of particular sites,   5
however, is the feeling among 'Ohana members that the bombing itself,
the very dedication of this island to destruction and war, violates a basic
religious and cultural feeling that they express in the term "Aloha 'Āina."
This implies a relationship to the land that precludes using it in a
destructive way.

Building on the history of Kaho'olawe, and on their knowledge of   6
their own culture, the 'Ohana is already showing that it is quite possible

to repossess the island as a place to study and further the Hawaiian heritage. This is something that proponents of military use of the island have claimed to be impossible.

In the final analysis, this clash between the 'Ohana and the military   7
cannot be mediated, because it represents a basic conflict of values. Since the military will not stand or fall on its use of Kaho'olawe, I favor the Hawaiian values here. The island is, for the Native Hawaiians, a unique resource. It cannot be duplicated anyplace else on earth for any amount of money. The military might be inconvenienced by not having access for training, but the same cannot be said of them. Kaho'olawe is, after all, part of Hawai'i, part of the heritage of its people. To continue to desecrate it is unconscionable. George Helm, who lost his life in an early occupation of the island, summed it up in this way: "I have my thoughts, you have your thoughts, simple for me, difficult for you. Simply . . . the reason is . . . I am Hawaiian and I've inherited the soul of my <u>kupuna</u>. It is my moral responsibility to attempt an ending to this desecration of our sacred <u>'āina, Kohe Malamalama o Kanaloa</u>. . . . What is national defense when what is being destroyed is the very thing the military is entrusted to defend, the sacred land of (<u>Hawai'i</u>) America?''

Considering only the overall structure, this paper is much clearer than the first one. Each sentence that begins a paragraph introduces a specific issue in such a way that the reader knows what to expect.

W R I T I N G   A C T I V I T Y

Begin your revision by going through your own paper this way, or have another writer do this. Discuss where the reader would have trouble following your argument as indicated by this first rough test. Do you need to combine paragraphs? Break them apart? Do you need clearer transitions and statements for the paragraphs?

Stage Two

After a quick look through the whole paper, the next step in revision is to read each paragraph separately to see if it is clearly developing part of the overall argument. Even when the overall paper is clear, individual paragraphs may still need work.

A more thorough reading of the first paper discussed above only strengthens the impression that it has serious problems. The second paragraph does have a reasonably clear statement, and its first half seems to relate to the idea of development (though someone who had not read the articles might have trouble understanding the talk about goats and fences and "areas with the most rainfall"). However, starting with, "These undeveloped and uninhabited areas," the paragraph goes in an entirely new and incomprehensible direction. Having read all the Kaho'olawe articles, you know where the information comes from, but a reader fresh to the subject would be totally lost. The next two little paragraphs (3 and 4) would be equally confusing.

All the material in paragraph 5 relates to military use, but with the mention of Lind it switches without warning from arguments favorable to the military to those against the military—a switch readers would find hard to follow.

Paragraphs 6 and 7 give the arguments for, and then against, historical value of the island. Although these arguments are a bit clearer than some of the others, there is not much help for the reader in understanding why this particular evidence is being used. All in all the paper gives the impression that the writer had some general idea of discussing the issues of development, military need, and cultural value but has given very little thought to helping a reader understand the issues. This is a very early draft. It needs a lot of revision.

WRITING ACTIVITY

The first task this writer needs to concentrate on is sorting out the material, including sorting out for the reader the pros and cons of the major reasons for the stand. Most important, the writer needs to show how all this material relates to the thesis. Discuss this paper with another writer and make some suggestions about sorting out the material. (Where should ideas be put into different paragraphs? Can any of these paragraphs be combined?) Try writing some new statements for either existing paragraphs or new paragraphs that could be made by combining existing ones.

Sometimes paragraphs from your first draft might need more than expansion or rewriting for clarity. Sometimes they need basic revisions in structure. The following excerpt illustrates that problem:

> I have no objection to strengthening the military force, yet I wonder if Kaho'olawe is so vital to that work. Firstly, we know in the modern age of warfare, Hawai'i is not locally defendable. An enemy would send a superior force to occupy the island or send a few nuclear missiles to Pearl Harbor. So, simply, the bombing training cannot cope with modern weapons.
>
> Secondly, according to Lind's argument, Kaho'olawe is an outmoded target compared with the "multi-million-dollar sophisticated"

ranges the military has constructed in Nevada, Arizona, and
California.

Thirdly, the investigation made on the island has presented it to
be one of the best preserved remnants of old Hawai'i. Up to now, sixteen historical sites have been found. Obviously bombing the island
does not at all help to preserve the historical remains but destroys
them.

Fourthly, military action on the island goes against the native
people's belief. As Mr. Hamasaki says, "The bombing of Kahoolawe is
a direct insult to the native Hawaiians who have always revered and
worshipped land—how sacred and precious it is amidst the watery
Pacific. To many Hawaiians, Kahoolawe is sacred as are so many land
areas and religious sites in Western and Far Eastern cultures." This is
reinforced in the following quotation from a pamphlet put out by the
Protect Kaho'olawe 'Ohana: "<u>Aloha 'Āina</u> is a traditional concept that
lays the foundation for Hawaiian religion, culture and lifestyle.
<u>Aloha</u> means love, and <u>'āina</u> means land. The two words together
express several levels of meaning. At the deepest level the presence of
our ancestors and gods of the land are acknowledged, respected and
cherished, through ceremonies both public and private" ("Kaho'olawe
and the PKO").

These four paragraphs actually present two arguments, and the paragraphing
and transitions should show this:

first: The military doesn't need the island because the training is not relevant
to modern warfare and better training facilities exist elsewhere

second: The military is destroying cultural relics and going against the religious
feelings of the Hawaiians.

The first two paragraphs should be grouped into one with a transition to show
their relationship. The statement that Hawai'i is not locally defendable needs to be
explained and supported more effectively. Likewise, the last two paragraphs need
to be grouped into one with a transition like: "Not only can we question
Kaho'olawe's importance to the military, but we can also make a stronger point:
The military is harming Kaho'olawe and, through it, the people of Hawai'i." The
statement that Kaho'olawe is "one of the best preserved remnants of old Hawaii"
needs to be recognized as a quotation, needs to be cited as such, and needs a context to make it more convincing.

Argument and Evidence

Besides checking the overall structure of the paper and examining each paragraph for clarity, you must also be looking at the quality of the argument and

evidence presented. The following paragraph is well structured and generally very clearly written, but it has problems with the argument:

> The navy has often said that they wish to keep the island of Kaho'olawe because it is the best place they can find to train their aviators. They have told state officials that they have looked for another site to practice, but there were no adequate facilities to be found. The point that the navy does not emphasize is that they have limited their search to the area only about 200 nautical miles away from their base in Pearl Harbor. It has been said that the navy does not want to give up the use of the island only because it is cheaper for them to maintain the island of Kaho'olawe than to move and set up at other sites that have been recommended. It is not necessarily true that the island is the only place for the military to maintain "combat readiness" or that the island is the only adequate place because of its advantage of being located near its base. If the navy would extend their search and pay a little more money, they could in turn find an adequate alternative site.

The problems in this paragraph relate to use of material and to the quality of analysis. The reader could follow this paragraph quite easily. However, the writer here, intentionally or unintentionally, has made her sources seem to be saying something they have not said. She says the "navy does not emphasize" that they looked within 200 miles of Pearl Harbor, but, in fact, it was a naval man, Commander Stone, who made that very statement. In the next sentence, the writer says, "It has been said that the navy does not want to give up the use of the island only because it is cheaper. . . ." Again it was Stone who indicated that the island was cheap, but a reader might get the impression that this was said by someone else as a criticism of the navy. Thus the writer has been somewhat careless in handling material.

From the point of view of argument, the paragraph shows an even more serious weakness: The argument for the military is stronger than the argument for the author's stand. She presents all the navy's arguments and then ends with the weak assertion that the navy could find a site if it looked. The paragraph below shows how a stronger and more accurate argument could be developed from the same material:

> The island is not necessarily the "best" site. Even Commander Stone cannot deny that with the use of "electronic simulators or targets," Kaho'olawe would not be needed. Ian Lind, who represents the American Friends Service Committee, points out that such facilities already exist, in Nevada, Arizona, and California (Nelson). It would be more reasonable to use the established facilities, and this would counter Stone's objection that it would be expensive to "duplicate"

the facilities here. Lind also shows that the navy's search was inadequate. The navy implied that a site that could replace Kahoʻolawe would have to be "within 200 nautical miles of Pearl Harbor," but he says that Culebra, an island in the Atlantic that was formerly used as a bombing target, is 1,310 nautical miles from the Atlantic headquarters. Further, Lind points out that although the navy once insisted that they could not do without that island, they are still operating in the Atlantic even though that site is no longer used for training. Stone doesn't help his case any when he admits that the Marines stationed in Okinawa sometimes train in the Philippines (Nelson).

Here, the arguments are attributed to their correct source and the writer's contention that the navy could find other sources is backed up both by her further reading and by her own analysis, not merely by assertion. You will recall that the section on analyzing sources told you that you should read all the sources skeptically, looking for the worth of the argument. The same is just as true when you look back at your own writing. Don't let yourself get away with sloppy arguments either.

Following the suggestions given in "Stage Two" and this section, examine each paragraph carefully, filling out, rewriting, and regrouping where necessary. Always keep in mind that your reader has not read your sources and that you must inform and convince him. All of this will strengthen your paper.

These examples demonstrate what we have often shown before in this textbook, that there are different reasons for revision and different ways to do it. Generally it is best to look first at overall structure and ideas, then to examine individual paragraphs, and finally to look at sentences. But revision is not that simple. Some writers revise even as they are writing the first draft. However, by calling attention to what might be called different levels of revision, this section attempts to give a strategy for revising as well as a means for checking a draft. If the strategy works, use it. If not, devise your own, but remember that your paper must work as a whole, and each of its parts must be clear and convincing.

Feedback from Other Writers

Since you are all working with the same material, you can help your peers make their papers more convincing and fully developed. However, you will have to make an effort to put yourselves in the place of readers who are not as familiar with the material to decide whether your papers are clear. Look at each other's papers as you looked at your own: first at overall structure and clarity and then at the clarity and completeness of individual paragraphs.

With a group of other writers, listen to a paper read in the way described earlier: Read only the first paragraph, the first sentence or two of each subsequent paragraph, and the conclusion. (Or trade papers with another writer and read the paper yourself in the way described.) On the basis of this reading, answer the following questions:

1. Do you feel confused at any point in the paper? Where?
2. Write what you take to be the thesis and a two-level outline of the paper showing its major arguments. If you cannot do this based on this quick reading, say so.

Now pick two paragraphs and read them carefully. Answer the following questions for each paragraph:

1. What is the purpose of this paragraph?
2. Does the paragraph have any evidence? Is it enough, and is the quality good enough to be convincing?
3. Look at the borrowed material (quotation, paraphrase, or partial paraphrase). Is it acknowledged? Used carefully and honestly? Worked into the text smoothly?

Finally read (or listen to) the whole paper carefully, and answer the following:

1. Are you still confused at any point? Where?
2. Are you convinced? Where do you need to be convinced more?
3. Do you think any of the paragraphs are in need of editing? Which?
4. What advice would you like to give the writer?

When you have completed this activity, discuss your answers with the other writers. If only one writer has read your paper and if there is time, getting this feedback from another colleague or two would be helpful. Use the feedback as a guide to revising the paper, always remembering that it is *your* paper. Think about what you have learned from this activity and what you saw of your colleagues' papers as you prepare a final draft.

Sentence-level Editing

Chapters 1 and 2 contain exercises to help you look closely at sentences for efficiency and effectiveness. Sentence-level editing is just as important in expository writing. You need to go through your paper one time looking only at your sentences. The best time to do this is after you have revised your paper and made sure that it is clear and well argued.

The following sentences were taken from a paragraph arguing that while Kaho'olawe could not support any development, it could be used for recreational purposes. How could you make this passage more effective? Remember how we have talked about combining sentences, eliminating repetition, and so forth.

The island doesn't have adequate natural water supplies and it is very costly to purify sea water. It is expensive to purify water, but it wouldn't cost much just to purify enough water for drinking instead of irrigation. If the navy would let the public have the right to visit the island there would be no need to produce water other than for drinking.

This paragraph has some of the same problems. How could you make it clearer and more efficient? Could you reduce it to one sentence?

Although there have been maybe 10,000 tons of bombs dropped onto the island, only certain areas have been used as bombing sites, leaving the other areas either clear or with just a small amount of ordnance. That means it wouldn't be costly for the navy or state to dispose of the unexploded ordnance since there are only a few in the areas that would be used by civilians.

Incorporating quotations into your sentences can cause problems with clarity. The quoted words must fit smoothly into your sentences. What is the problem in this sentence?

Lyman says by building "a one-acre, rubber-lined reservoir" will "produce about 500,000 gallons of water."

The writer of that sentence seems to have started another sentence after the quotation. Can you see that you can make a good sentence merely by removing one word? The next example has more serious problems. Rewrite this to make one smooth sentence:

Stearns says areas that can be developed into public recreation areas such as "picnicking, fishing, and camping." For example, Smugglers Cove, Waikahalulu Bay, and Ahupu Bay.

A common problem—working the name of one of the authors smoothly into a sentence—is illustrated here:

According to Farley Watanabe, who is a historic sites specialist for the state says that there is evidence indicating historical sites where the military have been bombing such as fishing shrines and temples but no sign of permanent human habitation.

Can you make a smooth sentence of this?

Finally, the following excerpt shows that inexperienced writers can have problems working paraphrases as well as quotations into their sentences. Work alone or with other writers to make this passage clearer and more efficient. Don't forget that sentences need to be corrrect as well as efficient. Are there any errors in the passage?

The important use of Kahoʻolawe and its proximity near Pearl Harbor makes it an appealing bombing target. It is this training that prepares young American pilots stationed at Pearl Harbor the skills needed during aerial attacks. This training and military presence in the Pacific go together. This presence, freedom to maneuver in the Pacific water and the protection of the American people are all the same thing.

8 *Final Research Project*

Statement of Assignment

The paper you write in this chapter will enable you to use much of what you have learned throughout the text. Most particularly you will adapt the skills learned in writing about Kahoʻolawe to a topic of your own. You will choose a subject that interests you and write a con/pro paper of at least 1000 words, in which you argue for one stand and discuss and refute the arguments for the other side. If you choose a topic that relates to your own experience, you might well include narrative like you wrote in the first part of the book.

Since this chapter will take you through a process similar to that in Chapter 7, you should review the sections there on organizing, writing coherently, and using borrowed material. This chapter will review some of these ideas and deepen your understanding of them by presenting a more complex and challenging context for them. As usual, this chapter presents sample papers showing the variety of subjects, approaches, and organizational strategies possible for con/pro papers.

Getting Started

Choosing a Topic

Your choice of topic is limited only by your knowledge, experience, and interests—and the word limit of the paper. You might want to start with a topic you already know something about. Or you might want to take this opportunity to learn more about something that has always intrigued you. Whether new or old, remember that you must choose a topic about which you can say something significant in 1000 words.

Note especially the last requirement. You must say something significant about your topic. You must have proof or evidence—some reason to show why an intelligent, reasonable person might be inclined to consider your ideas. You must not expect readers to believe something is so simply because you say it is. Along with the usual criterion—to write your paper in such a way that someone who is not familiar with your material will still understand its issues—here you must meet another: You should write this paper in such a way that a person who does not agree with your stand must at least give it respectful consideration.

Writing this paper will require you to make a series of choices about subject, material to collect and use, and argumentative and organizational strategies. The first choice, what subject to write about, may be the most important one. The success of the paper depends on your choosing a topic that interests you, that you can find plenty of fascinating information about, and that is limited enough to handle in the space you have.

One suggestion for limitation is that you pick a topic about which you can read almost everything that has been written, so that you can actually become an expert on the subject. Obviously topics like the war on drugs or abortion are simply out of the question. In five pages you could do nothing more than repeat the most obvious cliches about those topics.

You might, however, choose some specific subtopic related to these, such as whether public funding should be used for abortion, or whether mandatory drug testing of, say, airline pilots is proper or necessary.

Some local topic—an issue in your school, city, or state—might be just about the right size. For example, as I am writing this chapter, students at the University of Hawaii have formed an organization called Students Against Discrimination to convince the administration to move more quickly in hiring women and non-Caucasian faculty members. The university student body is more than 50 percent female and more than 70 percent Asian-American, yet the faculty is only 19 percent female and 25 percent non-Caucasian. Ironically, the least-represented ethnic group on campus (both faculty and students) is Hawaiians. Such a movement in your own university would make an excellent topic for a paper. For example, do you know what policy your school has (if any) on drug testing for athletics? How do women's sports compare to men's in financing, scholarship, and so on?

Looking through today's newspapers, I found the following topics of local interest: a debate on whether the state should develop a mass transit system; protests by Hawaiians who live near Volcano National Park about the development of geothermal power from the volcanos as an alternative to oil-fired electricity; a controversy about whether the state should build a convention center in Honolulu, and if so, where? The advantage of a local issue is that you can use your own knowledge and experience as well as facts from newspaper articles, interviews, official documents, even public meetings.

In the same newspaper, I also found some national issues that might be small enough for a paper like this: controversy about the tapping of Manuel Noriega's telephone conversations from prison; animals rights activists protesting fur coats;

the death of Nancy Cruzan, kept alive only by a feeding tube for eight years (an individual case that would allow you to pose some of the issues involved in the question of "mercy killing," which would otherwise be too broad); boycotts of Arizona for reversing its decision to honor Martin Luther King's birthday; arguments about oil drilling in Alaska's untouched wilderness areas; whether the University of Nevada at Los Vegas should be allowed to play in a bowl game while under suspension by the NCAA.

The daily newspapers and television news are excellent sources for topics. However, you need not deal with a public issue. Very good papers have been written on sports: Should weight lifters use steroids? Who was the better baseball player, Pete Rose or Ty Cobb? Should Rose have been kicked out of baseball for gambling? Other topics that have produced excellent papers include the cons and pros of karate as a means for self-defense, alternatives to the breast-feeding of babies, reparations for the Japanese who were interned during World War II, methods for eradication of fruit flies, survival of dolphins threatened by drag-net fishing. The topic need only lend itself to discussion from more than one point of view.

WRITING ACTIVITY

If you already have a topic in mind, skip this activity. If not, it might set you thinking. Write down one issue (more if you want) that is suggested by each of the following:

1. The subject I know the most about—in fact, I'm even a kind of authority—is . . .
2. Something that has always fascinated me is . . .
3. Something I might like to write about but don't think I know enough about is . . .
4. The thing I know best how to do is . . .
5. If I had to write a paper that would make the reader want to do something, I'd write about . . .
6. If I had to write an essay that would have a reader thinking how intelligent I was and how much I knew about my subject, I'd write about . . .

When you have some issues listed, talk to other writers, telling them what you know already, what you would need to know to write about the topic, where you might go to find out more or answer your questions about the topic. Perhaps they might be able to make some suggestions or tell you something you don't know about the topic.

When you have chosen a topic, you must begin to gather material. Chances are that you will know little about your topic. You might be confused about how you can come to a thesis of your own when so much has already been written. It will be tempting to let one or two of your sources do your thinking for you. However, keep in mind that this is *your* paper. You may not (and probably won't) come up with an idea that no one else has ever thought of. However, your task is to read the material, understand it, digest it, and *make your own sense out of the issue.* That sense will be your thesis. Maybe you'll borrow an analysis from writer A and a solution from writer C, even though you do not agree totally with either. You must think through your issue, considering it from different points of view, weighing whatever evidence you have, digging for more, and making your own conclusions.

Begin by asking a preliminary research question: Should a weight lifter use steroids? What are the dangers to an athlete in using steroids? Is there an alternative to breast-feeding that will give infants what they need? Do the dangers of geothermal power outweigh the advantages of not relying on oil (or vice versa)? Can the skills learned in karate be adapted for self-defense in unstructured conditions? A research question helps you focus your attention as you read and helps you judge what material is relevant.

Keep two things in mind: (1) You may have to do some reading before you can formulate a question, and (2) you may change the question as you begin to read. Maybe some other aspect of the issue will seem more interesting and pressing as you learn more about the topic. Keep your mind open and interested. Don't close your thinking down prematurely. You will have to walk the line between learning all you can about your topic and restricting your attention to save time.

Finding Material

The major written sources for information are newspapers, magazines, scholarly journals, and books. Information from the latter two sources will be more "processed"; information from newspapers will be relatively "raw." Neither source is intrinsically more useful, but each has its advantages.

In a book the author has usually thought through the issues and made her own sense out of her research. In newspapers the information is presented with less analysis and is more immediate. As you read newspapers and popular magazines, you will find contradictory and confusing ideas. Thus one advantage of these "raw" sources is that *you* will have to do the analysis, the *thinking*. And thinking is the major purpose for this paper.

You might want to begin by reading books for background. To find books on your topic look in the card catalog or the on-line catalog in your library. For many topics it may be best to think first of newspapers and magazines. Newspapers have a lot more than news items. They have editorials, columns, and special features. If you are working on a current public issue, opinion magazines like *Nation, National Review,* and *Atlantic* are helpful. If you are doing a topic from a particular area, such as sports or science, look for the many specialized popular or scholarly periodicals in that area.

The keys for unlocking information in newspapers and magazines are the periodical indexes found in the reference section of your library. Many of these are now on-line in various computer data bases. If you have never worked with newspaper and magazine indexes, your instructor can give you guidelines. Your university library will almost certainly have information, aids, even minicourses or orientation programs to help you.

Think beyond books and periodicals to original sources for your paper. For example, most governmental agencies keep minutes or journals on their proceedings. Sometimes you can get copies of these from the organizations concerned, or they might be available in libraries. The U.S. Congress, state legislatures, city councils, and even local school boards hold hearings on most of the proposals that come before them. Testimony from such hearings is usually available, either at the hearings themselves or from the proceedings mentioned above. You should inquire of these public bodies how to obtain such information. Legislation that is passed is published in various sources, such as state criminal and civil codes and local building codes. Your library can also help you locate and use these sources.

Don't overlook nonwritten sources such as television programs, public meetings, and interviews. Transcripts are often available for special programs on television (especially from educational channels). You can attend public meetings and hearings yourself and take notes on them. After the meeting you might even ask key speakers if they have copies of their testimony, or if you can get an exact quote from them.

Finally think of interviews. This often overlooked source can sometimes be the most valuable of all. In the revision section in this chapter, the paper about Kaho'olawe uses one interview extensively. Read that paper and note how much good information comes from this source. The Appendix contains an interview with Kaho'olawe activists who were imprisoned for their activities (Article 21). Reread that interview and others as you think about your own material. Some magazines (*Rolling Stone* is an excellent example) have regular interviews that would serve as good guides for interviewing.

Good interviewing requires that the interviewer know about the subject. If you go unprepared to an interview, you will simply waste your and your subject's time. Some specific guidelines are:

1. Have a purpose for interviewing this particular person and have in mind what information you want. That is, know the aspects of the issue with which this person is most familiar, and tailor your questions to those aspects.

2. Prepare questions in advance, based on the information this person can give, especially if she is the only one who can give it. However, don't be so narrowly focused that you cannot let the interview take on a life of its own. If it begins to go in unexpected directions, let it, at least for a while. If the interview becomes unproductive, it is up to you to get it back on track again.

3. Be prepared to ask follow-up questions if the answers to your original questions are not informative, wander from the point, or seem evasive. Make these questions sharp but not rude, to the point, and interesting.

4. Have information and knowledge that will enable you to ask good follow-up questions and go with the flow of the interview.

Prepare your questions in advance and show them to another writer (or writers), your teacher, or a kind friend. Better still, if a colleague is writing on your topic, or happens to have some knowledge about it, do practice interviews with each other. You may even collect information that will be useful for your paper.

Note Taking

You must take notes from all of your sources. The traditional way to do this is to use note cards—one note to a card, with each card clearly labeled. But some writers use notebooks or the backs of envelopes. Some writers are lucky enough to have portable computers they can use in the library. Notes go in and are printed out later—even sorted, by some programs!

Many inexperienced writers think that the photocopying machine and high-lighters have taken the place of note taking. Photocopiers have certainly changed the way research is done, but copying an article merely makes it more available; it does not digest and select material.

Selecting and digesting are the keys to good note taking. Unfortunately, you are at first faced with a Catch 22. You can't take efficient notes until you have read a good bit of material and begun to define your focus, but you need to take notes from the first so that you won't have to read things twice. Probably the best thing you can do to make note taking as efficient as possible from the beginning is to try to define a research question as soon as possible. This question should help you select what material you might need to take in your notes.

Look at the following information from the *9 to 5 Newsline*, Oct.–Nov. 1990: 1–2.

Average Working Person Faces the Big Squeeze

The U.S. economy grew during the 1980's, but only the richest 10% enjoyed the benefits. While these Americans got richer and paid fewer taxes, the average worker put in longer hours at lower real wages.

The income gap in the U.S. is bigger than it's ever been, bigger than it is in any competitor nation. Consider these facts about the decade:

The average income of working families dropped by $2000. In the same period the income of the richest 1% of Americans nearly doubled.

Real wages for the average worker dropped almost 10% during the 1980's. Families had to work longer hours or put more members to work just to stay at the same level.

While hourly wages in America's largest corporations declined by 5%, executive pay in those companies went up 149%.

One reason for falling wages is the growth in low-paying jobs. One in four American jobs paid poverty level wages in 1979. By 1987, that number was one in three.

Now legislators are debating whether to change the official definition of poverty. Economist Patricia Ruggles recalculated the poverty level using more accurate data—like the real cost of housing. By her count nearly one in four Americans is poor.

For example, a single mother of two who earns $14,000 a year is considered well above the official poverty level of $10,500 for a family of three. By Ruggles' figuring, that same family needs at least $16,685 to stay out of poverty.

Some politicians are calling for a commission to study whether to revise the poverty line. No action is expected soon.

For working families, however, the main issue isn't how to define the poor—it's how to stop the growing inequality in America.

Suppose you read this article to find information on a paper about poverty in the 1980s. If you had not defined the paper any more fully than this, almost everything in this short article would seem relevant. However, suppose you had decided to focus your paper more by asking the question: How should we define the poverty level? Your note taking would immediately become more efficient since the information at the beginning of the article, though interesting and important, would not be as relevant to your paper as the discussion at the end.

Suppose that you instead formulated the working question: What has caused the income gap to widen in the 1980s? The information in the beginning of the article would now be the most relevant. Further, since you would be seeking causes, the most important piece of information for you would be in the paragraph beginning, "One reason for falling wages. . . . " Some of the other information would also be worth taking, because you would need to establish that the wage gap existed before you could begin to ask why. However, the information on establishing a poverty level would not interest you. Thus a research question helps you select what material to take in your notes.

Using the research question will also help you decide how much of the material you need and how to take it down, in short, how to digest the material. Recall from Chapter 7 that borrowed material can be used as a direct quotation, as a partial paraphrase, and as a complete paraphrase. Obviously you will take your notes in one of these three forms. What parts of this article might you want to take as direct quotations, and what as some kind of paraphrase? Different writers might answer this differently. However, some general ideas might be helpful.

Succinct as the article is and interesting as the statistics are, you don't want to put all the information into your paper word for word. If your research question concerns the causes of the wage gap, the vital figures in this article are the comparisons, which you might paraphrase in a note like this:

statistics of gap

Income of working families went down $2000; that of the wealthiest 1% doubled. In the largest corporations working wages dropped 5% while executive salaries grew 149%.

9 to 5, page 1

The other information that would be relevant for your research question is the reason the article gives for the wage gap. A paraphrase might look like this:

reasons for gap

A major reason for drop in income is the growth in poverty level jobs: One in four jobs was poverty level in 1979, one in three in 1987.

9 to 5, page 1

You might want to take this last information down as a quote. You might also want to take down word for word the summary sentence, "The income gap in the U.S. is bigger than it's ever been, bigger than it is in any competitor nation." Another writer might have chosen to quote more or to use partial paraphrases throughout.

Observe that each of these notes has a source given after the information. *Always* put a notation, including the author's last name (and the date if there seem to be several articles by the same author), or a short form of the title and a page number, on every note you take. This will save you hours of backtracking in the library. All the information you use in your paper will need to be referenced, and you will have to provide a bibliography. If you have not taken down information on sources as you gather the information, you will have to find the sources again later on.

WRITING ACTIVITY

To help you become a more efficient note taker, try taking notes (direct quotations, partial paraphrases, and complete paraphrases) on one or two articles you will use for your paper. Show these, along with the original article(s) and your research question, to another writer or group of writers. Explain to them why you chose to take notes on the material you did and why you left some information alone. Also talk about why you chose the form you did (quotation or paraphrase). Your instructor may ask you to show him this work also.

Besides selecting and digesting material for your notes and identifying them clearly, you also need to begin sorting and labeling your notes. Look at the underlined headings on the sample notes above. Most writers give each note a heading or notation so they can tell at a glance what the note is about. As you begin to learn more about your subject, you will begin to define subissues or questions within your issue, just as we did with Kaho'olawe (military need, development possibilities, cultural value). These subissues might become the categories for labels.

You will work out your own most efficient way to take notes as you go. And your note taking will become more efficient as you learn more about your topic and begin to formulate your stand and the reasons for it. Whatever system of note taking you develop, remember these two important things:

1. Be extremely careful and honest. Keep in mind how a quotation differs from a paraphrase and how to make partial paraphrases. Remember: A quotation must be exact. Whenever you take down any quotation, put quotation marks around it. Don't count on remembering later which are your words and which the author's. If you paraphrase, do so completely. The honesty of your paper will depend on careful and honest note taking. If you take notes full of lazy writer's paraphrases, your paper will be made up of lazy writer's paraphrases.

2. Make sure that every note has a source indicated, including a specific page number. Remember that you will have to submit a bibliography with this paper, so get the information on all sources as you take your notes. The usual way to do this is to keep a separate list of your sources that contains all the bibliographic data. For books this includes author or editor (translator, compiler, etc.), complete title, edition, volume, place of publication, publisher, and date. For newspapers and magazines it includes author, title of article, name of publication, volume, date, and inclusive pages.

Analyzing Material

The quality of your paper will depend on the quality of your thinking as you begin to read, conduct interviews, listen, and so forth. Since you will be working with a controversial topic, you will find people arguing, disagreeing on interpretations of facts—even on the facts themselves. You will find many statements of the problem and many solutions. Your most important task in the paper is to make your own sense out of all this conflicting information. You may not come up with a unique analysis or a completely novel solution to a problem, but you must decide what to make out of everything available. What do you judge to be the situation? Why? What do you think should be done or not done? Who do you think was right, if anyone was? Is Ms. A's analysis the correct one, or is it Mr. J's? Are they both wrong? Partially right? We assume that there are more ways than one to look at this issue, but are there more than two ways? Just because we call it a con/pro paper does not mean that there are only two neat sides to the issue.

In other words, you must reconceptualize material gathered from various sources for use with your thesis and your structure. This does not, of course, mean you can do anything you want with the material you find. Everything we said in the last chapter regarding the careful and honest use of borrowed material goes double here. But you will use other people's material for your purposes. You did this in a controlled, maybe almost mechanical, way in your last paper. Here you will be on your own. You must decide what is your basic issue, how that breaks down into subissues, what material you read relates to what part of your paper, and so on. The first step in making such decisions is to read your sources critically and intelligently.

In Chapter 7 we analyzed some of the sources (primarily letters to the editor), noting where the arguments were questionable and where the writers substituted emotion for argument. In working with your material for this paper, such analysis will be vital. This section will consider articles like those you might find in newspapers and magazines. We will talk about how to get meaning and information from such sources, how to look for bias, and most important how to read one source in the light of others.

Every writer, every magazine, every newspaper has an editorial policy, which might be called a slant or even a bias. Some sources are quite open about this. *Ms.* Magazine, for example, has as its avowed purpose the presentation of a feminist point of view on political and social issues. *The Nation* is noted for presenting the liberal slant; *The National Review* has a conservative slant. Some newspapers identify themselves as conservative or liberal, but the majority of American newspapers, as well as the large circulation magazines such as *Time* or *Newsweek*, present themselves as "news" sources whose purpose is to report, not to comment. Nevertheless, a careful reading of most articles in such sources will reveal that they usually present a point of view and that this point of view affects the "news" as well as the "editorial" sections of those periodicals. The following passage from a *Time* analysis of the reporting on the 1988 national elections, recognizes this:

> More troubling was the fact that both the print and broadcast press frequently failed to point out the distortions in how the candidates painted each other's records. For instance, while many news organizations reported Bush's charge that Massachusetts furloughed a first-degree murderer named Willie Horton, who proceeded to rape a woman while on leave, few pointed out that the program had been instituted under a previous Republican Governor and that many states, including California under Governor Ronald Reagan, had similar furlough programs. . . . In their efforts to be fair and balanced, reporters were also reluctant to single out Bush for the negative tone of the campaign. Even though the Vice President was spending thousands more on negative ads than Dukakis and running them earlier, reporters generally blamed both sides equally for taking the low road. (Dan Goodgame and Naushad S. Mehta, "The Made-for-TV Campaign," *Time* 14 Nov. 1988: 71)

The last comment, that bias masqueraded as an attempt to treat the candidates equally, is especially compelling. As you read your sources, you need to be very aware of biases like this. Such bias does not make material useless, but you need to be aware of it so that you will know how such material can be used in your own argument.

WRITING ACTIVITY: BIAS

Take two or three articles, interviews, or other sources that you have collected for your paper. Read them carefully, noting any bias or slant given the "facts" and events presented. Does such a slant make the source unusable? What will you have to do when you use this information in your paper? Discuss your article and its bias with another writer or with a group. Your instructor may give you some sample articles to look at in class.

Besides watching for slant and bias, you must also be able to understand the implication of what you are reading and to understand how one article, interview, or argument relates to the others you will hear or read. When we worked with sources in Chapter 7, you wrote a comparison summary of two articles, showing where they agreed and disagreed. This exercise helped you think of one writer's opinions in the context of another's. The following analysis of two articles not only compares their ideas but also shows how they cast light or doubt on each other.

In the Sunday *Star Bulletin & Advertiser* of July 29, 1990, two Associated Press articles about Laos by David Brunnstrom were printed side by side. The first described in great detail the American bombing of that small nation during the Vietnamese war, saying, "More than 2 million tons of bombs were dropped on Laos altogether, surpassing the U.S. total in World War II" ("Villagers Wonder Why They Suffered So Much," A35). The World War II bombs were of course dropped over a much wider area, so the destruction in tiny Laos was much more concentrated.

The other article talks about the backwardness of Laos, comparing it with other Southeast Asian countries, such as "booming Thailand, across the Mekong River." The article quotes a Western "development expert" as saying "Asia's full of dynamism, but that's not Laos. . . . I think that, in the long term, it will remain a unique case, more like an African country than an Asian one." The writer then goes on to say that "Officials blame the malaise on the incentive-numbing central planning of the past and on inefficient use of aid from communist allies." Later the writer observes "Analysts say the unspoiled countryside and tropical climate provide great potential for tourism, but the government shows no enthusiasm for foreigners" ("Impoverished Laos' Future Dim," A35).

Can you see any way in which these two articles throw light on each other? Can you suggest any information from the first that might give an alternate analysis of Laos' "backwardness"? If you know that Thailand was not bombed in the Vietnam War and that Vietnam, which of course was, is also "backward" in its economic development, does that suggest anything?

Americans are often quick to stereotype other peoples. The statement that Laos's backwardness differs from the "dynamism" of the rest of Asia, and the implication involved in saying that Laos is more like Africa than Asia are examples of this.

Two articles, one in the *New York Times* and one in *Time* magazine, both reporting on *how* the 1984 election was handled by the media make an interesting study. One does not "refute" the other at all, but reading the second can cause one to reflect critically on what the first said. The title of the *New York Times* article by John Corry is "How TV Dilutes Political Debates" (21 Oct. 1984: 2, 31). The lead states, "Television is not just showing us the Presidential and Vice Presidential debates; television is determining how we score them, too." It goes on to indicate that candidates are judged more on their image than on the content of their presentation. The analysis and examples used to illustrate it are sharp and interesting. Then about halfway through the article, the writer returns to the subject announced in the title and in the lead:

> Television allows no pause for reflection. It is an intimate medium operating one on one. We look at the candidate; the candidate looks back at us. The appeal is visceral, reaching out to sentiment and predisposition, but not neces-

sarily to cognition and rationality. We may get a sense of how a candidate feels about a large issue, but never learn much about the issue. A candidate may persuade us he or she feels warmly, but not what they feel warmly about (31).

This is part of a common and widespread discourse about the problems with television as a medium. The ideas seems to be that the lack of content in political debates is tied to the medium of TV itself, rather than to any intention on the part of the candidates.

However, an article from *Time* magazine, reporting on the televised debate between George Bush and Geraldine Ferraro, candidates for vice president, shows that the supposedly more reflective medium of print journalism also pays inordinate attention to details of personality (David Beckwith and Melissa Ludtke, "Co-Stars on Center Stage," *Time* 22 Oct. 1984: 30–31).

Time conceded that Bush had "committed more factual gaffes than Ferraro," and of the issues summarized, Ferraro seemed to have given the better answer all but once, yet the writers of the article said that "Bush came out slightly ahead." This judgment was backed up by two paragraphs analyzing the candidates' speaking voices. This is followed by a quick summary of the content of the debate, but the article ends with another analysis of the speaking manner and appearance of the two candidates. Overall, only half of the article reports on the ideas in the debate, and both the beginning and the end, the parts most noted by readers, are devoted to details of personality, not to the content of the debate.

Again, the *Time* magazine article does not refute the *New York Times* article, but they comment on each other in interesting ways, and the two of them give us as readers a chance to think about the issue of television's effect on politics.

WRITING ACTIVITY

Take three or four articles you have been reading for your paper, and sketch a discussion like those above, examining possible biases, commenting on how the articles "talk to" each other and deepen your understanding of the possibilities and issues of your subject. Share this summary and commentary with another writer or with a group. If another writer is working on a related topic, you might work on such a summary together.

Thinking through Arguments

As you gather your material, you will inevitably be thinking about your issue. Perhaps you will have revised your original research question. You are probably beginning to break down your main issue into subissues, and you are also probably beginning to ask a number of questions.

At this point in Chapter 7 we had you take a stand and begin to prepare an outline. That rather simple procedure might be too simple at this point. You may have gathered so much material that you are not sure just where to go. The one thing you do want to be sure of is that you don't oversimplify complex material.

List, Group, Name. Several activities can help you think through what you already know and discover what you need to learn next. For example, if you are having a hard time seeing how things relate, you might begin by simply making lists.

For example, Edmund wanted to write a paper about a proposed resort development at a site called Queens Beach on the western coast of Oahu, Hawai'i. He read newspapers, attended public hearings at the Honolulu City Council, and talked to both supporters and opponents of the development. He collected pages of notes. Far from having a problem finding material, he had more than he knew what to do with.

Knowing that he had to write a con/pro argumentative paper, Edmund wanted to begin defining the subissues for his main issue, which he had stated in the form of a simple research question: Should the resort be built? He was not ready to formulate a thesis, but he wanted to see what he knew about the issue. He decided to write a list of all the reasons he had heard or read for or against building the resort. He produced this list:

1. The resort would help boost tourism, which is Hawai'i's main industry.
2. It would create a number of new jobs for the Native Hawaiians who live in nearby Waimanalo.
3. The coastline where the resort would be built is one of the last pieces of unspoiled coast on Oahu.
4. The area has a very popular beach that is used mainly by local people.
5. The developers, KOA, were promised that they could build the resort, and denying them this right would deprive them of their profit.
6. The actual property is owned by the Bishop Estate, whose money goes for educating Hawaiians. If they cannot have KOA build a resort, the value of their land would decrease and this would hurt the Hawaiians.
7. The area already has infrastructure like roads, sewer, and electricity, so the costs to the state in developing the resort would not be high.
8. The kinds of jobs that would result from the resort would be mainly low-paying service jobs.
9. That part of the island is already overdeveloped except for the coastline and has had severe problems with traffic and with sewage disposal. The resort would simply make the problems worse.

10. The resort would bring an additional five to six million dollars in tax revenues for the state.

11. The overall plans for development adopted by the state call for limiting resort developments to specific places on the island. This is not an area slated or zoned for such development.

12. Public costs of developing the hotel would involve widened roads, increased water supply, and fire and police protection.

13. The building of the hotel would damage the reef, which would be destroyed to make a sandy beach.

14. Tourism in Hawai'i is already overbuilt and the destruction of this natural beauty would hurt, not help, the industry. People come to Hawai'i to see scenery, not hotels.

15. This resort would be close to Waimanalo, a rural Hawaiian community, and would have a negative impact on the life-style there.

The list helped Edmund see what different people were saying about the development, but it was clear that he could not write a paper following this rather random order. Studying the list, he began to see that certain items could be grouped together, and he began to see that the overall issue of building the resort broke down into several subissues. For example, items 1, 2, 7, 8, 10, 12, and 14 all refer to economic issues like jobs, taxes, and tourism. Items 3 and 13 relate to environmental concerns; 4, 9, and 15 relate to life-style; and items 5, 6, and 11 might be considered legal problems.

As Edmund looked again at each of these groupings, he noted that the items under each subissue broke down into cons and pros. The economic items, for example, clearly broke down into arguments for (1, 2, 7, 10) and against (8, 12, 14) the development. Both items related to the environment were arguments against, as were all three related to life-style. In the group of legal issues, item 11 opposed development, while 5 and 6 were for it.

One other grouping occurred to Edmund as he looked over his list and thought back over the meetings and interviews. Many of the people who had been concerned about the development had been Native Hawaiians, because the proposed resort would be close to a traditionally Hawaiian area. Hawaiians had argued on both sides of the issue. Some had argued that many Hawaiians were economically disadvantaged and needed jobs (item 2) and that the landowner, Bishop Estate, was a Hawaiian institution (6). Others had argued that the jobs available would not pay enough to help the Hawaiians (8) and that the local life-style and environment would be adversely affected (3, 4, 9, 13, and 15). Thus the "Hawaiian" arguments complicated the issue even more, especially for Edmund, who was himself part Hawaiian.

So far Edmund had gone through a process that might be called list, group, and name. He had listed all his ideas, grouped ones that were related, and established a heading for each group (economic, environmental, life-style, legal, and Hawaiian issues). He had also grouped according to another set of labels: for and against.

Chart or Matrix.   As an aid in thinking through the issues, Edmund next constructed a chart, or matrix, like the one we made in the last chapter. It looked like this:

	For Resort	*Against*
Economic	Build tourism Add to tax base No cost for infrastructure	Tourism already overbuilt
Environmental		Destroy unspoiled coast Destroy reef
Life-style		Crowded roads, sewers, and local beach
Legal	Developer loses money already invested	Violate state planning
Hawaiian	Provide jobs Bishop Estate loses money for Hawaiian education	Jobs low-paying Negative impact on Hawaiian life-style and on agriculture

This kind of planning helped Edmund move from his first notion of arguing for the resort because of the money the Bishop Estate would make to his final stand against the development because of its negative impact on Hawaiians who live in the area.

Who, What, Why.   Another type of planning helped Kim think through the issues surrounding the Baby Doe case. Briefly, this case concerned a baby born with spina bifida, a small head and incomplete enclosure of the spine. Left alone, such a baby would live only a year or two. With surgery she might survive, perhaps severely handicapped mentally and physically, into her twenties (though some people with this condition have a less drastic prognosis).

The parents decided not to have the surgery done, but the federal government took jurisdiction and promulgated a regulation designed to protect the "civil rights" of handicapped infants. They threatened to cut off federal funding to any hospital that did not do its utmost for such infants. Hospitals saw this as an attempt to control medicine.

Surgeon General Everett Koop entered the picture with a recommendation that patient care review committees be set up to monitor such cases and aid the hospitals and doctors with them. Even this compromise seemed unacceptable to several professional groups who held that only the physician and the parents should be responsible for decisions about the care given to such infants.

The above summary simplifies the case considerably, but mentions the major people involved in the case: the baby, the parents, the federal government, the medical community, and Surgeon General Koop.

This list of interested parties makes it obvious that this is not a simple con/pro argument in which all issues fall on one side or the other. Clearly the parents and the doctors have much in common: Both think that the parents should have the major say. The government and Surgeon General Koop both want to limit the absolute rights of the parents, but Koop would also limit the role of the government. On the other hand, Koop and the government seem to be on the side of the baby since they are arguing for her civil rights. This is complicated by the fact that the parents argue that the baby's quality of life would be severely compromised and that she would undergo much suffering. However, the parents brought in the financial burden involved in caring for such a child, which might seem to compromise their position. Others say that the size of the burden makes it a justifiable argument and the government certainly has no right to intervene unless it assumes part of that burden.

Having gotten all this information from her reading, Kim realized that she had a complex issue. She needed to make sure she had thought it through thoroughly. To help with this process, she used a method that might be called dialoguing. This method assumes that one way for a writer to think through an issue is to carry on an internal dialogue. Thus Kim used a series of questions that required her to analyze what she had written, add more to it, and look at it from a different point of view. This technique is best used after you have done quite a lot of reading and know a good bit about the topic. It helps you think over what you know. It can also let you know when more reading and research are in order.

Dialoguing. A series of "dialoguing" questions is given below. You could use these questions to help you think through your issue, or you could develop your own list, perhaps with the help of other writers. Such questions can be used by one writer alone, but they are best used in a group, because the writer then must make her internal dialogue external and must respond to the questions in a way that will be clear and convincing to others. The questions can be asked in the order given; they can be asked randomly, each person in the group choosing one to ask, and the writer thinking through the answer out loud; or the listeners or readers can choose one that occurs to them as they consider a particular part of the paper.

Questions

1. What is one important point you haven't considered yet?
2. Is there a better argument for that point?
3. Is there a new way to think of this topic?
4. How could you make your main point clearer?
5. What criticism could be made of your paper?
6. Some readers might resist this idea; how could you make it more understandable or acceptable?
7. This argument isn't sufficient yet, what can you add?
8. What are your own feelings about this?
9. What is a good point on the other side of the argument?
10. What did you learn in your reading that surprised you?
11. What did you learn that you have not been able to fit into the paper yet?
12. How could you develop this idea?

By responding to such questions, Kim began to understand all the different points of view and to see how much she would have to deal with.

WRITING ACTIVITY

Try dialoguing either by yourself or with a group of writers. Start by summarizing the main points you have discovered in your reading. As you finish talking about each part of the paper, have one group member pick a random question, or choose a question relevant to one idea you presented. Respond to that question, trying to draw on the reading and thinking you have done. Let the questioner respond to your response if he wishes or challenge you again. Maybe something you say can be added to the paper. Most likely your answers will help you sharpen your thinking.

By the time Kim had read a lot of material and gone through exercises like the dialoguing, she felt that she had at least three stands to contend with. In order to find her way through the maze of arguments and analyses, Kim used a device that might be called who, what, and why, which is similar to the matrix Edmund used, except that it focuses on the arguments and questions posed by or associated with different individuals or groups. Her matrix looked like this:

Who	*What*	*Why*
Baby Doe	Should she have surgery?	Her severe handicap limits life.
Parents	Baby Doe should not have surgery.	The baby would be handicapped, and the financial burden enormous.
Government	Parents should not be allowed to have jurisdiction in this case; court should decide.	All infants have civil rights and parents are not capable of deciding.
Koop	Set up patient care review committees.	Committees can decide in lieu of parents and physician.
AMA and other professional groups	Only parents and physician should make decision.	Government interference sets a dangerous precedent.

Looking at the material in the schematic way helped Kim plan the paper. She decided to present her material in just this order since that is the order in which the players entered the real case. Her subissues became the arguments of each player, and the simple con/pro structure gave way to a side 1, side 2, side 3 analysis. She explained each stage, showing where each person or group stood and showing how the next person or group entering into the discussion commented on what had gone before and added new dimensions. She then concluded by arguing that the best interests of the child should be the first consideration, but that these should be determined by the parents with the help of a physician and a group like Koop's patient review committees. She felt that government interference was unwarranted. She further held that if the child was given the surgery, the parents should be helped with the ensuing financial burden. Only in this way, she argued, would the parents really be free to consider the child's best interest.

Diagrams. So far, we have talked about four methods for helping you sort through material: dialoguing; list, group, and name; building a matrix; and who, what, and why. Two other related methods, mapping and tree diagrams, accomplish the same thing, but add a visual component. For people who like to see a structure, these might provide attractive thinking strategies. In mapping you can start by drawing a circle with spokes out from it representing different issues, subdivided for this paper into con and pro. Edmund's paper might be represented schematically like this:

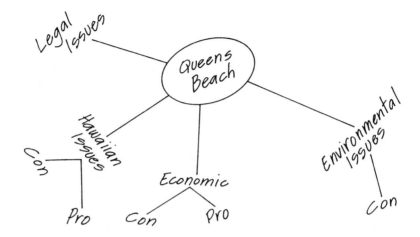

Finally, each spoke might become the center for another circle like this:

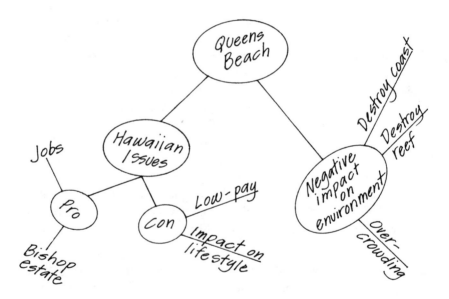

Another way of looking at the linking of ideas visually is to do tree diagrams. For example, in the Baby Doe case, you might start, as Kim did, with the parties involved:

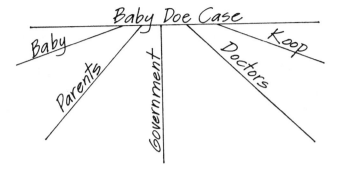

As you begin to think of the paper, some of the branches will grow branches, like this:

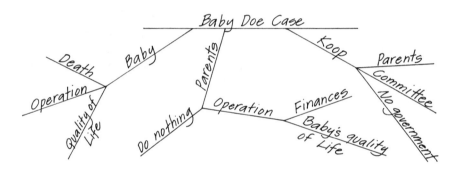

Devices such as all of these can be used for several different purposes as you write your paper. Mapping and tree diagrams, for example, can be useful for stimulating ideas early in the process. But, like matrixes and who, what, and why, they can also be used after most of the information is collected as a way of seeing relationships and moving toward a thesis and a structure. Finally these devices can be used to get feedback on drafts. For example, other writers might read or listen to your paper and see if they can sketch a tree diagram or build a who, what, and why matrix based on what they have read or heard. This would be a good way to check the clarity of your ideas. We will talk more about feedback later.

When you have read a lot of material, interviewed people knowledgeable on the topic, and thought about it yourself, choose one or more of these devices and use it to begin to sort through your material.

Thesis

By now you are probably beginning to form your own ideas, or to make your own sense out of your topic. You should be ready to decide on your stand and write a preliminary thesis. With the Kaho'olawe paper, this was the fairly simple process of deciding whether to support or oppose military training on the island or perhaps to offer the third choice of shared military and civilian use. The papers used so far in this chapter show that deciding on a stand may sometimes be more complex. Kim, for example, did not take a simple stand for or against Baby Doe's parents, but took ideas from several of the various groups involved. In thinking about the Queens Beach development, Edmund decided to focus on the effect it would have on one particular group, Native Hawaiians. When you begin to formulate your stand, be sure that it reflects the complexity of the issue.

The preceding paragraph used the term *preliminary thesis*. The thesis you write now may change in the process of writing your paper. For example, Pamela wrote a paper concerning development in Kaka'ako, an area of Honolulu filled with small businesses such as car repair shops. The area was slated for redevelopment, and both the city and the state had jurisdiction in the process. Plans for redevelopment had dragged on for ten years, and Pamela was wondering why it was delayed. As she collected material and began to think about it, she decided that inefficiency was to blame.

However, as she began to write the first draft, that catchall stand did not seem to fit. Some parts of the planning process seemed efficient enough by themselves. Looking back over her first draft and her material, Pamela rewrote her thesis as she began the second draft: "The reason for the delay in developing Kaka'ako is that the overlapping responsibilities and the hierarchical structure of the state and city governments prevent efficient decisions from being made in the area of planning." Once she had made this revision, she could account for things that she had not been able to cover in the first draft, and the paper came together in a more convincing manner.

Don't discount the fact that writing is a learning experience. Even if you have thought through your ideas thoroughly, when you actually put them into writing you learn even more. For example, when I was working on my M.A. project, one whole chapter never made its way into the final draft, because I started with a thesis almost exactly the opposite of the one I ended up with.

Nevertheless, when you have read, sorted, thought, resorted, and rethought, you should try to write out a thesis statement. It may be one, two, or three sentences. Remember Kim's thesis about Baby Doe: The child's rights should be paramount, but the decision about those rights should be made by the parents in consultation with a patient care committee. If the decision was made to care for the baby, and that would impose a financial burden on the family, help should be given them.

The Although Thesis.   When you have been studying a complex con/pro topic, it is not unusual to have mixed feelings about what you have read. Recall, for example, Stearns's compromise position concerning Kaho'olawe. If you want to do justice to all these feelings, consider what might be called an "although" thesis. For example, Judy, a student of Utah history, was interested in what has come to be called the Mountain Meadows massacre. At Mountain Meadows a group of California immigrants were massacred by Indians with the help of Mormon settlers. These immigrants were from the area in Missouri from which the Mormons had been driven, with a good deal of bloodshed, some fifteen years earlier. One Mormon elder, John D. Lee, was hanged for his role in the massacre.

As Judy read about the incident, she was convinced that Lee had taken an active part but felt he had not been the real power behind it. She finally came up with the following thesis: "Although John D. Lee took an active part in the Mountain Meadows massacre, he was unjustly punished when he was forced to take most of the blame, because there were other men far more guilty, he was not personally in favor of the massacre but responded to commands from superiors, and he was a victim of circumstances at his trial." It doesn't matter that this is not a particularly beautiful sentence. Your first thesis may never appear as such in the final paper. The thesis is written for you at this point, not for your reader.

Another writer assessing the blame of the dowager empress of China (the last powerful ruler from the Ching Dynasty before its defeat by Western powers) wrote this complex "although" thesis:

> Although the dowager empress is often held accountable for the Chinese Revolution of 1911 and its outcome, she cannot be blamed entirely. Though her deep-seated hatred of Western powers caused her to make unwise decisions, this was an understandable feeling shared by most of her people. Though her actions often seemed motivated by a love of power, she sometimes needed to exert power, because her entire country and her own government were in a state of rebellion and corruption. Though her actions were often irresponsible, unpredictable, and violent, she tried her best to keep the empire together.

Keep in mind one thing about an "although" thesis: It is not an excuse to avoid thinking, be wishy-washy, or fail to make hard decisions. Such a thesis does not say: "Although I think A has some good ideas, I think B has good ideas also." It recognizes complexity; it takes ideas from several viewpoints. But it takes a stand.

Other Thesis Patterns.   If the "although" pattern does not fit your needs, you might consider some other types of theses that would work for a con/pro paper, such as the "If . . . then" pattern. For example, the cons and pros of building golf courses on land presently earmarked for agriculture is a current controversy on Oahu. A student discussing one such proposal came up with the thesis: "If the site of the golf course is moved to avoid putting current small farmers off their land, and if no other development of resorts or condominiums is involved in the plans, I favor the development of a golf course."

One variant of this type of thesis is "If . . . then . . . ; however, if . . . then":

> If the state can give figures to show that projected ridership would enable a mass transit system to break even, then I am in favor of building one; however, if projected ridership would not be this great, then I would favor other solutions to the traffic problem, such as widening of existing highways and expansion of express bus service.

Another variant is: "If . . . then . . . because . . . ":

> If the state cannot give figures to show that projected ridership would enable a mass transit system to break even, then other solutions to the traffic problem should be considered because the state cannot afford to subsidize such a system permanently, and if the mass transit system attracted fewer riders than this, it would not really relieve the transportation problem.

One more pattern for a con/pro thesis is "Not only . . . but also . . . ":

> Not only should airline pilots be subjected to mandatory drug testing, but they should also be tested for alcohol blood levels.

This thesis could also, of course, be followed by a "because."

These patterns are not meant to be prescriptive or to limit what you can say in your paper. They are not so much models as devices to help you think about the kind of stand you might want to take.

WRITING ACTIVITY

Try now to write a working thesis for your paper. Make it as complex as your ideas about the material you have been reading. Write one, two, or three sentences. Don't write a dozen, or if you do write a dozen sentences, try to boil them down to three or four before you are satisfied. You are trying to get your ideas into their simplest form without distorting or belying complexity. If the "although" form, or any of the others, works for you, use it.

WRITING ACTIVITY

Share your thesis with another writer or with several. Ask them to talk your idea back to you in their own words so that you can see whether you are being clear enough to make sense to someone else. If someone else is working on the same topic or a related one, you can discuss the subissues involved in your larger issue and see if you understand them in the same way. However, you might well have different, even opposite, theses. There is no problem in that.

Tasks

You will recall from Chapter 7 that a good thesis helps you define the "tasks" your paper must do to convince your reader that your stand is reasonable and defensible and to refute other possible stands. Once you have your thesis, you should begin to do this kind of analysis. The two "although" theses we considered above are analyzed for tasks below.

Mountain Meadows Massacre

Thesis: Although John D. Lee took an active part in the Mountain Meadows massacre, he was unjustly punished when he was forced to take most of the blame, because there were other men far more guilty, he was not personally in favor of the massacre but responded to commands from superiors, and he was a victim of circumstances at his trial.

Pro tasks	Con tasks
1. Since she does not refute Lee's role in the massacre, no pro task.	1. Establish Lee's part in the massacre.
2. Establish that other people were more responsible.	2. Refute evidence against Lee at trial.
3. Show that Lee had tried to oppose the massacre but had given in to authority.	3. Refute evidence that Lee had led the massacre.
4. Show how the circumstances in the trial had kept the truth from being known.	

Dowager Empress of China

Thesis: Although the dowager empress is often held accountable for the Chinese Revolution of 1911 and its outcome, she cannot be blamed entirely. Though her deep-seated hatred of Western powers caused her to make unwise decisions, this was an understandable feeling shared by most of her people. Though her actions often seemed motivated by a love of power, she sometimes needed to exert power, because her entire country and her own government were in a state of rebellion and corruption. Though her actions were often irresponsible, unpredictable, and violent, she tried her best to keep the empire together.

Pro tasks	Con tasks
1. Show that her hatred of the West was shared by all Chinese.	1. Show how her hatred of the West caused unwise decisions.
2. Show her need to exert power.	2. Show how her actions were motivated by power.
3. Show how she tried to keep her empire together.	3. Show how she was violent and unpredictable.

Note that the defining of tasks is not exactly the same as deciding on an organization for the final paper. It happened that the author of the paper on the dowager empress wrote her paper following the order of tasks outlined above, except that she used the orthodox strategy of presenting cons first and then pros. However, Judy did not write the massacre paper in that order. She wrote first about Lee's involvement and guilt and then proceeded to defend his actions on all counts all at once.

WRITING ACTIVITY

Once you have your thesis and an understanding of the supporting issues involved in it, write out a list of the tasks you will have to do in the paper. Note that your paper must exclude as well as include. There will be issues involved in your topic that you do not handle. For example, Judy chose not to get into the problem of how a usually peaceable group like the Mormon settlers, whose record even in relation to Native Americans was a relatively peaceful one, could have countenanced, let alone participated in, a massacre. She simply took the massacre as a given and concentrated on the role of one man in it. Once you see the tasks involved in your paper, you can begin to plan for the organizational strategy that will work best.

Organization

In the last chapter, we presented a basic discussion on organization that centered around two simple types of structure for con/pro papers:

Type 1	*Type 2*
I. Con	I. Issue 1
A. Issue 1	A. Con
B. Issue 2	B. Pro
C. Issue 3	II. Issue 2
II. Pro	A. Con
A. Issue 1	B. Pro
B. Issue 2	III. Issue 3
C. Issue 3	A. Con
	B. Pro

To summarize briefly, in Type 1 the writer first discusses all the con points and then discusses all the pro points. In Type 2 the writer discusses the con and then the pro of each of a number of subissues. It should be clear from our analysis of sample projects in this chapter that this scheme is too simple for many papers, although the John D. Lee paper followed roughly the plan of Type 1, while the dowager empress paper followed Type 2. Thus, this simple description of organizational strategies still reveals two questions you must answer as you begin to plan for your paper:

1. How and when will I handle the con arguments?
2. In what order will I discuss the subissues in the paper?

The two questions are obviously related, but the question of how to order subissues must be answered individually. Recall that Kim in the Baby Doe paper chose to use a chronological order, that is, she presented subissues in the order in which they had come into the original case. Another strategy might be to present the subissues in order of ascending importance, that is, to save the strongest and most important arguments until last, because the reader would be most likely to remember the end of the paper. Sometimes different subissues must be presented in a particular order because the later issues depend on the former.

The first decision you must make as you proceed with your tasks is how to deal with the con arguments.

Handling Con Arguments. Recall from the last chapter that the con arguments are those your paper rejects or refutes. The pro arguments are those you support.

Generally, there are two ways to deal with con arguments: You can attempt to refute them, or you can concede them and go on to show why your side is stronger. In most papers you will do some of each. The John D. Lee paper above, for example, started by conceding that Lee was an important participant in the massacre. The writer had no argument with that. She then presented her three arguments about why he was not the most culpable participant: He was not the most responsible; he actually opposed the action at first; his trial was not fair. For her first two points, she refuted the con argument that Lee was the leader of the incident and had favored the massacre. This involved looking at evidence given at Lee's trial and showing from other accounts that this evidence was not reliable. Her third argument, lack of fairness at the trial, did not involve refutation of an opposing argument but did involve establishing that the trial was biased. In short this paper had a rather complex structure.

The paper on the dowager empress used a more straightforward structure. The writer simply presented three small con/pro arguments: The empress was anti-Western to a fault, but there was reason for this; the empress was a tyrant, but her realm was in chaos; the empress was violent and unpredictable, but she truly tried to help her country. In a sense, the writer conceded all the con points, then tried to show that the behavior of the empress could be seen in another light.

From reading the discussions above about each of these topics, can you see why the writers chose the structures they did? Think about this, discuss it with another writer, and read the analysis below.

Obviously the strategy you choose for handling your con arguments will depend on your material. If your material breaks down into two or three or four neat subissues about which reasonable readers and writers can disagree, you might use the strategy in the dowager empress paper. This is similar to the Kaho'olawe paper, where we isolated three subissues—military need, possibilities for civilian use, and historical and cultural value—and then argued con and pro on each.

However, where your material does not fit into such a neat package (probably in most cases), you will want to work out a variation of the two structures we have presented. Following are two papers which use different solutions to the problem of how to deal with the con arguments and how to structure the paper.

The following paper was written by a student nurse to argue against a proposal that all nursing students should be required to have four years of training instead of the current two years. Its structure might be described like this:

1. Introduction and thesis (paragraph 1)
2. Pro argument 1 (paragraph 2)
3. Pro argument 2 (paragraph 3)
4. Con argument 1 (paragraph 4)
5. Con argument 2 (paragraph 5)
6. Remaining pro arguments (paragraphs 6,7,8)

As you read the paper, note that the writer does not attempt to refute directly either con argument. She presents them in paragraphs 4 and 5 but then proceeds in her next paragraph to explain why these don't seem to her to be the deciding arguments.

Increasing Professionalism in Nursing

In mid-October of 1978, the Hawai'i Nursing Association met with   1
nursing representatives throughout the state and proposed that the legislature pass a bill making a four-year degree mandatory for all nurses
beginning in 1985. This bill will eliminate all the present two-year nursing programs that produce registered nurses after graduation. I feel this
bill would be detrimental to the public for several reasons.

First of all, today's cost of living is continuously on the rise. The   2
expense of a four-year college education is phenomenal. There are many
young people who would love to go to a university or college to seek a
four-year degree. However, due to the steady increasing costs for such an
education, they are turning to community colleges or vocational schools
for two-year degrees, such as the present nursing degree, because they or
their families cannot afford four years of college. The expense for the
present two-year nursing degree is only one-eighth the cost of a four-year
degree. Further, it costs the University of Hawai'i approximately $12,000
a year to educate a student in the current program. The cost to the school
triples for a four-year student, according to Pat Carolyn, nursing instructor at Maui Community College.

Because of the increased expenses, the mandatory four-year degree   3
will certainly decrease the number of prospective nursing students
throughout the state. Hawai'i will lose approximately 120 to 150 graduate
nurses a year. If the bill is put into effect in 1985, this loss will add to the
current shortage of nurses. Due to this, the demand for nurses will
increase and, in turn, nurses' salaries will increase. Consequently general
medical costs for the public will increase. Hospital rates will continue to
rise to accommodate the salaries for the much-needed nurses.

Those people who argue in favor of the expanded four-year program   4
point out that the two additional years of schooling would give a wider

background to potential nurses in various science courses and public health studies. This would make the two years of intensive nursing courses more meaningful. The outlook of the nurses who would be trained under the new program would be broadened through the in-depth addition of sociological and psychological concepts, as well as the study of the humanities. Since the scope of nursing includes not only recovery from illness but also disease prevention and the promotion of health in general, these wider studies would increase not only the variety of settings in which a nurse would be prepared to practice but also the level of health care she is prepared to provide.

The proponents also point out that no other profession involved in health care (occupational therapists, physical therapists, social workers, dieticians) requires less than a four-year university preparation. It is felt that nurses can't remain at the lowest level of education among the health care providers and still think they have a position of equal influence in the system.

However, aside from the financial questions discussed above, I think the ultimate question that should be asked is, will the added two years of non-nursing courses produce better nurses? In a recent study conducted by Ms. Carolyn at various hospitals in Honolulu, 85 percent of the patients asked were not aware that there were nurses with different levels of education taking care of them. The nursing skill and care, as far as the patients were concerned, did not have anything to do with a higher level of education. Further, the state board of nursing requires that all graduating nurses, whether two-year or four-year, pass an examination before they are licensed and able to work as registered nurses. The two-year and the four-year nurses take the same exam, and, in the past few years, the two-year graduates from Maui Community College have scored higher on these exams than the four-year graduates.

The kind of background knowledge in the various sciences and in 7
public health that a four-year program offers, can, I feel, be advantageous
if used in work where this knowledge will be beneficial, such as administration, supervision, or public health practice. However, I feel such
courses are not necessary for staff nurses working in the hospital doing
direct patient care. Like any other clinicians, nurses learn through
behavioral models. You can get the words from textbooks, and classrooms
provide some catalytic action, but being involved with an experienced
practitioner who knows the reality of care is the way to learn the practice
of nursing in the real world.

If the four-year program is put into effect, the ultimate outcome will 8
be poorer patient care. As explained above, the program will provide fewer
registered nurses, so they will be called on to fill head nurse and supervi-
sory positions. Who then will give direct patient care? That will fall more
and more to licensed practical nurses and nurses aides who have had far
less theory and practical training than the current two-year nurses. This
is surely not the answer to increasing professionalism in nursing.

Nona Irvine

The following paper on labeling rock lyrics uses a combination strategy. The
thesis for the paper is that a proposed system for classifying rock lyrics to indicate
objectionable material would be unwise and unworkable. The author starts by
considering the major argument of the proponents of such a system, that lyrics in
rock music are obscene. She concedes this point, but indicates that this is not the
whole story. On her other points, however, she gives a more direct refutation of her
opponents' arguments.

Rock Lyrics

Rock 'n' roll music always seems to have inspired an element of opposition to its "excesses": "Elvis's pelvis in the '50s; Beatles and drugs, sex

and Stones in the '60s; punk anarchy in the '70s" (Cocks 71). Now there's "pornographic rock," and a new group to condemn it, the Parents' Music Resource Center (or PMRC), headed by Elizabeth Mary "Tipper" Gore, wife of Sen. Alfred Gore, and Susan Baker, wife of Treasury Secretary James A. Baker III. The PMRC wants the record companies to systematically label records and cassettes that contain sexually explicit or graphically violent lyrics, including profanity, and to display the lyrics on the jacket sleeve so that consumers can see what sort of music they're going to listen to (Love 13). While these people obviously mean well, and are genuinely trying to protect children from bad influences, I think that they're going the wrong way about it.

First of all, I agree that some songs have extremely distasteful lyrics. Tipper Gore relates how, after buying a copy of Prince's "Purple Rain" album for her daughter, she became aware of the raunchy rock lyrics: "I was shocked when I heard the words to one of the songs, 'Darling Nikki,'. . . . It describes masturbation by Nikki, who's called a 'sex fiend'" (McBee). Baker adds that a friend exercised to another raunchy song "for hours before she became aware of the lyrics" (Gergen). Not to mention songs by heavy metal bands that deal explicitly with sadomasochism, oral sex, violence, the occult, and substance abuse. Among the bands fingered are the heavy metal groups AC/DC, Twisted Sister, Mötley Crüe, Judas Priest, and Black Sabbath, along with pop figures Prince, Sheena Easton, Madonna, and Cyndi Lauper (Love 13).

However, I think that the PMRC is wrong in pointing to these specific groups, with their specific songs, as a reason to impose a rating system on the entire recording industry. In the first place these "porn rock" bands are only a small part of the total picture—"a miniscule part of rock music, which is 26 percent of the . . . recording industry," a fact stressed by Recording Industry Association of America president Stanley Gortikov

(McBee). Secondly the recording industry and the Federal Communications Commission seem to be doing a pretty good job of keeping most of the airplay decent, in "an informal system of checks and balances," as a spokesperson for CBS Records says (Love 83). Last of all not everything that rock musicians turn out is bad for the public—for example, the "Live Aid" and the "U.S.A. for Africa" efforts to help the starving in Africa, and the "Christian rock" of Amy Grant and others (McBee). "Porn rock" is definitely not indicative of rock music in general, and should not be treated as such.

The second matter is the rating system itself. Originally, the PMRC wanted specific ratings: X for explicit lyrics, V for violence, O for occult, and D/A for drug or alcohol, along with the display of lyrics (Love 13). "We want a tool from the industry that is peddling this stuff to children, a consumer tool with which parents can make an informed decision on what to buy," says Gore (Love 14). The PMRC is opposed to the RIAA's proposed label, "Parental Guidance: Explicit Lyrics," because, says Gore, "If it's going to be a single rating, we would prefer an R or X because the general public is already oriented to the PG as being somewhat suitable for young teenagers." Having encountered a "no concessions" stand from Gortikov of the RIAA, the PMRC is now planning to join with the national Parent-Teacher Association, the National Education Association, and labor unions in a "state-by-state formation of a national organization" (Love 14).

Although the parents may be right in wanting unsuitable material to be appropriately labeled, a system of ratings comparable to the film industry's is very unfair to the music companies for a number of reasons.

First of all the very volume of record output makes such a rating system impractical: The movie industry "releases about 325 new movies a year"; the record industry has to deal with about 25,000 new songs

(McBee), all of which would have to be rated accordingly. To provide for such a massive job, a "very large staff of people" would be needed "to rate that many records," says RCS Records vice-president Robbin Ahrold (Love 15, 83). In other words, it would be a huge and expensive mess.

Secondly there is the problem of who would establish the standards and then interpret the music in question. How does one judge music? In film the "guidelines are quite specific; nudity and four-letter words require that a film get a certain rating" (Love 83). In music things are not always so clear. For example, John Fogerty's music was misunderstood and attacked in a newspaper column, "because the writer thought a line about a lawn was a reference to smokable grass" (Cocks 71). Adds Nikki Wine, a music broadcasting producer, writer, and director: "[A]rt is always a matter of highly personal and subjective interpretation" (Wine). Also there's the problem of slang: "Ratings would have to get into slang and language that no one understands," says Russ Solomon, the founder of the Tower Record retail chain. "When they finally realized what Jefferson Airplane's (later known as Jefferson Starship) 'White Rabbit' was about, the record was dead and gone for four years" (Love 83).

Possibly the most important reason for opposing a rating system is artistic freedom and integrity: For a country whose foundations lie in the right to free thought, speech, and expression, this sort of an action comes dangerously close to censorship. How can any artist—or anyone, for that matter—make his or her art true to his beliefs if he is always worried about how a small, conservative group of people is going to interpret his work? This is not to say that the metal bands are really "art," but to point out the fact that the PMRC's attitude toward rock music in general bodes ill for artists of all sorts. "I don't believe these mothers speak for anything resembling the majority," says Danny Goldberg (president of Gold Mountain Records), and I agree with him.

Last of all, it seems to me that the PMRC is barking up the wrong tree, so to speak. The real problem with these rock lyrics is young children's response to them, so why is the PMRC pressuring the record companies? Parents have the direct responsibility for the upbringing of their children, and RIAA's Gortikov says, "you cannot substitute supervision of the record industry for supervision of the child" ("Next: R-Rated"). Even if the PMRC's demands are met, what sort of an effect, if any, would a rating system have on the young audience? Terence Moran writes, " . . . most [kids] would probably be tempted to get their ears into the tunes their parents think most dangerous, and the tunes themselves might get raunchier under the cover of an R or X rating" (Moran 16). Nikki Wine adds: "There's no end to the possible combination of ways in which underage children might 'accidentally' hear or see objectionable material, even after it's clearly rated and labeled" (115).

In practice, a rating system would clearly be a big hassle, a counterproductive measure, and an infringement of our basic rights. Although this ratings suggestion is a well-meant gesture, the parents of PMRC should take into careful consideration all the positive and negative aspects of their proposal, including future repercussions on rock music's role in society. After all, freedom is a very precious thing, and the first step towards censorship of liberty—even one made in the name of good taste—can tilt the precarious balance between freedom and oppression.

Works Cited

Cocks, Jay. "Rock Is a Four-Letter Word." Time 30 Sept. 1985: 70–71.

Gergen, David. "X-Rated Records." U.S. News and World Report 20 May 1985: 98.

Holden, Stephen. "Recordings Will Carry Advisory about Lyrics." New York Times 9 Aug. 1985: C10.

Love, Bob. "Battle over Rock Lyrics Heads for Round Two." Rolling Stone
12 Sept. 1985: 13–15, 83.

McBee, Susanna. "Now It's Labels on 'Porn Rock' to Protect Kids."
U.S. News and World Report 26 Aug. 1985: 52.

Moran, Terence. "Sounds of Sex." The New Republic 12 Aug. 1985: 14–16.

"Next: R-Rated Record Albums?" Newsweek 26 Aug. 1985: 64.

"Nineteen Big Record Firms Agree to Warning Labels." Wall Street
Journal 12 Aug. 1985: 8.

Wine, Nikki. "R-Rated Rock Needs Only Some PG." Los Angeles Times
7 Oct. 1985: 115.

Charlene S. Gima

WRITING ACTIVITY

Now is the time for you to look back over all your work—your notes, your thinking exercises (matrixes etc.), your thesis, your list of tasks—and plan a strategy for your paper. It might be that your preliminary thinking has produced an obvious structure, and you are now ready to write. Maybe you have even begun to write. If you are not clear yet about how your paper will come together, take time now to make a plan for yourself. This might take the form of an outline (using sentences for the major entries in the outline helps you see how your ideas are fitting together). It might be something else, like a short written account of what you will do:

> First I will write an introduction that explains this and this. Then I will present my thesis. Then I'll present my first argument, then the con exceptions to it, and so on.

You might simply redo a matrix or a tree diagram that you made earlier and use that as a plan.

Whatever form your plan takes, do spend some time organizing as you begin to write. Then discuss your plan with another writer or with a group. Give them copies of your outline or whatever planning device you are using. Ask them to tell you whether the plan looks clear and interesting. Your instructor may ask you to show him your plan.

Ask your colleagues to do another dialoguing exercise with you at this point. If they concentrate on the questions that force you to defend your arguments and analyze your issues, they can be very helpful to you.

Writing a Draft

So far this chapter has been broken into separate sections for thinking about the paper and organizing the paper. Now we will discuss writing the paper, but it would be a mistake to think that you do all your thinking before you begin to organize and all the organizing before you begin to write. Organization and thinking through your material go hand in hand, and writing is not a separate activity. Although this section is called "Writing a Draft," a writer is not necessarily through thinking, organizing, or even reading, when he or she starts a first draft.

Most writers are more comfortable starting a draft after they have done some preliminary planning and have at least a rough idea of where they are going. This is usually a wise plan for an inexperienced writer. But some writers begin to draft out of complete confusion, using the writing itself to clarify and organize. Even those who plan ahead often go back and forth between planning and writing. I myself most often prepare a rough general outline before I begin writing and then do more detailed and exact outlining as I write. I often interrupt my drafting to spend some time writing freely on the subject as a way of thinking. Indeed I often write before I begin the rough outline, not as a draft, but as a way of thinking. You will work out your own method.

Once you have begun drafting, review Chapter 7, especially the discussion on coherence and paragraphing. Remember that you must write your paper so that a reader who is not familiar with your material will still understand your argument. This means that the reader must know what you are doing at any given point. Clarity is extremely important in an argument paper, because you won't convince anybody of anything unless they can understand your points and follow your logic.

The Introduction

The first chance to help your reader understand the paper comes in the introduction. An introduction generally does two things: (1) It gives whatever background is needed to understand the paper, and (2) it presents a thesis or statement of intent. In addition, it must be interesting enough to make the reader want to continue reading the paper.

Introductions are hard to write. Many writers write a working introduction to define what they are doing and to get started. They then write the paper and finally return and rewrite the introduction. That is not a bad strategy. If you would prefer to craft a wonderful introduction at the beginning, do so, but don't get hung up. If you are having trouble making it perfect, leave it for now—or finish it roughly as a guide for yourself—and plan on coming back to it later.

An important question to ask yourself as you begin to write is: How much background do I need? Can I jump right into my argument, or do I need to spend some time explaining the situation to my readers? No one can answer that question but you. The sample papers we have looked at so far all have simple introductions. They state the problem and get right to the analysis. However, the writer of the paper below chose to write a long, leisurely introduction that sets the tone and prepares for the con/pro discussion that follows. The thesis in this paper does not come until paragraph 4, but the paper works.

This paper grew out of a situation that almost caused a confrontation between farmers and activists on one side and developers and police on the other. Many articles were written in local newspapers and magazines, but I think this paper, written by a college freshman, presented the issues as clearly and forcefully as anything on the subject. As you read the paper, note first how the introduction sets up the problem for the reader. Then note how clearly the author moves from point to point, and how his voice is always there, telling the reader what is going on at any point and letting us know how he feels about the situation.

Waiahole-Waikane: The Price of Development

The Waiahole and Waikane valleys lie about midway along the wind-   1
ward coast of Oahu. They are basically a rural retreat, away from all the
hustle and bustle of the city. The mood of the two valleys is felt in the
Honolulu Advertiser's article "Time Stands Still in Waiahole" by Arnold Kishi:

> In more than fifty years Waiahole Valley on Windward Oahu
> hasn't changed much. It's like taking a walk down a road into a
> departed era. A thin white arrow on a small black "Waiahole School"
> sign on Kam Highway points toward the Koolaus to this hidden bit of
> small farm rural Oahu. Trees line both sides of the valley road often
> blocking out the sunlight (E23).

The total population of the area is about 900, mostly small farmers,
retirees, and their families. There are deep ties between the residents and
the valleys. Forty-one percent of the residents are maintaining land that
has been in their family name for more than twenty years. The average
age for the farmers is fifty-three (Tune, "Issues" A13). Older people have

stayed to farm the land as their sons and daughters have left to make more money in the city.

What then is the problem confronting these two valleys that contain   2
a bit of old Hawai'i? To answer this question we can look a little to the south at Kaneohe. The original sparse development of the shoreline of Kaneohe is now dense and continuous from the boundary of the naval air station, now the Kaneohe Marine Corps Air Station, to Kahalu'u. Subdivisions have enlarged the town inland into what were agricultural areas and have sprung up to the north as far as Waiahole. The original town center is now an urban shopping district and a large new shopping center has been created a mile northeastward in what were agricultural lands.

Now the thrust of housing development, which made Kaneohe lose   3
its rural character and become a suburb of Honolulu more than a decade ago, is turning to these valleys. Present residents are well aware of this, and they know that the present informal life-style and agricultural activities are incompatible with the more urbanized community structure that will come with more development. Therefore the Waiahole-Waikane struggle is a classic confrontation between a developer and rural residents. In the past when confrontations like these arose, the landowner almost always won. Because of this the small farmers were pushed back further and further until these two valleys are one of the few remaining rural areas on the island.

The principal characters of this struggle are Mrs. Lester Marks, prin-   4
cipal heir to the McCandless lands, which make up most of the valleys; Joseph Pao, developer and head of Windward Investors, who want to build there; Robert Fernandez, president of the Waiahole-Waikane Community Association; and of course the government. About two years ago the residents learned of the McCandless heirs' plan of seeking to change the land zoning from agricultural to urban. This met with staunch opposition from the residents as rumors spread that much of the McCandless land

was about to be sold to a North Carolina developer with Joe Pao acting as
an intermediary. Eventually a group of investors, headed by Joseph Pao,
bought much of the McCandless land with Mrs. Marks retaining management. The tentative plan presented before the Land Use Commission consisted of 6,700 housing units for low, moderate, and high income groups.
The housing mix would be composed of 850 garden apartments and townhouses for low-income families, 2,150 garden apartments and townhouses
for moderate-income families, 2,000 single family homes for moderate-
income families, 400 half-acre estate lots for high-income families (Lynch
A3). Later both the proposed development plan and the rezoning were
rejected as the residents gained a "victory" in the struggle. The celebra-
tion was short lived, however, as Joe Pao submitted another plan similar
to the first, but labeling the development an "agricultural" subdivision.
This plan was also rejected. Now Mr. Pao, though still wanting the urban
zoning, looks to developing the area but making each lot two acres; this
can be done under the present agricultural zoning, though the results
would destroy any real farming in the area. The rejections of the earlier
proposals, backed by the state and city, bring into focus the strong and
sound reasons for keeping the area agricultural and are therefore in conflict with the current proposal for two-acre residential lots. These reasons
provide a firm base in supporting the residents' opposition to the
developments.

First of all the proposed developments run counter to the city's new   5
general plan, which proposes to prevent development on this part of the
island and to retain its agricultural potential. Even in the older general
plan, though there was slated to be much more development in Windward
Oahu, the city left almost all of the Waiahole and Waikane valleys in
agriculture and preservation. Therefore it has always been the city's
intention to leave the two valleys undeveloped ("Waiahole-Waikane Fate"
B2). The state's plan for the area also conflicts with developer Pao's plans.

John Farias, state agriculture chairman, stated that his department
would continue to oppose the plan because "it runs counter to the
Ariyoshi Administration's goal of more agricultural diversity and self-
sufficiency." Farias continued to say that "The land now under small-
scale agricultural use has the potential of an expanding agricultural
base" in Windward Oahu (Schlenk A3).

This potential can be seen when one looks into agricultural activities   6
in the valleys. A survey from the Department of Agriculture and figures
from the Crop and Livestock Reporting Service indicate that commercial
farmers use about 240 acres in Waiahole-Waikane and part-time farmers
use an additional 50 to 60 acres. The commercial farmer is an asset to the
state in a very real economic sense. Eighty-two percent of the sweet potatoes on Oahu are grown in Waiahole-Waikane valleys. Thirty percent of the
Oahu papayas are from this area. The Crop and Livestock Reporting Service goes on to say:

> . . . the valleys produce about 28,000 pounds of papayas per acre per
> year, or roughly $5,000.00 per acre per year. . . . Some individual
> farmers have been producing more than 50,000 pounds per acre or
> almost double the State's average. The papaya crop in the two valleys
> is valued at $73,000.00 each year. The two valleys also produce
> bananas, snap beans, cucumbers, flowers, and hogs. Total value in
> 1972 was $303,000.00 (Tune, "Issues" A13).

Until recently the farmers have been on month-to-month leases, which
have discouraged any long-term investments and therefore kept the
farmers from expanding their farms even more.

Another factor that would argue against development of the valleys is   7
the question of water. The State Department of Agriculture is concerned
that any development of Waiahole and Waikane valleys in Windward Oahu
may eventually take back water that is now transported to the valuable
agricultural lands of Central Oahu. The Waiahole Ditch Tunnel supplies

much of the water for Central Oahu's rich sugar and pineapple lands. Any development will increase in density as the years go by and though at first water from surrounding sources may be adequate, the pressure to take water from the Waiahole Ditch Tunnel will increase as the population increases. In this way development on the windward side of Oahu will have a definite impact on all parts of Oahu.

A major consequence of development, which is often overlooked but   8 which I feel would be one of the main priorities in considering develop- ment, is the social impact of the development upon the present residents of the area. As stated earlier the residents of Waiahole-Waikane are mainly small farmers and retirees, mostly long-time residents. Because of this, many of the people, self-sufficient and set in their ways, would find it hard to move. Their attachment and fondness for the land are deeply ingrained, so they are not just numbers or dots on the map that can be erased and put somewhere else by the wave of a hand. Thus in consider- ing this problem one cannot assess eviction or noneviction by simply acknowledging the economics of the situation.

The main social impact of developing the Waiahole-Waikane valleys   9 would be the destruction of the life-style of the people there. Whether development forces them to move or not, their life-style will be drastically disrupted. The most likely result if developments come will be the eviction of the present residents. Due to their self-sufficiency and their paying of one of the lowest rents on Oahu, the residents will find it impossible to find comparable housing. Robert Fernandez points out that "if they (residents) have to move, they will lose their life-style completely because there is nowhere for them to go" (Lynch A3). Calvin Hoe, owner of a Hawaiian artifacts store in Waiahole, expresses similar sentiments, "a lot of them (residents) built their own homes. Where would they go? I can just see these people wilting just sitting on a concrete balcony ("500 Gather" A2). Robert Fernandez adds, "Life-style is not something you can pack up in a suitcase when you move to public housing'' (Tune, ''Windward Development Opposed'' A2). Nothing could be more true. How can one expect to live in one-bedroom housing (probably the only thing the residents could afford) with the absence of a backyard farm, after living for all or much of your life in a rural community? The lives of the people of Waiahole-Waikane will certainly deteriorate if they are forced to move.

Even if many of the people are able to stay in the valleys after the   10
developments, the pressure on them to conform to the incoming residents' life-style will be great. In this case not only will the present leaseholders of the McCandless Estate feel the effect but also the small landowners in the area. Restrictions against farm animals, social pressures, and tax increases will undoubtedly affect all living in Waiahole-Waikane presently. ''It's a funny thing,'' says WWCA President Fernandez, ''whenever a lot of new people move into an area, there is pressure on older residents to change their life-style. Even if you have lived here all your life and these people just came in, you are going to have to live their way'' (Lynch A3).

Despite these many reasons backing the residents in their fight   11
against the urbanization of Waiahole and Waikane valleys, Joseph Pao and the McCandless Estate continue to seek urban rezoning and approvals of their development plans. Why and what are their reasons in favor of the developments? When the McCandless Estate first sought rezoning from agriculture to urban they justified their decision because of ''the low agricultural value of the land and the need for housing'' (''Waiahole Residents'' A3). However, as seen in the survey done by the Department of Agriculture and the Crop and Livestock Reporting Service, the valleys are important to the state in a very real economic sense. Low agricultural value? On the contrary, Waiahole and Waikane valleys are highly valued by the state agriculturally because of the potential both valleys hold in agricultural activities of the future.

The developers also cite the need for housing. There is no doubt that   12
Oahu is in need of housing. It is low-cost housing, however, which is
sorely needed, not high-priced housing which would certainly make up
the bulk of this development. Granted there were plans for low-cost housing in the plans Joseph Pao submitted, but the majority of the housing
units were for moderate- and high-income families. Also, in the past
developments that supposedly involved low-cost housing suddenly were
transformed into communities out of the price range of low-income families when the building was done.

Finally, the owners of the land contend that a current rise in tax   13
assessment makes the development necessary. However, figures from the
State Tax Office show that this is not as substantial as is claimed. These
figures show the following:

* The total area of the development - 1337 acres
* The old assessed valuation - $1.3 million
* The new assessed valuation - $4.1 million
* The new actual valuation (used to compute the taxes) - $2.8 million

Using these figures we find that the actual tax increase on the property
comes out to about $27,000 (Tune, "Windward Development Opposed"
A3). So the question is asked, "Should the landowners who have been
receiving a tax break for years because of underassessed land be allowed
to develop that land just because taxes jumped up sharply to reflect the
current higher values on the land?" (Tune, "Windward Development
Opposed" A13). I believe that profit, not taxes, is really behind the push to
develop. Joe Pau and his investors have, after all, purchased much of the
McCandless land, and they now seek return on their investment through
development. Other than this profit motive I personally see no other reason for the development of the Waiahole and Waikane valleys. If this reason is the driving force behind the development, it is an extremely selfish

motive for not only economics are involved but also the welfare of many people as stated earlier.

Recently the tide has changed in favor of the landowner-developer as 14 Circuit Court Judge Arthur S. K. Fong granted a summary judgment allowing Mrs. Marks to evict nine tenants and reclaim her property in Waiahole valley. This is a severe blow to the entire community as this decision will make it possible for Mrs. Marks to evict the rest of the residents based on the law of precedent. Therefore the future of the residents of Waiahole and Waikane valleys looks bleak indeed. Despite the sound reasons against the development, the government seems to be headed back into the winner-loser formula in which the landowner always ends up being the winner. If it does come to this it will truly be a sad sight, for the credibility of the government will suffer, not to mention the residents of the valleys.

Bibliography

"City Rejects Pao's Waikane Plan." Honolulu Star Bulletin 11 Mar. 1976: A6.

Harpham, Anne. "Pao Buys McCandless Land." Honolulu Advertiser
    22 May 1975: A3.

Haugen, Keith. "Judge Fong OKs Waiahole Eviction." Honolulu
    Star Bulletin 21 Apr. 1976: A8.

Hawai'i Environmental Simulation Laboratory, University of Hawaii.
    Kaneohe Alternatives: An Application of Impact Methodology.
    Honolulu: Hawaii Office of Environmental Quality Control, 1974.

Kishi, Arnold. "Time Stands Still in Waiahole." Honolulu Advertiser
    9 Aug. 1970: E23.

Lynch, Kay. "Waiahole Residents Oppose Rezoning." Honolulu Advertiser
    15 July 1974: A3.

Pellegrin, David. "Governor, Mayor Oppose Pao Plan to Develop Valleys."

Honolulu Advertiser 18 July 1975: A1.

Schlenk, Jill. "Ag Chief Criticizes Waiahole Rents, Pao." Honolulu

Advertiser 5 June 1975: A3.

Scott, Nadine W. "Group to Battle Waiahole Ouster." Honolulu

Star Bulletin 20 Apr. 1976: A7.

Tune, Jerry. "Issues at Waiahole-Waikane." Honolulu Star Bulletin 28

Sept. 1974: A13.

———. "McCandless Deal Nearly Sealed." Honolulu Star Bulletin 27 Sept.

1974: D7.

———. "Water and Development at Waiahole." Honolulu Star Bulletin 22

Mar. 1975: B1.

———. "Windward Development Opposed at Land Use Meeting." Honolulu

Star Bulletin 9 Aug. 1974: A9.

"Waiahole-Waikane Fate." Honolulu Advertiser 15 June 1975: B2.

"Waikane Group Rips Pao Project." Honolulu Advertiser 31 May 1975: B1.

Gene Asahina

Besides having an unusually long introduction, this paper has an unusual organization. The general rule in con/pro papers is to present the pro last, on the principle that the last argument presented will be remembered. However, this paper does not do that. The structure of the paper might be presented like this:

Paragraphs 1–4 Introduction: thesis ends paragraph 4

Paragraphs 5 and 6: Pro point 1

Paragraph 7: Pro point 2

Paragraphs 8, 9, and 10: Pro point 3

Paragraph 11: Con point 1 with a refutation

Paragraph 12: Con point 2 with a refutation

Paragraph 13: Con point 3 with a dismissal

Paragraph 14: Conclusion

Considering what was said earlier about this controversy—its intensity and importance to the island of Oahu—can you think why the writer used this organization? What is the effect of piling up all the reasons against the development before beginning to present the reasons for it? Discuss the organization and impact of this paper with another writer or with a group.

Coherence and a Writer's Voice

As you read the paper, you probably noted how easily and clearly it moved from point to point. Again, the long explanatory introduction sets up the situation so that the reader understands it. Then the writer makes sure that the reader stays with him through each point by writing clear statements and transitions. Look at the scheme of the organization given above, then go back and look at the paper again, noting especially the beginning of each paragraph that introduces a subissue in the paper (paragraphs 5, 7, 8, 11, 12, 13). Note how the reader is always kept informed of what the writer is doing.

For that matter, look at each paragraph. Remember in Chapter 7 we said that every paragraph in an argument paper is like a small argument: It always has a statement, some kind of proof, and some analysis or explanation of that proof. You will see that this is true of each paragraph in this paper. Paragraph 5, which presents the first pro argument, that development of the valleys runs counter to city and state planning, is especially strong in this regard. The first sentence is a clear statement of the subject of the paragraph. The rest of the paragraph is an explanation of planning, plus quotations that support the contention that the valleys were meant to be agricultural. Paragraph 6 then moves this argument one step further by presenting a wealth of statistics about farm production in the valleys.

Remember what we have said before: As you are drafting your paper, think of each paragraph as a unit of the paper that presents an important element of your argument. Remember to write the draft paragraph by paragraph, thinking of what each paragraph will add to your paper.

Another element in the clarity of this paper is the strong and continual presence of the author's voice. The writer of this paper clearly knows what he is talking about and cares about the issue. I often hear students say they are afraid to state what they believe strongly, because they should be "objective" in their writing. Objectivity is a good characteristic, but it need not be understood as not caring or not feeling strongly about an issue. Objectivity requires a writer to be careful of facts, present clear and rational arguments and analysis, and try to be as honest as possible. It does not exclude commitment. One can, of course, be more or less neutral in presenting a con/pro paper. But if you feel strongly about your subject, write strongly. Whatever tone you take your voice must be clearly present in the paper. This is *your* paper. You must take control of it from the first, guiding the reader from point to point, explaining and analyzing facts and judgments, bringing

your reader along. One of the major strengths of the paper we have been considering is that strong voice.

Related to the personal voice is the use of personal experience or narrative.
Many topics will not lend themselves to this, but some may. At the beginning of
this chapter, I said this paper would be the culmination of a whole semester's work.
Sometimes your paper can be strengthened by a scene. For example, a paper that
argued for a seat belt enforcement law mainly by citing statistics and other objective evidence ended strongly with the following scene and commentary.

People can tell you to wear seat belts and give you odds about survival, but it never sinks in or hits home until <u>you</u> know someone involved
in an accident and can see for yourself how their lives are altered.

A very serious car accident occurred while I was organizing my ideas
for this paper. Five days before Thanksgiving a 1985 black Monte Carlo
failed to negotiate a turn on rain-slicked pavement. Before the accident
the car held five minors who, that night, were out for fun. After the accident the car held two girls with minor injuries, two other girls who were
later to be hospitalized in guarded condition and in critical condition, and
a boy—the driver of the car—whose life ended at the age of seventeen.
None was using a seat belt at the time of the accident.

I see no issues of rights in the senseless killing and injuring of people in accidents like this. The girl in critical condition, whom I know personally, was very lucky not to have any permanent physical paralysis.
However, after her internal injuries and her broken jaw, wrist, and palate
heal; and after the swelling of her face disappears along with the gash on
her cheek; and even after she gets her front teeth replaced, the
unpleasant memories of that event will leave a physical and psychological
scar—especially since on that night she lost one of her friends forever.
It's too bad that the seventeen-year-old boy isn't still alive today to tell
people how important it is to wear seat belts. If his death had to stand for
something, let it be a lesson about safety to those who think it only hap-

pens to the "other guys." It is particularly for this reason I support the enforcement of seat belt laws.

Writing the draft of this paper will be the longest and probably the hardest writing task you have done this semester. But keep going. Remember that it is a draft and can be made clearer and stronger later on. Nevertheless, keep your reader in mind as you go. Write paragraph by paragraph, keeping your overall thesis in mind, and keeping your reader in mind also. Remember to write your paper so that someone who is not familiar with the issues will be able to understand it. Also remember to include enough interesting and convincing proof, experience, and data that someone who did not agree with your stand would still have to respect your paper.

How and When to Give Credit

Chapter 7 had a great deal of information about ways to make sure that you are using borrowed material honestly, and that information will not be repeated here. However, you would do well to review that section. Remember particularly the three acceptable ways of using someone else's ideas and words: direct (and exact) quotation, partial paraphrase, and complete paraphrase.

What does need discussing here is how to give credit to your sources. The sample papers presented earlier in this chapter illustrate the method we will use for giving credit: parenthetical references. In this system (look at "Rock Lyrics" or "Waiahole-Waikane," for example), the writer uses the author's last name plus a page number—or simply a page number if the author's name is given in the text—in parentheses after the quotation, partial paraphrase, or paraphrase. Then the writer provides a Bibliography or a List of Works Cited at the end of the paper so that the reader can note the full information for the sources mentioned in parentheses. The two papers at the end of this chapter also use this method.

Parenthetical references are simpler than traditional footnotes or endnotes, and they are being adopted now by scholars in most fields. Bibliography entries in these papers follow the forms given in the *MLA Handbook for Writers of Research Papers*, third edition. Your instructor may ask you to use these forms or may refer you to forms found in another handbook or some other source. When you write papers for other classes, your instructors there will almost certainly ask you to follow the forms used in the discipline in which you are working. The important thing is not so much that you follow one particular form or another as that you follow the chosen form consistently.

Perhaps more important than a detailed discussion of bibliographic forms is a consideration of the question: When do I cite a reference? Forms are relatively easy. Deciding when to footnote is more difficult and requires you to make a judgment.

It may help you decide when to use footnotes or parenthetical references if you keep in mind that there are essentially two reasons for them:

1. Citations give credit where it is due.
2. Citations guide your readers to further information. By this time in your work, you are certainly aware of how useful a good bibliography can be to a researcher.

Most of the evidence you will be using in your paper will come from reading or interviewing. Does this mean that you must give credit for every thing you say? Not really. A good rule of thumb is this: If the information you are giving is background information, that is, the kind of thing that you can read about in a lot of sources, you need not footnote it. You do need to give credit for the following kinds of information:

- Someone's particular theory or interpretation of events
- Someone's particular research or statistics
- All exact quotations and partial paraphrases (because they contain short quotations)

For example, generally you would not need to cite a source for a date. However, suppose that the date for some event is in dispute, and one of your sources has come up with a date because of some particular research she has done. You would need to footnote that date.

To footnote or not to footnote: Usually it's a judgment call. Just remember to be honest and informative and to think of the needs of your readers.

Reworking the Draft

The best thing to do with a completed draft is to set it aside for a day or two, and then return to it to see what else it needs. Be sure to leave yourself time to do this. Recall one strategy for revisions suggested in Chapter 7:

- First check the whole paper to see that your thesis is clear and that the parts work together to support that thesis.
- Then check each paragraph, making sure that it does what it sets out to do clearly and fully.

- Next look at the sentences to see that they are clear, efficient, even beautiful.
- Finally edit grammar, spelling, typos, and so on.

Stages of revision will rarely be so discrete or efficient, however. As you look for overall clarity, you will find sentences that need rewriting and individual paragraphs that need attention. Nevertheless this suggested procedure gives you a plan for what can be a daunting task.

In the last chapter you read through your draft in a special way to check quickly for global clarity. You might do that kind of reading again as a first step in revision. Read your introduction; read only the first sentence or two in each paragraph; and then read the conclusion. This is a good test for clarity. It can sometimes reveal problems with structure.

For example, Joan wrote a paper concerning the building of a proposed freeway across the Ko'olau Mountains on Oahu. This project has been held up for more than fifteen years because of opposition by environmentalists and Native Hawaiians, who say that its route would destroy historical ruins. Reading Joan's draft as we have suggested, we would find the following:

The H-3 Controversy

The H-3 freeway has been a controversial issue since it was first con-   1

ceived of over twenty years ago. The freeway was originally proposed to

connect Pearl Harbor to the Kaneohe Marine Corps Air Station but has

undergone several changes due to environmental and cultural concerns.

Instead of passing from Aiea through the Moanalua Valley and then

through the Ko'olau Mountains to the Kaneohe Station, the H-3 is now

planned to cut through North Halawa Valley and the Ko'olaus at a point

above Haiku Valley. This route, however, is as controversial as the origi-

nal. Environmentalists against building H-3 have been battling the state

since the very beginning. There have been many issues raised, which have

caused more than a ten-year delay in the completion of the highway and

have cost the state millions of dollars (as the case has been tied up in

courts). I feel that a freeway as controversial and useless as H-3 should

not be built.

Supporters of H-3 claim that the highway is needed to alleviate traffic   2
problems on the Pali and Likelike Highways. . . .

The H-3 freeway, however, will not run from the windward side into   3
Honolulu town but will connect Kaneohe with Pearl Harbor. Most residents, however, do not work in the Pearl Harbor area. Only a small percentage of commuters will even use this freeway during peak hours . . . On
the windward side, H-3 would not alleviate traffic on the Kahekili Highway, another problem area. . . .

Building the H-3 also means cutting through several areas of   4
historic, cultural, and environmental importance. . . .

[Proponents] state that the highway will cause no damage. . . .   5

These claims, however, have been proven wrong. . . .   6

Concerning the aesthetics of the H-3, even the state agrees that   7
visually it wouldn't be attractive. . . .

The H-3 freeway would emerge on the windward side of the Ko'olaus   8
at a point above the Omega Station in Haiku Valley, a federal navigation
transmitting station. . . .

Studies are being done to determine the consequences of   9
gasoline spills or collisions on the highway near the Omega Station
since "electromagnetic radiation from the station's antenna, under
which the freeway would be located, would far exceed federal safety
standards." . . .

The H-3 would also puncture the Ko'olaus in the area where there   10
are "significant water dikes." . . .

Furthermore, Windward Oahu is slated to be a rural area by the   11
Oahu Development Conference. Building the H-3 freeway would facilitate
the movement of people from Honolulu to Windward Oahu. This would
increase the growth of that area. . . .

H-3 is expected to cost the state seventy-four million dollars by its   12 completion. This would make it one of the most expensive highways built in the history of the United States. . . .

The state argues that this money would create jobs and thus be good for Hawai'i. However, much of the money to be spent will be to drill the tunnel through the Ko'olaus "which will require specialized equipment and operators who will be brought in from the mainland." . . .

13

There are many alternatives to building the H-3 freeway, but the state seems to ignore all of them. . . .

14

Their latest attempt to complete the H-3 freeway has been to ask Congress to exempt Hawai'i from federal environmental laws, such as the law currently prohibiting the state from building the highway near Ho'omaluhia Park, an area of important archaeological value. This latest attempt by the state is unjustified. They are asking that the laws apply to every other state except Hawai'i. If Congress should grant their petition, it would set a precedent whereby other states could be exempt from laws also. Our judicial system would soon be undermined and weakened. Instead of trying to find ways around the law, I believe the state should direct its energies toward studying alternatives to H-3. This highway, where the costs far outweigh the benefits, is not worth building.

15

A reader would have no serious trouble reading through this paper. He would understand that there were several objections to the freeway and that the writer opposes it. Joan seems to have adopted the strategy of presenting and refuting con arguments (those for the freeway), rather than presenting all the cons, then all the pros.

However, the paper gives a scattershot impression. Its objections to the highway seem to be a loosely related list rather than a unified argument. One way to bring the individual arguments together is to show how they are all related. For example, the arguments for H-3 have to do with the economics of development: The building of it will create jobs, and once it is built it will facilitate people's movement to jobs. The arguments against it have to do with environmental concerns: H-3 will create possible health hazards to users, destroy cultural sites, adversely affect the environment because it may affect water resources, place an unaesthetic structure in a lovely valley, and facilitate growth in what is now a rural area.

On rereading her draft, Joan felt that she needed to make such connections clearer. She felt that the first key to this would be a more thoughtful introduction. Thus, she wrote:

I came to the island of Oahu fifteen years ago just in time to read in the headlines that environmental groups had taken the state to court to stop progress on the third transisland highway proposed to connect Pearl Harbor to the Kaneohe Marine Crops Air Station. That highway, H-3, is still in the headlines, and the state is still in the courts trying to get permission to proceed.

The question whether to build the H-3 freeway between Honolulu and Windward Oahu presents the classical clash between progress and concern for the environment. On one side the state argues that increasing traffic problems make the highway mandatory. They add that its construction, a complex, long-term project, would create jobs. The opponents downplay such benefits and argue further that the environmental and cultural damage that will be the inevitable cost of the project far outweigh any benefits.

Why has the state persisted, despite years of court battles, in its plans for the highway? Mainly they claim that the continually growing problem of traffic congestion as workers commute daily to jobs in Honolulu can be solved in no other way.

This introduction sets the problems out more clearly and prepares the reader to visualize the two sides in a larger context. Joan kept essentially the same organization that she had in the first draft. However, she put her second con argument, concerning jobs that would be created by building H-3 (paragraph 13 in the original draft), right after the first con argument, the discussion of alleviating traffic (paragraph 2), since there was really no reason for separating them as had been done in the first draft. This gave her a standard type 1 organization: all cons followed by all pros.

When she was ready to switch to the pro side, she felt she needed again to let her "voice" guide her reader to a larger understanding of her reasons for opposing the highway:

> This highway has been opposed for twenty years by people willing to spend time and a good deal of money on court battles. They have had very strong reasons for doing so. Their opposing arguments have taken several forms, but they boil down to a strong commitment to preserving environmental and cultural resources that could never be replaced.
>
> First, Windward Oahu is slated to be a rural area by the Oahu Development Conference. The opponents of H-3 realize that the major result of building a new highway in this area would be that it would facilitate development of suburbs in this area. This would bring the usual detrimental effects on the water and the aesthetic appearance of the area, but it would also bring two unique problems in this case: danger from radiation and destruction of important Hawaiian cultural sites.

Joan then developed the environmental concerns, leaving the cultural one for the last. She placed the material about exemption from environmental laws after the cultural discussion. This reinforced her conclusion because it showed the lengths to which the state would go to build this highway.

She concluded with a brief discussion of alternatives that summed up what she had said and went one step further in suggesting alternate solutions to the traffic problem.

> Anyone who drives from Windward Oahu in the morning realizes that the state's concern with traffic is not a misplaced one. However, their solution is. I think my discussion of the problems involved in such a project show this. However, perhaps the most puzzling aspect of the situa-

tion is why the state continues to ignore the many feasible alternatives to H-3 that have been put forward. The federal funds currently earmarked for H-3 could be transferred to other projects almost intact (90 percent federal funding for H-3; 85 percent for other proposed projects). Further, such alternatives would also provide jobs.

Alternatives include building a third lane on the present Likelike Highway where it goes through Wilson Tunnel, joining with current street-widening projects on the road leading up to this tunnel. Interchanges to ease the flow of traffic into Likelike and into Kahekili Highway on the windward side are another possibility. These projects, which would be aimed at increasing the capacity of the current highways, would not create the environmental damage of the proposed H-3. One wonders why they are unheeded.

Joan's revision helped her redefine her focus and make the overall issue clearer to her readers, even though the change in the structure of the paper was minimal.

In a paper on the eradication of fruit flies, a major problem for farmers, Carol made more basic changes in structure in her second draft. She wrote her first draft using the structure:

I. Con
II. Pro

She was arguing against a three-part proposal for getting rid of these pests. In the first draft, she first presented all three proposals for eliminating the flies, then went back and presented the arguments against each. The result was confusing for the reader as you will see by reading the excerpt from her draft below. After an introduction about the problem, Carol began discussing the methods for killing the flies:

The U.S. Department of Agriculture has proposed an eradication plan that includes three methods aimed at getting rid of the pests: aerial spraying of malathion pesticide; male annihilation, which uses chemical attractants to lure flies to toxic compounds; and sterile male release.

The first of the plans considers spraying malathion over the entire state, either through aerial or soil application. Many of the state's agriculture and households use this chemical today.

The second part of the plan involves a technique called <u>male annihilation</u> which uses certain chemicals to attract male pests to the lure toxicant. As the male population decreases, so does mating and reproduction until finally, the species is wiped out. Methyl eugenol has been found to be the best lure available for male oriental flies; cuelure for melon flies; and Trimedlure for the medfly. Furthermore, Robert Metcalf, an entomologist-chemist-author on male annihilation says that through this method it may be possible to develop crop varieties changed enough so that insects don't attack them.

The next step proposed to eradicate the Tri-Fly involved a more biologically sound process. It involves a technique of sterilizing male lab-reared flies by radiation. When the sterile male is released to mate with a fertile female, her eggs do not hatch. In time the population would diminish.

Obviously each of the proposed methods introduces complications that outnumber the benefits by far. The reasons for my strong opposition to the Tri-Fly Eradication Program are explained in the following paragraphs.

Beginning with the proposal to use chemicals for spraying or for annihilation, we must consider its underlying lack of reliability. There is no guarantee that all flies, especially the ones that live in "hilly terrains" deep within mountain forests, will be destroyed. Also the costs of such methods run very high. . . .

Hampton Carson, professor of genetics, does not believe the proper engineering exists yet for complete eradication. The technique of releasing sterile males to the wild proposes implications.

A quick reading of this excerpt reveals the problem with this type of organization, that is, presenting the proposed methods first and then presenting the objections to each method. In a feedback session colleagues told Carol they had trouble following the paper and asked her why she had separated the refutation of each method of eradication from the discussion of how it would work. She replied that the refutation for the first two methods was the same since both of these methods used the spraying of chemicals. Thus it would not work to follow each method of eradication with objections. The comments persuaded her to use a compromise organization. Starting again after the introduction, Carol's next draft read:

The U.S. Department of Agriculture has proposed a Tri-Fly Eradication plan that employs three methods (to be used in sequence) to exterminate the pests. The plan is broken up into chemical and radiation usage. The first and second methods (use of chemicals) include aerial spraying of malathion pesticide and male annihilation. The third method calls for the release of sterilized males into the wild population for mating.

Edward Shiroma of the USDA Animal and Plant Health Inspection Service is coordinating efforts of the Tri-Fly Eradication plan. He proposes to begin the program by spraying malathion throughout the state. He supports this rather ambitious plan by stating that much of the state's agriculture and many households already use malathion. In addition, experience with this product in California supports its use, since it was effective there.

The second part of the chemical process, male annihilation, uses other chemicals to attract male pests to the lure toxicant. As the male population decreases, so does mating and reproduction until finally, the species are wiped out. . . .

Despite the arguments for these two steps, however, chemicals, whether for spraying or for male annihilation, have many adverse side effects. There is no doubt that the use of pesticides will harm valuable plants and animals. Many endemic species, such as the Drosophila fly, which is an important insect to evolutionary research, would also be eliminated. Moreover, the general health of the people will be affected. . . .

In addition to possible environmental effects, there is no guarantee that spraying of chemicals will be effective. Chemicals may be unreliable because there is no guarantee that all flies, especially the ones that live in "hilly terrains" in mountain forests, will be destroyed. Moreover, the costs of chemical methods run very high—$70 million to $80 million, with treatment covering a long period of time, 15 years or more.

Whereas the two first steps just discussed use chemicals, the third part of the plan involves using radiation to sterilize male flies born and raised in a laboratory. When sterilized, they are released to the wild population. Hopefully, these sterile males will mate with the fertile females, after which the eggs will not hatch. If enough of the population's eggs do not hatch, the species would eventually self-destruct. Many opponents of the chemical side of the Tri-Fly Eradication program support this technique because of its more "natural" course of action.

However, the technique of releasing sterile males is perhaps premature at this time. Hampton Carson, professor of genetics, does not believe the proper engineering exists yet for eradication by this method. Because the males are lab-reared, he claims, they lack knowledge of "correct" and often learned mating behaviors of the wild. When the sterile males are released, females often "do not recognize courtship patterns and thus, no mating occurs." Instead, the females continue to mate with the wild insects. Furthermore, according to Carson, even if mating did occur, the females would still need fruit to lay eggs in. Fruit will continue to be damaged with eggs, regardless of whether they are "dead" or "live" eggs. Thus the sterilization technique would provide little immediate help to agriculture. Besides its ultimate ineffectiveness, this method, like chemical spraying, is very expensive.

Obviously, Carol has done more in her revision than rearrange materials, although the rearranging has made the structure of her argument clearer. She has also made her individual paragraphs much more effective by clearer statements and transitions. When she talked to her readers about why they could not follow her explanations, she realized that she was sometimes expecting them to know information that was not in the paper. Since she was so close to the material, she did not realize this. She had to remember, as you will have to as you write and revise, what we said so often in Chapter 7: You must write so clearly that someone who has not read the original material will still understand your paper.

With another writer, compare some of the original paragraphs with those in the revised draft and discuss what has been done to make them clearer. Note that several of the paragraphs end with an ellipsis (. . .), which indicates that not all of the supporting information has been included. Nevertheless you can see how much clearer the discussion is. Note how supporting quotations and data are also used more effectively.

WRITING ACTIVITY

In doing the paper on Kaho'olawe in Chapter 7, Clete became interested in the subject. He did further research, including talking to a fellow student, Keoni Fairbanks, who had actually gone with the 'Ohana to work on developing the island. He wrote a more extensive paper on the subject.

Clete's third draft is given below. You can see that it is in fairly good shape. However, you may find that you want to know more about some of the things Clete discusses, and that you still need some points clarified. Since you and your colleagues are familiar with the material, you should be able to discuss the draft in some depth. With another writer, or with a group, consider Clete's draft, discussing where you would add, subtract, rearrange, and so forth. Consider all the stages of revision we have talked about. That is, first consider the overall structure of the paper, deciding whether each part is clear or needs clearer transitions and statements. Then look at individual paragraphs. Do some need clearer explanations? Finally look at the sentences. Pick out two or three sentences that could be written more elegantly. Work on making them more effective. If you wish, use the questions in the peer feedback section to help you.

Kaho'olawe (Third Draft)

Kaho'olawe is about eleven miles long and six miles wide. Ever since 1953, the navy has claimed complete control of Kaho'olawe. Since that time, the navy has fired practically every type of conventional artillery onto the island. However, since 1980, the Protect Kaho'olawe 'Ohana has organized protest against the yearly bombings of Kaho'olawe during the RIMPAC naval exercises. What RIMPAC does is invite countries located on the rim of the Pacific to practice bombing on Kaho'olawe. These countries include the United States, Australia, Japan, Canada, and New Zealand. This program got started back in 1971, and today it is the largest naval exercise in the Pacific-Indian Ocean region. The 'Ohana has been successful in talking to various countries involved with RIMPAC and changing their minds about bombing Kaho'olawe. At this time, therefore, only Canada and the United States bomb Kaho'olawe. Today the 'Ohana members are doing various activities on the island. One such activity is building halaus (long houses) for the annual Makahiki gathering. Another of their most recent activities is guided tours that the University of Hawai'i students are able to get involved with. All of these projects are sponsored around the pride and heritage of Kaho'olawe that still live on in the Hawaiian people's hearts. That is why, I feel, Kaho'olawe should be given back to the 'Ohana.

Kaho'olawe is very dry and thought to have no chance of decent development. Furthermore, the island has a low elevation, which in effect loses much valuable water from the winds and water making development altogether nearly impossible. The history of Kaho'olawe dates back from the early 1800s. Further evidence from this time has shown that the island was never developable back then, too. The island was used as a penal colony for prisoners. One report has cited that the prisoners found so little food on Kaho'olawe that, in desperation, several of them swam the eight-mile channel to Maui in 1841, where they took canoes and food to bring back to Kaho'olawe.

However, today the Kaho'olawe 'Ohana members are changing the views of this so called nondevelopable island. Keoni Fairbanks, a graduate student at the University of Hawai'i and key member of the 'Ohana, said that projects to get the land back in shape are starting right now. On one part of the island, he said, the Native Hawaiian Species Society is planting some pumpkins and exotic and Hawaiian plants. Also, halaus and even a hula mound, where hula performances are presently held, have been constructed. Keoni Fairbanks also mentioned that if successful planting should start on the island, the goat population has to be controlled. He said they are shooting the goats today because they are ruining the vegetative land. Furthermore, this year the 'Ohana has gotten 75,000 dollars to hire experts to start projects on water systems development. The key experiment will be trying to collect the scarce water and distributing it usefully on the island.

State and federal officials are also doing some planting of their own. Today a tree called the tamarisk is being planted experimentally. Ronald Walker, chief of the State Division of Forestry Wildlife, says that "Tamarisk is hardy, and although it is not a native plant, it will stay where it is planted. While there it creates a wind break, allows debris to pile up and enhances conditions for the creation of soil in which other things may grow" (TenBruggencate, I4).

Much research going back to the early 1800s has shown that only a few archaeological sites have existed on Kaho'olawe. These early sites were simply fishing grounds, heiaus, and shrines where fishhooks were found. These materials apparently came from other islands, brought by fishermen who paid respect at the shrines in later times. Thus, some people believe that no connections can be made today that Kaho'olawe could sustain human population on the island.

However, recent archaeological discoveries show that Kaho'olawe is an island with many valuable sites. "The 'Ohana sees Kaho'olawe as the

focal point for the revival of Hawaiian religious beliefs and practices''
(Yamaguchi, A3). Today, with more than 2,000 archaeological features on
the island, it is placed on the National Register of Historic Places.
Recently, the founding of ''[a] halau was erected at Hakioawa, believed to
be the site of an ancient settlement'' (Yamaguchi A-3).

Kaho'olawe, which possesses many sacred and cultural sites today, is
an island that must be viewed and preserved. Keoni Fairbanks sees an
island that thrives with historical sites and expresses that the Maui
County Plan take effect. The Maui County Plan is, today, the ultimate goal
of the Protect Kaho'olawe 'Ohana. Through this plan, nine bays, Hakioawa, Ahupu, Kuhe'e'ia, Keana Keiki, Kamapau, Hanakanai'a, Kaaulana,
Hoonokoa, and Kamohio, will be used for guided tours for the general
public. On each of the nine bays, there will be heiaus, which will have
restrooms and facilities for the people. Connecting each bay will be hiking
paths leading up to the archaeological sites. Through these guided tours,
the people could experience the land features, fishing divergence, and
other historical Hawaiian traditions. Fairbanks says that this project will
take years to develop, but once it's started, their sacred island will be
saved forever.

Today the military is not allowed to bomb in the new National
Historic District on Kaho'olawe. However, they still bomb other parts of
the island, and they still maintain that the bombing is essential to their
training. Adm. Robert Reimann, commander of Pearl Harbor Naval Base,
''stressed the importance of being able to deliver ordnance with precision,
as air strikes on Libya have shown'' (Yamaguchi A3). Presently new tech-
nologies of practice bombing are in working form. However, R.H. ''Dick''
Brady, deputy public affairs officer at Pearl Harbor, had this to say:
''While technological advances have somewhat reduced the need for the
kind of training that Kaho'olawe offers, there still comes a point where

you must get in an airplane or ship and practice against something that resembles a real target. You cannot simulate land targets in the water'' (Tanji A9). Lt. Cmdr. Gary Shrout said, ''The navy has helped with replanting areas of the island, which is severely eroded.'' Shrout also said that ''the navy worked with the state forestry division and the Native Hawaiian Plant Society in planting 23,000 native plant species in seven one-acre sites, as well as planting 41,500 trees.'' Brady followed up by saying the navy might provide help for the state water resource study of Kaho'olawe, providing a helicopter on a space available basis (Tanji A9).

Despite this extensive cooperation, however, currently RIMPAC naval exercises still pose threats to Kaho'olawe as shellings still occur. Maui County Mayor, Hannibal Tavares, who is also in charge of Kaho'olawe, said, ''[T]he navy is able to maintain bases in other parts of the country without requiring a bombing range such as Kaho'olawe'' (Tanji A16). He further stated that Kaho'olawe, which is listed on the National Register of Historic Places, is the only area being bombed. The navy says that they are restricted to certain areas of Kaho'olawe to bomb and do not touch the archaeological sites. However, on July of last year, ''ten cluster bombs (with 5-8 shells each) were dropped directly onto five archaeological sites and near to five other sites in the vicinity of the mauka planting site at the head of Kaneloa Gulch'' (Kaho'olawe Aloha 'Āina 34). Luckily, no explosions occurred, and no damage was done. The navy had apparently missed their targets by over a mile. This incident exposed how the monitoring of training by the navy is poor. Another concern is that the already endangered humpback whales are threatened by the shelling near the waters of Kaho'olawe. Furthermore, the navy today has options to use simulated exercises that would replace training and stop the bombing of Kaho'olawe.

Keoni Fairbanks told me that his dream of Kaho'olawe would be for the military to return Kaho'olawe to the 'Ohana, pay for the clearing of ordnance, revegetate the land, and start helping with water programs. His concern, however, is that, even if the military gave up the island, the state would take over. He feels that Kaho'olawe should be given to the 'Ohana and that the federal and state government should support them. Fairbanks also expresses that he doesn't want the Department of Land and Natural Resources to turn the island into a hunting place, nor does he want resorts or any improved settlements on Kaho'olawe. The reason for this is because the island has both religious and cultural significance tied as one, and modernization would break the bond.

In conclusion, the island of Kaho'olawe is too valuable to be bombed by the navy. The Hawaiian people's long struggle to gain their heritage back is a lesson we must all follow and learn. We should support these people and help carry out their long-awaited dream to gain back Kaho'olawe. It is difficult to understand the importance of the island if you're not Hawaiian yourself, but think, always, in terms of being in their place. The island of Kaho'olawe is their land, their soil, their heritage. As Hawaiian activist George Helm wrote before he died: "I am a Hawaiian and I've inherited the soul of my <u>kupuna</u> [elder]. It is my moral responsibility to attempt an ending to this desecration of our sacred 'āina . . . for each bomb dropped adds further injury to an already wounded soul" (Yamaguchi A3).

[Bibliography omitted.]

Clete Yokoe

Feedback from Other Writers

Throughout this text, we have suggested various methods for getting feedback from your colleagues. Some have been oral, some written. Any of these would be helpful here.

Oral Draft. Your instructor might ask you to do an "oral draft." This would probably be most useful in the drafting stage, and could be done either in a small group or in the larger class. An oral draft is not a reading of your paper, but a "talking" of it. Your listeners can respond in several ways.

They might, for example, write a two- or three-level outline (or draw a tree diagram) of the paper as they listen, trying to see if they understand your point and your argument. Alternately, they might "tell back" your argument to see if they have understood it.

You might also ask some of your colleagues ahead of time to prepare one of the dialoguing questions we discussed above. Their task would be to listen to your oral draft, and then choose a question that they think might help you develop some idea more fully.

You might ask your colleagues to answer, orally or in writing, questions such as: What did you hear in my oral draft that you needed to hear more about? Did you hear anything you didn't need to hear? Did you learn anything that surprised you? Were you convinced by the presentation of this point? Where did you want to argue with me? Do you think you would win the argument? If so, what needs to be added or subtracted to convince you? What was the most interesting thing you learned from the paper? You and your listeners will think of other such questions.

Feedback on a Completed Draft.   When you have a good draft, you might like to get some written feedback from your colleagues. Below is a suggested set of questions that your readers could use to evaluate a draft. Some of the questions given above might also be used.

1. What is the thesis of the paper?

2. What are the major arguments and organizational structure of the paper? Write an outline showing them.

3. Are you confused at any point in the paper? Where? (Indicate paragraph and sentence.)

4. Look at each paragraph. Does it have a clear statement around which the paragraph is organized? Is there anything in the paragraph that does not relate to this central idea? Is the purpose of each paragraph clear? If any paragraph does not meet these criteria, indicate that below.

5. Look at each paragraph again. Does it have evidence? Is it persuasive? Indicate any paragraph that does not persuade.

6. Which is the strongest paragraph (or section) as far as persuasion goes? Which is the weakest?

7. Are you convinced by the argument? Where do you need to be convinced more?

8. Which paragraph is the best written in your opinion? Can you say why?

9. Do you notice particular editing problems? Is there a specific paragraph or section that needs editing?

10. What advice would you give the writer to help her write a stronger, more persuasive argument?

Here is a group activity that can accomplish the same things as the questions.

WRITING ACTIVITY

Have three other writers read your paper according to the following instructions:

Reader 1. Write a two-level outline of the paper. Be sure to begin with a thesis.

Reader 2. As you read the draft, take a red or blue pencil and underline the statement in each paragraph. Then put brackets around each reference to a piece of information. Finally, tell whether the paragraph has a clear voice to let the reader know why the information is used and how that paragraph relates to the overall structure and thesis of the paper.

Reader 3. Check the documentation for the paper. Tell the writer where you think it is not correct. Don't forget to check the bibliography.

After each reader finishes, discuss the paper and his or her comments. Then write a response, telling *specifically* what you plan to do in response to what the readers have said.

Sample Papers

We have discussed several papers so far in this chapter to illustrate a variety of possible strategies and topics. We include two more just for you to read. As you read them over, note the different kinds of material used, the clarity of the writing, and how much you learn from reading them.

Should Marijuana Be Legal in Alaska?

In early 1975 the legislature of the state of Alaska passed a law legalizing marijuana. This law allowed all adults eighteen years old or over to possess up to four ounces of marijuana in their homes for personal use. This law was eliminated March 3, 1991, when the state's voter-approved marijuana recriminalization law took effect. This law made any possession or use of marijuana illegal. I believe that the history of marijuana use since it was legalized and the new information on the drug more than justify the Alaska state legislature's action in recriminalizing use of this drug.

As can be expected, many Alaskans oppose the recriminalization. They think that the original reasons for making it legal still obtain. However, one of the major arguments for the law is clearly outmoded. In 1975 the state was not aware of how widespread the use of this drug was or would become. In 1966 the National Institute on Drug Abuse sponsored a nationwide study on the extent of drug use in the United States. Alaska, however, was not included since the study covered only the forty-eight contiguous states. Because of the lack of information on drug use in Alaska, the state didn't consider drug use a "significant problem" and believed that legalization wouldn't cause extensive drug use (Municipality of Alaska Task Force 2).

Further, in 1974 the state of Alaska began the construction of the trans-Alaska oil pipeline. The state thought that since drug use hadn't been a problem for the state that the legalization of marijuana would be helpful to the pipeline workers. They believed that the workers were confronting a "potential non-normal crisis situation, and will have to adopt unusual methods to cope with this unusual situation" (Task Force 4).

However, this situation proved unusual in an unexpected way. During the construction years (1974–1978), the state began to realize that the pipeline had had an adverse impact on "drug-related arrests, deaths, accidents, treatment admissions, etc." (Task Force 9). The pipeline workers developed drug habits and were able to buy large quantities of drugs due to their large paychecks from the state (Task Force 6). By the time the state realized the major drug abuse, the pipeline construction had ended and many of the effects beyond the pipe workers were not "immediately noticeable." However, it is now clear that there has been a general increase in crimes, drug abuse, tolerance for drugs and alcohol, and drug abuse among minors (Task Force 6, 8). The state has realized that they have to "address drug use" immediately, so they have begun to set up substance abuse centers to try to eliminate some of the drug abuse and problems that have occurred (Task Force 9).

Despite these problems, opponents of recriminalization argue on constitutional grounds that marijuana should be legal. The Alaska Supreme Court did unanimously rule that "possession of marijuana by adults at home, for personal use, is protected by the constitutional right to privacy" (Croft and Futch 1A). Using this decision, James Garhart, a resident of Wasilla, Alaska, argues that recriminalizing marijuana takes away his "freedom and liberty." He argues further that marijuana should fall under the same category as "alcohol, tobacco, sex, and handguns." These are legal for an adult under some circumstances and clearly illegal under others (Garhart 3).

In January 1991, David Jurco filed a lawsuit against the state to keep marijuana possession legal. Jurco said his suit is based on "the state constitution's guarantee of the right to individual liberty and the prohibition of cruel and unusual punishment" (Croft and Futch 1A). A nonprofit group called Alaskans for Privacy is helping with Jurco's case, for they also feel that the recriminalization of marijuana violates their "natural and fundamental right to liberty" (Croft and Futch 7A).

However, such arguments ignore more pressing concerns. The constitution does protect individual privacy, but the effects of marijuana use go beyond the rights of individuals. I agree with Wesley Jones that marijuana users who support legalization in Alaska are also "supporting ter-rorism, murder, and corruption on an international scale" (Jones 3A)—because drug use literally brings these things in its wake.

Another questionable argument for legalization comes from the many critics who compare it to the "legal drugs" alcohol and tobacco (DuPont 11). If alcohol and tobacco are legal, they argue, then so should marijuana be. They point to the many studies that show that alcohol and tobacco are also very addictive. When users of these drugs are unable to obtain the drug they develop withdrawal symptoms that include anxiety, restlessness, and insomnia. The symptoms occur until the user receives the drug or some substitute (Task Force 115). In addition, statistics show that 30 percent of all Americans are dying at an early age because of alco-hol and tobacco use. With these statistics in mind critics ask how mari-juana can be considered a dangerous and illegal drug when the legal drugs, alcohol and tobacco, are killing so many people (DuPont 11).

However, research shows that marijuana can be even more harmful than alcohol. Equally large numbers of people are not dying from its effects simply because it has not been as widely used. In a newsletter on marijuana by the Insurance Bureau of Canada, Dr. Hardin Jones points out that the chemical makeup of marijuana makes it potentially more harmful than alcohol. He states, "Marijuana is a cannabis plant made up of over 200 chemical compounds, with the main ingredient being THC (tetrahydrocannabinol)." Alcohol, however, is "an extremely uncompli-cated drug," which the body breaks down into carbon dioxide and water, with the main ingredient being ethanol. Dr. Jones has researched exten-sively on the ethanol in alcohol and the THC in marijuana. He has con-cluded that "50 grams of ethanol produces mild intoxication and is metabolized in about five hours, while only .005 grams of THC are required to produce the same degree of intoxication." Further it requires months for the THC to be removed from the body, so that in effect, Dr. Jones states that "the marijuana user is under the influence of the drug even between highs" (Insurance Bureau of Canada 3). A 1978 brief on alcohol and drug concerns published in Canada said that even eight days after smoking marijuana 20 percent of the THC is still present in the body. Since 1978, the dangers of the drug have increased, since all kinds of marijuana "on the street today have a higher concentration" (Insurance Bureau 3). Ann Landers emphasizes this fact when she quotes from a Chicago Tribune article that states, "a potent and expensive form of marijuana called sinsemilla . . . up to 18 times more powerful than the marijuana of 1960s" is now available (Landers 10G).

Marijuana appears to affect automobile driving just as alcohol does. In England studies have shown that ten out of fifty-four motorists killed in a ten-month period were found to have THC in their bodies (Insurance Bureau 3). In 1977 the Boston Accident Investigation Team found that "16% of drivers involved in fatal accidents had used marijuana" (Insurance Bureau 3). Psychologists believe that this is due to the usual effects of marijuana: distortion of time and space perception, vision impairment, loss of analytical thinking, and the decline in concentration and manual dexterity (Insurance Bureau 4).

Marijuana is also more dangerous than tobacco. Both cause damage to the tissue in the lungs. Marijuana, however, causes more than tobacco does. Researchers say that "5 marijuana cigarettes cause as much damage as 12 ordinary tobacco cigarettes." Therefore, marijuana users have a "50% higher chance of getting lung cancer than a regular tobacco user" (Insurance Bureau 6).

While some scientists have said that marijuana is not physically addictive, much research suggests that marijuana is just as addictive as alcohol and tobacco. Dr. Norman Panzica has said that "withdrawal of marijuana, especially in the chronic user, may evoke a psychic response in that the individual feels the need for the drug, somewhat like the symptoms of cigarette smokers.'' He also says marijuana use psychologically stimulates the desire for other "harder" drugs (Task Force 115). In one California drug abuse clinic, "99% of the heroin addicts under treatment used marijuana first and believed it would not lead to harder drugs when initially taken" (Insurance Bureau 2).

The legalization of marijuana for adults can also cause negative effects on minors. Marijuana is available today in Alaska to almost any kid who wants it. Because of its "ease of portability and transfer, the detection of this drug is virtually impossible." It is very difficult to "restrict its presence in the school or anywhere" (Insurance Bureau 2). Kids see it used in the schools by peers, and even by their parents. Legalizing the drug simply makes it even more available to minors and thus increases peer pressure to smoke it because kids feel grown-up to be doing what the adults can do legally. Teachers and counselors have testified that "academic performance drops in the students who use marijuana regularly." Such students have a lack of motivation that carries over even into sports and other activities "where there is the opportunity to learn and experience achievement" (Insurance Bureau 2).

Despite its dangers, marijuana has proved useful in the medical field. In 1971 the Federal Food and Drug Administration legalized THC, cannabinoids, and marijuana for medical uses. Marijuana was found to have a bronchodilating effect on the lungs and has been proven useful in the treatment of asthma. The drug has also helped with cancer, anorexia, depression, anxiety, muscle spasms, and even epileptic seizures (Insurance Bureau 4). Dr. Robert DuPont said that THC and other cannabinoids have "proved to be excellent research tools, and they have helped the medical profession with many ideas for further research" (DuPont 11).

This is not an argument for general legalization, however, and there is some concern about its use even in medicine, since it is a very dangerous drug. Ann Landers quotes from the National Security Intelligence Report that states, "Long-term use of marijuana damages your immune system and affects genetic structure of new cells" (Landers 10G). The THC from marijuana gathers in the fatty cells that are present in sex glands and brain cells. It interferes with the normal production of DNA and causes chromosome breakage, which produces birth defects (Insurance Bureau 3).

Overall marijuana is a dangerous and unhealthy drug. The Alaska legislature was correct in recriminalizing it. This law should help prevent premature death due to the effects of marijuana on the body.

Bibliography

Crater, John. Letter. Anchorage Daily News 3 Oct. 1991: 3A.

Croft, Jay, and Futch, David. "Pot Law Ignites 1st Challenge." Anchorage Times 5 Jan. 1991: 1A, 7A.

DuPont, Robert, MD. "Marijuana Is a Health Hazard." Listen Mar. 1982: 11.

Garhart, James. Letter. Anchorage Daily News 1 Oct. 1990: 3A.

Insurance Bureau of Canada. "Viewpoint," in The Marijuana Issue: A Headmaster's Perspective. Ontario, Canada: Ontario Secondary School Headmasters' Council, 1980.

Jones, Wesley J. Letter. Anchorage Times 31 Dec. 1990: 3A.

Kezer, Robert. Letter. Anchorage Times 11 Dec. 1990: 3A.

Landers, Ann. "Marijuana a More Powerful Drug Today." Editorial. Anchorage Daily News 14 Apr. 1991: 10G.

Municipality of Alaska Task Force. Task Force on Drug Use in Alaska. Alaska: 1990.

Rich, Kim. "Citation May Test Pot Law." <u>Anchorage Daily News.</u> 6 Apr.
    1991: 1A, 8A.

State of Alaska Legislature. <u>Relating to Penalties for Unauthorized Posses-
    sion and Control of Certain Drugs.</u> Alaska: 1975.

State of Alaska Legislature. "Chapter 71: Controlled Substances." <u>Alaska
    Statutes Supplement.</u> Alaska: 1990.

Suzanne M. Epperson

Making Amends

On February 19, 1942, President Franklin Roosevelt signed Executive
Order 9066, which gave any military commander the legal right to remove
anyone from any area. The mass internment of 120,000 persons of Japanese ancestry followed. Including both American citizens and Japanese
nationals, the internees were stripped of their freedom, property, and
livelihoods and condemned to crowded, unclean, and often half-completed
detention camps. They were never charged with any crime, but the
general public, which had been bombarded by prejudiced propaganda,
held them guilty by race.

Since then, President Gerald Ford has annulled Executive Order
9066, admitting that a national mistake had been made, and the Commission on Wartime Relocation and Internment of Civilians, set up by Congress in 1980, has suggested measures to compensate the victims. The
commission's recommendations have been written into a bill by Senator
Spark Matsunaga, which would establish the following if passed:

* a $1.5 billion fund to provide, initially, a one-time per capita payment
  of $20,000 to each of approximately 60,000 surviving internees
* a fund for humanitarian and public education related to the wartime
  events which would use the remaining monies of the $1.5 billion
* a law proclaiming that a grave injustice was done and making a
  national apology.

* presidential pardons to individuals convicted of violating wartime laws imposing a curfew on American citizens based on ethnic makeup.

* a liberal review by federal agencies of applications for restitution of positions, status, or entitlements lost in whole or in part because of wartime acts or events (Morse A9).

The redress of America's internment of the Japanese is long overdue.

Opponents of this redress have argued that internment was necessary, as the Japanese in the United States posed a threat to the war effort against Japan. William Blanchard, in the article, "Alien Internment Defended," noted that in California there had been a large number of Japanese nationals living in close proximity to an area in which 90 percent of America's aircraft industry was situated. Because of this, he had seen a great potential for an invasion of a "literally defenseless" California coast by Japanese troops intending to damage U.S. air strength (A13). Earl Warren, the attorney general of California at that time, held that Japanese-American citizens were more to be feared than alien Japanese (National Committee 11).

Such suspicions of Japanese-American disloyalty are refuted by a 1941 report by Curtis B. Munson, who had been assigned by the State Department to investigate the climate of Japanese-American communities on the West Coast and Hawai'i. The report "certified that Japanese-Americans possessed an extraordinary degree of loyalty to the United States, and immigrant Japanese were of no danger" (National Committee 9). The FBI and navy intelligence had been covertly monitoring Japanese-Americans for years and had found that "almost 100% of the Japanese American population was perfectly trustworthy," confirming Munson's report (National Committee 9). It should also be noted that although the defeat that Japan suffered at Midway in June 1942 left it incapable of invading the West Coast or Hawai'i, the building of durable mass detention camps in the United States was still in progress (National Committee 15).

Some try to justify the suffering of the Japanese in the detention camps by pointing out that everyone faces hardships during a war. In his editorial, "Reparations to AJAs," A. L. Goulart brings up the casualties and destruction caused by the bombing of Pearl Harbor and the atrocities that POWs faced at the hands of the Japanese military. He insists that victims from such Japanese military offensives should be compensated before redress of the interned Japanese takes place.

Compensating veterans for wartime injuries and paying restitution to the interned Japanese are two distinct issues. Veterans have served their nation and therefore receive benefits. In the case of the internees, about two-thirds were citizens wronged by their country. Most of the interned Japanese nationals "were permanent U.S. residents" (National Committee 3), which made them eligible for U.S. naturalization. Both groups are deserving of redress, as they were clearly discriminated against, being the only people with the ancestry of an enemy nation to suffer mass incarceration during the war. In 1942 there were 1,100,000 aliens in the United States from the countries with which America was at war, and less than 4 percent were Japanese. However, the majority of German and Italian nationals were restricted only by a curfew, and they did not encounter an extensive roundup, like that which the Japanese nationals and Japanese-American citizens faced. German- and Italian-American citizens maintained all their rights (National Committee 13).

The strongest argument that Japanese-Americans have for redress is that their most basic constitutional rights as U.S. citizens were violated with their incarceration. The Fourteenth Amendment of the Constitution reads as follows:

> No state shall make or enforce any law which shall abridge the privileges or immunities of citizens of the United States . . . nor shall any state deprive any person of life, liberty, or property, without due

process of law; nor deny to any person within its jurisdiction the equal protection of the laws.

The Fifth Amendment assures that one is not required to answer for a crime unless charged by a grand jury, and a quick, just trial for each citizen is stipulated by the Sixth Amendment (Malalis A19). All of these rights were usurped from Japanese-Americans, as they had to comply immediately with a military order of evacuation, forcing abandonment of property. They were thrown into a world totally lacking privacy and full of humiliation and uncertainty. Community toilets, contaminated water, rationing, and barbed wire were but a few of the indignities suffered. Some of the internees even lost their lives.

Of course, the Japanese-Americans have not been the only people ever subjected to injustices by a government. Although German Jews faced a higher level of inhumanity in the Nazi concentration camps, they shared a similar plight of Japanese-Americans, having been imprisoned without charge but on the basis of ''race.'' West Germany has made a restitution payment of approximately 35 to 40 billion dollars to Jews and Jewish institutions (National Committee 23). The U.S. government has a precedent to follow in dealing with questions of redress. To make amends for the broken treaties and other unjust acts it has committed against American Indians, our government has restored extensive acres of land to the various Indian tribes and spent millions of dollars on such things as an Indian Business Development Program (Jackson and Galli 140–141). Therefore, compensation of the Japanese internees is entirely within reason.

Some members of the Japanese community have shown indignation at the idea of redress, for in the Japanese character there is a strong affinity to endure hardship, suppress emotion, and work independently to better oneself. However, the interned Japanese have clearly been wronged—discriminated against for no justifiable purpose. Moreover, the majority of the internees were betrayed by their own nation, which willfully deprived them of the constitutional liberties of U.S. citizens. Restitution, therefore, is not an act of charity but the fulfillment of justice.

Bibliography

Chuman, Frank F. The Bamboo People. Del Mar, Calif.: Publisher's, 1976.

Blanchard, William. "Alien Internment Defended." Honolulu Advertiser
18 July 1981: A13.

"Governors and AJAs." Honolulu Advertiser 4 Aug. 1983: A12.

Hartwell, Jay. "Interned AJAs Must Be Compensated." The Sunday
Star Bulletin & Advertiser 16 May 1982: A9.

———. "Japanese-Americans Urged to Lead." Honolulu Advertiser 28 Apr.
1982: A4.

Hosokawa, Bill. JACL in Quest of Justice. New York: William Morrow and
Company, 1982.

Jackson, Curtis E., and Galli, Marcia J. A History of the Bureau of Indian
Affairs and Its Activities Among Indians. San Francisco: R & E
Research Associates, 1977.

Malalis, Carolyn. "How Japanese-Americans Were Denied Their Rights."
The Sunday Star Bulletin & Advertiser 30 May 1982: A19.

Morse, Harold. "Testimony Supports Reparations for AJAs." Honolulu
Star Bulletin 21 Mar. 1984: A9.

The National Committee for Redress. The Japanese American Incarceration:
A Case for Redress. San Francisco: Japanese American Citizens'
League, 1978.

Okubo, Mine. Citizen 13660. Seattle: University of Washington Press, 1983.

"Reparations to AJAs." Honolulu Star Bulletin 22 July 1981: A17.

"When the US was Wrong." Honolulu Star Bulletin 1 Aug. 1981: A7.

Zimmerman, Carl. "Reparations for Interned AJAs." Honolulu
Star Bulletin 24 Aug. 1981: A19.

student paper

We add one professional con/pro paper. This one is from *The Nation* 14 May 1990. In this article, as in most pieces from large-circulation magazines, there is no formal documentation. Note, however, that the sources are worked into the text. Note also that the author refutes con arguments as he presents the arguments for his thesis.

Professional Paper

Throwing Away the Key: Justice's War on Drug Treatment

Dick Thornburgh should meet Charles Cash, and he should do so at the latter's office in the Arthur Kill Correctional Facility for men on Staten Island. Cash, a former heroin addict and an ex-convict who is now a counselor in one of the country's most successful prison drug rehabilitation programs, is eager to pose a question to the Attorney General: Why has the Justice Department slashed out of its Bureau of Justice Assistance (B.J.A.) all funding for drug treatment in jails?

Given that the official price tag of the federal government's War on Drugs is $9.5 billion for the current fiscal year, Thornburgh's move to excise a few million dollars for jailhouse drug rehab may seem incidental. But it is a forceful statement of his department's monolithic "just deserts" approach to crime fighting: tough law enforcement and more prisons. To Cash, who well understands the criminal justice system and the despair of addiction, the decision to cut the funds is a perplexing and counterproductive action, one that leads him to question just how serious Washington is about drugs and crime.

The B.J.A., which functions like a foundation within the Justice Department, is supposed to encourage improvements in the criminal justice system by awarding grants to state and local governments. Eighty percent of its money flows to the states in the form of block grants, which can be used more or less as the states wish in such areas as law enforcement, victim assistance, drug testing, domestic violence programs and prison management. The rest of the funds are distributed as discretionary grants to specific programs the B.J.A. wants to promote. From 1987 through 1989, the B.J.A. dispensed almost $10 million in such awards to drug rehabilitation programs for convicts—a modest amount considering most states do not provide adequate treatment and, according to state governments, 60 to 85 percent of the people under correctional supervision require drug treatment services.

Much of the B.J.A. money for drug rehab supported experimental programs in several states, many modeled on Stay'n Out, the state-funded program at Arthur Kill prison, of which Charles Cash is a graduate. Cash was a high school basketball star in Brooklyn who used his reputation to pursue a career dealing drugs and invested his profits in his habit. He tried several times to clean himself up. But counseling at Phoenix House didn't work, nor did a stint in a methadone program, where he used fake names to obtain extra methadone to sell. He ended up in Arthur Kill on a felony extortion charge, and in 1979 entered Stay'n Out. After getting out of jail that same year, Cash found a job doing menial work at a meatpacking plant, and rose during the next seven years to become an assistant manager. He also received an associate degree in child behavior from Long Island University, and in 1987 he returned to Arthur Kill and Stay'n Out as a counselor. "Some people in Washington may not believe in rehabilitation," Cash says from behind his desk at the facility. "But this is where the truth lies. I am a spitting example."

Stay'n Out, pioneered by Ronald Williams, a former heroin addict who helped start Phoenix House in 1967, takes convicts with a history of drug abuse who are within two years of parole and places them in units segregated from the general prison population. Discipline in the wards is strict; those who enter the program are responsible for the appearance and some operations of their unit. For anywhere from nine months to two years, they attend seminars and counseling sessions on subjects ranging from how to find an apartment to how to understand what led to their addiction. "The jailhouse mentality stops at the door," Williams says. "They are residents, not inmates."

Arthur Kill prison is a grimy and depressing place, just a few miles from one of the nation's largest garbage dumps. But walk down a hallway and into the Stay'n Out wing and the atmosphere changes. The relations between guards and prisoners appear relaxed. The area is clean and the bunks are neat, the "residents" better groomed than their fellow "inmates."

At an orientation session in one ward, a counselor explains the hard-and-fast rules of the program: no fighting, no drugs or booze, no lying. Violate one of these and you're out. In another ward a group encounter session produces shouts and even roars; participants in the program must refrain from confrontations with one another until such meetings, where they can let it all out. In the meeting room of a third ward Hank Fury, a former judge who served seventeen months in a federal prison for a $2 million bank fraud, holds sway. He is now working for Stay'n Out, conducting seminars on values, among other things. "To keep off drugs and crime when they get back out (which will make them less of a threat to you and me), these guys are going to need a lot of inner strength," he says before the session. The convicts take it all quite seriously, asking Fury tough questions. If he could go back to his past life of wine, women and fast Cadillacs, why wouldn't he? They want to know how you can avoid feeling that you're only worth what you own and how much money you make. Clearly, the guys in this room are thinking hard about how to keep straight when they leave Arthur Kill.

The residents display a lot of pride in the program. When informed of the B.J.A. cutbacks, they get angry—angry that prisoners in other facilities won't get the chance they have had. Bill Mangot, a mountainous man sentenced in 1983 to nine to eighteen years for armed robbery and looking forward to his first furlough, shakes his head: "It's so obvious. Prison perpetuates low self-esteem. In this program you're treated as a human being, not a piece of junk." Other residents join in. "If you lock up a guy and give him nothing but hard time, he'll be back," says Mike Finch. "Stay'n Out taught me a lot and to think about what I did to end up here. I couldn't deal with that if I was just locked in a cell." Albert Nelson adds, "The folks in Washington should be looking at how to come up with solutions to the crime and drug problems. They have us here in prison. These are problems that can be addressed while we are incarcerated. I used drugs for twenty years and never stopped to look at what I did until I got here. I knew drugs were bad—they say, 'Just Say No'—but I still chose to do drugs."

These men can recite backward and forward all the standard arguments for treatment: the high recidivism rate, the budgetary burdens of building prisons, the cost-benefit case for rehab, how hard time breeds hardened criminals who will be back on the street someday. "Washington is taking the easy way out," gripes Matt Whitfield. "You just lock up the person and try to forget about him." And when Robert Ellevy declares, "I know I'm not the same person who came into the penal system," all the others nod in agreement.

One hundred forty-three men are enrolled in Stay'n Out at Arthur Kill, and forty-six women participate in its program at the Bayview Correctional Facility in Manhattan. The waiting list for Arthur Kill is several hundred names long, which allows the program to accept those convicts who seem most likely to benefit from it. One unit at Arthur Kill serves as a training ward for officials and counselors from other states interested in developing similar plans. Stay'n Out claims a success rate of 78 percent, based on a study that found that three-fourths of its alumni stayed off drugs and were not arrested during their parole period.

Last summer, when the B.J.A. staff in Washington compiled a program plan for this year's discretionary grants, it called for devoting about 20 percent of these awards to prison drug treatment and other correctional programs. In November, according to a Justice Department official who would likely become unemployed if named here, the program staff at the B.J.A. received a sharp message from the higher regions of the department that said, in effect, "Thank you very much. Now we're going to do what we want." And they did.

This year's discretionary budget totals $49.6 million, but not a dime of it is for jailhouse drug rehabilitation. There is, however, up to $2.7 million reserved for the National Citizens' Crime Prevention Campaign, best known for its mascot Mcgruff, the sleuthing hound who urges us all to "take a bite out of crime." In previous years the program staff, made up of midlevel career employees, went through a very careful and deliberate process in determining who would receive discretionary grants. This year the professionals were cut out of the loop, according to department sources, and the higher-ranking political appointees took over. "The politicals suspect the career employees are not ideologically pure," one Justice official says.

The two political appointees directly responsible for the Office of Justice Programs, which includes the B.J.A., refused to comment on the funding cut. But their public remarks provide clues to the decision. In 1989 Richard Abell, the assistant attorney general in charge of the Office of Justice Programs, contributed an article on the crisis of prison overcrowding to *Policy Review*, the journal of the conservative Heritage Foundation. "Criminal rehabilitation usually doesn't work," he wrote. What will? More prisons. In an address last year to the Federal Bar Association, Clifford White 3d, the deputy assistant attorney general for the Office of Justice Programs, focused on the shortage of prison beds as a key challenge for the criminal justice system. His answer: more prisons.

Since Abell and White—and their boss Thornburgh—are so concerned about the lack of prison space, one might assume they would be interested in a program that could ease overcrowding. About 75 percent of those released from state prisons are rearrested. Stop the revolving door at the jailhouse, and the crisis becomes manageable. Both Abell and White pay lip service to the need to explore innovative solutions, but what they have in mind are the "innovations" of boot camps, house arrest and cheap modular prisons. "Criminal justice people think treatment is coddling, that it's sweet time," one Justice Department official says. "They would like treatment to be surgery—take a piece out of someone's brain and make him a good citizen in thirty days."

Within the department, the political appointees justified the B.J.A cuts by arguing that such programs should be the province of the Department of Health and Human Services and its National Institute on Drug Abuse. But no such programs yet exist in those agencies; moreover, prison treatment is not a field that the public health sector has much experience in. The Justice Department is simply dropping the ball.

Discretionary funds are bucks with big bangs. The intent has been for the B.J.A. to use them to create a chain reaction within the criminal justice community. Cut them off, and the reaction slows. "We are dismayed by [the cuts]," says Diane Canova, the public policy director of the National Association of State Alcohol and Drug Abuse Directors. She speaks of the fierce competition among state law enforcement and corrections officials for block-grant money and state resources, noting that the money "is usually gobbled up by law enforcement activities. It's hard for state criminal justice planners to trade in money for new radios or police gear for a new rehab wing; it's difficult to wean them away from their past practices."

Stay'n Out's Williams recalls that federal funding was crucial to his program's takeoff in 1977. "At that time there was a lot of resistance within corrections," he says. "To make the program palatable to the New York State corrections officials, we had to have federal funds. Corrections received a gift of a program and personnel. That made it easier for them to give it a shot."

The very success of jail treatment programs may have led to their defunding. "What we apparently did was catalyze a lot of thinking about rehab, and not just for drug abusers but for all offenders," says Dr. Douglas Lipton, director of research of Narcotic and Drug Research Inc., which received $1.3 million in B.J.A. grants, in part to help states develop prison drug-treatment programs. "That may have triggered a response in that part of the Justice Department that doesn't believe in any rehabilitation."

Treatment in general has not been a top priority of the Bush Administration's crusade against drugs. Of the $10.6 billion proposed for next year's federal antidrug budget, 70 percent is reserved for law enforcement, corrections and interdiction; only 14 percent is earmarked for treatment. Dr. Beny Primm, director of Health and Human Services' new Office for Treatment Improvement, has actually called for a moratorium on new money for treatment, claiming that many publicly funded treatment programs are not spending all the available funds.

At the same time, the National Association of State Alcohol and Drug Abuse Directors estimates that only 13 percent of the 10.6 million Americans who need treatment are receiving it. Still, no one has yet come up with a grand plan for a national treatment-on-demand program, and even some drug policy experts sympathetic to the concept note that any such program would face daunting obstacles, not least among them the reluctance of many addicts to apply for treatment and then stick with it.

Studies do show that a great number of substance abusers come into contact with the criminal justice system and that the success of drug rehabilitation is often contingent on the length of treatment. In fact, a recent study funded by the Justice Department estimates that as many as 1.3 million recent arrestees in major metropolitan areas are cocaine users—more than the 620,000 to 1.2 million weekly cocaine users the National Institute on Drug Abuse estimates exist in the entire nation. This makes jail an ideal spot for rehab. Even the White House cannot avoid conceding this, at least on paper. The National Drug Control Strategy it released last September notes that prisons "can provide an opportunity for treatment, and more such programs should be designed, demonstrated, and evaluated." The report hails Stay'n Out as a program that has produced encouraging results and that should be replicated by states using federal grants. The Justice Department didn't get the message.

Prison drug rehabilitation is no magic solution. The Stay'n Out counselors acknowledge that most residents, even after they complete the program, still don't realize what they are going to face on the outside. Some, but not all, will obtain post-release treatment. Stay'n Out is planning to open its first residential treatment center in the Bedford-Stuyvesant neighborhood of Brooklyn, but it will have only forty to fifty beds. When inmates leave Arthur Kill, all that New York State gives them is a suit, $40 and a subway token.

These men are going to be out on the street one way or another. Our choice is between an ex-con who has had treatment and one who has spent his time in the general prison population. Bill Mangot, the armed robber now just nine credits short of a Bachelor of Arts degree in sociology from St. John's University, knows that drug rehab programs won't work for all convicts: "But for most it gives them a better chance. If they were not here they'd be on even shakier ground when they get out."

One need not have sympathy for criminals to realize that taxpaying and law-abiding citizens (especially those most likely to be crime victims) are better off if the ex-con makes it, if the addict remains clean. Those in the Justice Department and elsewhere who talk tough about fighting crime and prosecuting a War on Drugs but then cut a program that demonstrably reduces the number of substance abusers and criminals are hypocrites. They are hard on criminals, but soft on crime.

David Corn

Appendix: Research Materials

Kaho'olawe is a currently uninhabited island in the Hawaiian chain. Since World War II it has been used by the United States Navy as a target area for training pilots. Several years ago, various groups in Hawai'i began protesting that the island should not be used in this way, but should be returned to the state, or to the Hawaiian people, for civilian use of one kind or another. Items 1 and 27 in this section give histories of this controversy. See also Chapter 7 for a more comprehensive discussion of the issues involved.

The following articles, selected from newspapers in Hawai'i and other sources, discuss the pros and cons of this issue. Read them through carefully since they will form the raw material for several assignments in this text. The articles are numbered and given in chronological order (except for number 20). The bibliographic information for each is given after the number. Because of the way in which the controversy developed, the last articles give the most complete picture of the Hawaiian activists' point of view. Thus you must read the whole packet of articles to get a complete view of the controversy.

Some of the articles are abridged. Where that is done, it is indicated by an ellipsis. Article 7 is adapted from the original. All others are as in the original sources except that a few typographical errors have been silently corrected. The name of the island is Kaho'olawe, with the ' indicating a glottal stop common in the Hawaiian language between two vowels. Many articles give the name without this indication. The articles contain several Hawaiian terms, which are defined below.

Glossary

Note: Because usage varies, the spelling of certain terms and place names may vary in the readings in this section.

Aloha 'Āina: "Āina" means land; "Aloha 'Āina" implies spiritual links to the land. See Article 27 for a definition.

Heiau: Temple or shrine.

Haole: Foreigner, used mainly for Caucasians, especially those from the U.S. mainland.

Kama'aina: Someone who has lived for a long time in Hawai'i—literally, "child of the land."

Kamehameha Schools and Bishop Estate: The estate comprises the lands that were privately owned by the Kamehameha dynasty chiefs. They were left by the last heir for education for Hawaiian children. The estate supports the Kamehameha Schools for Hawaiians.

Kahuna: Expert of a particular art, craft, or practice, whose talent was believed to be endowed by the gods, thus a priest.

Kupuna: Elder, male or female.

Mana: Personal power or strength that is rooted in nature and the gods.

'Ohana: A family, especially an extended family; used by Hawaiian organizations that seek to work together using traditional Hawaiian procedures rather than Western organizational methods.

shibai: A shady and dishonest deal.

List of Articles

1   MacDonald, "Fixed in Time: A Brief History of Kahoolawe"

2   Stearns, "Pre-Navy Kahoolawe"

3   Nelson, "Can Kahoolawe Be Cleared for Habitation?"

4   "Bomb Ban Sought for Kahoolawe"

5   Bakutis, "Kahoolawe: Little Island, Big Find"

6   Tong, "Kahoolawe 'Needed'"

7   Stearns, "Kahoolawe in the Raw"

8   Midkiff, "Kahoolawe from the Beginning"

9   Bakutis, "The Two Faces of Kahoolawe"

10   Haugen, "A Tale of Two Target Islands"

11   Altonn, "Kahoolawe Uncovered"

12   McCoy, "Navy Protects Kahoolawe Sites"

13   Sawyer, "Sites Weren't Protected, Sawyer Says"

14   Daugherty, "Isle Needed for Training Says Marine"

15   Hamasaki, "The Hawaiians and Kahoolawe"

16   Kim, "Reply to Daugherty"

17   Nelson, "Kahoolawe Tug-of-War Cost Navy $572,000"

18   Altonn, "Lyman Enlists in Fight to Rescue Kahoolawe"

19   Kakesako, "Navy Spells Out Why It Uses Kahoolawe"

20   Smith, "Kahoolawe: Hawaiians on Trial"

21   Westlake, "Behind Bars: An Interview with Richard Sawyer and Walter Ritte, Jr."

22   Ashdown, "Once-Green Kaho'olawe Can Be Revived"

23   Altonn, "Kahoolawe Trees Thriving"

24   Aluli, "Why the Bombing of Kaho'olawe?"

25   *Aloha 'Aina: Ending Military Use and Control of Kaho'olawe*

26   McGregor, "Myths Cloud Pro-Military Thinking on Kahoolawe"

27   *Kaho'olawe and the Protect Kaho'olawe 'Ohana*

ARTICLE 1

MacDonald, Peter. *Fixed in Time: A Brief History of Kahoolawe.* Honolulu: Hawaiian Historical Society, 1972.

Kahoolawe, the smallest of the eight main islands in the Hawaiian group, is dry, barren and seemingly abused by both man and his gods. Loneliness is the characteristic that must be emphasized in any description of the island. High winds deflected from Maui's Haleakala Crater sweep over the isle's terrain with a force which sends clouds of red dirt miles over the ocean—an effect that resembles a colorful, mystical storm. The island's sounds are almost exclusively produced by rustling pili grass, creaking cactus and keawe and the splash of Pacific surf. Nature's right to govern Kahoolawe's mood is periodically challenged by United States Navy aircraft and ships which bomb and shell the area. At night flashes from the detonations can be observed from neighboring Lanai, Molokai, Maui and Hawaii.

Geologists describe the volcanic origin of Kahoolawe as occurring during the early Pleistocene Epoch about 1.5 million years ago. It is speculated that west Maui, east Lanai, east Molokai and Kahoolawe were at one time all interconnected. But erosion and a 250 foot elevation of the shoreline during the Aftonian Interglacial submerged those areas that had been adjoined. Currently, with the elements and man daily wearing away its surface, Kahoolawe is 10.9 miles long, 6.4 miles wide, 1,472 feet in altitude with a total area of 45 square miles.

Hawaiian legend gives another interpretation of the island's creation. In the chant of the high-priest, Kahakukamoana, chiefly families from Nuumea, Holani, Tahiti and Polapola (Bora Bora) settled on various islands in Hawaii, thus poetically bringing them to life. According to native myth,

> Kahoolawe is said to be the child of Keaukanai, the man, and Walinuu, the wife, from Holani; and the epithet of the island-child is "the farmer," he lopa. Molokini (a small islet in mid-channel between Maui and Kahoolawe) has no separate settlers but is called navel-string-lewe-of Kahoolawe.

In the centuries prior to the white man's arrival the western point of Kahoolawe gained considerable importance as the landmark indicating the direction of Tahiti. For this reason the cape was called Ke-ala-i Kahiki (the route to Tahiti).

The Hawaiian historian, Malo, explained that the natives managed to plant potatoes, yams and sugar cane on the island. An absence of taro cultivation was due to the extreme aridity of the area. More recent evidence indicates that the Hawaiians living on Kahoolawe prior to Cook's discovery were never more than semi-permanent residents. Fishing and not agriculture was the principal source of food. Kahoolawe served as a base for a fishing population which never totaled more than 150 persons before 1778.

Early European explorers left brief descriptions of the island. Noticeably absent are favorable impressions concerning Kahoolawe's beauty or capacity to support life. . . .

The Imperial Russian Navy's Lieutenant Von Kotzebue presented evidence of human life on the island. During the night of November 25, 1816, his ship fell into a trade wind which took him and his crew so close to Kahoolawe that they sighted a number of fires along the coastline.

Contact with Western civilization did not change conditions or the population on Kahoolawe immediately. It continued to serve as a fishing station for native canoes well into the 19th Century. Beginning in 1830 the island would be used as a penal colony for the monarchy. . . . After Kahoolawe's designation as an isle of exile, most of its fishing population steadily moved to Honuaula, Maui. . . .

Most of the convicts were suffering from dysentery due to a steady diet of kupala, a feed for hogs. They resolved to reduce their discomfort and in late February, 1841, the exiles began the first of a series of foraging trips northward across Alalakeiki Channel. . . .

The convicts made more raids upon Kalepolepo, Maalaea, Ukemehame, Olowalu and Waikapu—all on Maui. With each trip they procured enough canoes, potatoes and taro to make survival certain. . . .

During the British occupation of Honolulu, February to July 1843, the law banishing criminals to Kahoolawe was abrogated. With the restoration of Hawaiian independence on July 31, royal pardon was extended to the Kahoolawe exiles as well as others imprisoned during the period of British control. . . .

Leases of the island to various politicians, businessmen, and ranchers were secured between 1858 and 1910. At the latter date Kahoolawe was proclaimed a forest reserve. . . . *[There follows a description of three such leases, all unsuccessful. The lessees introduced plants, but they also brought grazing animals, with the result summarized below.]*

The plight of Kahoolawe's investors was in large part due to the island's natural characteristics. Strong northerly winds are redirected off Haleakala toward Kahoolawe making it the windiest of the eight major Hawaiian islands. Maui robs moisture from the northeast and its southern neighbor is dependent upon Kona storms for rain. Rainfall recorded on the island has ranged from 8 to 27 inches per year. In addition, the introduction of livestock upset the ecology of Kahoolawe. A subsequent loss of plant life accelerated the island's erosion. C.S. Judd wrote in 1916,

> The innumerable sheep and goats cropped the grass and other herbage so closely that the sod cover was broken. This gave the entering wedge for the wind to exert its influence on the light top soil. This unprotected and exposed soil could not stand the force of the strong trade wind but was lifted little by little and carried southwest across the island many miles out to sea in a great red cloud. In this manner the top of the island which was once covered with four to eight feet of good soil has been reduced largely to hardpan. . . . The area affected in this manner by aeolian erosion covers, fortunately, only about one-third of the island on the higher elevations. One-third, as already has been stated, in the more sheltered parts is covered with pili and other grasses in which there is growing up a fine stand of young algaroba trees. The remaining one-third, toward the southeast is at the lower elevation and is very rocky and barren.

Profit and Loss

Governor Frear proclaimed the island a Territorial Forest Reserve in 1910. After he briefly visited Kahoolawe late in 1911, it was decided that the area could only be saved by the elimination of grazing animals. Eben Low was employed in the double task of ridding the island of his own livestock and thousands of wild sheep and goats.

A research expedition undertaken by Charles Forbes in 1913 for the Bishop Museum revealed that Kahoolawe had 16 native plants and 15 introduced species.

A tree tobacco (*Nicotiana Glauca*) was the most common species probably because the animals would not eat it.

By 1918 the Territorial reclamation project had proven itself unsuccessful. On January 1, 1918, Angus MacPhee, a cowboy from Wyoming and ex-manager of the Ulupalakua Ranch on Maui, secured the Kahoolawe lease for 21 years at $200 a year. Terms of the lease stipulated that in 4 years all the goats and sheep would be removed. In time, MacPhee hoped that the island's vegetation would support cattle.

At the end of two years MacPhee managed to slaughter or capture and sell over twelve thousand goats and sheep. Twelve Hawaiian cowboys under Jack Aina were recruited for the extermination. The last of the herds became harder to track and some animals were able to find refuge along the cliffs and caves of the island's eastern sections. Thus, in spite of the preparation and work, the first phase of the island's recovery was not a complete success. The sheep and goat population, though considerably reduced, was not thoroughly destroyed.

The attempt to build Kahoolawe into a profitable enterprise was initiated with the erection of ten redwood water tanks of 10,000 gallons capacity. In addition, there were several 5,000 gallon tanks built. Fencing and corrals were constructed and 5,000 trees planted. Also, hundreds of pounds of Australian salt-bush and grass seed were spread over the island. In time, the plants began to thrive in the rich volcanic soil irrigated by trapped water. When two years had expired, Governor Wallace R. Farrington inspected MacPhee's accomplishments and extended the island's lease to 1953.

But Kahoolawe's misfortune, seemingly the island's dominant trait, was soon to drive MacPhee to the brink of financial ruin. First, a young Hawaiian cowboy was killed one day when the surf was exceedingly high. His comrades, still influenced by superstition, were certain that his ghost remained on the island and some of them decided to leave. Not long after, a recently built 50,000 gallon cistern lacked the proper amount of cement and collapsed under a storm's downpour. MacPhee was close to losing the $90,000 he had invested in Kahoolawe. Luckily, he was able to form a partnership with Harry Baldwin of the Maui Agricultural Company and was saved from bankruptcy. Another $90,000 was put into the island and the owners renamed their project Kahoolawe Ranch.

The middle and late 1930s saw the reclamation of the area progressing at a slow but seemingly steady pace. A new sampan was built to haul cattle and water between Kahoolawe and Maui. Named the *Mazie C.*, the small boat was launched in April 1937. By 1938, 600 head of cattle were being fattened on the island as rains drenched the soil and the planted brush and grasses were watered. A total investment of more than $190,000 had been spent by January of 1941. But a small annual profit was also being made. Both MacPhee and Baldwin were confident of success.

The events of December 7, 1941, were to drastically determine the future of Kahoolawe. The military commandeered the MacPhee sampan and forbid anyone to go to the island. Patriotism helped move Baldwin and MacPhee to sublease the island to the Army, Navy and Marines. Years of destructive bombing followed. Worse, numerous undetonated explosives made any future agricultural project almost impossible. Kahoolawe gained the somewhat sad distinction of being "the most shot at island in the world."

The end of the war did not bring the re-establishment of the Kahoolawe Ranch. By the terms of contract with the Territorial Government, MacPhee and Baldwin had rights on the island until 1953. But the Navy was able to convince administrators in Honolulu that the demands of military preparedness should be met before those of private interest. Late in 1945, MacPhee and his daughter were allowed to go to Kahoolawe to survey the damage but the Navy refused to release the custody of the island. The old rancher filed an $80,000 suit against the Navy in 1946 when it appeared that Washington was neither allowing him to reclaim his properties nor compensating for his financial losses. MacPhee was never able to regain his holding and died in 1948. . . .

The Battle for Kahoolawe

[An executive order February 20, 1953, directed the Navy to assume complete control of Kahoolawe. This section starts with a description of early protests against the bombing. Prominent in this early movement was Elmer Cravalho, mayor of the island of Maui.]

However reduced the acreage used for target practice, by mid-November 1970, there was still no appreciable slackening of Navy bombing operations. In late January of next year, Pearl Harbor officers stated that the surrender of Culebra Island target site to Puerto Rico ws not indicative of a similar policy in Hawaii . . . for the future. At about the same time, Senator Inouye received a letter from the Assistant Secretary of Defense for Installations and Logistics, Frank Sandars. Inouye was informed that "it is not intended to make the island (Kahoolawe) excess to the needs of the Navy in the foreseeable future" since it would cost $1,000,000 to conduct a reasonable 70% surface clearance and less than 50% water clearance of undetonated explosives. In the senator's opinion the Department of Defense credibility was still questionable and he remarked,

> It would appear that the Navy continues to insist that no such rehabilitation is possible and further—or perhaps therefore—there is no need to determine the (total) cost or feasibility because the Navy has no intent to ever return Kahoolawe to the State of Hawaii, even if the Navy's need should diminish . . . With all the knowhow the Department of Defense has accumulated on explo-

sives and detection, I just cannot believe that this is an impossible task. We did it in World War II in such bombed population centers in Berlin, Tokyo and elsewhere. Who are they trying to dissuade? . . .

In late July, Cravalho and Life of the Land, a local ecology group, filed a suit against Secretary of the Defense Laird, Secretary of the Navy Chafee and Rear Admiral Hayward. The plaintiffs contended that the defendants had failed to abide by the National Environmental Policy Act of 1969, which required that the military submit detailed reports on the effects of bombardment on Kahoolawe's terrain to Hawaii's public. . . .

In mid-May of 1972, the Navy submitted a report which deemphasized the effects upon the target site and instead claimed, "The environmental effect of weapon exercises upon the ecology or ecological system of other nearby islands of the Hawaiian archipelago will remain negligible." This was apparently enough for Judge Tavares who dismissed the suit of Cravalho and Life of the Land on May 16, 1972. . . .

Red Dust in the Sunset . . .

[This section gives a summary of the situation as of 1972.]

Kahoolawe's bombardments alternate between sea barrages and aerial bombing. Sea-to-surface missiles and high-caliber gunfire from Navy vessels pound the island an average of two days and two nights a week. Navy and Marine aircraft drop 200–500 pound bombs three days and two nights a week. A termination of the target practice tomorrow, next week, next month or next year is highly unlikely. If the attention devoted to the issue by Honolulu's newspapers is a fairly accurate index, then public interest concerning the Kahoolawe dispute has already begun to wane within the last year. Likewise, Congress has had to deal with its usual assortment of world and national problems so that a careful study of Inouye's bill of April 27, 1971, has been neglected. . . .

Naval officers and the animals of Kahoolawe have exhibited a strikingly similar streak of stubbornness. At times, one could almost suspect an unannounced alliance between the two groups. The Navy has not been eager to conduct the complete extermination of the goats and sheep, and for their part, these durable inhabitants of the island have not complained about the target practices. If the animals continue to multiply and destroy Kahoolawe's vegetation, full rehabilitation would be impossible, but the Navy's position more secure.

Naval personnel express hurt astonishment when there is any suggestion of placating Maui's hunters and fishermen at the expense of "national defensive readiness." Yet, below the surface, the military mind is not likely to be very troubled. Custom is on the Navy's side since customarily the Department of Defense has not been inclined to give up its holdings. The State revegetation program on two thirds of Kahoolawe might be viewed as a partial capitulation to Hawaii's government, but the Navy continues to retain full authority over the island. Finally, Naval policy makers are possibly comforted by the fact that any monetary backing for Gundersen's proposal (perhaps the only practical and realistic reclamation plan in existence for Kahoolawe) is out of the question. . . .

[MacDonald's impression that public interest was lessening was probably true at the time, but less than three years later, a group of native Hawaiians started another even more active protest. The following articles detail this. For another historical summary, written by this group, see Articles 25 and 27.]

ARTICLE 2

Stearns, Harold T. "Pre-Navy Kahoolawe." *Honolulu Star Bulletin* 20 Jan. 1976: A15.

[The author is a former district geologist with the U.S. Geological Survey and the author of "Geology and Groundwater Resources of Lanai and Kahoolawe." Hawaii Bulletin 6, Hawaii Div. of Hydrography, 1960.]

We were tossed violently about in a sampan the day in March 1939, when James Y. Nitta, my assistant, Stanley, my young son, and I were put aboard a dingy and rowed ashore to Kahoolawe. Having looked at the island for years from Maui, I was excited to have a chance to explore it.

Harry Baldwin, who had leased the island from the Territory of Hawaii for a cattle ranch, had provided us with transportation and horses for my survey in the hope that water supplies could be found for his cattle.

An Ecuadorian, Manuel Pedro, the manager of the ranch and a colorful character, lived on Kahoolawe, and we slept in his cabin during our work on the island. He kept us awake nightly with stories about his exploits on the island and elsewhere. Near the cabin was a rain catch and a storage tank which supplied us with drinking water.

We rode all over the island and spent several days hiking along the spectacular cliffs and circling the island in a boat. Manuel said that about 500 cattle, 200 wild sheep, 25 wild goats, 17 horses, three mules, and 500 wild turkeys were on the island.

Abundant schools of bright tropical fish could be seen easily from the shore, and the rocks were covered with opihi. It was a fisherman's dream. I gathered up a gunny sack full of glass floats which had drifted in from Japanese fishing fleets in the north Pacific.

Kahoolawe is seven miles long, six miles wide, 1,491 feet high and covers 45 square miles or about the same size as Saipan (48 sq. mi.). The island lies 6¾ miles from Maui and is part of Maui County. In late geologic time it was submerged to a depth of 850 feet, which left most of the land bare and rocky, but in the Dust Cap area on the leeward side ½ to 1 foot of loose dust covers most of the rocks. . . .

I named the red cap above 850 feet the Dust Bowl because on every windy day a streamer of red dust extends eastward from it for miles out over the sea. Evidence exists that this cap once supported trees, but the introduction of goats in the Hawaiian Islands in 1778 by Capt. James Cook ultimately spelled doom for the trees.

A drive to rid the island of goats was started in 1918. Most were eliminated but some remained, and I saw a number on the cliffs above Kanapou Bay in 1939 and am told that they became numerous again after the Navy took over the island.

Kiawe trees were introduced about 1900 and successfully reclaimed most of the barren slopes and, in some places, formed dense groves. Two plots of ground had been fenced for a period of five years as an experiment, and these plots had grass and flourishing haole koa growing knee-high when I mapped the island, indicating that reclamation by nature would be possible if the wild goats and sheep were eliminated.

The rainfall averages about 25 inches per year, which is enough to keep vegetation alive. Unfortunately, most of the rain falls during a few heavy kona storms although "Naulu" storms are common. The trade winds are cut off from Kahoolawe by Haleakala.

Rain is the only source for fresh water supplies. Seven dug wells existed late in the 19th century. These supplied water for stock until about 1900 when the water in the wells became brackish. By 1939 the water in the Ahupa well contained 3,250 particles per million and in the Hakiowa well 12,600 ppm of chlorides, much too salty to drink.

Several shallow wells formerly had supplied 25 to 80 Hawaiians with brackish water during the period from 1823 to 1858. Baldwin built two 10,000 gallon tanks at Papakanui Beach, which he filled with fresh water boated from Maui.

Occasional flood waters are available from Kuhei Gulch, but it is obvious that extensive rain catches would have to be built or water would have to be brought from Maui to support any practical future use of the island. Kahoolawe contained numerous fishing shrines in the early days and was a source of stone for adzes as I found large abandoned quarries there. The archaeology has been described by J. Gilbert McAllister in Bishop Museum Bulletin 115.

No coral reefs occur, but the spectacular coastline and sea cliffs, reaching 800 feet in height, lapped by the blue Pacific, give Kahoolawe a special beauty and serenity. No other State in the union would permit so wonderful an island to be used for bombing.

Whatever excuses may have been valid during World War II expired at the end of the Vietnam war. The Navy should relinquish Kahoolawe and return it to the people of Hawaii for a State or national park. It would make a unique public park if cleaned up, restored and opened for recreational use.

A landing field can be easily constructed and a dock for small boats would make the island accessible to people from all over the State with especial value to Maui with its rapidly growing developments along the nearby coast.

If officially requested, the cleanup program could be done by the Navy with modern techniques in a matter of a few months. The recent invasions of Kahoolawe by occupying Hawaiians is an understandable protest against regulations which deny the people of Hawaii the full use and the enjoyment of one of their Islands.

ARTICLE 3

Nelson, Lyle. "Can Kahoolawe Be Cleared for Habitation?" *Honolulu Star Bulletin* 24 Mar. 1976: F8.

By July the Navy and State should know whether Kahoolawe is a "bomb" that eventually will hurt someone.

The man heading a study to determine to what extent Kahoolawe is an arsenal of buried, deadly duds declined to discuss his preliminary estimates of conditions on the target Island.

Wendell Webber, president of Marinco Ltd., spent the first week of March on Kahoolawe on a field trip.

He was accompanied by an earth-moving heavy equipment expert.

In a telephone interview from his office at Falls Church, Va., Webber said, "It is too early to discuss costs of cleaning it up but we will have a better idea by July. Then it's up to the Navy or Congress to release our findings," he said.

Webber has a Navy contract to undertake clean-up feasibility studies of several bomb targets.

His men are back on the Island today resuming a survey to determine what needs to be done to clear the Island of 35 years of shelling.

Rear Adm. Donald C. Davis, when he was 14th Naval District commandant in 1969, estimated there were 10,000 tons of shells and shrapnel fragments on the Island.

The potential danger of the Island was cited last week by Davis's successor, Rear Adm. Ralph Wentworth.

"The big problem is under the earth where, if a fuse is hit the wrong way, it's going to go off," he said.

Wentworth said he read with interest the opinions of Richard J. Keogh, a retired Army explosives expert who wrote about Kahoolawe for the March issue of Honolulu magazine.

Keogh points out that:

Ten percent of all bombs dropped are duds which means 90 percent, consisting of bomb fragments, will confuse electronic detection instruments.

Clearing the surface of ordnance will not make the Island safe for nonmilitary uses.

Bombs dropped vertically from aircraft have been known to penetrate 90 feet below the surface and that almost all holes of entry soon disappear with time and rain.

What will be the impact on the ecosystems of Kahoolawe if the entire Island is dug up?

Rear Adm. Davis made a brief survey on the Island in 1969 after a Navy bomb was found on Mayor Elmer Cravalho's West Maui pastureland.

Davis estimated 50 trained ordnance specialists could clear 70 percent of the surface in 200 days. He did not include offshore areas where bombs missed the target.

From his 1969 survey Davis concluded the Island was beyond saving, unfit for future human habitation.

This upset Sen. Daniel K. Inouye who questioned Defense Department and Navy credibility and candor, saying that the 1953 presidential order called for restoration, when no longer needed for national security, of the land to its earlier condition. . . .

ARTICLE 4

"Bomb Ban Sought for Kahoolawe." *Sunday Honolulu Star Bulletin & Advertiser* 14 Oct. 1976: A7.

Thirteen persons and the Protect Kahoolawe Association yesterday filed suit in Federal court seeking an end to military bombing practice over Kahoolawe. . . .

The suit says that the continued use of live ordnance on Kahoolawe pollutes the environment, endangers lives, interferes with religious practices and destroys historical sites. . . .

The suit says that the defendants have violated the National Environmental Policy Act because they have failed to file "statutorily required environmental impact statements" with their budget requests for funding of the Kahoolawe bombing.

The suit says further that under the Federal Water Pollution Act each depart-ment of the executive branch of the Federal Government must comply with requirements for the control and abatement of water pollution.

"The discharge of bombs and munitions into the State ocean waters surround-ing Kahoolawe renders such waters unreasonably harmful and detrimental to pub-lic health, safety, recreation, welfare, aquatic life, thereby creating water pollution," the suit says.

The plaintiffs also say that the bombs and munitions have caused soil erosion on the island and "the movement of sediment into the coastal waters of the island."

The Clean Air Act is violated, the suit alleges, because the use of live ord-nance . . . "generates fugitive dust which is carried by winds from Kahoolawe to the island of Maui."

Aluli, De Fries, Helm, Maxwell, W. Ritte and L. Ritte allege in the suit that their First Amendment rights to freedom of religion have been violated because they have not been allowed to practice the Hawaiian religion on Kahoolawe. . . .

[Joel] August [attorney] said yesterday that the plaintiffs will also file a motion for a preliminary injunction to halt the bombing practice while the present suit is being resolved.

The U.S. Attorney's Office, which represents Federal defendants, would not comment on the suit yesterday. They had not yet been served with a copy.

Some of the plaintiffs in the suit earlier this year were allowed to go to Kahoolawe for a religious ceremony.

Walter Ritte and Emmett Aluli were not given permission by the Navy, how-ever, because of their previous unauthorized visits to the island. However, they did attend the ceremony and Aluli was later arrested.

Aluli was acquitted of trespass charges in September and Federal Judge Dick Yin Wong said the Navy's refusal to allow Aluli to attend the February religious ceremony was "arbitrary and capricious."

Ritte earlier had been acquitted of trespass charges by Federal Judge Samuel P. King. Ritte was arrested and charged after two "occupations" of Kahoolawe in January.

A R T I C L E 5

Bakutis, Bunky. "Kahoolawe: Little Island, Big Find." *Sunday Honolulu Star Bulletin & Advertiser* 23 Jan. 1977: A2.

Kahoolawe has "flabbergasted" two members of a State historical site study team who returned to Oahu Monday after a fourth week-long field trip to the small controversial island which is being used as a Navy bombing target.

"I had no idea how rich in historical and cultural findings Kahoolawe would be," said Dr. Rob Hommon, State archaeologist who has been with the study since February.

"I look forward to working on the island for 100 years or more," said an exuberant Dr. Maury Morgenstein, a geologist and president of Hawaii Marine Research.

Both scientists agreed that this most recent trip to Kahoolawe is one of the most exciting archaeological discoveries they have found in Hawaii.

"For a little island we weren't expecting to find much on, it's completely flabbergasted us," Morgenstein said.

Hommon said 12 archaeological sites were found in a three-mile-long coastal area around Ahupu Bay on the northwest side of the island.

And there are more than 50 structures within those 12 sites which were used for either habitation or work, Hommon said.

Among the most exciting finds were an underground mine for basaltic glass, the first of its kind found in Hawaii, and an eroded gorge face with Hawaiian history preserved some 85 centimeters deep (between two and three feet).

"There is no doubt now that people inhabited this island and the population density was equal to Lanai during early Hawaii," Hommon said.

"And the sites found are equal in quality and second in density to the Kona coast of Hawaii," said Morgenstein.

Morgenstein, also a marine life specialist, said the reef habitat around Ahupu Bay "is in the pristine condition of early, early Hawaii, a state which is unique in the State."

With less than a third of the island covered in the joint State-Navy study, a total of 28 sites has been found.

"Pending further analysis, all of those sites look eligible for the National and State historic registers," said Hommon, adding that the study team hasn't even touched the previously recorded big sites in the northeast corner of Kahoolawe.

After the third week-long excursion in November, the team returned amazed with discoveries which included a basaltic glass workshop, an adze quarry and agricultural site—all of which were on the upper midplain of the island.

Hommon speculates the basaltic glass was used for making a cutting edge on tools. But the glass also has an important archaeological feature as it can be used in dating its cultural use.

Samples of the glass taken on the November trip preliminarily show the upper part of the island was inhabited around 1300 to 1600, Hommon said, adding that Hawaiians may have lived in the area past that time.

Hommon speculates that findings on the most recent trip indicate that the Ahupu coastal region of Kahoolawe was settled from 900 A.D. to 1400. The earliest reliable dates for Hawaiians inhabiting the islands is 600 A.D., he said.

Both Hommon and Morgenstein said the 12 new sites are well preserved and had not suffered from vandalism like areas on other islands.

However, many of the sites had been hit during ship-to-shore firing practice by the Navy, Hommon said.

"We saw fresh craters and shattered rocks in the middle of sites," he said.

But recently the Navy has stopped shelling practice in the area because of reports of possible historic sites there, Hommon said.

What is intact, however, has opened up new material and knowledge about Hawaiians' ancient life-style in all respects, the scientists agree.

Most habitation sites are located at the mouths of gullies opening to the sea and perched terrace-style on the sides of the gorges, Hommon said.

Many of the living sites have rock retaining walls and rock overhangs and appear to be cave-like dwellings, he said.

The study team also found "at least two fishing shrines and two structures that might be heiaus," Hommon said.

The basaltic glass mine is located in one of three lava tubes found on the expedition.

"It's the first underground basaltic glass mine found in the Islands and is interesting in that we had no evidence before that Hawaiians had technology in underground mining," Morgenstein said. It is a complete facility with a support pillar and two stopes, he said.

But most exciting is "the thickest known section" of Hawaiian culture preserved layer after layer through stratification, Morgenstein said.

The 85-centimeter-deep time sequence shows almost every facet of daily life, Hommon said.

"We found rare sea shells, unusually large fish bones, bird bones and charcoal, which indicates fireplaces and cooking," said Hommon.

Hommon said the Kahoolawe study might wind up at the end of this year depending how much time the group is able to spend on the island.

At the end of the study the group will submit forms to the Navy and National historic site review board recommending the different sites to be entered in the National Register of Historic Places.

A R T I C L E 6

Tong, David. "Kahoolawe 'Needed.'" *Honolulu Advertiser* 28 Jan. 1977: A3.

Not enough has been publicized about the military importance of Kahoolawe, according to Adm. Maurice Weisner, commander of American armed forces in the Pacific.

Speaking to a group of news executives and reporters, Weisner said he has not seen much media coverage of why Kahoolawe "is needed" by the military.

The island, which lies south of Maui, has been used by the military as a bombing target for many years. Hawaiian activists have criticized its use as a bombing target and want the island returned to the State.

Weisner stressed the importance of Kahoolawe as a means to maintain combat readiness of the military.

"We have reviewed all the alternatives to Kahoolawe, and we haven't been able to come up with one," he said.

The island now is being used almost on a daily basis by the military for shore bombardments and aerial strikes.

According to Lt. Cmdr. Scott Stone of the U.S. 3rd Fleet, the projected use of Kahoolawe through 1979 calls for target practice there 285 days and 123 nights every year.

Military use of the island is suspended during the weekends, when the area is used by fishermen. Military use has been suspended also during survey operations that the State and the Navy are carrying out to make an inventory of cultural resources on the island.

Areas of archaeological significance on the island no longer are used as bombing targets, Stone said. . . .

ARTICLE 7

Stearns, Harold T. "Kahoolawe in the Raw." *Honolulu Advertiser* 2 Feb. 1977: A9.

Senator Inouye plans to introduce legislation for an appropriation to cover costs of a one-year pilot project to remove unexploded ordnance from a part of Kahoolawe, as recommended in the Marinco Report.

The report calls for remote controlled bulldozers and other equipment to doze the ground to a depth of 4½ feet in order to remove all the shrapnel and unexploded ordnance. The report implies that the ground could then be used for golf courses and farming.

The Marinco Report is faulty for two reasons. First, those who visit the island can see for themselves that the land is not suitable for farming or development. No developable ground water exists in Kahoolawe and the cost of desalinizing sea water is prohibitive for farming or golf courses.

I was impressed with the lack of change there during the last 37 years. The Navy fenced an area near the summit eight years ago and had the State plant rows of different kinds of trees. All have grown very poorly. The eucalyptus and ironwoods did better than the others but even they are miserable-looking shrubs no more than eight feet high, obviously the victims of thin soil, strong winds, and very little rain. Goats have increased in great numbers in spite of sporadic efforts by the Navy to keep them under control.

Second, in an earlier Commentary . . . I stated that the Marinco Report was a "snow job" and my return trip to Kahoolawe confirmed this opinion. I was impressed with the fact that digging up the island to locate buried bombs would be disastrous and unnecessary. If Kahoolawe's thin top soil was worked with a bull-dozer, it would become loose and broken up and be blown or washed into the sea within 25 years. Furthermore, many of the cities in Europe were cleaned up, after World War II where live bombs were considerably more numerous, by conventional methods.

The Marinco Report appears to have been written to exaggerate the difficulty, danger and cost of cleaning up the island in order to justify continued use for a bombing practice range. The Navy, to date, has given no indication that Kahoolawe is to be returned to the state for civilian use. The reason is not due to clean-up problems, but is simply because the island is the best place for practice bombing in Hawaii and the Navy intends to keep it, or at least a part of it, until another place as good or better has been made available. Kahoolawe is used as a firing range for training purposes for both airplanes and ships and has the advantage of being close to Pearl Harbor.

However, the Navy neither needs nor uses the whole island and might be expected, reasonably, to relinquish those parts most suitable for civilian use and enjoyment. Smugglers Cove, for example, on the west tip of the island, has a good coral sand beach but it is exposed to open sea.

About two miles east of Smugglers Cove is Waikahalulu Bay. It is a sheltered cove bordered by cliffs which affords good anchorage when the trade winds are blowing. This bay, as well as gray sand beaches which lie at the mouth of some of the gulches on northeastern shores, could be checked for safety and released to the public for picnicking, fishing and camping. Ahupu Bay lies in this area. If unexploded ordnance exists in any of the bays, it could be towed out to sea and disposed of safely. It would not take long to clean up the underwater ordnance because only strays have ever been dropped in the bay areas.

If those parts of Kahoolawe which are safe, or which can be made safe at small cost, were released by the Navy to the State for public use, civilian resentment against the Navy would diminish.

The State could negotiate a compromise with the Navy to declare at least the western tip around Smugglers Cove as a public marine park. A chain link fence could mark the boundary so that people would not hike into the target areas. The government might sponsor free guided tours over the jeep road to the summit on weekends and holidays and on such week days as are not scheduled for bombing practice. Such limited use would not be equal to return of the island to the State but would indicate good will from the Navy and would give as many citizens as cared to look an opportunity to see Kahoolawe in the raw.

ARTICLE 8

Midkiff, Frank F. "Kahoolawe from the Beginning." *Honolulu Advertiser* 15 Feb. 1977: A7.

The Island of Kahoolawe is situated in the lee of Mt. Haleakala. Winds flow by and over Haleakala and thereby lose the water they have picked up from the trough of the trade winds and the Japan Current. Kahoolawe in this situation never has had adequate water to sustain human habitation.

In a book written by S. M. Kamakau entitled *Ruling Chiefs of Hawaii* there are a few references to Kahoolawe but none indicating any considerable importance except as a point of departure for fishing craft. At pages 356–357 in Kamakau's book there is the following reference to Kahoolawe showing that it had in early days . . . been made a penal colony and Lanai also, in part, was included:

> To this island were committed law breakers to punish them for such crimes as rebellion, theft, divorce, breaking marriage vows, murder and prostitution. Kahoolawe was the prison for the men and there was no protection for them; the government furnished them with food, but they suffered with hunger and some died of starvation and some few in the sea. Death by starvation was so much more common than by sea that some of the prisoners swam at night from Kahoolawe to Honua'ula, stealing canoes from the people there and paddling to 'Olowalu where they stole food at night.

The important reference from Kamakau . . . shows that although all the other islands except Kahoolawe and parts of Lanai were occupied and capable of producing crops and food, Kahoolawe never had any permanent inhabitants. The fact that all the other islands were heavily populated, often to the extent of interisland and intervalley warfare for food, indicates that the Hawaiians must have made conscientious and even desperate efforts to convert Kahoolawe into a place of human habitation.

However, it's clear that these efforts never were successful. It is probable that during short periods, when the first settlers landed in Kahoolawe, they may have erected their temples or heiaus. Ruins of these would still be found in a few places on Kahoolawe. Ruins of the fishing heiaus are found in various places, but this makes no substantial comparison of Kahoolawe with the islands that were capable of sustaining human population.

There is a small portion of Lanai [a neighboring island] that rises to 3,300 feet. This raised the breezes high enough to cause some fresh water precipitation when tall trees were planted and established. However, the highest point of Kahoolawe is 1,477 feet. The island also is more in the lee of Mt. Haleakala and is more fully deprived of moisture in the trade winds.

So whereas Kahoolawe will not be able to provide agriculture, it has a really great use:

Kahoolawe provides an economical part for the wonderful and most essential national defense system.

Our airplanes and artillery without this most serviceable defense factor (training) would be inadequate to train our national defense forces.

Although the ordinary leasehold, commercial and agricultural activities could never exist on Kahoolawe, the island has proved to be a wonderful place to train aviators and other types of troops. In the Pacific we have a number of aircraft carriers. Hundreds of young men flying the planes have to be taught how accurately to deliver their bombs and engage in evasive action in order to avoid enemy missiles. This requires very thorough preparation and training.

For some years the Soviets have been increasing the number of ships of their navy and planes of their air force throughout the Pacific. They have been considering Saipan, the Palaus, Truk, Western Samoa, Tonga and various other places in order to establish fishing bases and canneries, but more particularly for the purpose of creating hostile Pacific fleet bases.

The responsibility of the Department of Defense and our armed forces to maintain the freedom of the ocean lanes is a very serious one. From my experience as high commissioner of the Trust Territory of the Pacific Islands for two years I am very certain that the build-up of the strength of the Soviets in the Pacific has been going on rapidly and is becoming a serious menace. We have to maintain equality. To become No 2 in strength would invite possible disaster.

For all these reasons it is recommended that people responsible for the safety and growth of our nation and responsible for peace in the Pacific should not jeopardize the Navy's use of Kahoolawe to train our forces for national defense until an adequate alternative site is established.

ARTICLE 9

Bakutis, Bunky. "The Two Faces of Kahoolawe." *Honolulu Advertiser* 15 Feb. 1977: A3.

Unexploded bombs and white-sand beaches glitter in the sun.

Playful whales blow water puffs next to the shoreline of steep cliffs, and dummy bombs raise puffs of white smoke on red-dirt targets.

Incongruities abound on a first brief visit to the Navy target island of Kahoolawe.

From a distance, while you approached the island by helicopter on yesterday's Navy tour, Kahoolawe could be mistaken for any other leeward coast in the Hawaiian chain.

It looks dry and rough — unlike the usual tropical paradise pictured on Hawaii travel posters.

But according to recent finds by a State Historical site study team, the island is one of the best preserved remnants of old Hawaii.

Hawaiians inhabited the island mostly in the mouths of ravines next to the shoreline, and they even grew sweet potatoes in the upper regions of the island, the study group says.

Signs of the ancient culture, which reportedly flourished in a density equal to Lanai's population, cannot be seen from a Navy helicopter.

The adz quarry, basaltic glass mine, religious sites and cave dwellings are hidden now — covered by years of erosion and neglect.

What can be seen is a large top section of hard red dirt in the middle of the island.

It is riddled with erosion ravines which deepen and gather vegetation as they twist their way toward the sea.

Unexploded ordnance and bombing targets punctuate the barren red areas of the island.

Small dirt roads crisscross much of the island's 28,000 acres that have been used as a military bombing target for more than 30 years.

A Navy spokesman estimates that 10,000 tons of bombs have lacerated the island since 1941.

But in contrast to the barren midplain, there are numerous vegetated ravines and white beaches.

Small coves dot the coastline. The coves usually are backed with sloping gullies of kiawe and haole koa.

As the helicopter pulled close to the southern cliffs, two whales played just off shore in a cave lined bay. The water and reef areas are crystal-clear, with the ocean colors varying from deep blue tones to light green and brown in the shallows.

The waters surrounding Kahoolawe are described to be in pristine condition — like what existed in the days of old Hawaii, according to a member of the State study team. That team completed its fourth week-long excursion to the island in January.

Does the island have any growth potential?

The military has established a conservation area near the top of the island.

The trees planted there at the 1,500-foot level were surrounded by a fence to keep out the numerous goats which inhabit the island.

A Navy spokesman said the trees aren't doing too well.

"They were planted there because that is the place where there is the most rainfall," he said.

However, it is also the hottest place on the island and the area most exposed to wind. The Navy has not planted anything in the ravines where most of the vegetation is growing.

Asked what he thought of the island, U.S. Representative Dan Akaka said:

"It's drier than I thought it would be.

"But even though it is arid, there's a strong beauty here.

"In fact, it's much like other leeward areas in the Islands."

It's this strength that members of the Protect Kahoolawe Ohana want to be returned to public use.

The Navy says aridness makes the island an ideal bombing target because of the good visibility year round.

A R T I C L E   1 0

Haugen, Keith. "A Tale of Two Target Islands." *Honolulu Star Bulletin* 24 Feb. 1977: C8.

Culebra, Puerto Rico and Kahoolawe, Hawaii—two islands that for years were bombed and shelled by the Navy.

Puerto Ricans launched a campaign to oust the Navy in 1970.

By that time, the Navy was already accustomed to complaints from Hawaii's residents—especially those on nearby Maui—about the shelling of the uninhabited Kahoolawe.

It took five years to convince the Navy that it should stop ships from using the 10-square-mile Culebra as a weapons target range.

In the case of Kahoolawe, the Navy still is not convinced.

In both cases, the Navy said there are no alternatives to using the "target" islands.

In fact, Navy officials argued that Culebra, used as a target since 1917, was an "irreplaceable keystone" to its $300 million Atlantic fleet weapons range.

And the Navy is still searching for a replacement.

In Hawaii, Navy officials say there is no place that can substitute for Kahoolawe as a target range for the Pacific fleet and its many Oahu-based Navy and Marine units. The Island has been used since World War II.

Although there are strong similarities between the two situations, there are differences.

Culebra has about 1,400 residents.

Kahoolawe is uninhabited.

Ramon Feliciano, mayor of the tiny Puerto Rican island, said his constituents centered their protests on the fact that shrapnel from exploding shells sometimes hit the streets of a section of the island municipality called Dewey.

And John Vincent, a retired Methodist minister who has lived on Culebra since 1946, said one child and nine sailors were killed and numerous others wounded as a direct result of Navy target practice sessions.

No deaths have been reported as a result of target practice on the 45-square-mile Kahoolawe.

The major thrust of complaints against the continued military use of Kahoolawe six or eight years ago was that the bombing bothered Kihei, Maui, residents whose homes are only seven miles from the Island being shelled.

Maui Mayor Elmer F. Cravalho, in whose County the Island lies, complained bitterly. He warned of dangers to his constituents and waged a battle with the military that eventually led to the use of smaller ordnance.

He questioned their accuracy—especially when a bomb intended for Kahoolawe was found on Maui.

It was only recently that Hawaiians introduced the concerns over the destruction of heiaus (ancient temples) and other artifacts that would help them trace and better understand their own unwritten history and their culture.

But the young Hawaiians who voiced their concerns had no rank or station from which to command public attention. They had to attract attention and bring the Island into focus in the only way they knew how.

On Jan. 3, 1976, nine young Hawaii residents—most of them part-Hawaiian—landed on the Island and left two men on the barren arid landscape.

"They touched the aina (land) and felt her pains upon seeing the desecration brought about by the military bombing," a spokesman for the group said later.

The two young men—Dr. Emmett Aluli and Walter Ritte Jr.—were arrested and charged with trespassing.

On Jan. 12, 1976, the two returned. With them were Ritte's wife, Loretta, and his sister, Scarlet.

"The Kahoolawe issue is serious," a spokesman said after that visit.

They appealed to then-President Gerald Ford. He did not reply. The Department of the Navy and Hawaii's congressional delegation also refused to meet with them to "talk story."

Then in February 1976, while Ritte and Aluli were under court orders not to return to the Island, the Navy permitted 65 persons to visit one site on the Island for a religious ceremony. The young protesters called on their kupuna (elders) and kahuna (priests) to bless the Island and "clear the pathway toward making right the wrongdoings."

By now, the abuse of the Hawaiian land, the desecration of the aina—sacred to the Hawaiians—had become the focal point.

The State sent in an archaeological team and experts confirmed there are sites that need to be preserved.

By this time, Ritte and Aluli had gone to trial and had been acquitted of trespass charges.

The Protect Kahoʻolawe ʻOhana had been formed and positions taken reflected a Hawaiian unity against "the values of haole (non-Hawaiian) materialism." The young protesters continued to protest the bombing and call for a return of the Island to the State.

But their pleas fell on deaf ears.

They asked that a knowledgeable Hawaiian kupuna be allowed to accompany the non-Hawaiian archaeologists on fact-finding visits to the Islands, but to no avail.

Again they took the only action they felt would be effective.

On Jan. 30, 1977, five young men—all part-Hawaiian—landed on Kahoolawe and vowed they would stay until the Navy permanently halted the bombing.

Several days later, three of them let themselves be captured and be charged with trespassing so they might tell their story. They are George Helm, president of the ʻOhana; Charles Warrington, a social worker, and Francis Kauhane, a second-year law student at the University of Hawaii.

The others—Ritte and Richard Sawyer—remained on the Island.

Two others from Molokai—Karl Mowat and Glen Davis—landed on the Island, but soon gave themselves up and were similarly charged by the federal government. Letters and telegrams were fired off to President Carter. The Maui County Council also appealed to the President.

The Navy responded by inviting both the news media and Hawaii's congressional delegation to the Island for demonstrations and briefings. No lives are in danger, they said.

But the Hawaiians are not content.

Legal Aid attorneys took the case to federal court seeking an injunction against the Navy—in the interest of the safety of the two men. The court ruled against them and the bombing continues.

Helm and Kauhane flew to Washington and joined forces with three other Hawaiians, representatives of the Council of Hawaiian Organizations, in an attempt to bring the issue before the President.

"Kahoolawe will become the model of an alternative value structure for the Hawaii people of today, as well as for the entire State and the rest of the world," Helm said.

Since then, there has been still another invasion of the target island. An additional 10 persons—including two women—joined Ritte and Sawyer in their "occupation." Eight of them have been found and arrested on trespassing charges.

Four others—including Ritte and Sawyer—are still on the island.

Still there has been no indication the Navy will give up the Island or any part of it.

In Puerto Rico, the protest snowballed and drew congressional support from Sens. Henry Jackson, D-Wash., Edward Kennedy, D-Mass., and Hubert H. Humphrey, D-Minn.—none of them from Puerto Rico.

But Hawaiians have not had such support.

In fact, Sen. Daniel K. Inouye, Hawaii's senior representative in Washington and long a supporter of the return of Kahoolawe to the State, has said he doubts now that such a return will ever take place.

It is fear of economic reprisal from the Department of Defense—the potential relocation of Navy and Marine units and the loss of jobs and federal money coming into Hawaii—that prevents many politicians from taking a position against any military decisions affecting Hawaii.

Military spending in Hawaii ranks second only to tourism in the amount of money it adds to the economy of the State.

In that aspect the Kahoolawe and Culebra situations differ.

The other major difference seems to be that, as of this writing, no one has been killed as a result of the Navy's operations on Kahoolawe.

Not yet.

[In 1977 two young men, George Helm and Kimo Mitchell, disappeared while occupying the Island. Their fate is still unknown.]

A R T I C L E   1 1

Altonn, Helen. "Kahoolawe Uncovered." *Honolulu Star Bulletin* 24 July 1977: C1, C15.

Barren, bomb-riddled Kahoolawe has turned out to be a mecca for archaeologists, revealing unexpected information about settlement patterns in ancient Hawaii.

"It's incredible," says State archaeologist Robert J. Hommon. "Kahoolawe offers archaeological data no other island has."

Hommon is leading a field survey of Kahoolawe's archaeological sites under a contract between the Navy and the State Department of Land and Natural Resources.

The survey began in May, but Hommon began preliminary explorations of the island in January last year.

"We never expected to find such a richness of archaeological data," he said. "It's a very important island in Hawaii, with all kinds of interesting questions. We are really itching to do more work."

Hommon said the vast erosion of Kahoolawe and the fact that it has never been bulldozed for agriculture afford advantages for tracking the past that aren't possible on other islands.

Describing findings to date, Hommon said it's clear that Kahoolawe's arid environment was once far more attractive to humans than it is now.

The island at one time was well populated by Hawaiians "and I'm quite certain it was permanently occupied," he said.

The earliest settlement date established so far at coastal sites is about 1150 A.D. and the earliest dates in the interior are in the late 1300s, Hommon said. He believes earlier dates will be determined eventually. . . .

The archaeologists so far have found 70 sites—complexes with more than 250 individual structures or features.

Hommon said the majority of the features identified by his group are associated with habitation, including platforms, house terraces and activity areas.

There are also quite a few fishing shrines, or evidence of such shrines, along the coast and further inland than usual, he said.

The scientists found hummocks of topsoil surrounded by artifacts, seashells, and branch coral at several activity areas in the interior.

Coral was not used by the Hawaiians as a tool but often was a symbol of sanctity, Hommon said.

The team concentrated on one site, retrieving all of the shells and artifacts without digging. Hommon said the material was scattered over an area of about 100 by 100 feet.

But, he said, "It was totally eroded, very unimpressive when we found it." Normally, he said they would have walked right over it. "We are learning to look for sites with very subtle clues."

He said artifacts from the site date from about 1400 A.D. to 1650 A.D reflecting 250 years of occupation. "It was not constantly occupied but for some reason they came back to that site." . . .

The goats on Kahoolawe probably were responsible for much of the erosion, but Hommon also suspects the early settlers may have started the erosion cycle.

He said explorers reported seeing Hawaiians burning vast areas on other islands, perhaps to clear land for planting crops or to obtain better pili grass.

One site buried at the edge of a gulch, Hommon said, is intriguing because it has a layer of gray soil, instead of the usual red, which extends about one-quarter of a mile.

The gray soil could have resulted from burning, he said, adding that perhaps the area in the past was not a steep gulch at all but a gently sloping valley.

"What was Kahoolawe like then?" he asked. "We are just beginning to ask questions."

Each trip brings surprises, such as petroglyphs—very simple figures of dogs and people.

"The person who found the petroglyphs didn't know there weren't supposed to be any and he just casually mentioned them," Hommon said.

A R T I C L E   1 2

McCoy, Jim. "Navy Protects Kahoolawe Sites." *Honolulu Star Bulletin* 13 Sept. 1977: B5.

The United States military is taking a "reasonable, responsible and very concerned attitude" toward protection of historical sites on Kahoolawe, a government attorney argued yesterday.

The attorney for the Protect Kaho'olawe 'Ohana countered, "We feel there is no question that their operations are causing irreparable injury to historic sites on Kahoolawe."

In between the volleys of denials and claims, one of the men who brought the Kahoolawe issue to a head was bitter.

Emmett Aluli, a Molokai physician who, with Walter Ritte Jr., was one of the first "invaders" of the military controlled Island more than 20 months ago, was standing outside the courtroom during a recess.

He was watching the smattering of Ohana members who were waiting for proceedings to get under way. Their numbers were small compared to previous court hearings, such as last Friday's sentencing of Ritte and Richard W. Sawyer Jr., both now in the Halawa Correctional Facility serving time for trespassing.

Once again, Aluli, who had spear-headed the current lawsuit on behalf of the Ohana, sensed the government was winning its case.

He feels the State officials are as much to blame as the military is.

"The State and the Navy are making plans to celebrate another victory over the Hawaiians as they are probably celebrating the overthrow of Queen Liliuokalani today," he said bitterly.

Yesterday was Queen Liliuokalani's birthday.

Testimony in the Ohana's lawsuit to stop the bombing of the Target Island ended yesterday.

Federal Judge Dick Yin Wong took under advisement the Ohana's request for a preliminary injunction and summary judgment which would halt the bombing until all historical sites are surveyed.

Wong gave no indication when he would issue his written decision.

Vice Adm. Samuel Gravely and Navy Capt. C.B. Crockett took the stand to testify that Kahoolawe was not only strategically important, but that the Navy was doing a good job of protecting historic sites formed hundreds of years ago by Hawaiians who lived there.

Gravely testified that if Kahoolawe were not available for military use, the readiness of Pacific forces would be reduced by 30 to 40 percent.

"We have checked into all alternatives (bombing sites) available to us and have found that none are acceptable," Gravely said.

He said that moving to Mainland bombing sites would not only be expensive, but it would produce a "morale problem" among crew members who would feel it unnecessary to leave their home port and families to participate in the exercises.

Going to the Mainland would leave Pacific forces undermanned, Gravely said.

Crockett also testified that regulations such as the National Historic Preservation Act of 1966 which the plaintiffs claimed the Navy had broken were only "advisory" in nature and were not mandatory.

The Ohana, led by Aluli, claimed the military was violating such laws intended to protect the 89 historic sites already found on the Island. State archaeologists have surveyed 34 percent of Kahoolawe since they began making the expeditions in May 1976. They expect to finish surveying in 18 months.

The Ohana wants the bombing stopped so the surveying can be done on a full-time basis, instead of the present five-days-a-month schedule. Inherent in this action is the Ohana move to permanently halt the bombing.

Crockett testified that State efforts to survey archaeological sites, coupled with the increasing use of inert ordnance and the Navy's cooperation in removing target ranges if the State deemed they would endanger the sites, indicated the Navy's willingness to preserve sites.

Joel August, Legal Aid attorney for the Ohana, said that the Navy had not followed certain regulations before 1976 and questioned whether ship and plane bombing would preserve sites.

August, citing recently obtained military data which showed the maximum error rate for plane to surface bombardment does not exceed half a mile (or about 880 yards), wondered how the military could protect historic sites when targets were located within 300 meters of a site.

August argued the defendants have fallen down in their duty to submit the 89 historic sites already found to the National Register of Historic Places.

He said the Navy has not only found itself in the "unfortunate circumstance where they (Navy) assume they are above the law," but is also playing the "shell and pea game" where everyone points fingers at each other saying it is your responsibility to protect sites.

"We feel there is no question that their operations are causing irreparable injury to historic sites," August argued.

ARTICLE 13

Sawyer, Richard, Jr. "Sites Weren't Protected, Sawyer Says." *Honolulu Star Bulletin* 17 Sept. 1977: A11.

The Protect Kahoolawe Aloha Aina Ohana finds the Navy's allegation Sept. 3 that it is trying to protect Hawaii historical sites to be a totally ludicrous and deceitful attempt to cover up the trail of desecration and destruction that it has left on Kahoolawe for the following reasons:

For the last 36 years that it has bombed the Island, its position has always been that the Kahoolawe target complex has no historic value. As of Sept. 1, with the filing of our civil suit, its position has suddenly changed.

Capt. Crockett's blank refusal to allow kamaaina witnesses to accompany the State archaeologists to help them to identify and validate their findings in addition to giving positive assistance in locating unidentified sites is a direct hindrance to creating a valid study.

Naval personnel on Kahoolawe have told us about their simulated A-bomb test there which destroyed nearly an entire bay area located somewhere between Smuggler's Cove and the lighthouse area. How did the Navy go about protecting the historic sites located there?

How does the Navy protect historic sites on Kahoolawe during its annual operation RIMPAC in which naval forces from New Zealand, Australia, Canada and other Allied forces are invited here to play naval war games? Does it instruct those invited foreign powers where our Hawaii historical sites are located?

The archaeological teams themselves admit to finding a basalt glass mine as well as many other obliterated sites on the hard pan area adjacent to the Navy's painted bull's eye targets. Just ask them.

While on the Island on two different occasions, we observed cowrey shells (he'e lures), as well as fragments of other types of shells and pieces of coral in the midst of large *pohaku* and wall-like formations to be painted white and, therefore, designated and blasted as a specific target area.

Despite the Ohana's efforts to educate the public about what is really happening to our historical sites, our State government continues to allow the Navy to deceive the public. As long as the State government continues to pass "shibai" resolutions without any attempt at implementation or follow-up action to at least check on the Navy's compliance with Navy promises, the Navy will continue to drop 100 percent live bombs as we of the Ohana observed while we were there.

ARTICLE 14

Daugherty, Dick. "Isle Needed for Training Says Marine." *Honolulu Star Bulletin* 17 Sept. 1977: A9.

A plumber does not become a master plumber overnight. A combat infantryman does not become an expert in land warfare overnight. An electrician does not become a master electrician overnight. A combat pilot does not become an expert in air warfare overnight. All must have time, and place, to practice their trades, to become proficient; become efficient.

Kahoolawe is the issue. I, for one, am sick and tired of reading and listening to the drivelings of the Rittes, the Sawyers, and now the Greensteins, et al., members of the Protect Kahoolawe Ohana as concerns use of the Island of Kahoolawe for military target purposes. . . .

We all are well aware of the Ritte and Sawyer charade as pertains to Kahoolawe. Now Mr. Greenstein is quoted in your Sept. 7th edition as stating "The Island is no longer necessary for naval defense since we are presumably not at war. As commander-in-chief, the President has the authority to stop this nonsense."

Mr. Greenstein, Mr. Ritte and Mr. Sawyer, we were "presumably" not at war on the early morning of December 7, 1941!

Thank God, I wasn't in Hawaii on that date, but I'm certain that there are many native Hawaiians living today who well remember it.

Now, Mr. Greenstein, if this newspaper quoted you correctly, am I correct in concluding that since you are currently having no plumbing problems, you don't believe there is a need for practiced, experienced plumbers for you to call if and when you do experience such problems? Am I correct in concluding that since we, as a nation, are not currently at war with another country, it is your observation that we don't need any practiced, experienced military force?

Or just what are you saying? Are you saying, "Mr. Plumber, don't practice your trade in my house." Are you saying, "Military persons, go practice your trade somewhere else." Without having the guts to say who else's house or where else?

God forbid that this should happen, but, Mr. Greenstein, Mr. Sawyer or Mr. Ritte, singularly or as a group, answer me this one hypothetical question.

If some day in the future a young Hawaiian mother should approach you, seriously wounded herself and with her dead babe in her arms, the result of an attack by an enemy such as on December 7, 1941 and ask you, "Why? Why did this happen? You were part of a driving force which resulted in our military having no place to adequately train, to prepare to defend us against an enemy. Why?" What would be your answer to this young Hawaiian mother?

Gentlemen, I've read all of your quoted claptrap. I would now like to know in a "quote-unquote" statement, what would be your word for word answer to this young mother.

You may call it nonsense, Mr. Greenstein, and Messrs. Ritte and Sawyer may share in that assessment, and I may be calling the shots wrong (as I don't know you from Adam), but you don't have a last name that would indicate to me you should be calling the shots for native Hawaiians who were around on December 7, 1941 (or the survivors of native Hawaiians who died on that day).

Since you all share a common problem, I recommend a common solution. Shut up! But not until, of course, you have answered the hypothetical question I have posed.

God willing, in spite of the Greensteins, the Rittes, and the Sawyers, the sound, intelligent thinking of the majority of American people will, from this day forward, ensure that it remains a hypothetical question.

ARTICLE 15

Hamasaki, Richard. "The Hawaiians and Kahoolawe." *Honolulu Star Bulletin* 24 Sept. 1977: A9.

Not only did Maj. Dick Daugherty miss the entire point of the Kahoolawe issue, but he has demonstrated a most naive, arrogant and typically careless attitude concerning the Hawaiian Islands and the rights of native Hawaiians.

Item One:

Ever since the Hawaiians lost control of their own land and heritage there has been a greedy scramble to exploit any and everything that could show a profit, be it beachfront property, lush valleys, mountain slopes, etc., thereby destroying or burying the cultural roots that were the basis for the Hawaiians' rich and healthy civilization.

Item Two:

Civilization is relative to the people who inhabit their environment—given the lush rain forests, abundant reefs, temperate weather and ocean, was not the Hawaiian Islands called "paradise" by her Caucasian discoverers—indeed, the Polynesian civilization thrived.

Item Three:

There never would have been a "Pearl Harbor Day" if the military had never stepped foot on the Hawaiian Islands. Today the military not only pours billions of dollars into the island economy, but employs thousands of local residents. The Hawaiians have paid a costly cultural and ethnic price to the military establishment here; however, so has every local citizen.

The military is here supposedly to protect and prepare the rest of America from the threat of, or in case of, a nuclear war. As a result, if there ever is a nuclear war, every living person on Oahu, man, woman and child, will be in jeopardy of their lives—because of the very nature in which the military has fortified itself here on this island.

What Major Dick Daugherty and others are not aware of in the arrogance in their own attitudes, beliefs and actions is that the military is a guest. They are guests of the people of Hawaii—we are a state and we possess what is called state's rights.

I feel that the bombing of Kahoolawe is a direct insult to the native Hawaiians who have always revered and worshipped land—how scarce and precious it is, amidst the watery Pacific. To many Hawaiians, Kahoolawe is sacred as are so many land areas and religious sites in Western and Far Eastern cultures.

Is it not time for us to respect and recognize the Polynesian civilization as it was and still is in the Hawaiian people that have survived the great shock of modernization and military encroachment and disease (to name a few)?

Some members of Protect Kahoolawe Ohana may not have Hawaiian names as Maj. Dick Daugherty points out, but they certainly have Hawaiian blood flowing through their veins. The Sawyers, the Rittes, the Helms (we could go on and on)—these people feel and understand the injustice and unnecessary presence of the military on Kahoolawe.

These are the people who were the grandfathers or grandmothers or mothers and fathers, uncles and aunties, sons, daughters, brothers and sisters, and cousins of those Hawaiians that chose to intermarry with other races not for profit or gain but for love—love for people, love for the land.

Aloha Nui Manu.

Aloha Aina.

ARTICLE 16

Kim, Charles. "Reply to Daugherty." *Honolulu Star Bulletin* 24 Sept. 1977: A9.

Mr. Daugherty's letter on Kahoolawe (Sept. 17) deserves a reply, especially his emotional appeal concerning a young Hawaiian mother. The basic question is: Why is anyone in Hawaii threatened by military attack? The answer is the military presence here makes us the biggest target in the Pacific.

Mr. Daugherty suggested that Kahoolawe's use as a military practice target helps defend Hawaii. I have never heard of a Phantom jet shooting down an ICBM Missile, which today is the threat, not prop-driven planes as was the case 36 years ago. Thus, training on Kahoolawe cannot help defend Hawaii against modern weapons.

ARTICLE 17

Nelson, Lyle. "Kahoolawe Tug-of-War Cost Navy $572,000." *Honolulu Star Bulletin* 30 Sept. 1977: A14.

The Protect Kahoolawe Ohana's assorted activities have cost the U.S. Navy $572,000 in the tug-of-war over the Target Island, the Navy said yesterday in answer to *Star Bulletin* queries.

Beside the tab for the military, 3rd Fleet spokesman Lt. Cmdr. Scott Stone said the Navy and Marine Corps lost 46 full or partial days of training through August because of the Ohana. . . .

In answer to a *Star-Bulletin* query, Stone said the Navy is not looking now for any alternatives to Kahoolawe as a bombing target.

When it did look for alternatives, it confined the search to within 200 nautical miles of Pearl Harbor.

Navy comment was sought by the *Star-Bulletin* on this and other points in response to a new critical assessment of Kahoolawe made by Ian Lind, a pacifist representing the American Friends Service Committee.

Lind's special report charges that the Navy made no serious search for an alternative to Kahoolawe, that the Island plays a small role in the total military training picture, and that superior training facilities are available elsewhere.

Stone said the Navy's on-site examination of places such as Kaula Rock southwest of Niihau were made and reported in an environmental impact statement of 1972.

He denies Lind's claim that less than 7 percent of the military's target training time is spent at the Island. He says Lind included Air Force and Air Guard flying time that is unrelated to Kahoolawe in his total target training time.

Lind's assessment suggested that Kahoolawe is an outmoded target compared with the multimillion-dollar sophisticated electronic warfare test ranges the military has constructed in Nevada, Arizona and California.

Stone said Kahoolawe's value is that it costs only about $10,000 a year in maintenance and that to duplicate the West Coast ranges at astronomical expense "is contrary to common sense."

And besides, he said, it's Kahoolawe's proximity to Pearl Harbor and Kaneohe which makes it attractive.

Stone repeated the Navy's contention that the tactical range at Barking Sands, Kauai, is unsuitable as an air-to-ground or surface-to-surface substitute for Kahoolawe.

Stone did say the Navy cannot rule out the possibility that electronic simulators or targets may at some future date make Kahoolawe operations unnecessary. . . .

Lind also noted that the Navy once said it could not get along without using Culebra, situated off the east coast of Puerto Rico, as a target island; but it was shut down in 1975 and the Atlantic Fleet is still in business.

Culebra is 1,310 nautical miles from the Atlantic Fleet's headquarters in Norfolk, Va.

Stone said that Marine Corps elements based on Okinawa often go to the Philippines for air and naval gunfire support training. . . .

A R T I C L E   1 8

Altonn, Helen. "Lyman Enlists in Fight to Rescue Kahoolawe." *Honolulu Star Bulletin* 14 Oct. 1977: A2.

Richard Lyman Jr., the first person to turn Big Island lava into agricultural production, has his sights on another wasteland—bomb-riddled Kahoolawe.

The 74-year-old president of the Bishop Estate board of trustees believes Kahoolawe can and should be rehabilitated "as a laboratory for the rest of the world. . . . "

He says the Hawaiian native claims—which he admits he considered "frivolous" up to a year ago—can be the key to the Island's reclamation. . . .

Lyman recently visited Kahoolawe with a group including 10 civilians and seven military officials. . . .

"It was a Hawaiian atmosphere," Lyman commented, discussing the visit and his impressions of the Island in an interview.

While noting that he spoke only for himself, he said he believed everyone in the group felt something should be done with Kahoolawe.

"I like to believe—and I may be an old damn fool—that Kahoolawe could be a symbol of man being able to reverse forces of destruction, to turn them around to be useful to man," he said.

"With the help of the (Protect Kaho'olawe) 'Ohana and the government, Kahoolawe could be a laboratory to the rest of the world that we could do things."

Lyman said he became interested in the Island because some of the 'Ohana members protesting its use by the Navy as a bombing target were graduates of Kamehameha Schools.

"I felt I had a duty, a responsibility, to find what caused them to protest. Now I find these young people did have a gripe," he said.

"I believe the young Hawaiians protesting the issue of Kahoolawe . . . should be given credit by other Hawaiians for what they've done. . . .

"I'm very excited about the possibilities of the Island, despite the lack of water," said Lyman, who received an award two years ago for his achievements in recycling barren lava beds for agricultural growth.

He said grass and trees also can be grown on the dry, barren Island of Kahoolawe, even with just 24 inches of rain annually.

He suggested the possibility of a one-acre, rubber-lined reservoir to catch the rainfall to produce about 500,000 gallons of water.

If men can be sent to the moon, he said, "It should be no trick at all to do what I'm dreaming about. But first, we've got to get rid of the goats."

He said windbreaks also would be needed to prevent further erosion by wind and water.

Lyman said he recognizes the Navy's need "to improve its techniques" but was told the entire Island isn't used for bombing.

"So why can't we start a laboratory of reclamation and reforestation now on the land they are not using for bombing sites?"

He said he gets "speechless" when told the costs of clearing the ordnance and rehabilitating the Island would run up to $150 million.

He thinks it can be done much cheaper, perhaps "using the forces of destruction to help man," such as charges to blast holes for trees.

He said there must be types of trees that will flourish on the Island and hold the soil, but they must be tended like children. "You can't just walk away and leave them."

He observed that perhaps some "old-fashioned" methods of agriculture would work on Kahoolawe, noting how the Indians taught the Pilgrims to grow corn by putting down one grain and then a fish. The fish became fertilizer, he said.

Hawaiian ways of growing things also might be tried, he said, pointing out that the Hawaiians were able to exist in extremely difficult conditions, growing taro between rocks and in swamps.

"Experts say it can't be done, but I say it can," he said.

He said the Navy can't be blamed for all the "desecration" of Kahoolawe. Much of it was created by the people who went there more than 100 years ago, taking animals which ate plants to the roots and caused the erosion.

"But the big problem is who's going to be responsible for cleaning up the Island of all the danger.

"There are lots of things that can be done," he added, "but it will take the combined efforts of many people . . .

"I feel if we all sit down together, the Ohana and the government, we could come up with a workable solution." . . .

A R T I C L E   1 9

Kakesako, Gregg K. "Navy Spells Out Why It Uses Kahoolawe." *Honolulu Star Bulletin* 14 Nov. 1977: A2.

Washington—The Navy has publicly acknowledged for the first time that its reason for regarding Kahoolawe as the only acceptable target range in the Pacific is because it would take too much time and money to deploy its forces to the West Coast for training.

The Navy said the only alternative site on the West Coast would be San Clemente Island, and said the "significant deterrent to the use of the Southern California island by ships based in Hawaii is the round-trip transit time and related expenses."

"Current estimates, just for naval gunfire support ships, are 12 to 15 days of steaming at an average fuel cost of $120,000 per ship per exercise, as compared with one-day transit from Pearl Harbor to Kahoolawe and return, at an average cost per ship of $10,000," the Navy said.

The only other possibility would be to relocate the entire Honolulu-based fleet to another base, the Navy said, and that seems out of the picture at this time.

Several weeks ago, Sen. Daniel K. Inouye forwarded to Adm. T.B. Hayward, Pacific fleet commander, an assessment of the situation involving the 45-square-mile island, used by the military as a bombing range since 1941, done by Ian Lind, a pacifist representing the American Friends Service Committee in Honolulu.

Inouye said the responses made by a Pearl Harbor spokesman to the *Honolulu Star Bulletin* on Oct. 20 concerning Lind's study were inadequate, and he asked the Navy to substantiate its claim that it has conducted a thorough search for an alternative target site.

In a six-page letter to Inouye, Hayward said the answers supplied by Lt. Cmdr. Scott Stone, 3rd Fleet spokesman did not constitute an official Navy response. Stone had said that the Navy is not looking for any alternative to Kahoolawe at this time.

Hayward said 131 islands in the Pacific have been examined and rejected as possible alternative sites because they are inhabited or too close to inhabited islands, or are too small or too far away, or contain unsuitable terrain and climate or are either a state or federal wildlife refuge.

"As for target areas outside of the Hawaiian area, one has to look either to the West Coast or to the Western Pacific," Hayward said. "I do not believe anyone would seriously recommend sending Hawaii-based ships, aircraft or ground forces to the Western Pacific for such training—when they do deploy to the Western Pacific the intent is that they deploy in an operationally ready status."

Hayward said that if combined arms training is to be accomplished at a place other than Kahoolawe, then San Clemente Island off Southern California is "the only site which may reasonably be considered."

He said the Southern California island is also unsuitable because "unlike . . . Kahoolawe, the full range of combined arms training cannot be conducted at San Clemente. San Clemente's environmental restrictions and the restraints imposed because of commercial air traffic in the vicinity limit its usefulness."

As to Inouye's question whether the Navy has studied the cost and feasibility of relocating operations away from Kahoolawe, Hayward said the answer "depends on what types of relocations are being considered."

Hayward said that if the relocation involves sending the ships, aircraft and ground forces to other locations and then returning them to Oahu, then it is a simple matter to compute these costs, as was done with the possibility of using San Clemente.

"Computing the cost of relocating forces to another base is obviously much more complicated, but it can be done," Hayward said. "We have not compiled an extensive cost comparison of all the possible alternative sites, since most of them have been rejected based on other factors."

Hayward also took exception to Lind's contention that Kahoolawe plays only a minor role in the training of military forces in Hawaii: "I would point out that, without the Kahoolawe target facility, certain types of training could not be completed by military forces in the mid-Pacific region."

The admiral said the most significant type of training done there is the Marines' combined arms training. In addition, he said, Kahoolawe is "the only place in the mid-Pacific area where surface ships can practice naval gunfire support."

Hayward said Lind's other assertion, that the Navy considers Kahoolawe so unimportant because it requires little funding compared with other firing ranges, also is erroneous.

He said no comparison can be made with other Navy or Marine test ranges or bases because they all serve a different purpose. "For that matter, the Pacific Missile Range Facility at Barking Sands (on Kauai) represents a tremendous investment when compared with Kahoolawe for entirely different training needs," he said.

He added that the Navy has rejected Barking Sands as a target site because it is "an open-sea, bottom-instrumented range, totally unsuited for combined arms exercise of the type conducted on Kahoolawe."

A R T I C L E   2 0

Smith, Pam. "Kahoolawe: Hawaiians on Trial." *Hawaii Observer* 28 July 1977: 14–15.

[Following is the last part of an article talking about the trial of the members of the Protect Kahoʻolawe ʻOhana on trespassing charges.]

The real drama of the trial centered around the question of criminal intent. Since Judge Thompson had already upheld King's ruling that motive for entry on the Island did not apply, the defendants' position—that they had gone to the Island because of their religious beliefs—was no longer arguable. However, Thompson decided to allow introduction of such testimony in order to "preserve the record" should the defendants lose the case and appeal to the Ninth Circuit Court. In the exchanges that followed, Special Prosecuting Attorney Robert Manekin tried to extract from the defendants an admission that their motives were political:

Manekin: "Is it not true that you were politically, as well as spiritually, motivated to go on the Island?"

Ritte: "I was motivated because I am Hawaiian."

Manekin pointed to the fact that some of the defendants were currently involved in an environmental lawsuit concerning the Navy's use of the Island and that they had participated in the activities of a political organization—the Protect Kaho'olawe Ohana. To this came the inevitable reply: The Ohana is a family—not a political organization—which has spiritual roots in the concept of "aloha aina." All five spoke movingly of the ways in which the plight of Kahoolawe had awakened them spiritually to a rich, cultural tradition; they visited Kahoolawe not to defy the law but to bring their *ho'okupu*, their blessings, to the desecrated Island.

The defense called two "religious experts," Emma de Fries and Edward Kelana-hele, and an anthropologist, Dr. Steven Boggs, to buttress the testimony of the five defendants. All three testified that a deep spiritual relationship to the land lay at the roots of Hawaiian culture. The prosecution, in a surprise move, called for the first time a rebuttal witness to testify about Hawaiian religion. Charles W. Kenn, an elderly Part Hawaiian, is a consultant at Kamehameha Schools and has made a life-long study of Hawaiian archaeology. Kenn, who admitted having a missionary church background, stated that there is "no such thing as Hawaiian religion today." He identified "aloha aina" as a political concept that became popular around the time of Annexation. Kahoolawe, he said, has no special significance other than as a temporary shelter for fishermen. His replies provoked the first chorus of indignation from the hundred or so Ohana members who filled the courtroom.

These conflicting interpretations of Hawaiian religion, culture and history are not likely to be settled in court. Nor is it within the scope of the court, in Judge Thompson's opinion, to legislate on the moral issues involved in the Kahoolawe case. Prefacing his ruling with the comment that he had "great empathy" for the group and found "the desecration of the Island by bombing deplorable," Thomp-son stated that "a court of law may arrive at a decision that it does not want to make." He said that it "defied logic" to presume that any of the defendants were not completely aware of the advance permission needed to go on Kahoolawe. Since all of the defendants had failed to seek permission, he found the motive for their entry irrelevant. The group's desire to see the bombing stopped was, he concluded, "a political purpose, not a religious one," and he urged the Ohana to pursue legal political means in achieving their goal. So saying, he found the five Hawaiians guilty of a "technical trespass" and scheduled their sentencing for July 25.

"A fair decision," commented Walter Ritte, "but when you know you're not guilty, it's a heavy trip." Spirits daunted, and eyes tearful, the Ohana members crowded into the halls, where they were greeted by the irrepressible Aunty Clara. "No sadness, now," she shouted. The Betsy Ross of the Ohana, she rallied the troops together in an endless conga line stretching through the halls and back to bite its own tail. Smiles and tears alternated as they followed her barrel voice in a rendition of "Hawaii Aloha."

A R T I C L E   2 1

Westlake, Wayne Kaumualii. "Behind Bars: An Interview with Richard Sawyer and Walter Ritte, Jr." *Hawaii Observer* 17 Nov. 1977: 18–23.

Recently, Amnesty International, the worldwide organization working on behalf of political prisoners, was awarded the 1977 Nobel Peace Prize for its 16-year efforts to free prisoners jailed for their racial, religious and political beliefs. The Nobel Committee has called 1977 "the year dedicated to prisoners of conscience." Amnesty International has over 5,000 case files on men and women all over the world who are jailed for what they think, not for what they do. According to a Honolulu AI spokesman, State Senator Anson Chong (D-6th), the case of Walter Ritte and Richard Sawyer of the Protect Kahoʻolawe ʻOhana is now in the investigatory stage. Ritte and Sawyer are serving a six-month sentence behind bars at Halawa Correctional Facility for trespassing on Kahoolawe. Chong said the question of their imprisonment may be moot, due to their imminent release. But there will be others.

Observer: The aim of political imprisonment is to weaken an insurgent movement by depriving it of its leaders, and to weaken those leaders through physical, psychological and emotional punishment. Have you or the Ohana been weakened in any way by your imprisonment?

Ritte: No way—imprisonment has helped to strengthen my personal self, as I have learned much here at Halawa Hale. I do not consider myself the leader of the Ohana. There are many leaders within the Ohana; everyone picks up and takes responsibility when it is time. We follow the deep message which comes from the *na'au* (gut). An honest statement would be that our jail term has strengthened the Ohana and their goal to stop the destruction of Kahoolawe.

Sawyer: In one sense, Ohana means family. We have worked as a large family giving freely of ourselves for the love of an island, for the love of our culture as taught to us by our kupunas, and for the love for each other. When there is trouble in the family, everyone shares our frustrations; but the family, our Ohana, remains strong because, if they fall down, then all our efforts are *poho* (for nothing). We have not been able to keep up with our Ohana, but we know they have become stronger. We feel it emanating in the strength displayed by our pregnant wives. The Ohana has been quiet but they have been busy. . . .

[Sawyer is responding to a question about who is responsible for their imprisonment.]

We have only taken our love to that Island in the form of *moha'i aloha*. Every single time we visited the Island we have taken young coconut plants, ti-leaf stalks, taro and other plants to replenish the aloha in the aina that the navy has blown away with their 500-pound-plus bombs. Our Federal court system does not recognize the native rights of the Hawaiian people to express our love for our land. The real criminals are those people in high command, the President, the high-command of the navy, our senators, our State Government officials—all those who don't give a damn about what happens to an entire Hawaiian Island—45 square miles of primitive beauty—where the unwritten history of the Hawaiian people lies partially intact, and partially devastated and desecrated.

Observer: Several Hawaiians have publicly labeled you two as misguided radicals who don't really speak for most Hawaiians. What about these moderates, this so-called silent majority of Hawaiians? Why do they remain docile and complacent?

Ritte: I don't speak for all Hawaiians—I only speak as *a* Hawaiian. It would be a dream come true if the majority of Hawaiians would speak their *mana'o* (mind). Learning about ourselves is not easy; we are at many different levels of trying to become living Hawaiians today. I have never been in jail before in 32 years; I have been a "good citizen" and my actions for Kahoolawe have made me a proud Hawaiian. I apologize to those kupunas I have offended. . . .

Observer: Your attorney Hyman Greenstein states: "The Hawaiian conscience has only smouldered into protest during the last couple years or so." What happens if this smouldering protest erupts into violence? What would you do?

Ritte: Aloha aina has no room for violence. I don't speak for all Hawaiians. The teachings of our kupunas have not included violence. The world already knows about violence. What the Hawaiians have, and what the world needs, is the essence of aloha. We should nurture it and allow the essence of aloha to once more guide our lives in Hawaii. Aloha aina is a start.

Sawyer: The Hawaiian conscience has been smouldering on the grassroots level of Hawaiian awareness much longer than most people realize. If the politicians on both the Federal and State level continue to ignore the plight of the aboriginal Hawaiian people and the wrongs done to them; if the tourist industry continues to crowd local people out of their peace of mind; if the attitudes of Big Business and the navy continue to disregard the value and the beauty of Hawaii by blatant desecration of Hawaiian land and culture by bombs and over-development; if working within the system continues to result in zero improvement of the situation of the Hawaiian environment and people—*anything is possible!*

Violence is hardly possible in a movement based on aloha aina principles. It is not the way of the Hawaiian people as taught us by our kupunas. I don't know what I'd do. I would probably take my immediate family and head for the peace and quiet of the secluded valleys and live off the land like I originally planned to do.

Observer: Do you feel that continued trespassing on the Target Isle is a viable means of political protest and change?

Ritte: My continued action for Kahoolawe is due to the lack of response from the politicians. I am very disappointed in Dan Inouye. He wants to play the middle-road and thus end up doing nothing to stop the daily destruction of Kahoolawe, who is near death environmentally and who carries our heiaus, *ko'as* (fishing shrines), and precious history and roots. Well, Kahoolawe is just much too precious to allow the one man who can stop the destruction to play the middle-road political game. Inouye is The Man—this I have learned. His inaction or negative action will cause many others to suffer and our culture to be altered and rearranged by daily bombs. Many criticize me for being so harsh and turning Inouye against us. I speak what I feel is the truth, and I do not think like a politician. I don't care if Inouye hates me, but I feel his greatness will allow him to see the truth of aloha aina. I speak only out of concern for Kahoolawe, not out of spite for Inouye. He is the man who can stop the destruction of Kahoolawe—all that happens concerning Kahoolawe rests with him. I just don't understand the apathy and lack of action on the part of our elected officials. We are not trespassing on Kahoolawe—we visit the aina of our ancestors. Strange laws keep us from embracing our Island Kahoolawe.

Sawyer: Judge Sam King is a Hawaiian and should be respected in his capacity as a Federal judge. However, it is becoming obvious that people are not treated equally under the present system of laws. The laws seem to be designed to protect money and those who have lots of money. It's almost as if, when you have more money, you have more human rights. It is also becoming obvious that the U.S. Navy must be exerting some sort of control over the U.S. judicial system because the law is not enforced upon them when they violate Federal environmental laws. In our civil suit against the navy, they were found to have broken the law but allowed to continue what they were doing because they are the U.S. Navy, and therefore above the law. The big question in my mind is, "Does the Department of Defense actually control the U.S. judicial system?" What happened to our government for the people? Change will come about when our politicians get off their okoles and start earning their salaries by doing their homework and learning about what Aloha Aina Kahoolawe really means. If people and politicians continue to be complacent with things as they are today, one *gigantic* visit should be made to Kahoolawe by the many people who really care about Aloha Aina Kahoolawe.

Observer: What happens when you get out of jail? Will you go back to Kahoolawe?

Ritte: I will do all that is necessary to stop the destruction of Aina Kahoolawe. It is wrong to destroy aina, the "giver of life." We should be sitting down with government officials to solve this problem. I will always go back to Kahoolawe — it is a Hawaiian Island and I am a Hawaiian. The bones of my ancestors are on Kahoolawe along with the proud history of their great endeavours. *Kalani Ua Maui A Mamao*, my son, will also go to Kahoolawe. I sit here, a prisoner at Halawa Hale, thinking of Kahoolawe. The desire to return burns as bright as the volcanoes of Pele.

Sawyer: The return of Kahoolawe to the people is inevitable, but it will not happen if we just sit back and talk about it. We must all exert our individual mana and express our love for our battered Island. I envision the Island becoming a place where the children can learn the historical significance of this land and the aboriginal Hawaiian people who first lived here: a historic park not to be used for resorts or hotels, not a place to visit with hotdog and hamburger stands. A place for children to feel the mana of the aina. A *pu'u honua* — a place for the enlightenment of future generations.

A R T I C L E   2 2

Ashdown, Inez MacPhee. "Once-Green Kaho'olawe Can Be Revived." *Honolulu Advertiser* 19 Nov. 1977: A11.

A clipping titled "Once upon a time Kaho'olawe was Green" was brought to my desk today. I was asked to write a reply because I have known Ulupalakua since 1908, and Kaho'olawe since 1916.

Many kama'aina of long ago have related how, in their youth of the 1870s and later, Kaho'olawe still had a strong covering of verdure, a "forest land" as it was described. . . .

As for Kaho'olawe: Eben Parker Low took my father and me to the island in 1916. "Uncle" Eben had the island as a sheep ranch along with his sheep ranch at Humu'ula on Hawaii. The territorial Board of Agriculture and Forestry had taken the island from him in 1910 with the intention of removing remaining goats and sheep and going ahead with reforestation. Nothing had been done because the $75,000 appropriation asked for by the board was not forthcoming.

My father, Angus MacPhee of Wyoming, told the governor and others that he would reforest, provided they leave the island to him. He obtained the lease in 1917, for a term of 25 years. We had four years in which to remove the goats and sheep and start reforestation, or lose the lease. I remember that we sold 13,000 head of goats in that period, to say nothing of the animals shot.

We also planted 5,000 trees, indigenous varieties with a guard row and windbreak of eucalyptus which, later, we would use to replace fence posts etc.

Governor Wallace R. Farrington, Delegate to Congress Harry A. Baldwin and other officials came over in 1922. They were so amazed and pleased with what my father and the rest of us had done that the lease was extended till December 1954 with option to re-lease as long as he wanted the island. . . .

The hundreds of pounds of Australian salt bush, pili and maninia grass and red-top seeds we planted thrived wonderfully. The trees were protected by fencing. We sold 900 head of fine cattle in 1939 for $81,000, and I could show photos to prove that the island was so covered with verdure that the "dust cloud from the island of death" no longer was flying westward with the winds. . . .

I might add that the name Ka-ho-o-la-we means Gathering Driftwood. The oldest name is Aina o Kanaloa. The name given the island by the first discoverer Hawai'i-loa long before Columbus was Ko-hema-lama-lama, meaning Southern Beacon because he used the island as part of his navigational triangle for traveling to and from Ku Kahiki, the Horizon.

Yes, Kaho'olawe was green, when it was Aina Kanaloa or the Southern Beacon. We called it Kanaloa and everything thrived.

Give back to me that Land of Kanaloa and my family will make it green and thriving even now. We lost thousands of dollars. Maybe we could earn it back, with interest. We could do as good a work for the State of Hawai'i as we did for the former territory. I promise!

ARTICLE 23

Altonn, Helen. "Kohoolawe Trees Thriving." *Honolulu Star Bulletin* 19 May 1979: A4.

State forestry division plantings are thriving on barren, bomb-riddled Kahoolawe because of goat control measures by the Navy, Libert Landgraf, division chief, said yesterday.

"They have kept the goat population down substantially," the state forester said. "It's the best I've seen in umpteen years."

The forestry division last year developed a 12-year tree planting program designed to protect 1,200 acres in the higher areas with windbreak plantings and to beautify the seacoast with rows of coconut trees and other lowland plantings.

The Island has serious erosion problems because of the goats and drought conditions.

Lt. James Davidson, Navy spokesman on Kahoolawe matters, said goat hunts are being conducted on the Island about every six months.

A 10-day hunt began Monday with Navy ordnance demolition experts and Marines participating.

"It's a conservation effort—not a sporting event," Davidson said.

He said it is difficult to estimate Kahoolawe's goat population, but it may be about 1,000.

He said crews who are working on an environmental impact statement for the Island report that the plants "are gaining, which shows we are keeping the goats under pretty good control."

Goats normally don't like tamarix trees, one of the main species being planted, he said. "But, still, if they get hungry enough, they would probably eat those."

He said the environmental impact statement, being done by the Environmental Impact Study Corp. on contract, is expected to be completed late this summer.

The initial impact statement was produced in 1972 and revised in 1976. The new one is a final draft on that, Davidson said.

Landgraf said Maui foresters planted 1,200 trees on the Island in February and when they checked them last month only 43 had died. "That's really good for Kahoolawe—fantastic," he said.

He said the division hopes to put another 5,000 plants on the Island by the end of the year.

ARTICLE 24

Aluli, Noa Emmett. "Why the Bombing of Kaho'olawe?" *Honolulu Star Bulletin* 25 May 1984: A15.

. . . The Protect Kaho'olawe 'Ohana is a community-based statewide organization of native Hawaiians and supporters of diverse ethnic, educational and economic backgrounds, drawn together in an effort to perpetuate Hawaiian cultural traditions and values for future generations.

We are firmly committed to protect Kaho'olawe from further bombing and other forms of destruction and misuse. Through a legal agreement signed between the 'Ohana and the Navy in 1981, the Protect Kaho'olawe 'Ohana is recognized as stewards and guardians of the Island and now works with the Navy to develop programs to manage, restore and preserve the cultural and natural resources on Kaho'olawe. However, the agreement does not in any way waive the 'Ohana's right to protest the military use of the Island. . . .

Our opposition to the RIMPAC shelling of Kaho'olawe is rooted in a number of concerns.

First, we believe that the *'aina* (land) is a gift from the *Akua* (god) and must be treated with respect and dignity. The *'aina* and all its bounty is the source of life, nurturing our bodies and spirits.

The Hawaiian expression for this spiritual and life-sustaining relationship to the land is *aloha 'aina* (love for the land). *Aloha* embodies the life and spirit of Hawaii and its people. To love the land therefore is not an empty directive, especially when one considers the importance of the *'aina*. It is within this spiritual-philosophical context that we oppose the RIMPAC shelling of Kaho'olawe.

Second, Kaho'olawe has achieved national significance by being the only Island placed on the National Register of Historic Places, thereby recognizing Kaho'olawe as a cultural, archaeological and educational treasure.

Kaho'olawe is the only Hawaiian Island where the total prehistoric and historic settlement system is known to be preserved. The Island contains thousands of archaeological sites and features, including one of Hawaii's major petroglyph fields, the second largest adze quarry discovered in the Islands, numerous fishing shrines, religious temples, house structures and burial sites.

Together, the archaeological resources of Kaho'olawe illustrate the detailed and complex record of nearly 1,000 years of habitation by the Hawaiian people. Kaho'olawe connects us to those who have come before us. This link with our past is essential because it provides us with a foundation to understand our cultural heritage as Hawaiians, which helps us to define who we are today and what to seek for the future of Hawaii.

Third, the shelling of Kaho'olawe poses an immediate threat to two of the most important archaeological sites on Kaho'olawe. The ships' guns will be firing directly over Ahupu Valley, the location of one of the richest petroglyph fields in Hawaii. The Pu'u Moiwi adze quarry complex is located within the Navy's target zone. . . .

Fourth, Kaho'olawe is used as a site of religious ceremonies by native Hawaiians. With information recalled from ancient chants and legends, we know that historically Kaho'olawe has played an important role in Polynesian religion. Over the last eight years, these traditions have been revived on Kaho'olawe through the practice of numerous religious rituals, from small private ceremonies by individual native practitioners to more elaborate public rituals, such as the traditional Hawaiian Makahiki.

The Makahiki rites are especially important because of the association with the god Lono, Hawaiian god of the peace, prosperity and fertility that we pray will be returned to Kaho'olawe.

Fifth, Kaho'olawe now serves as an educational center for the perpetuation and practice of Hawaiian culture.

Under the stewardship of the Protect Kahoʻolawe ʻOhana, Kahoʻolawe's cultural integrity is being restored through the revival of traditional Hawaiian practices.

We utilize ancient skills, artisanship and knowledge to build traditional Hawaiian settlements. We pursue research using native resources to reveal the Hawaiian significance of Kahoʻolawe. In an attempt to revitalize the land, the ʻOhana is beginning a revegetation program using native plant species suitable for Kahoʻolawe to rejuvenate the native ecological system which has been lost through countless years of abuse and neglect.

Over the last three years, the ʻOhana has brought over 4,000 people to Kahoʻolawe to experience for themselves the beauty and spirit of the Island.

Sixth, environmentalists have warned that the bombing of Kahoʻolawe and the accompanying marine activities associated with it could have dire effects on the endangered humpback whale population. The waters near Kahoʻolawe are the traditional breeding location for the humpback whales. They begin to arrive from Alaska in November and remain in Hawaii as late as June or July. During this period pregnant whales give birth, nurse their newborn and mate again. . . .

ARTICLE 25

Aloha ʻAina: Ending Military Use and Control of Kahoʻolawe. Honolulu: The Protect Kahoʻolawe ʻOhana Fund, Nov. 1987.

A. Significance of Kahoʻolawe

Kahoʻolawe—Kohe Malamalama O Kanaloa—is a microcosm of Hawaiian history that reflects the many problems and issues concerning the Hawaiian people. The island continues to be a focus for Native Hawaiian political action to end external use and control of Hawaiʻi's native resources. Kahoʻolawe is one of the eight major islands in the Hawaiian archipelago, located 8 miles south of the Maui island. It encompasses 45 square miles of varied terrain including hills and plateaus rising to 1500 feet, valleys, beaches and reefs.

Over the past eleven years since the Protect Kahoʻolawe ʻOhana has assumed stewardship of the island, it has become a center for the perpetuation of Native Hawaiian spiritual beliefs and practices. As Native Hawaiians we believe that all ʻaina is sacred and should not be abused or desecrated. Our genealogies trace our origin to the various life forces of nature—Papa, the earth; Wakea the sky; Kane, life sustaining waters of our springs and streams; Lono, our makahiki rains; Kanaloa, the deep foundation of the earth and ocean; Ku, the luxuriant growth of the forest; Pele our volcano—and their multitude of body forms in our native plants, fish and birds. We honor and respect our 'aina in chants, poems and myths. We worship our akua who are the life forces of nature with ho'okupu or offerings. Our ancestors lovingly named the various features of our 'aina as they named their children. By attuning ourselves to the rhythm and pattern of nature in planting, fishing and healing, we provide for the basic needs of our families. The 'aina is the source of mana.

Each of our islands have unique significance and characteristics. Each are special, significant and sacred for different reasons.

Called in ancient times *Kohemalamalama O Kanaloa* (sacred refuge of Kanaloa—a major Polynesian god), Kaho'olawe is sacred to our god Kanaloa. Ancient chants and archaeological evidence indicate that Kaho'olawe was inhabited for over a thousand years. Hawaiians fished, farmed and lived in coastal and interior settlements across the entire island. It is a place where *kahuna* (priests) were trained to read the currents, winds, clouds, earth and sky. It was a navigational center for early Pacific migrations. Kaho'olawe is the site of the second largest basaltic glass quarry and adze production area in the Hawaiian Islands. Thousands of archaeological features including petroglyph clusters, fishing shrines, temples, dwelling and camp sites and burial sites illustrate the detailed and complex record of habitation by the Hawaiian people.

The island was continuously inhabited from approximately 1000 A.D. to 1941. In 1832 the Hawaiian Kingdom banished several political prisoners to the island but the local residents refused to leave because of their attachment to the place. 1858 saw the first of many ranch leases. Unfortunately due to the introduction of European herbivores and overstocking during the ranch period, much of the island is severely eroded.

In 1941 Kaho'olawe was seized by the U.S. military while Hawai'i was under Martial Law, to be used as a bombing target. While first promising to return the island after the war, the military kept delaying until President Eisenhower issued Executive Order 10436 in 1952 officially taking Kaho'olawe for Naval operations until such time as they no longer needed it. The Navy has maintained that Kaho'olawe is indispensable to national security, and that it will never be returned to the people of Hawai'i. The Navy's abusive bombing and shelling, coupled with their total lack of environmental management and subsequent population explosion of goats and sheep has resulted in a severely eroded and degraded island environment.

In 1976 Native Hawaiians on the neighboring island of Moloka'i looked across at Kaho'olawe and decided to go rediscover that part of their native land. The resulting awareness of the island's beauty and cultural/spiritual significance versus the abuse at the hands of the Navy led to direct action by hundreds of Native Hawaiians and a civil suit against the government to stop the bombing and return the island. The suit, contending violations of environmental and historic preservation laws and invoking the Native American Religious Freedom Act, resulted in a 1980 Consent Decree which forces the Navy to survey and protect historic sites, begin soil conservation and revegetation programs, and allow regular religious and educational access to the island. A complete archaeological survey revealed the importance of the island and the entire island was placed on the National Register of Historic Places as a National Historic District in 1981.

B. The Consent Decree

Under the Consent Decree the Navy is required to comply with federal environmental and historic preservation laws and to acknowledge the rights of Native Hawaiians to practice our religion on the island. The 'Ohana is acknowledged to be the steward of the island and in that capacity responsible to monitor the Navy's compliance to the Consent Decree. The 'Ohana is also provided access to the island during ten days of ten months of each year for religious, educational and scientific purposes. Negotiation sessions are held with the Navy every six months to review the Navy's compliance with the Consent Decree and to arrange accesses to Kaho'olawe.

Regarding military operations on the island, the Navy is required to limit the expenditure of live ordnance to 25 percent of the total expended within one year; abide by noise level standards; and adopt standard operating procedures which would protect the various archaeological sites and features of Kaho'olawe. The Navy is required to develop a cultural resource management plan to provide for preservation of the invaluable historic sites on the island and for the island as a whole, which is a national historic district. The Navy is required to implement a land management plan which would conserve soil; reforest the island; eliminate the goats; and clear one-third of the island of ordnance. The Navy is also required by the court to assure proper ocean management by restricting ordnance falling into the waters surrounding Kaho'olawe.

We have found the Navy to be cooperative up to the point that we do not begin to assume fuller responsibility as stewards of the island or fully exercise our rights to practice our Native Hawaiian religion. There is an ongoing tension over who is the primary steward of the island.

We feel that over the past seven years we have maximized the capacity of the Consent Decree to protect the island. At this stage the Consent Decree cannot provide for the stabilization and preservation of the invaluable historic and cultural sites of the island for our children and our children's children over the next seven generations. It cannot afford us the ability to fully practice our Native Hawaiian religion. We find that we have reached a point where we must go beyond the Consent Decree to protect Kaho'olawe and practice Aloha 'Aina. With this in mind we share the following update on the implementation of the Consent Decree to provide the foundation for our assertion that military use and control of the island must end altogether.

1. Military Operations. The Navy readily provides us with detailed statistics on rainfall; goats killed; percentage of live to inert ordnance used on the island; number of persons who have gone on access to Kaho'olawe; and amount of hours that the island is used by each branch of the U.S. armed services and any foreign government, which since 1984 has only been Canada.

However, the really critical data regarding the hit and miss statistics for training on the island is not available to us. This makes it extremely difficult to determine how the archaeological sites are being protected from ordnance during training exercises. We have also requested the Standing Operating Procedures for protection of the archaeological sites that the Navy is required to utilize under the terms of the Consent Decree. These have not been provided as the Navy informs us that the briefings are given verbally. Without such information we cannot verify that the Navy is taking adequate measures to protect the national historic district of Kaho'olawe.

In July ten cluster bombs were dropped directly onto five archaeological sites and near four others. The Navy could not explain which armed service was responsible for dropping the bombs; why they were dropped one mile away from the nearest air or ground target; why the bombs didn't explode; and why a report had not been filed. We still await the written report of the findings of the investigation to receive this information.

We are concerned with the training scenarios used by the U.S. marines when they conduct training exercises on the island. We have requested that they discontinue depicting the island as "enemy" territory or as American territory controlled by the "enemy" or terroristic forces such as was used in Beachthunder '85. In those exercises an "Alliance for an Independent Kaho'olawe" supposedly took over the island, held American citizens hostage and received assistance from a communist group on Kaua'i. It is one thing to use Kaho'olawe for target practice and another matter altogether to use a scenario depicting the island as territory controlled by "local insurgents." This casts a dehumanizing stereotype upon the island and upon the people associated with it—the Protect Kaho'olawe 'Ohana and others. Exercises should be devoid of ideological trappings that conjure up negative images of the island, the 'Ohana and local people.

The percentage of live ordnance to inert has decreased from 1982 to 1986. The total amount of ordnance expended by aircraft has decreased by 50 percent but the amount expended by ships has remained the same. The total number of hours scheduled for military use of Kaho'olawe has declined over 30 percent from 2.2 million hours in 1983 to 1.5 million hours in 1986.